CHILDREN WITH LEARNING PROBLEMS

CHILDREN WITH LEARNING PROBLEMS:

A Handbook for Teachers

LARRY A. FAAS

Arizona State University

HOUGHTON MIFFLIN COMPANY

BOSTON

Dallas   Geneva, Illinois   Hopewell, New Jersey   Palo Alto   London

Text Credits

Pages 7, 27–28 Excerpts from *Educating Exceptional Children*, 3rd ed., by Samuel A. Kirk and James J. Gallagher. Copyright © 1979 by Houghton Mifflin Company. Reprinted by permission.

Pages 69, 315–321 Excerpts from *A Word or Two About Learning* by Doreen Kronick. Academic Therapy Publications, San Rafael, California, 1973.

Pages 167–168 Adapted from *Language Experiences in Communication* by Roach Van Allen. Copyright © 1976 by Houghton Mifflin Company. Reprinted by permission.

Pages 186–188, 190 Excerpts from *Structures and Techniques—Remedial Language Training: Multisensory Teaching for Alphabetic Phonics* by A. R. Cox. Educators Publishing Service, Cambridge, Massachusetts, 1975.

Pages 191–194 Excerpts from *Teachers' Manual for Alphabetic Phonics Workbook I* by G. F. Green. Educators Publishing Service, Cambridge, Massachusetts, 1971.

Page 208 Slightly adapted from *Spelling: Structure and Strategies* by Paul R. Hanna, Richard E. Hodges, and Jean S. Hanna. Copyright © 1971 by Houghton Mifflin Company. Reprinted by permission.

Printed in the U.S.A.

Library of Congress Catalog Card Number: 79-89741

ISBN: 0-395-28352-3

Contents

Preface

Children with Learning Problems: A Handbook for Teachers supplies readers with a wide range of diagnostic and remedial suggestions for use in providing free, appropriate educations for children who have trouble learning. The handbook is designed for use (1) as a basic text in methods courses for those who are preparing to teach children with learning problems; (2) in inservice training programs to update and extend the skills of teachers who wish to become more proficient in working with students who have learning problems; (3) as a valuable reference book for special and general educators when the needs of a student call for a rarely used technique or procedure; and (4) as a source of information for school administrators, social workers, counselors, psychologists, and others who are called on to participate in the development and administration of individualized education programs.

This text advocates an instructional approach that combines task analysis and process analysis. *Task analysis* procedures make it possible to break down instructional activities into sequences of small steps that can serve as the basis for determining *which* tasks have been mastered and *what* skill should be taught next. *Process analysis* focuses on the child's ability to receive, associate, and remember as well as to retrieve and to express various types of information. Information that is obtained from studying an individual's ability to process visual, auditory, and tactual-kinesthetic material is helpful in determining how to structure instruction to facilitate learning.

Throughout this book the term *learning problems* is used in place of *learning disabilities* to offer readers a broader, more flexible frame of reference that tends to highlight the similarities—rather than the differences—among those who have trouble learning because of factors such as limited mental ability and specific learning disabilities. Many of the techniques and procedures commonly associated with programs for learning disabled children are also frequently used in remediating the learning problems of children with other types of difficulties.

Each of the diagnostic procedures discussed in this handbook is designed to answer certain specific questions and each is effective when used for its intended purpose. No single diagnostic instrument answers every question that may arise about a student's learning problems. Similarly, each of the remedial techniques and procedures is effective when used correctly in the appropriate situation as described in the text. No one procedure is effective in all conceivable instructional situations. When providing diagnostic and remedial services, teachers should be able to select and use with ease a wide range of instruments and procedures. They should be able to adapt their instruction to the specific needs of each student; the student should not have to adapt to the one or two types of intervention a teacher feels comfortable using if the selected approach is not the most appropriate one available.

The text is organized into six parts. Part One focuses on types of learning problems and their prevalence; legal provisions; diagnostic and remedial considerations; writing individualized education programs (IEPs); and selecting the least restrictive, most productive services for a child. Part Two discusses the diagnosis and remediation of various social, behavioral, perceptual, and language difficulties of children with learning problems. Topics in Part Three include diagnosis of reading problems, instructional approaches for various problems, and visual/sight-word and auditory phonetic approaches to remediation. A criterion-referenced reading test is also featured in this section. Diagnosis and remediation of spelling and handwriting problems are discussed in Part Four, which also includes a handwriting skill analysis and check list. Part Five concentrates on diagnosing and remediating arithmetic and mathematics problems and presents a criterion-referenced arithmetic test. Part Six includes chapters that focus on working with parents of children who have learning problems, record keeping, teaching study and location skills, selecting instructional programs for adolescents, and providing career education for children with learning problems. The appendixes include a glossary and lists of publishers and professional journals and periodicals.

I am especially appreciative of the efforts of Jean Cooper, Kim Senee, Pauline Tsang, Sue Browning, Terry Gallegos, Nancy Bergman, Eve Mantel, and Jane Miller who assisted with the typing and proofreading of the manuscript. I would also like to extend my thanks to those reviewers whose criticism and suggestions helped refine the manuscript. They include T. Patrick Mullen; Anita L. Herman, University of Wisconsin at Milwaukee; and Samuel A. Kirk, University of Arizona. Particular gratitude is expressed to my wife Patricia and my children Rachel, Eric, and Audra for their understanding and support during the long hours required to develop this handbook.

L.A.F.

PART ONE

*Introduction to the Diagnosis and
Remediation of Learning Problems*

ONE

Children with Learning Problems

TYPES OF LEARNING PROBLEMS

Students with learning problems are found in nearly every classroom of every school. These problems vary from student to student in terms of type and severity. More than one or two students in a classroom rarely exhibit the same specific type of learning problem.

Students who have difficulty learning may have problems related to limited mental ability, social and emotional problems, sensory impairments, and specific learning disabilities. Educational deficiencies in students can also be attributed to a lack of educational opportunity or to the fact that instruction is being provided in a language other than the student's own.

Limited Mental Ability

Some students have learning problems due to retarded intellectual development ranging from a mild discrepancy from the average or norm of the population to very severe or profound mental retardation. The causes of limited mental ability can be traced directly to many factors, including Down's syndrome and other chromosomal abnormalities; inherited metabolic errors, such as phenylketonuria and galactosemia; blood incompatibility; cranial abnormalities, such as hydrocephaly and microcephaly; premature birth; birth injury; prenatal irradiation; prenatal infections, such as rubella; postnatal infections, such as encephalitis and meningitis; and ingestion of toxic substances.

Diagnosing limited mental ability is easy when the student's level of performance is severely reduced. This is particularly so when the child's low ability

3

accompanies a visually definable condition such as Down's syndrome. Diagnosing mental ability that is only mildly limited is much more difficult. For example, the academic performance of children whose learning problems are primarily due to emotional disturbance may closely resemble that of children with mildly limited mental ability. It is also very easy to confuse lack of prior experience with the inability to profit fully from experience.

The selection of a test for evaluation purposes is an important step in the measurement of a child's mental ability. In choosing devices to measure mental ability, caution must be exercised in the following areas:

Avoid the problems that frequently occur when a test of verbal ability is administered in a bilingual child's second language.

Avoid selecting an instrument that calls for performance in only one skill area. For example, the assessment of the mental ability of children with visual perceptual problems should not depend entirely on their performance on nonverbal items that call for matching or discriminating between visual figures.

Avoid confusing an inability to process one type of information with a general reduction in mental ability. Use a variety of instruments or a single instrument that contains a number of subtests, each of which assesses specific skills. This practice makes it possible to examine the differences in a student's performance on various tests and subtests. Information regarding intraindividual differences that occur within a student's performance may be more helpful to a teacher than information that compares a student's performance with that of other students.

Instructional techniques and sequences selected from this book can be used to provide instruction for children with reduced mental ability. In teaching these children, one should focus on their actual abilities and what they should be taught next, instead of on what they have not learned or may not be able to learn.

Social and Emotional Problems

Students who experience trouble adjusting socially and emotionally often have learning problems. These problems are caused in part by the tendency of such students to waste time trying to avoid or delay facing the material they should be studying.

Some students attempt to manipulate their teachers into forgetting to have them read or complete their assignments by causing disturbances or trying to become teachers' pets. These disturbances usually take the form of aggressive behavior directed toward the teacher, other class members, or the school's equipment and property. Students who tend to become aggressive when faced with a frustrating situation often find themselves devoting so much time getting into and out of trouble that they have little time left to concentrate on school work. They spend much of their time between confrontations reliving past conflicts and preparing for possible future situations.

Students who try to become teachers' pets may offer to do something for their teachers in place of the feared tasks. For example, they may offer to take the milk money to the office each day when the task they want to avoid is scheduled. Other students who find it difficult to cope with the pressures involved in performing the assigned learning tasks tend to withdraw from participation. These students seem to find it safer to dream and fantasize than to interact with their teachers and classmates. When this occurs their academic performance often falls far below their potential.

Students who have trouble adjusting tend to impose either too much or too little structure on their behavior. Those who overstructure their performance tend to devote so much time to the unimportant details that they have no time left to perform the assigned learning tasks. Those who are unable to structure their behavior often fail to attend to tasks long enough to complete them.

Students who have trouble adjusting stand a much better chance of working out their problems when they are succeeding academically than when they are failing. Procedures selected from this book can help teachers design and deliver appropriate instructional experiences to students who have social and emotional problems.

Sensory Impairments

The learning problems of students with sensory impairments are related to a partial or total inability to see or hear. Sensory impairments should be distinguished from the failure to gain meaning from what is seen or heard. Students with sensory impairments are usually referred to as partially sighted, or blind, and hard-of-hearing, or deaf.

Students with limited vision or hearing may also have difficulty gaining meaning from the stimuli they do see or hear. Those who have a combination of limited vision or hearing and information-processing disabilities are among the most difficult students to teach. Special techniques have been developed to educate children with limited vision and hearing. In some cases the task sequences and procedures described in the following chapters can be adapted for this use. In other cases more specialized techniques will be needed. For example, teachers who wish to become thoroughly acquainted with the specialized techniques available for teaching students who are hard of hearing or deaf should begin by referring to Moores (1978). One of the most comprehensive coverages of the special techniques used in teaching blind and partially sighted students is found in Lowenfeld (1973).

Specific Learning Disabilities

The *learning disabled* population is a heterogeneous group whose learning problems do not fit neatly into the traditional categories of the handicapped (Kirk and Gallagher, 1979). Children who are learning disabled have average, near average, or above average intellectual ability. Their academic performance is characterized by a significant discrepancy between their achievement and their ability to achieve (Bateman, 1965). They have the visual acuity needed to see but may lack the ability to receive, organize, store, and remember visual stimuli efficiently. Similarly, they have the auditory acuity needed to hear but may lack the ability to receive, organize, store, and remember auditory stimuli efficiently. They are not physically handicapped but may be awkward, poorly coordinated, or inefficient in the use of their hands and fingers.

The most widely accepted definition of learning disabilities during the 1970s was formulated in 1968 by the National Advisory Committee on Handicapped Children. It states:

> Children with special learning disabilities exhibit a disorder in one or more of the basic psychological processes involved in understanding or in using spoken or written language. These may be manifested in disorders of listening, thinking, talking, reading, writing, spelling, or arithmetic. They include conditions which have been referred to as perceptual handicaps, brain injury, minimal brain dysfunction, dyslexia, developmental aphasia, etc. They do not include learning problems which are due primarily to visual, hearing, or motor handicaps, to mental retardation, emotional disturbance or to environmental deprivation.

This definition was adopted by Congress as part of the Children with Specific Learning Disabilities Act of 1969. It was included, with a few minor changes, in the 1975 Education for All Handicapped Children Act.

Kirk and Gallagher (1979) state that the 1968 National Advisory Committee definition "has been accepted by many and criticized by others. One objection was that it could be interpreted to exclude inadvertently children with learning disabilities among the mentally retarded, the disadvantaged, the emotionally disturbed, and those with sensory handicaps" (p. 283). They report that in February 1972 the Professional Advisory Board of the Association for Children with Learning Disabilities clarified the 1968 definition by adding the following paragraph:

> Children with specific learning disabilities who also have sensory, motor, intellectual or emotional problems or are environmentally disadvantaged, should be included in this definition, and may require multiple services.

According to Kirk and Gallagher (1979), three criteria or factors must exist before a child can be diagnosed as learning disabled: (1) A discrepancy must exist between the child's abilities or between potential and achievement. (2) The child must have a learning problem that excludes, or is not due to, general mental retardation, auditory or visual impairment, emotional disturbance, or lack of an opportunity to learn. "The exclusion factor does not mean that children with hearing and vision impairments or children who are diagnosed as mentally retarded cannot *also* have learning disabilities. Those children require multiple services" (p. 284). (3) The child must require special education services. Students who have not had an opportunity to learn but who can learn by ordinary methods of instruction are not learning disabled.

The following definition of specific learning disabilities fulfills these three criteria:

> A specific learning disability is a psychological or neurological impediment to spoken or written language or perceptual, cognitive, or motor behavior. The impediment (1) is manifested by discrepancies among specific behaviors and achievements or between evidenced ability and academic achievement, (2) is of such nature and extent that the child does not learn by the instructional methods and materials appropriate for the majority of children and requires specialized procedures for development and (3) is not primarily due to severe mental retardation, sensory handicaps, emotional problems, or lack of opportunity to learn. (Kirk and Gallagher, 1979, p. 285)

Kirk and Gallagher (1979) divide the learning disabled population into two broad groups: academic disabilities and developmental disabilities. They use the term *academic disabilities* when the student's performance in reading, writing, spelling, and arithmetic falls below the expected level. The rules and regulations for learning disabilities developed by the Bureau of Education for the Handicapped of the U.S. Office of Education defined academic disabilities as problems in oral expression, listening comprehension, written expression, basic reading skills, reading comprehension, mathematics, and mathematics reasoning (*Federal Register*, December 29, 1977, Section 121a. 541).

Developmental learning disabilities as described by Kirk and Gallagher (1979) involve the lack of those skills that are prerequisites to successful performance. Developmental learning disabilities include "(1) disorders of attention, (2) perceptual and receptive disorders, (3) limited use of mental operations of memory, seeing relationships, generalizing, associating, and so forth, and (4) language disorders including limited ability to decode and encode concepts, either verbal or motor" (p. 290).

Lack of Educational Opportunity

Students who have not had an opportunity to obtain an education should not be confused with those who have failed to respond to quality instruction. Students may have lacked the opportunity to receive an education for many reasons: they live in isolated, sparsely populated areas where bad roads and weather prevent regular school attendance during certain times of the year; they move too often to become familiar with any one instructional series; they miss school frequently due to poor health; they have been living in a location where instruction was unavailable or of substandard quality; they attend schools that are overcrowded, underequipped, and/or understaffed; or they must drop out of school during part of the school year to harvest fruit and vegetables.

Some students have trouble learning new material because they have not been taught prerequisite skills. These students do not lack mental ability, they do not suffer from vision or hearing loss, and they are able to process information. Their primary reason for failure is poor curriculum and ineffective instruction. Some instructional procedures and task sequences described in this book will be helpful to teachers who are responsible for helping these students catch up.

Instruction in the Student's Second Language

Students who enter the American school system without basic proficiency in English almost always experience difficulty learning material that is presented by their English-speaking teachers. Teachers should not take these students' failure to learn the material presented as an indication that they lack the ability to learn.

However, teachers should not automatically assume that the only reason a student has a learning problem is because he or she uses English as a second language. Other factors, such as decreased visual and auditory acuity, should be checked. Also, a qualified bilingual examiner should conduct a thorough psychoeducational evaluation. This evaluation should include a check of the student's proficiency in his or her first language, level of educational attainment in his or her first language, general ability level, and learning style.

Examiners should assess a student's proficiency in his or her first language before assuming that that language can be used for communication, psychoeducational assessment, and instruction. Some students who appear to be using English as a second language are not proficient enough in their first language to use it functionally in an academic setting. They may speak a combination of the two languages without being proficient in either. It would be unjust to expect these nonlingual children to display their educational potential on an examination that is administered in either language.

Students who are proficient in their first language should be examined by a bilingual psychoeducational diagnostician. The student's level of performance in the first language provides a good indication of the potential for performance in the second language.

Teachers need information about how these students receive and process information if they are to present efficiently and effectively the material they want the student to learn. Students are much more likely to catch up with their classmates when instructional inputs are introduced through their most functional channel. Teachers cannot assume that all bilingual and nonlingual students will learn best visually. Some may be experiencing learning problems because of a combination of visual perceptual problems and the fact that instruction has been provided in their second language.

A number of approaches to teaching English as a second language and to bilingual instruction are currently available for use with students who lack proficiency in English. These approaches may be supplemented with some of the remedial techniques and procedures described in this book.

PREVALENCE OF LEARNING PROBLEMS

Attempts to determine the prevalence of learning problems in the school-age population have been frustrated by the wide variations existing among the individuals and problems being studied. The question of how severe a student's problem must be to be referred to as a learning problem has not been answered satisfactorily. Myklebust and Boshes (1969) estimate that 15 percent of the population they studied were underachieving. Meier (1971) reports that 15 percent of a group of 2,400 second graders were having learning problems.

The U.S. Office of Education (1975) estimates that 2.3 percent of the population age 19 and under are mentally retarded. Hallahan and Kauffman (1978) report that actual surveys tend to show a prevalence figure of about 3 percent, while 2.27 percent of the population falls two standard deviations below average on the normal curve.

The number of children who show signs of emotional problems is estimated by the U.S. Office of Education (1975) at 2 percent. Wood and Zabel (1978) indicate that between 2 and 3 percent of the school population have serious, recurrent, or persistent problems requiring special services for extended periods of time.

The U.S. Office of Education (1975) estimates that 0.575 percent of school-age children have hearing handicaps and that an additional 0.075 percent are considered deaf. It is impossible, however, to estimate the number of students whose hearing may be limited from time to time because of the congestion that accompanies transient conditions like head colds and allergies. An estimated 0.15 to 0.56 percent of the population is legally blind, according to a 1971 report by the Committee on Rehabilitation of the National Institute of Neurological Diseases and Blindness. It is easy to recognize the problems and special needs of blind students; it is much harder to determine the effects on achievement of subtle factors such as the need for new lenses in eyeglasses.

The general nature of definitions of learning disabilities makes it difficult to determine their prevalence in the school population. Wissink, Kass, and Ferrell (1972) estimate the prevalence of learning disabilities at between 2 and 20 percent with an average of 5 percent. Kirk and Gallagher (1979) estimate that between 1 and 3 percent of the school-age population are learning disabled. These disabilities range from very mild problems, noticeable only when the student is asked to function academically, to problems that are so debilitating and severe that they are easily recognized by everyone.

Although studies of prevalence do not give exact percentages of students with learning problems, they do provide an indication of the overall magnitude of the problem. The most important concern is to identify those who have special needs and to provide appropriate assistance, regardless of the number of students involved.

LEARNING PROBLEMS OR LEARNING DISABILITIES?

There are many more similarities than differences among the groups described in this chapter. Educators have traditionally emphasized techniques that are unique to each group without recognizing that many of the instructional procedures and materials used in teaching members of all these groups are the same. I have used the term *learning problems* in place of *learning disabilities* throughout this book because it provides a broader, more flexible frame of reference within which to discuss remedial instruction.

Teachers should vary their techniques and procedures according to the needs of each individual student. The student should not have to adjust to the one or two techniques the instructor knows how to use. No one diagnostic approach answers all of the questions asked about the many different kinds of learning problems found in schools. No single instructional approach is effective for all types of problems.

SUMMARY

1. Students with learning problems of varying types and degrees of severity are found in nearly every classroom of every school.
2. Many of those who have difficulty learning have problems related to limited mental ability, social and emotional problems, sensory impairments, or specific learning disabilities.

3. Some learning problems can be attributed to a lack of educational opportunity or to the fact that instruction is being provided in a language other than the student's own.

4. Attempts to determine the prevalence of learning problems in the school-age population have been frustrated by the heterogeneous nature of the individuals and problems being studied.

5. It is far more important to provide appropriate services for students who have special needs, regardless of the number involved, than to worry about the percentage of the population that is having problems.

6. The techniques selected for instruction should match the student's specific needs.

7. No one diagnostic approach answers all of the questions that arise in the schools.

8. No one instructional approach is effective for all types of problems.

REFERENCES

Bateman, B. 1965. "An Educator's View of a Diagnostic Approach." In *Learning Disorders.* Ed. Jerome Hellmuth, vol. 1. Seattle: Special Child Publications.

Hallahan, D. P., and J. M. Kauffman. 1978. *Exceptional Children: Introduction to Special Education.* Englewood Cliffs, N.J.: Prentice-Hall.

Kirk, S. A., and J. J. Gallagher. 1979. *Educating Exceptional Children.* 3rd ed. Boston: Houghton Mifflin Company.

Lowenfeld, B., ed. 1973. *The Visually Handicapped Child in School.* New York: John Day Company.

Meier, J. 1971. "Prevalence and Characteristics of Learning Disabilities Found in Second Grade Children." *Journal of Learning Disabilities,* 4 (January), 6–9.

Moores, D. F. 1978. *Educating the Deaf: Psychology, Principles, and Practices.* Boston: Houghton Mifflin Company.

Myklebust, H. R., and B. Boshes. 1969. *Minimal Brain Damage in Children.* Final Report. Contract 108-65-142. Neurological and Sensory Disease Control Program. Washington, D.C.: Department of Health, Education, and Welfare.

National Advisory Committee on Handicapped Children. 1968. *First Annual Report, Subcommittee on Education of the Committee on Labor and Public Welfare, U.S. Senate.* Washington, D.C.: U.S. Government Printing Office.

Report to the Subcommittee on Rehabilitation. 1971. Washington, D.C.: National Institute of Neurological Diseases and Blindness.

U.S. Office of Education. 1975. *Estimated Number of Handicapped Children in the United States, 1974–75.* Washington, D.C.: U.S. Government Printing Office.

U.S. Office of Education. 1977. "Education of Handicapped Children: Implementation of Part B of the Education of the Handicapped Act." *Federal Register,* Part II, 42, No. 163, August 23. Washington, D.C.: U.S. Government Printing Office.

U.S. Office of Education. 1977. "Assistance to States for Education of Handicapped Children: Procedures for Evaluating Specific Learning Disabilities." *Federal Register,* Part III, 42, No. 250, December 29. Washington, D.C.: U.S. Government Printing Office.

Wissink, J., C. Kass, and W. Ferrell. 1975. "A Bayesian Approach to the Identification of Children with Learning Disabilities." *Journal of Learning Disabilities,* 8 (March), 36–44.

Wood, F. W., and R. H. Zabel. 1978. "Making Sense of Reports on the Incidence of Behavior Disorders/Emotional Disturbance in School Populations." Mimeographed. Minneapolis: University of Minnesota.

TWO

Legal Provisions for
Handicapped Children and Youth

HISTORICAL ASPECTS

Society's approach to educating and caring for the handicapped has evolved gradually from the pre-Christian period, when neglect and mistreatment were common, to the current time, when free appropriate education is mandated for all handicapped children. This evolution can be divided into five periods, characterized by neglect and mistreatment, protection and pity, development of institutional services, development of public school programs, and mandated services in least restrictive environments.

During the pre-Christian period, society tended to either neglect or mistreat people whose physical appearance or abilities deviated noticeably from average. The Spartans reportedly killed their deviant or malformed infants (Kirk and Gallagher, 1979). Others routinely placed their handicapped infants high on the rocks in the mountains to perish from exposure or the attacks of wild animals and birds.

From the early Christian era until the early 1800s, there was a growing tendency to protect and pity the handicapped. Many of the religious orders that came into existence during this period provided havens for the handicapped in monasteries and convents. However, these havens served mainly to protect the handicapped from the harshness of society rather than to provide education and training. The use of handicapped individuals as court jesters during the Middle Ages suggests that they may have been exploited for the purposes of entertaining the rulers and wealthy of that time.

During the 1800s publicly supported institutions for the mentally retarded, emotionally disturbed, blind, and deaf members of society were established throughout Europe and the United States. For example, the American Asylum for the Education and Instruction of the Deaf, a residential institution now known as the American School for the Deaf, was established in Hartford, Connecticut, in 1817. The predecessor of the Perkins Institution for the Blind was organized in 1829 in Watertown, Massachusetts. The growth in the number of residential facilities for the handicapped in the United States was particularly rapid during the last half of the nineteenth century. Although initially their purpose was to provide a life-long protective environment, as they developed, these residential facilities began offering specialized training for their handicapped residents.

The development of these residential facilities made it possible to remove the handicapped from the poorhouses and prisons. The National Advisory Committee on the Handicapped (1976) estimates that in 1850, 60 percent of the people residing in poorhouses were deaf, blind, insane, or mentally retarded.

The period between the last part of the nineteenth century and 1975 has been characterized by the establishment of public school classes for the handicapped. The first day class for the deaf was established in 1869 in Boston, and the first special class for the mentally retarded was organized in Providence, Rhode Island, in 1896 (Kirk and Gallagher, 1979). Since that time special classes have been organized throughout the nation. The most rapid growth in special services for the handicapped in the United States has occurred in the last fifteen years, an explosion that has been encouraged by state and federal legislation.

The passage in 1975 of PL 94-142, the Education for All Handicapped Children Act, signaled the beginning of a new era in the education of handicapped children. Under this law, the nation's schools must provide free appropriate education in the least restrictive possible environment for all handicapped children. This mandate is in sharp contrast to the permissive legislation that preceded PL 94-142, which had allowed school districts to decide if they would provide services to their handicapped students.

THE EDUCATION FOR ALL HANDICAPPED CHILDREN ACT

The Education for All Handicapped Children Act, which became law on November 29, 1975, has been referred to as the "bill of rights for handicapped children" (Abeson and Zettel, 1977, p. 121). Weintraub (1977) reports that PL 94-142 represents the standards that have been laid down by courts, legislatures, and other policy bodies since 1970. As described by Ballard and Zettel (1977), the act has four main purposes:

1. guaranteeing the availability of special educational programming to handicapped children and youth
2. assuring fairness and appropriateness in decision making with regard to providing special education to handicapped children and youth

3. establishing clear management and auditing requirements and procedures regarding special education at all levels of government
4. providing financial assistance of state and local governments through the use of federal funds.

Let us now turn to a discussion of the major requirements and provisions of PL 94-142.

Definitions and Eligibility for Services

All handicapped children between the ages of 3 and 21 who require special education and related services are entitled to the provisions and rights described in PL 94-142. The act defines *handicapped children* as children who are "mentally retarded, hard of hearing, deaf, speech impaired, visually handicapped, seriously emotionally disturbed, orthopedically impaired, other health impaired, deaf-blind, multi-handicapped, or as having specific learning disabilities, who because of those impairments need special education and related services" (*Federal Register,* August 23, 1977, Section 121a.5).

Ballard and Zettel (1977) point out that the criteria for determining a child's eligibility under the act are two-pronged. First one must determine if the child actually has one or more of the disabilities listed in the definition. Then one must determine if the child requires special education and related services. They remind us: "Not all children who have a disability require special education; many are able to and should attend school without any program modification" (p. 178).

Special education is defined in PL 94-142 as "specially designed instruction, at no cost to the parents, to meet the unique needs of a handicapped child, including classroom instruction, instruction in physical education, home instruction, and instruction in hospitals and institutions" (*Federal Register,* August 23, 1977, Section 121a.14). The term *related services* means "transportation and such developmental, corrective, and other supportive services as are required to assist a handicapped child to benefit from special education, and includes speech pathology and audiology, psychological services, physical and occupational therapy, recreation, early identification and assessment of disabilities in children, counseling services, and medical services for diagnostic or evaluation purposes. The term also includes school health services, social work services in schools, and parent counseling and training" (*Federal Register,* August 23, 1977, Section 121a.13).

Priorities

PL 94-142 specifies that first priority in the delivery of services be given to handicapped children who are not receiving any education. This group includes children who have been excluded from school and children who were not known to school authorities prior to passage of PL 94-142. Second priority is to be given to severely handicapped children within each disability group who are not receiving an adequate education.

Funds made available by the federal government to pay the excess costs of educating handicapped children cannot be claimed for more than 12 percent of a district's population. No more than one-sixth of this group, or 2 percent of the school population, may be children who are diagnosed as learning disabled. These limits do not mean that only 12 percent of a district's population can be diagnosed as handicapped or that only 2 percent can be diagnosed as learning disabled. They were included in PL 94-142 to insure that federal funding would be used to serve those who have the severest problems. State and local funds must be used to pay the costs of any services in excess of these limits.

Child Find

Each state and local education agency is required to develop and implement procedures insuring that all handicapped children, regardless of the severity of their handicaps, are located, identified, and evaluated. The agencies must also develop and implement practical methods for determining which children are currently receiving special education and related services and which are not receiving the services they need.

Appropriate Educational Services

The term *appropriate* is not defined in PL 94-142. Ballard and Zettel (1977) indicate that the definition is inherent in the individualized education program (IEP) that is written for each child. (See later in this chapter and Chapter 4 for discussion of the IEP.) In other words, the services agreed on by those who prepare the IEP become what is appropriate for the particular child.

Chapter 5 covers the range of possible service delivery models commonly available, as well as the advantages and disadvantages of each approach. It is particularly important to select a model that provides services of an intensity level that is appropriate for the child.

Free Educational Services

PL 94-142 states that all handicapped children who require special education or related services are to receive these services without cost to the parents or guardian. The only exceptions are those incidental fees that are commonly covered by the parents or guardian of nonhandicapped persons. Therefore, the services of private day schools and public or private residential facilities must be free, and nonmedical care and room and board must be provided when needed. However, parents who enroll their child in a private day school or a public or private residential facility when appropriate services are available at the district level may be expected to cover the costs of these additional services themselves.

Due Process Provisions and Procedural Safeguards

The procedural safeguards and due process provisions of PL 94-142 have the following stipulations:

1. Regular consultation with the child's parents or guardian is required in all cases.
2. Disagreements between parents or guardians and local public school officials may be resolved by due process hearings.
3. Parents or guardians must be given prior notice regarding the identification, evaluation, and placement of their child.
4. All contacts with parents and guardians must be made in their native language.
5. Parents and guardians must be advised of their rights under PL 94-142.
6. The terminology used in all notices must be understandable to the general public.
7. An independent appraisal of the child may be made at no cost to the parent under certain conditions.
8. Parental consent must be obtained on the basis of informed understanding.
9. Confidentiality of information must be carefully maintained.
10. The parents' or guardian's written consent must be obtained before the child is evaluated, when the child is placed in a program, when the child's IEP is approved, and when significant changes are made in his or her program.
11. Parents or guardians and students who are 18 and older have the right to examine all of their records.
12. Surrogate parents must be assigned to serve as advocates for all children who are not represented by parents or guardians in due process hearings.
13. Appeals may be made by parents or guardians to an impartial hearing officer or panel whenever there is a dispute regarding the process of identifying, evaluating, placing, or releasing a student.

Parent Participation and Involvement

Parents must be invited to participate in developing their child's individualized education program (IEP). This invitation should be delivered far enough in advance of the appointed time to give the parents sufficient time to make arrangements to attend. Parents should be actively involved in the preparation of the child's IEP, not merely observers who are called in and told what the program will be like.

Personnel Development and Inservice Training

Each state is required to develop and implement a comprehensive system of personnel development that includes inservice training of general and special educational and support personnel. This system should provide enough trained personnel to offer the services promised by PL 94-142. It should also include procedures for disseminating significant information derived from educational research and demonstration projects.

Each local education agency is also required to establish procedures for implementing an inservice training program. A portion of the PL 94-142 funds made available to state education agencies and local school districts can be used to cover the costs of inservice training.

Least Restrictive Environment

Handicapped children should be educated with nonhandicapped children to the maximum extent possible. Ballard and Zettel (1977) note, however, that this provision "does not mandate that all handicapped children will be educated in regular classrooms. . . . It is not a provision for mainstreaming. . . . It does not abolish any particular educational environment, for instance, educational programming in a residential setting" (p. 183). The student's IEP must indicate the extent to which the child will be able to participate in regular educational programs, and should clearly justify any movement of the child toward a more restrictive environment. Chapter 5 contains an in-depth discussion of the least restrictive types of programs that are appropriate for different groups of handicapped children.

Individualized Education Programs (IEPs)

An individualized education program (IEP) must be developed, approved, and implemented for each handicapped student requiring special education or related services. The components that should be included in each student's IEP are discussed in Chapter 4.

Nondiscriminatory Evaluation

PL 94-142 specifies that the testing materials and procedures used in determining if a child is handicapped must be nondiscriminatory. For example, verbal test items must be presented in the child's native language. Children who use Spanish as their primary language must be evaluated in Spanish. Children whose primary language is Apache, Pima, German, and so on must be evaluated in their native language or with a procedure that does not require language-based communication.

Children who are being evaluated for possible placement in a program for the handicapped must be presented with tasks that permit them to respond through a functional mode of communication. For example, they might give a blind child items involving auditory inputs and vocal responses. Or the child who cannot use either hand might be asked to respond verbally rather than by assembling a puzzle. The potential of many handicapped individuals has been underestimated because they failed to respond to items that required them to perform through a mode of communication that was not functional. This provision is designed to eliminate this source of error.

Confidentiality

The right of the handicapped to have their records handled in a confidential manner is granted by PL 94-142 and by the Educational Rights and Privacy Act of 1974. This latter law, which is commonly known as the *Buckley Amendment,* is discussed in detail in Chapter 19.

Surrogate Parents

Public agencies are required to assign an individual who is not an employee of the agency to serve as a surrogate parent for those children whose parents cannot be located or who cannot attend parent conferences. Surrogate parents serve as child advocates who fill in for the missing parents. Those selected to serve as surrogate parents may represent the child in matters related to identification, evaluation, and educational placement.

Surrogate parents should not have an interest that conflicts with the interests of the child they represent. They should have the knowledge and skills needed to insure adequate representation of the child.

Preschoolers and Young Adults

Handicapped children who are aged 3 to 5 or 18 to 21 are entitled to free appropriate education in those states where such requirements do not conflict with state law or court decree. States will receive a $300 incentive grant entitlement for each preschool handicapped child served. This additional funding is provided to encourage the development of preschool programs for handicapped children.

SECTION 504 OF THE VOCATIONAL REHABILITATION ACT OF 1973

Section 504 of the Vocational Rehabilitation Act of 1973 (PL 93-112) is a basic civil rights provision designed to end discrimination against handicapped persons. It requires many of the same guarantees and provisions as PL 94-142. Section 504 states, "No otherwise qualified handicapped individual in the United States shall, solely by reason of his handicap, be excluded from the participation in, be denied the benefits of, or be subjected to discrimination under any program or activity receiving Federal financial assistance." In keeping with this goal, Section 504 calls for providing all handicapped Americans with appropriate educational services, guaranteed access to the physical facilities where services are being provided, preschool and adult education programs that do not discriminate against people on the basis of their handicaps, services that start immediately rather than sometime in the future, services that are located in facilities that are near the person's home, due process and procedural safeguards, and nondiscriminatory assessment.

SUMMARY

1. Society's approach to educating and caring for the handicapped has gradually evolved from the pre-Christian period, when neglect and mistreatment were common, to the current time, when a free appropriate education is mandated for all handicapped children.
2. The Education for All Handicapped Children Act (PL 94-142) has been referred to as the "bill of rights for handicapped children."
3. PL 94-142 calls for the provision of free and appropriate education in the least restrictive environment for all handicapped children between ages 3 and 21.
4. The unserved handicapped members of the population are to receive first priority under the provisions of PL 94-142. The most severely handicapped underserved members of each disability group are to receive second priority.
5. Due process provisions and procedural safeguards are outlined in PL 94-142.
6. Parents must be invited to participate in the development of their handicapped child's individualized education program.
7. Nondiscriminatory evaluation procedures must be used to identify handicapped children.
8. Surrogate parents must be appointed to serve as a handicapped child's advocate when the child's parents cannot be present.
9. Section 504 of the Vocational Rehabilitation Act of 1973 contains specific safeguards designed to protect the rights of handicapped citizens.

REFERENCES

Abeson, A., and J. Zettel. 1977. "The End of a Quiet Revolution: The Education for All Handicapped Children Act of 1975." *Exceptional Children,* 44, No. 2, 115–128.

Ballard, J., and J. Zettel. 1977. "Fiscal Arrangements for Public Law 94–142." *Exceptional Children,* 44, No. 5, 333–337.

Education for All Handicapped Children Act (PL 94-142). 1975. 20 U.S.C. 1401.

Family Rights and Privacy Act (PL 93-380). 1974. *The Education Amendments of 1974.* 20 U.S.C. 821. Sec. 513.

Kirk, S. A., and J. J. Gallagher. 1979. *Educating Exceptional Children.* 3rd ed. Boston: Houghton Mifflin Company.

National Advisory Committee on the Handicapped. 1976. *The Unfinished Revolution: Education for the Handicapped, 1976 Annual Report.* Department of Health, Education, and Welfare, U.S. Office of Education. Washington, D. C.: U. S. Government Printing Office.

U.S. Office of Education. 1977. "Education of Handicapped Children: Implementation of Part B of the Education of the Handicapped Act." *Federal Register,* Part II, 42, No. 163, August 23. Washington, D.C.: U.S. Government Printing Office.

Vocational Rehabilitation Act of 1973 (PL 93-112). 1973. 29 U.S.C. 701. Sec. 504.

Weintraub, F. J. 1977. "The End of the Quiet Revolution: The Education for All Handicapped Children Act of 1975." (Editorial) *Exceptional Children,* 44, No. 22, 115–128.

THREE

Diagnostic and Remedial Considerations

Diagnostic-remedial procedures should begin as soon as it appears that a student is having a learning or behavior problem. Remedial assistance and evaluation of progress should continue until the student no longer needs special assistance. Diagnostic-remedial procedures usually consist of eight steps: (1) determining that a problem exists, (2) obtaining parental permission for psychological testing, (3) performing a psychoeducational evaluation, (4) determining the physical, environmental, and psychological correlates of the student's problem, (5) formulating the diagnostic hypothesis, (6) developing an individualized education program (IEP), (7) using clinical teaching procedures to operationalize the IEP, and (8) conducting program evaluation and systematic follow-up.

DIAGNOSTIC PROCEDURES

Diagnostic procedures may be initiated by the student's teacher, the student's parents, the student, or other concerned persons. These procedures may also be initiated as a direct result of the student's poor performance during screening procedures or achievement testing.

Step 1. Determining That a Problem Exists

Collecting information to determine the existence of a learning problem should begin as soon as a student is suspected of experiencing difficulty, a student requests help, or another individual or agency expresses concern about the student. The procedures involved at this stage should consist of discreet inquiries regarding the student's background, academic performance, history, health record, school attendance, and performance on school-administered screening tests of auditory and visual acuity, achievement, and speech. Questions that require answers before deciding that a student has a learning problem include the following:

Does the student have the auditory acuity needed to hear?

Does the student have the visual acuity needed to see?

At what level is the student performing in reading, spelling, writing, and arithmetic?

Is there an educationally significant discrepancy between the student's estimated intellectual ability and his or her actual level of performance?

Teachers can often use informal assessment procedures to determine whether a student has a learning problem. These procedures may be incorporated into the student's regular instructional program without drawing attention to the purpose of the assessment. The following informal procedures may prove helpful:

observing the student's performance in various types of learning situations

collecting samples of the student's daily work

assigning seatwork exercises that emphasize specific tasks in areas of possible difficulty

administering exercises orally in areas of possible difficulty

administering criterion-referenced tests individually that cover the areas of possible difficulty

preparing anecdotal notes regarding the student's performance

using check lists and rating scales to evaluate personality traits, behavior, attitudes, opinions, and interests

tape-recording and reviewing the student's speech and reading performance

timing the student's attention span and rate of work

observing the student's work habits and organizational skills

conducting individual conferences with the student and his or her parents

The importance of the student's teacher in these activities must be emphasized. Teachers who are qualified to administer diagnostic tests should be encouraged to evaluate their own students whenever possible. It must also be determined at this stage whether the student's teacher is able to provide special services for the student without further information and assistance.

The principal and inhouse consultants should be called on for advice before asking the student's parents for permission to refer the student for a psychoeducational evaluation.

The information collected at this stage often enables one to make minor modifications in the curriculum and instructional procedures. However, these modifications should be handled discreetly and whenever possible, without the student's knowledge. In many cases, assistance can be provided without subjecting the student to the embarrassment of realizing that others know he or she is having difficulty.

Step 2. Obtaining Parental Permission for Psychoeducational Testing

After it has been determined that a student's learning problem is severe enough to require an in-depth psychoeducational evaluation, a conference should be held with the student's parents. The classroom teacher will usually be accompanied by the principal or the principal's representative. Also, older students may sit in on this conference so that they can provide input and participate in the decision-making process.

Teachers should structure Parent conferences so that they can accomplish the following:

Express the school's concern about the student's learning problem and its desire to provide appropriate assistance.
Gather input that will help the school understand and better serve the student.
Discuss the need for additional information about the student.
Discuss what is involved in a psychoeducational evaluation and how the data it will produce will contribute to understanding the student's learning problem.
Determine if a psychoeducational evaluation is needed.
Obtain the parents' written permission to refer the student for evaluation by a qualified psychoeducational diagnostician.

The involvement of the parents and older students in the decision-making process is consistent with both parent and student rights. It is also helpful in securing their cooperation and support of remedial services that may need to follow.

Referral procedures should be described in each school's policies and procedures. A prescribed referral form is used in most districts. The person filling out the referral should include summaries of all relevant classroom test scores, behavioral observations, anecdotal notes, and reports of daily written lessons, and so on, which were collected during step 1. A description of the interventions that have already been attempted and their effectiveness should also be included. (See Chapter 20, pp. 330–331, for an example of a referral form.)

The way a referral is written has a great deal to do with how the psychoeducational evaluation will be handled. A referral that contains clearly stated questions about the student's suspected learning problems is much more likely to result in helpful answers than the referral that does not indicate what is desired. Specific referral questions and an accompanying summary of previously collected information will help the diagnostician focus on the problem area without needing to spend valuable time searching for answers to questions that have already been answered by the student's teacher or the school's principal.

Step 3. Psychoeducational Evaluation

The assessment procedures included in a psychoeducational evaluation should provide data that confirm or disprove the existence of the problems tentatively identified during step 1. Step 3 procedures should provide comprehensive information about the student's intellectual ability, skill mastery, and learning style. Both process analysis and task analysis procedures should be included.

Process Analysis   Process analysis is the evaluation of the student's proficiency in one or more of the following psychological, perceptual, and academic processes: intelligence, psycholinguistic abilities, tactual cutaneous-kinesthetic perception, visual perception, auditory perception, reading, handwriting, and arithmetic. Standardized, norm-referenced tests are usually used in this type of evaluation, and the data obtained are generally in the form of grade equivalents, or standard scores that can be used in comparing the student's performance with that of his or her peers. Differences among students are called *interindividual differences.* Differences within a single individual's performance, on the other hand, are called *intraindividual differences.* They are identified by comparing a student's performance in one area (for example, visual processing) with his or her performance in another area (for example, auditory processing).

For example, a student may process visual material easily while experiencing difficulty processing auditory material. Simple logic tells us that this student is much more likely to learn material presented visually than auditorily. Process analysis in this case, then, provides information on *how* instructional material should be presented for the student to receive and learn it most efficiently. Analysis of the student's information-processing abilities is also helpful in determining if the student is receiving, storing, remembering, and expressing concepts effectively.

The Wechsler intelligence scales (Wechsler, 1955, 1974) and the Stanford-Binet Intelligence Scale (Terman and Merrill, 1960) are the instruments used most frequently to evaluate intellectual processes. The Illinois Test of Psycholinguistic Abilities (Kirk, McCarthy, and Kirk, 1968) is the main instrument used to determine *how* students receive, organize, and express visual and auditory material.

In a standardized test designed to cover a wide range of performance levels, it is not possible to include items representing every specific task in a general process. As a result, the items used in most standardized tests assess only a portion of the tasks that would be found if a process were broken down into a sequence of steps. For example, a detailed task analysis of basic addition skills (a subprocess of the general arithmetic process) might produce a list of twenty-five specific tasks. Items 1, 5, 10, 15, 20, and 25 from this list would probably be the only addition items included on the standardized test. This feature makes it possible to produce grade equivalent scores on a standardized arithmetic or reading test without providing information regarding all of the specific tasks that the student has mastered and must still master.

Task Analysis   Task analysis consists of breaking a process down into a sequence of specific subprocesses, steps, or tasks. For example, when the *CRD Arithmetic Test* (see Chapter 17) was being written, the general process *arithmetic* was first task analyzed into eight subprocesses, or task areas (addition, subtraction, multiplication, division, place value, fractions, money and decimals, and measurement). Each of these subprocesses was then task analyzed further until twenty or more specific tasks were identified in each subprocess area. An objective or criterion statement was written describing each specific task. One test item was then written for use in assessing the student's mastery of the skill described by each of these criterion statements. The items corresponding to all of the criterion statements for each area were then typed, creating eight *criterion-referenced tests.*

Bush and Waugh (1976) provide the following example of a task analysis of the auditory association process (a subtest from the *Illinois Test of Psycholinguistic Abilities):*

1. *Attention.* Attention to vocally produced auditory sound units (i.e., noises, speech sounds, words, phrases, sentences).
2. *Discrimination.* Discriminate between auditory-vocal sound units found in two sets of sentences or phrases.
3. *Establishing correspondences.* Establish reciprocal associations between the auditory-vocal sound units and objects or events.
    a. Retrieve and identify auditory-vocal sound units as meaningful auditory-language signals. Substitute auditory language signals of the two sets.
    b. Establish word order sequences and sentence patterns of the two sets.
4. *Automatic auditory-vocal decoding.*
    a. Shift attention from the auditory-language signals to the total meaning that is carried by the signal sequences.
    b. Retrieve a common denominator term (aud-vocal symbol) that makes association between the two sets.
    c. Retrieve the auditory-vocal symbol that stands for the common denominator to fit set two.
5. *Terminal behavior.* Respond with appropriate auditory-vocal symbol to complete set two.

Criterion-referenced tests, based on detailed task analysis of a process or subprocess, are useful for determining *which* skills a student has mastered and *what* skill should be taught next. In their current state of development, they lack the standardization needed to prove that the items they contain are properly sequenced. Criterion-referenced tests that will be accompanied by norms for each item are currently being developed.

Combined Process-Task Analytic Approach   The recommended approach is a combination of process and task analysis. During the initial evaluation of the student, more time is usually devoted to the administration of instruments that produce data for use in process analysis. Following this initial evaluation, the day-to-day assessment used by the student's teacher should be largely criterion referenced in nature.

Tailor-made evaluations should be designed for each student being examined. It is unlikely that any one test instrument or evaluative procedure will work for every student suspected to have a learning problem; therefore, it is absolutely necessary for those who are performing psychoeducational evaluations to be able to use a wide range of techniques and instruments.

The psychoeducational evaluation of a student believed to have a learning problem usually calls for a team effort. Rarely is one person able to handle all the specialized psychological and educational tests, vision tests, hearing tests, and speech and language evaluations the student may require. Referral for a medical examination is also frequently necessary.

The individual needs of the student must not be forgotten during the evaluation process. Teachers and evaluators should make every possible effort to minimize the trauma that the student may experience as a result of being repeatedly pulled from the classroom for one type of evaluation or another.

Step 4. Determining the Physical, Environmental, and Psychological Correlates of the Student's Problem

Kirk and Gallagher (1979) describe *correlates* as factors within the student or the student's environment that are frequently related to learning problems and their remediation. For example, a sound-blending problem may be related to an inability to learn to read words. As a result, sound blending would be considered to be a correlate of the inability to learn to read. Kirk and Gallagher (1979) divide the correlates of learning problems into physical factors, environmental factors, and psychological factors, as follows:

Physical correlates

visual defects
auditory defects
confused spatial orientation
mixed laterality

hyperkinesis
poor body image
undernourishment

Environmental correlates

traumatic experiences
conditioned avoidance reactions
undue family pressures
bilingualism
sensory deprivation
lack of school experience or instructional inadequacies

Psychological correlates

attention disorders, distractibility
poor visual or auditory perception and discrimination
slow understanding and interpretation of verbal or nonverbal concepts
poor organizing and generalizing ability
inability to express concepts vocally or manually
minimal motor and verbal skills
defective short-term visual or auditory memory
poor closure and sound blending

Step 5. Formulating a Diagnostic Hypothesis

At this stage, any relevant observational and test data are organized into a written summary of the student's current level of educational performance and an explanation of why the student is not learning.

Each person who provided services during the diagnostic process should provide input into this summary. The summary should include an interpretation of the relationships among the symptoms and correlates defined during the preceding steps, and should be stated in educational terms that can be easily understood by all members of the school faculty and the student's parents. In some cases this step may be combined with step 6. In others it serves as preparation for step 6.

Step 6. Developing an Individualized Education Program (IEP)

An individualized education program (IEP) should be prepared for each student who has a learning problem. The August 23, 1977 *Federal Register* outlines the specific legal requirements regarding the development of IEPs and includes a listing of those who are to participate in IEP planning conferences. IEP planning conferences and the preparation of IEPs are discussed further in Chapter 4.

Step 7. Using Clinical Teaching Procedures to Implement the IEP

The remedial prescription contained in the student's IEP must actually be used before evaluators can determine whether it will produce the desired results. Furthermore, it should be used over a long enough time to give it a chance to work. Lerner (1976) suggests that a *clinical teaching* approach be taken during remediation. The primary goal of clinical teaching is to tailor the learning experience to the needs of the individual learner. In clinical teaching, diagnosis does not stop when treatment procedures begin. Lerner describes it as an ongoing alternating teach-test-teach-test process.

Clinical teaching requires continual decision making by the person doing the planning and teaching. Lerner (1976) describes clinical teaching as a five-phase cycle, consisting of diagnosis, planning, implementation, evaluation and modification of the diagnosis, and planning of new interventions. She summarizes her discussion of clinical teaching by stating that "clinical teaching differs from regular teaching because it is planned for an individual child rather than for an entire class; for an atypical child rather than the mythical average child" (Lerner, 1976, p. 104). Clinical teaching procedures should continue until re-evaluation indicates that the student no longer needs special assistance.

Step 8. Conducting Program Evaluation and Systematic Follow-up

Every student who has a learning problem should be followed up on a regular basis to determine if additional assistance is needed. This follow-up is usually conducted by the district office personnel responsible for supervising the preparation and implementation of IEPs and for determining that the services needed by the student are actually being provided. Follow-up procedures should also assess the effectiveness of the remedial prescription and remedial services.

REMEDIAL CONSIDERATIONS

Teachers of students who have learning problems should keep the following considerations in mind. The techniques mentioned can contribute to the success of attempts to assist students. Used improperly, they can also reduce the effectiveness of these efforts. Teachers should review these considerations to evaluate the procedures they are using to plan and deliver instruction.

Diagnostic-Based Planning

Remedial programs that are based on thorough psychoeducational diagnosis and systematic planning have a much better chance of success than those that are formulated at the last minute. Careful study and planning makes it possible to fulfill the following goals:

Collect and thoroughly review the data and observations contained in the psychoeducational evaluation.

Determine *how* the student learns by examining his or her learning strengths and weaknesses.

Determine *what* specific skills the student needs to master in each academic area.

Formulate a set of instructional objectives and procedures that is appropriate for use with that student.

Involve the student's teachers and parents in the formulation and eventual implementation of the remedial procedures.

Locate or design and construct any instructional materials that will be needed during the remedial process.

Prepare possible alternative procedures that will be available if the remedial program needs changing or restructuring.

Establish a systematic procedure for evaluating and recording the student's progress during remediation.

The Starting Point

Many students who have a learning problem have experienced years of repeated failure. As a result, it is natural that they enter remedial programs anticipating that these new experiences will also end in failure. Remediation should start with tasks at an easy enough level that the students cannot fail. It should continue at this level until they have had a chance to experience the feeling of success. As soon as a pattern of success has been established, instruction can move on to the more difficult tasks.

Sequencing

Teachers who are working with problem learners should direct much greater attention than usual to the detailed step-by-step sequence of the skills they are trying to teach. Students who are not having trouble learning often possess sufficient closure ability to fill in any steps that might be left out during instruction. For those students who are having trouble mastering the material, however, seemingly minor omissions may become major barriers to success.

Remedial and Compensatory Teaching

Minskoff and Minskoff (1976) suggest that instruction of students who have learning problems should be divided into remedial teaching and compensatory teaching. They indicate that "The aim of remedial teaching is to have the learning disabled child reach a basic level of competence in his disability areas so that he can meet the minimal and social demands made upon him to use these processes in school, at home, and in adulthood" (p. 218). However, they also point out that it is sometimes necessary to use students' learning abilities to help them master subject matter content as close to grade level as possible, a technique called *compensatory teaching*. They feel that the academic deficits that accompany some learning problems make it necessary to provide remedial and compensatory teaching at the same time. Compensatory teaching, which is discussed in greater depth in Chapter 22, is a temporary procedure that is phased out as soon as students begin to develop competence in their disability areas (Minskoff, Wiseman, and Minskoff, 1972).

Value of Tasks

The prior failure of students with learning problems to acquire as much information as their age mates makes it necessary to include as much content as possible in the remedial activities and materials. However, Minskoff, Wiseman, and Minskoff (1972) remind us that the content of the remedial program must have social and academic value and relevance to the students. For example, teachers should consider the ages and interests of the students when selecting the content of the remedial program. Also, actual spelling words or reading material that students need to study are of much greater value than a series of nonsense words or a fairy tale.

Frustration Level

Teachers of children with learning problems are constantly faced with the question of how much to expect during an instructional session. It is easy to build a case for a warm, supportive, nonthreatening approach that glosses over the tasks that are proving troublesome to students. However, it is also easy to rationalize that an intensive crash program is essential if the students are to catch up with their age mates.

The problem with the first approach is that the expectancy levels are usually too low to cause much of a change in the student's performance. Those who follow the second approach, on the other hand, tend to pressure students to perform at levels that produce failure and frustration. A warm, positive approach that sets high expectations while providing for recognition of step-by-step progress toward skill mastery usually works much better.

Attention Span and Distractions

Children whose learning problems involve a short attention span and the inability to ignore distractions require special management. Their teachers should be sensitive to a variety of environmental factors that can help or hinder them. For example, children who are easily distracted auditorily can be helped by carpeting and by acoustical treatment of classroom walls and ceilings. Classroom dividers and study carrels that have been covered with sound-absorbing materials are also helpful in reducing the amount of stimuli that must be processed by those children who are easily distracted auditorily. Some stereo headsets shut out enough sound when they are worn but not plugged into a sound source to help these children.

Children who are tactually defensive are also easily distracted. They tend to feel uncomfortable when they are touched, crowded, or brushed against. Teachers who are in the habit of placing a reassuring hand gently on the shoulder or back of a child they are helping will find that this practice is particularly distracting to tactually defensive children. These children also can find it very distracting to have other class members frequently passing by their desks. They should therefore be seated away from the flow of traffic and with their backs to a wall.

Students who are easily distracted by visual stimuli may also require special management. When there are more visual stimuli present than they can handle, they often find it helpful to sit facing a blank wall or to retreat to a study carrel.

Cluing

Teachers who work with problem learners should examine the cluing system (hand gestures, pointing, color coding, verbal prompting, and so on) they are using to insure that it does not interfere with or distract from the material the student should be learning. Conflicting teacher clues are particularly difficult to handle. For example, the student may become very confused if the teacher's hand signals direct attention to one task while the verbal instructions call for response to a different task. The system of hand clues used in the DISTAR Arithmetic Program (Engelmann and Carnine, 1969) is an excellent example of a carefully structured set of clues to direct students' attention to specific tasks so that the desired responses can be obtained.

Overloading

Overloading occurs when teachers are unaware or insensitive to the problems that can occur when students are bombarded with more stimuli than they can handle. Children with relatively sound central nervous systems usually respond by "turning off" or "tuning out" the excess stimuli. Those who have sustained minimal brain injury tend to have somewhat lower tolerances for one or more types of stimuli. As a result, they are particularly vulnerable to overloading.

Furthermore, if a student is seizure prone, overloading may bring on a seizure. If a student tends to be overly anxious, overloading may bring on an anxiety reaction. The anxiety reaction may be expressed in the form of hostility, acting out, or a loss of self-control.

Teachers should accept responsibility for stressing a student to the point where he or she becomes overloaded. They should immediately remove an overloaded student from the task or situation that is causing the overloading. Sometimes it is best to give the student a much easier task on which success is guaranteed; at other times the student should be removed entirely from the stimuli-producing situation until he or she regains control. The guilt that is often felt by the student who "blows" or loses control during overloading can be eased by a discussion and explanation of what has happened.

Teachers who have students who become overloaded easily need to teach these students how to monitor their own behavior so that they can recognize when they are becoming overloaded. Regular classroom teachers of these students will find that it is sometimes necessary to permit them to withdraw from the task or classroom group when they find themselves becoming overloaded.

Flexibility and Restructuring

Teachers who are conducting remediation must be prepared to restructure a task if the student does not master it in the form in which it is originally presented. Minskoff, Wiseman, and Minskoff (1972) suggest the following procedural modifications as possibilities:

Rearrange the stimulus.
Give additional clues in the same channel.
Give additional clues in a different channel.
Lead the child to discover the correct response.
Use a cue at a lower difficulty level.
Give the correct response. (p. 24)

All teachers must be prepared for those days when the student will make very little progress and those days on which the movement through the assigned tasks will be faster than anticipated. As a result, they must be able to vary the pace to fit the student's readiness or lack of readiness for the next task. They may also have to modify the motivational procedures being used in order to elicit more intense involvement.

The length of the remedial session should be varied from time to time. A general rule suggests that the instructional period should end before the student wants it to stop, instead of after the student insists that it end. Also, it is best for the student to end each remediation period with successful performance of the last task that is attempted. To facilitate this, teachers can drop back to an easier level when formulating that task.

Integration

Many students who have learning problems also have trouble recognizing how new skills and content relate to material that has been learned previously. Therefore, each remedial plan should provide not only for teaching students new skills and content but also for teaching them how to integrate this new material with material learned earlier. If students cannot integrate the new skills with the old, the skills learned during remediation may become isolated splinter skills that have little to do with the student's total thought and response systems.

Teaching to the Automatic Level

Many problem learners exhibit noticeable inefficiency in their thought and decision-making processes. They often slow down or stop to think through decisions that should be handled by habit at the automatic level. For example, a student with a grammatic closure problem may have to stop and mentally review the rules for changing a word from its singular to its plural form rather than responding automatically.

Error Analysis

Careful analysis of the errors made by students often provides valuable clues that can be used while planning future instructional materials and activities. Keeping a record of the specific tasks that the student fails makes it possible to locate specific problems and faulty response patterns. These clues make it possible to identify important factors that may have been overlooked during earlier diagnostic and remedial efforts.

Feedback

Students receiving remedial instruction should be provided with immediate and regular feedback about their successes. This provision is especially important with students who have a history of repeated failure. Every student needs to succeed at least 51 percent of the time. Many people require a success rate that is much closer to 80 or 90 percent.

Record Keeping

The record-keeping procedure used should be easy to understand and to keep up to date. If not, teachers will either stop using the system as soon as they get a chance or end up spending time keeping records that should be spent providing remediation. Record keeping is discussed in Chapter 20.

It is helpful to both teachers and the students receiving remedial instruction if the students record their own scores and plot their own progress. This way, the students can quickly monitor their own progress without needing detailed explanations. The use of a record-keeping system that can be understood by the student's parents will add greatly to their awareness of their child's progress and to their support of the services their child is receiving. A complex system that is highly technical and difficult to understand often turns off both the teachers who are asked to use it and the parents who cannot understand what it means.

SUMMARY

1. Diagnostic-remedial procedures should begin as soon as it appears that a student is having a learning or behavior problem.
2. Diagnostic procedures may be initiated by the student's teacher, the student's parents, the student, or other concerned persons.
3. Diagnostic-remedial procedures involve a sequence of steps extending from determining that a problem exists through systematic follow-up and evaluation of program effectiveness.
4. Those responsible for providing remedial instruction should keep in mind such factors as basing their planning on diagnosis, carefully selecting the starting point, proper sequencing, and selecting tasks that are of value to the student.
5. Those providing remedial instruction should also keep the student's frustration level and attention span in mind.
6. Cluing procedures, the avoidance of overloading, flexible assignments, integration of new information with previously learned information, teaching to the automatic level, and error analysis are other important remedial considerations.

REFERENCES

Bush, W. J., and K. W. Waugh. 1976. *Diagnosing Learning Disabilities.* 2nd ed. Columbus, Ohio: Charles E. Merrill Publishing Company.

Engelmann, S., and D. Carnine. 1969. *DISTAR Arithmetic I.* Chicago: Science Research Associates.

Kirk, S. A., and J. J. Gallagher. 1979. *Educating Exceptional Children.* 3rd ed. Boston: Houghton Mifflin Company.

Kirk, S. A., J. J. McCarthy, and W. D. Kirk. 1968. *Illinois Test of Psycholinguistic Abilities.* Urbana: University of Illinois Press.

Lerner, J. W. 1976. *Children with Learning Disabilities.* 2nd ed. Boston: Houghton Mifflin Company.

Lerner, J. W. 1967. "A New Focus for Reading Research—The Decision Making Process." *Elementary English,* 44 (March), 236–242.

Minskoff, E. H., and J. G. Minskoff. 1976. "A Unified Program of Remedial and Compensatory Teaching for Children with Process Learning Disabilities." *Journal of Learning Disabilities,* 9 (April), 21–28.

Minskoff, E. H., D. E. Wiseman, and J. G. Minskoff. 1972. *MWM Program of Developing Language Abilities.* Ridgefield, N.J.: Educational Performance Associates.

Terman, L. M., and M. A. Merrill. 1960. *Stanford-Binet Intelligence Scale.* Form L-M. Boston: Houghton Mifflin Company.

U.S. Office of Education. 1977. "Education of Handicapped Children: Implementation of Part B of the Education of the Handicapped Act." *Federal Register,* Part II, 42, No. 163, August 23. Washington, D.C.: U.S. Government Printing Office.

Wallace, G., and J. M. Kauffman. 1973. *Teaching Children with Learning Problems.* Columbus, Ohio: Charles E. Merrill.

Wechsler D. 1955. *Wechsler Adult Intelligence Scale.* New York: Psychological Corporation.

Wechsler, D. 1974. *Wechsler Intelligence Scale for Children–Revised.* New York: Psychological Corporation.

FOUR

Writing Individualized
Education Programs (IEPs)

An individualized education program (IEP) is required by PL 94-142 for each handicapped child enrolled in public or private school who requires special education or related services. An IEP is a written document that must be prepared and approved prior to the student's placement in a special program.

Before an IEP can be prepared, it must first be determined that the student actually has a problem, and a conference must be held with the student's parents to obtain permission to evaluate the student. These procedures and other steps involved in the diagnostic process are discussed in Chapter 3. The procedures described in this chapter begin with the IEP planning conference.

THE IEP PLANNING CONFERENCE

An IEP planning conference must be held for each handicapped student who is placed in a special education program or scheduled for related services. Furthermore, an IEP review meeting must be held at least annually to revise and update the IEP. These meetings should be scheduled at a time and place that is mutually agreed on by the participants. Communication with parents who do not read or speak English, including any printed materials and forms, must be in their native language or through a mode of communication they understand. The following people must attend the IEP planning meeting:

1. the parent(s), guardian(s), or a surrogate parent (Attempts to gain their participation should be carefully documented if they decline an invitation to attend or if they fail to appear after accepting an invitation.)
2. the student, when appropriate

3. the teacher(s)
   a. the regular classroom teacher and prospective special education teacher if initial placements are being considered
   b. the special education teacher if the IEP for a student that has already been placed is being revised
   c. special therapists (for example, speech and language clinicians or physical therapists) if the student's problem lies in their areas
4. a local education agency (LEA) representative (other than the teacher) who is authorized and qualified to supervise the program designed to meet the handicapped student's special needs; usually a special education program administrator, consultant, or principal
5. a member of the team that evaluated the student if the IEP is being prepared for a newly identified student
6. any other person the parent(s), guardian(s), surrogate parent, student, or school wishes to invite

THE CONTENT OF AN IEP

Each student's IEP should include the following information and components:

1. a statement of the student's present level of educational performance, including academic achievement, social adaptations, prevocational and vocational skills, psychomotor skills, and self-help skills.
2. a description of the student's learning style
3. a statement describing the annual goals to be reached by the end of the school year under the student's individualized education program
4. a statement of short-term instructional objectives, which must be measurable intermediate steps between the present level of educational performance and the annual goals
5. a statement of specific educational services needed by the student (determined without regard to the availability of those services), including a description of
   a. all special education and related services needed to meet the unique needs of the student, including the type of physical education and career education program in which he or she will participate.
   b. any special instructional media and materials needed.
6. a statement giving the dates when services will begin and end
7. a description of the extent to which the student will participate in regular education programs
8. a justification for the type of educational placement the student will have
9. a list of the individuals who will be responsible for implementing the individualized education program

10. a statement of the objective criteria, evaluation procedures, and schedules that will be used to determine, at least annually, whether the short-term instructional objectives are being achieved

Present Level of Educational Performance

The IEP planning committee must determine what the student already knows and what he or she needs to learn before it can develop annual goals and short-term objectives. The description of levels of current educational performance should include a discussion of the student's strengths and weaknesses in the various curricular areas. It should also include data and information on the student's academic achievement, social adaptation, prevocational and vocational skills, psychomotor skills, and self-help skills.

A file containing all the information available about the student should be assembled before the IEP conference. This file might include:

the referring teacher's report
previous special education teachers' reports when the conference is being held for
    a student who has been serviced previously
medical reports
speech/hearing/language evaluation reports
the reports of remedial reading, adaptive physical education, and other education
    specialists who have worked with the student
a history of the student's previous educational evaluations
the student's developmental and social history
a report of a social worker or teacher who has visited the student's home
recommendations from the various people who have evaluated and worked with
    the student

The information needed to determine the student's present level of educational performance can be obtained through a variety of formal and informal assessment procedures, which should be completed before the IEP planning conference. The following information-gathering procedures are among those most frequently used.

Informal Assessment   Informal assessment usually consists of teacher-directed attempts to determine which skills have been mastered and which have not. For example, the teacher might see if the student can "sound out" an unfamiliar word or add numbers that require carrying.

Informal Diagnostic Tests   These include informal inventories and check lists prepared for use in determining a student's performance level and error patterns on a specific academic task or group of tasks. Informal diagnostic tests should be designed so that they produce information that will be useful to those who must select the methods and materials that will meet the student's needs. They are often criterion-referenced tests, and provide information regarding what portions of the academic skill sequence the student has mastered and what portions remain to be mastered. The *CRD Arithmetic Test* (see Chapter 17), the *CRD Reading Tests* (see Chapter 10), and the *Handwriting Skill Analysis and Check List* (see Chapter 15) are examples of informal criterion-referenced diagnostic materials.

Systematic Observation   Systematic observation can be used to gather data on specific student behaviors such as attention to task and study and work habits. It is also a key factor in the assessment of perceptual motor skills such as balance and posture, coordination, body flexibility and rhythm, and perceptual motor match.

Formal Diagnostic Tests   This group of diagnostic instruments consists mainly of commercially published, standardized norm-referenced tests. These tests make it possible to compare the student's performance with that of his or her peers. The data they provide are usually expressed as age or grade equivalents. The *Woodcock Reading Mastery Tests* (Woodcock, 1973), the *Stanford Diagnostic Arithmetic Test* (Beatty, Madden, and Gardner, 1966), and the *KeyMath Diagnostic Arithmetic Test* (Connolly, Natchman, and Pritchett, 1971) are examples of formal diagnostic tests.

Diagnostic or Clinical Teaching   Teachers often have to work with the student in a one-to-one teaching situation to assess the relevance of information obtained from tests. Diagnostic or clinical teaching permits them to determine how well a student responds to various teaching methods and materials. This additional information helps the IEP committee select the most effective instructional strategies for that student. Diagnostic or clinical teaching sessions also give teachers an opportunity to determine how rapidly the student learns new material.

The material contained in this section of the student's IEP should follow an orientation that indicates the skills the student has mastered in each area. The following listing of content areas might appear on a district's program planning form (adapted from Hayes, 1977).

Area 1: Reading skills

readiness
comprehension
vocabulary
word attack

Area 2: Arithmetic skills

addition
subtraction
multiplication
division
place value
money and decimals
measurement
fractions

Area 3: Language arts skills

handwriting
spelling
grammar
speech

Area 4: Perceptual motor skills

auditory and visual acuity, memory, sequencing, discrimination, association
eye-hand coordination
fine motor development

Area 5: Gross motor skills

large muscle activity
general physical health
body localization
directionality
laterality

Area 6: Social skills

social acceptance
responsibility
self-control
self-concepts
general behavior
self-help skills

Learning Style

Each student's IEP should contain a discussion of his or her learning style. This discussion should indicate how the student processes information most efficiently. It should also describe how to structure instruction so that the student will be most likely to learn the skills being taught.

Annual Goals

The annual goals section of a student's IEP should contain global statements of what the student is expected to learn in each academic area during the school year. The goals should be arranged in order of priority, from most to least important. Factors such as the severity of the student's handicap, and the student's general ability level, special abilities, attention skills, and past rate of learning must be considered when annual goals are being selected. The goals may be expressed as projected growth in the student's grade equivalent or age equivalent scores on standardized diagnostic tests, or as projected levels of attainment on specific sequences or hierarchies of skills for each of the instructional areas.

Short-Term Objectives

The short-term objectives listed in the student's IEP should describe the sequence of steps through which the student will advance as he or she progresses from the present level of skill development to the level projected in the annual goals. Planners are encouraged to use commercially published lists of objectives whenever they are applicable to the student's needs. It is often easier to select or modify objectives from these lists than to write a new set of objectives for each student.

Major subtasks should be listed in order of priority on the student's IEP. These subtasks can be task analyzed further during the instructional process as needed. Undue emphasis on listing every minute task while preparing an IEP can require so much time that little time remains for instruction.

The objectives that accompany the handwriting check list and the criterion-referenced diagnostic arithmetic test contained in Chapters 15 and 17 are designed for use as short-term objectives in IEPs. The code that appears beside each arithmetic objective (for example, A1 = addition objective number 1; $3 = money and decimals objective number 3) can be used when listing short-term objectives for the student. The student's parents should receive a complete set of the written objectives whenever a code of this type is used in their child's IEP.

Specific Education and Related Services

The specific related services the student will require in order to benefit from the special education being provided might include special transportation arrangements, parent counseling and training, medical services, physical therapy, occupational therapy, counseling services, and services of the school nurse or social worker. This list should also include an indication of any special kits, talking books, films, filmstrips, and other instructional materials needed by the student, as well as any special equipment such as projectors, desk magnifiers, and home-school telephone connections. Each IEP should include provisions for career education and regular or adaptive physical education for the student.

Other Requirements

Duration of Services   The date on which each type of service will begin and the estimated length of time it will require should be stated in the student's IEP. "Special transportation services will start on March 3 and continue until the end of the school year" is an example of an adequate statement.

Extent of Participation in Regular Education   PL 94-142 requires that handicapped students be educated to the greatest extent possible with nonhandicapped students. The hierarchy of possible placements discussed in Chapter 5 includes the various types of service delivery models that are usually considered in selecting the least restrictive, appropriate placement.

Justification of Placement   A statement must be included in each student's IEP that justifies the degree to which the student is restricted from contact with nonhandicapped children.

Individuals Assigned to Provide Services   This section should clearly indicate who will provide each type of service and instruction the student needs, and describe each person's responsibilities. For example, it should include a detailed description of the contributions to be made by the regular classroom teacher and the special education teacher. This description might indicate which teacher will provide instruction in reading, handwriting, and in each of the other specific skills. It is not usually necessary to be this specific about the services of a speech therapist or physical therapist.

This section should also describe the contribution expected from the student's parents. Finally, older students' IEPs might include the specific contributions they have agreed to make to their own progress.

Evaluation of Instructional Effectiveness   This section of the IEP should describe in detail the objective criteria, evaluation procedures, and schedules for determining, on at least an annual basis, if the short-term instructional objectives are being achieved. It should also state what methods will be used to determine whether the annual goals described in the student's IEP have been reached. If the procedures used to assess the effectiveness of the services at this stage are the same as the procedures used during the pretest to determine the student's "present level of performance," it is much easier to determine that growth has occurred.

AN EXAMPLE OF AN IEP

The following example of an IEP was developed to guide those who desire assistance in learning how to write IEPs. The form includes provisions for recording data required by PL 94-142. Information regarding the student's learning style is in the final paragraph of the section describing the student's present educational levels.

INDIVIDUALIZED EDUCATION PROGRAM PLAN

Student's Name: Rachel Lawrence

Grade/Program: Grade 4

Birth Date: October 5, 1967

Teacher(s): Mrs. Matson

Present Date: February 1, 1977

School: Hope Elementary School

Primary Assignment(s):	Date Started	Expected Duration of Services	Special Media or Materials
Regular Education 4th Grade and resource room attendance (3 times per week, 50 min. each time.)	4-15-77	Until June, 1978	Talking books, tape recorder
Physical Education			

Extent to which the child will Participate in Regular Education

Rachel is working easily in all areas of the 4th grade, both socially and academically, except for her deficits in reading. The resource room, through on-going diagnostic-prescriptive procedures, will attempt to strengthen her reading skills sufficiently to enable her to remain in the regular class environment at least 50% of the time.

Services:

Bus Transportation	4-15-77	on-going	

IEP Planning Meeting Participants: Name
  *Local Education Agency Representative: Mr. Donald Klein
  *Parent, Guardian or Surrogate Parent: Mrs. Kathleen Lawrence
   Student:
  *Teacher(s):   Mrs. Gray
 **Evaluator(s):   Mr. Robert Smith
   Other(s):

Dates for review and/or revision of the Individualized Education Program Plan: January 31, 1978

Person responsible for the maintenance and implementation of the IEP plan: Building Principal -- Mr. Bell

* Must attend. If the parent, guardian or surrogate parent does not attend, documentation of attempts to gain their participation should be attached.
** Must attend if the student is newly identified as exceptional.

SOURCE: Reprinted with permission of the Bureau of Special Education, Department of Education, Harrisburg, Pennsylvania.

PRESENT EDUCATION LEVELS

DIRECTIONS: Using as many pages as necessary, describe the student's present educational levels in appropriate curricular areas. These may include but are not limited to:

Academic Achievement   Pre-Vocational Skills

Emotional Maturity   Vocational Skills

Self-Help Skills   Psychomotor Skills

Social Adaptation   Other:

Academic Achievement:

GENERAL ACHIEVEMENT TESTING:

Stanford Achievement Test

Word Meaning	2.1
Paragraph Meaning	2.4
Spelling	1.4
Word Study Skills	2.2
Arithmetic Computation Skills	4.6
Arithmetic Concepts	4.9
Social Studies	2.8
Science	2.9

READING AND LANGUAGE ARTS:

Daniel's Word Recognition List

Level	Untimed	Timed
PP	100%	100%
P	90%	95%
1	80%	90%
2	75%	75%
3	60%	65%

Houghton Mifflin Pupil Placement Inventory (Informal Reading Inventory)

Level	Oral	Silent	Average	Word Recognition in context
PP	100%	100%	100%	100%
1	100%	100%	100%	99%
2	90%	100%	95%	95%
3	75%	75%	75%	89%

Hearing Comprehension

4	85%
5	75%
6	70%

Botel Spelling Inventory

Level	Score
PP	85%
P	80%
1	75%
2	60%

Results of the Stanford Achievement Test indicated that Rachel is having no difficulties in math. Indeed, an informal math inventory revealed that Rachel had mastered the basic math computation skills. It was quite apparent, however, that word problems were very difficult for her. This was not because of the mathematical reasoning or computation skills required but because she was not able to read the words of the problem. Once they were read to her she could complete the problems with ease. The same thing occurred when the social studies and science sections of the Stanford Achievement Test were read to Rachel. Her scores went up to 5.2 in Social Studies and 5.8 in Science. The low scores in Word Meaning, Paragraph Meaning and Spelling, and Word Study Skills further demonstrated that Rachel's academic problems were primarily due to a reading problem. Additional testing was completed with the following results.

Rachel's reading evaluation indicates a youngster whose primary difficulty is in word recognition. Her sight vocabulary, her word analysis skills and her word recognition in context skills are all adequate at a 2nd reader level. Her comprehension, despite the difficulties she has reading words, is adequate at the 3rd reader level. In addition, when information is read to her (hearing comprehension), she is able to comprehend material as high as the 5th reader level.

An Informal Writing Sample revealed that Rachel has an excellent background of information to draw upon, good sentence structure, and imaginative writing, all of which are severely hampered by her difficulty in spelling (which is only adequate at a first reader level). In analyzing the errors in spelling and word recognition, the following strengths and weaknesses were revealed. Rachel knows all the consonants in both their initial and final positions. She is well aware of long vowels, but has difficulty with short vowels (hād/hăd). Consonant blends consisting of 2 letters present no problem to her no matter where they are located in a word. However, 3 letter blends (spr/str, etc.) are difficult for her. Rachel understands that a final silent "e" at the end of a word will make the vowel long and knows how to pronounce long vowels. However, the open syllable ("me") and the closed syllable ("met") concepts are not known to her, which further complicates her problems with short vowels. Of course, words with unusual spellings and words that do not follow any rules are quite confusing to her.

Results from some of the sub-tests on the Detroit Test of Learning Aptitude and the Gates Associative Learning Battery, indicate that Rachel has no difficulty making the associations necessary for word learning. In addition, she learns more easily when words are presented to her through more than one sensory channel (visual, auditory, and kinesthetic).

SOURCE: Reprinted with permission of the Bureau of Special Education, Department of Education, Harrisburg, Pennsylvania.

Instructional Area: Reading and Language Arts

Annual Goal: Rachel will increase sight vocabulary.

SHORT-TERM OBJECTIVE	INSTRUCTIONAL METHODS MEDIA/MATERIAL TITLE(S) (OPTIONAL)	EVALUATION OF INSTRUCTIONAL OBJECTIVES	
		TESTS, MATERIALS EVALUATION PROCEDURES TO BE USED	CRITERIA OF SUCCESSFUL PERFORMANCE
1. Rachel will pronounce words containing open syllables.	1. As often as possible Rachel should be provided with the opportunity to learn words by seeing them, hearing them and by writing them all at the same time. This can be accomplished by having Rachel say the word she is learning to read, write and say its parts and say the word again after she has written it. (Visual, Auditory, Kinesthetic technique to word learning as developed by Grace Fernald).	1. Given 20 words (10 of which will be open syllables like "me", "I", "go", etc.) Rachel will select and write down the words that demonstrate the open syllable concept; will mark the vowel to indicate that it is pronounced with a long vowel sound and will pronounce the words to the teacher.	1. 90% accuracy on each task.
2. Rachel will pronounce words containing closed syllables.		2. Same as #1, except that closed syllables will be used, selected, written, etc.	2. 90% accuracy on each task.
3. Rachel will pronounce words containing 3 letter consonant blends (spr, str, etc.) in the initial position.		3. Given a list of 20 words, Rachel will underline all the triple letter consonant blends and say the words containing these blends to the teacher.	3. 90% accuracy.

SOURCE: Reprinted with permission of the Bureau of Special Education, Department of Education, Harrisburg, Pennsylvania.

An Example of an IEP

Instructional Area: Reading and Language Arts

Annual Goal: Rachel will be able to spell words she is currently learning to read.

SHORT-TERM OBJECTIVE	INSTRUCTIONAL METHODS MEDIA/MATERIAL TITLE(S) (OPTIONAL)	EVALUATION OF INSTRUCTIONAL OBJECTIVES	
		TESTS, MATERIALS EVALUATION PROCEDURES TO BE USED	CRITERIA OF SUCCESSFUL PERFORMANCE
1. Rachel will spell words containing: a. open syllables b. closed syllables c. 3 letter consonant blends 2. Rachel will spell words of her own choosing that do not follow any phonic or spelling principles.		1. Given weekly tests in which 5 words are dictated, Rachel will write the words. At the end of each month, she will be given 20 words to write. 2. The above weekly test will contain 2 additional words of Rachel's choosing. Rachel will write these 2 variant spelling words at the end of each weekly list. At the end of each month, Rachel will be asked to spell five of these words on the monthly spelling test.	1. 80% accuracy on 6 of the monthly tests. 2. 80% accuracy on 6 of the monthly tests.

SOURCE: Reprinted with permission of the Bureau of Special Education, Department of Education, Harrisburg, Pennsylvania.

Instructional Area: Reading and Language Arts

Annual Goal: Rachel will read 2 to 3 sentence math word problems in the regular 4th grade class.

SHORT-TERM OBJECTIVE	INSTRUCTIONAL METHODS MEDIA/MATERIAL TITLE(S) (OPTIONAL)	EVALUATION OF INSTRUCTIONAL OBJECTIVES	
		TESTS, MATERIALS EVALUATION PROCEDURES TO BE USED	CRITERIA OF SUCCESSFUL PERFORMANCE
1. Rachel will identify basic sight vocabulary used in beginning word problems. 2. Rachel will read 2 sentence word problems. 3. Rachel will read 3 sentence word problems.	1. Words selected from the math text book used by Rachel's 4th grade class.	1. Given a list of 25 commonly used words in beginning math word problems, Rachel will read these words orally. 2. Rachel will read 10 math word problems, 2 sentences in length. 3. Rachel will read 10 math word problems, 3 sentences in length.	1. 75% accuracy. 2. 95% of the words contained in the problems are to be read accurately. 3. 95% of the words contained in the problems are to be read accurately.

SOURCE: Reprinted with permission of the Bureau of Special Education, Department of Education, Harrisburg, Pennsylvania.

An Example of an IEP

Instructional Area: Reading and Language Arts

Annual Goal: Rachel will explain social studies concepts dealing with understanding the Pilgrims in America. These are the same concepts as those to be learned by her peers in the regular 4th grade class.

SHORT-TERM OBJECTIVE	INSTRUCTIONAL METHODS MEDIA/MATERIAL TITLE(S) (OPTIONAL)	EVALUATION OF INSTRUCTIONAL OBJECTIVES	
		TESTS, MATERIALS EVALUATION PROCEDURES TO BE USED	CRITERIA OF SUCCESSFUL PERFORMANCE
1. Rachel will explain: a. Why the Pilgrims came to America. b. What problems they encountered getting here. c. What problems they had establishing themselves in the various colonies. d. How problems were solved in each of the colonies.	1. The following choices of methods and materials are to be used to accomplish this goal: a. Teacher prepared materials on the same topics as her peers but adapted for Rachel's use. b. Easier textbooks and other commercially prepared materials using an easier text, but on the same topics. c. Talking books. d. Taping the appropriate sections of the regular 4th grade social studies text book for Rachel to listen to in order to obtain the necessary information. (Rachel can comprehend material read to her as high as a 5th reader level.)	1. Rachel can take the same tests the other children take except that they must be: a. Read to her; or, b. Put on tape for her; or c. Written on an easier level for her.	1. The criteria can be the same for the rest of the children, provided that she: a. Tell her responses to the teacher; or b. Tape her responses on the tape recorder; or c. Write her responses, given additional time to do so. (Spelling is not to be counted.)

SOURCE: Reprinted with permission of the Bureau of Special Education, Department of Education, Harrisburg, Pennsylvania.

Instructional Area: Reading and Language Arts

Annual Goal: Rachel will observe and record data as related to the scientific method.

SHORT-TERM OBJECTIVE	INSTRUCTIONAL METHODS MEDIA/MATERIAL TITLE(S) (OPTIONAL)	EVALUATION OF INSTRUCTIONAL OBJECTIVES	
		TESTS, MATERIALS EVALUATION PROCEDURES TO BE USED	CRITERIA OF SUCCESSFUL PERFORMANCE
1. Rachel will read words in the science experiments.	1. SAPA - Modules # 33, 40, 46	1. Given a list of 25 words used in the science experiments Rachel will be required to do, Rachel will read these words orally.	1. 75% accuracy.
2. Rachel will record the data she observes.	2. SAPA - Modules # 33, 40, 46	2. Using correct spelling, Rachel will record the data she observes.	2. 75% accuracy.

SOURCE: Reprinted with permission of the Bureau of Special Education, Department of Education, Harrisburg, Pennsylvania.

SUMMARY

1. An individualized education program (IEP) is required by PL 94-142 for each handicapped child enrolled in public or private school who requires special education or related services.
2. Each student's IEP should be developed in a planning meeting attended by specific individuals including the student's parents, teachers, and the administrator responsible for seeing that the IEP requirements are carried out.
3. A description of the student's current level of educational performance must be included in the IEP.
4. Annual goals and short-term objectives must be outlined in the IEP.
5. The specific education and related services and the people who will provide each must be listed in the IEP.
6. The date services will begin and end and a justification of the type of placement selected must be included in the IEP.
7. An objective procedure for evaluating the effectiveness of the instruction provided by the program outlined in the IEP must be included in the IEP.

REFERENCES

Beatty, L. S., R. Madden, and E. F. Gardner. 1966. *The Stanford Diagnostic Arithmetic Test.* New York: Harcourt Brace Jovanovich, Inc.

Connolly, A. J., W. Natchman, and E. M. Pritchett. 1971. *KeyMath Diagnostic Arithmetic Test.* Circle Pines, Minn.: American Guidance Service.

Hayes, J. 1977. "Annual Goals and Short-Term Objectives." In *A Primer on Individualized Education Programs for Handicapped Children.* Ed. S. Torres. Reston, Va: The Foundation for Exceptional Children

U.S. Office of Education. 1977. "Education of Handicapped Children: Implementation of Part B of the Education of the Handicapped Act." *Federal Register,* Part II, 42, No. 163, August 23. Washington, D.C.: U.S. Government Printing Office.

Woodcock, R. W. 1973. *The Woodcock Reading Mastery Tests.* Circle Pines, Minn.: American Guidance Service.

FIVE

Selecting the Least Restrictive
and Most Productive Type of Program

A number of different types of program options should be available for students with learning and behavior problems who require special educational services. The availability of these different options makes it possible to select a program for each student that will be the least restrictive and most productive for that particular student. The hierarchy of alternative program options or types developed by Reynolds (1962) is shown in Figure 5.1.

The broad base of Reynolds's hierarchy shows that the largest number of students with special needs are those with mild problems. The narrow top of the model indicates that the portion of students with severe problems is much smaller.

Each program option restricts or segregates the problem learner from his or her age mates to a different degree. This degree ranges from minimal segregation —for example, when the child's problem can be handled in the regular classroom —to the obvious restriction and segregation of placing the child in a residential or hospital school program. Most educators believe that the student with mild learning and/or behavior problems should be educated in the regular classroom whenever possible. The movement of the student from the more restrictive types of programs toward placement in a regular classroom is called *mainstreaming*.

Each program option allows for services of a certain degree of intensity. Regular classroom teachers who have students with learning problems in their classrooms are obviously limited in the amount of time they can devote to indivi-

Dr. L. Kay Hartwell, assistant professor of special education at Arizona State University, Tempe, Arizona, coauthored this chapter.

FIGURE 5.1   *The Reynolds Hierarchy of Services*

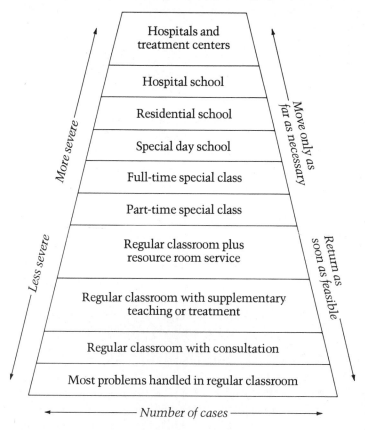

SOURCE: Reprinted from "A Framework for Considering Some Issues in Special Education" by M. C. Reynolds in *Exceptional Children* by permission of the Council for Exceptional Children. Copyright © 1962 by the Council for Exceptional Children.

dual students; therefore, these students must be able to function with limited one-to-one assistance. The program provided in a residential or hospital setting, however, may be more intense.

The first option to consider in selecting the least restrictive and most productive type of educational placement for students with learning problems should be regular classroom placement. Other, more restrictive, types of programs should be considered only when regular classroom placement cannot provide the intensity of services necessary to produce the desired change in the student's behavior. A program that is not intense enough tends to sacrifice the student's academic progress for the sake of the least restrictive environment; a program that is more restrictive than necessary tends to sacrifice the student's social needs for the sake of academic productivity. Educators must maintain a balance between the two goals of productivity and least restriction when planning or adjusting students' programs.

The special educational placements of students should be considered temporary, and they should be reviewed regularly. However, services provided in the program selected should continue until sufficient academic and social progress has been made to justify moving students to a less restrictive, less intense type of program.

Adamson and Van Etten (1972) suggest that one of two decisions can be made when a student fails to show progress within ten weeks after placement in a program: either the program can be continued for an additional ten weeks if there is reason to think that a solution can be found, or the student can be reassigned to another type of program. In some cases the student needs a more intensive type of program. In other cases the delivery model is appropriate but the instructional technique needs to be changed.

No one type of program delivery model is suitable for all students who have special needs. The following program options were listed in Reynolds's (1962) hierarchy. Each of these alternatives has its unique advantages and disadvantages.

PROBLEMS HANDLED BY THE REGULAR CLASSROOM TEACHER

The largest group of students with special needs consists of students with very mild problems that can be handled in regular classrooms. They can be taught by regular classroom teachers who have special training in such areas as individualizing instruction, managing behavior, and correcting reading and arithmetic problems. This delivery model serves students with learning and/or behavior problems who are able to succeed while remaining in the mainstream of the school. Their teachers provide assistance in the form of adjusted curriculum, special instructional techniques, and supplemental instruction for groups of students with similar problems. The advantages of this model include the following:

1. The students remain fully integrated with their classmates.
2. The students have the opportunity to learn and interact with their nonhandicapped peers.
3. Services can usually be provided without overt identification of the students.
4. It is regarded as the least restrictive of the available program alternatives.

The disadvantages of this model include the following:

1. The large enrollments and overcrowding in many regular classrooms leaves teachers without the time necessary to individualize instruction.

2. Children with problems are often rejected socially by their peer group.
3. The nondisruptive student with special needs is easily overlooked and may not receive appropriate instruction.
4. The instruction being provided for the other students in the regular classroom may not be appropriate for the student with special needs.
5. Regular classroom teachers are often not prepared to work with students who have special needs that vary significantly from the needs of the other members of their classrooms.

REGULAR CLASSROOM PLACEMENT WITH CONSULTATION

Many students with learning problems can be educated in regular classrooms if their teachers are assisted by special consultants. These consultants are usually district office staff members who are responsible for assisting teachers in several schools. This assistance may include educational diagnosis, development of IEPs, parent counseling, and selection of appropriate instructional materials, methods, and techniques. The advantages of this approach to delivering appropriate services to students with learning and/or behavioral problems include the following:

1. The student spends the entire day in a regular classroom.
2. The student's placement involves minimal or no segregation from his or her nonhandicapped peers.
3. Other members of the class may not even know the student has been identified as having special educational needs.
4. The student's teacher has an identifiable source of special assistance.
5. The consultant can often expedite the procurement of necessary materials and the scheduling of other services that may be needed by the student or teacher.
6. The consultant may be able to schedule the follow-up services needed to insure that the student's special needs are actually being met.
7. More students can be served by the regular classroom teacher when supplemental assistance is provided, making this model the most cost efficient.

The disadvantages of regular classroom placement with consultation include the following:

1. The consultant may be unavailable during the crisis periods when assistance is most needed.
2. The consultant's range of expertise may not include the skills needed to meet the student's or teacher's specific needs.

3. The presence of a consultant in the classroom greatly reduces the chance that other class members will remain unaware that the student has a problem.
4. Most states do not provide funding for this service alternative.

REGULAR CLASSROOM PLACEMENT WITH SUPPORT SERVICES

Some students with learning and/or behavior problems, particularly students whose problems are mild to moderate, are able to perform successfully when regular classroom attendance is supported with supplementary teaching, tutoring, or treatment. The services of speech clinicians, physical therapists, remedial reading and remedial arithmetic specialists, and academic subject tutors are among those used in this approach.

These supplementary services are usually delivered on a regularly scheduled basis by specially trained personnel who devote 50 percent or more of each week to providing direct services to students. This feature of regularly scheduled, direct services to students distinguishes this approach from the approach that uses consultant services. (However, the specialists or itinerant teachers who provide these supplementary services may also devote a portion of their weekly schedules to providing consultant or administrative services.) The treatment of tutorial services provided may consist of from one or two hours of instruction for a student per week to one or more class periods each day. They may be provided on a one-to-one basis or to small groups of students with similar problems. The person providing these services may be responsible for students with special needs attending one school or for several attendance centers.

Students receiving these types of services must often move from their regular classrooms to another room for tutoring or therapy. At other times the tutor or itinerant teacher may join the regular classroom teacher in the classroom to work with a group of students with special needs. This team-teaching approach makes it much easier for the tutor and the regular classroom teacher to correlate their efforts.

Tutors or itinerant teachers may also observe students, diagnose, prepare IEPs, and prepare special instructional materials. They tend to concentrate on assisting students who are having minor problems with the academic tasks involved in a specific academic area or subject. Following are some of the advantages of this approach to delivering special services.

1. Direct services are provided for students on a regularly scheduled basis.
2. The regular classroom teacher is assisted by supplementary support personnel who have special training.
3. It is often possible to assist students without removing them from regular classrooms.

4. The primary responsibility for instruction remains with regular classroom teachers.

Some disadvantages of placing children who have learning problems in regular classrooms and providing supplementary teaching, tutoring, or treatment are as follows:

1. The pressure on itinerant teachers to help students catch up academically may cause them to give too little attention to the underlying causes of the problems.
2. The tendency of tutors to specialize in one academic or subject matter area may result in undue emphasis on problems in that area at the expense of other types of problems.
3. Short-term tutorial services directed toward development of a few skills may be substituted for the comprehensive, in-depth services that are actually needed by some students.
4. The tutor or therapist may be too overloaded to help any one student significantly.
5. Tutors may have to spend excessive amounts of time traveling between schools.
6. Equipment and materials must often be transported from school to school.
7. Itinerant teachers often lack sufficient contact with the faculties of the schools they serve to develop a feeling that they are accepted members of these faculties.

REGULAR CLASSROOM ATTENDANCE PLUS RESOURCE ROOM SERVICES

Some students with special needs require more special assistance than a tutor or itinerant therapist can provide. Included in this group of students are those who are able to succeed in the regular classroom program if they are also receiving the services of a resource room and resource teacher. These students receive most of their instruction from their regular classroom teachers. They leave the regular classroom for from one or two periods a week to one or two periods a day to receive the special instruction available in the resource room.

A well-equipped resource room contains a wide variety of instructional equipment and material. Resource teachers may concentrate on providing services for students who have one type of learning problem—for example, limited vision—or they may provide services for students who have several different types of problems.

They usually engage in screening, diagnosis, parent counseling, writing IEPs, preparing instructional materials, conferring with regular classroom teachers, and arranging student follow-up. They should be free to spend at least 20 percent of their time in these activities, with the remaining time devoted to providing direct services to students. The effectiveness of this type of service delivery model depends heavily on the development of close, cooperative working relationships between regular classroom teachers and resource teachers.

The advantages of using resource rooms to serve students who have learning problems include the following:

1. The students are given special assistance without being segregated from their age mates for extended periods of time.
2. The students are able to benefit from the services offered in the resource room while continuing to benefit from the program being offered in the regular classroom.
3. Special equipment and materials that are not usually found in the regular classroom are available in the resource room.
4. The unscheduled time included in resource teachers' weekly schedules enables them to offer diagnostic, parent-counseling, and other support services.

Some of the disadvantages of the resource room and resource teacher approach to delivering special services are as follows:

1. Some students require more hours of special instruction per day or week than can be provided in a resource room.
2. Students must miss part of the instruction that is being provided in the regular classroom to receive instruction in a resource room.
3. It is very difficult to locate teachers who possess the range of remedial, diagnostic, and human relations skills needed for successful performance as a resource teacher.
4. Some school districts tend to view resource rooms as cure-alls capable of handling problems of all types and degrees of severity.
5. Some schools tend to use resource rooms for students who need services of a type and intensity that can be provided only in full-time special classrooms.
6. Conflicts often occur between resource teachers and regular classroom teachers regarding the specific times the student will be permitted to attend the resource room.
7. It is not always clear which teacher is responsible for reporting to the parents on the student's progress.

PART-TIME SPECIAL CLASSES

Some students have to divide their time between regular class attendance and part-time special class enrollment. The special classes usually serve as these students' home rooms. They leave the special classrooms for a portion of each day to participate in selected parts of the regular school program or for work-study experiences. Teachers of part-time special classes may devote the entire day to working with these part-time students or they may spend half of each day working as consultants or resource teachers.

The advantages of part-time special class enrollment include the following:

1. The students are provided with the security of home rooms that have a small enrollment and easily identifiable, specially trained teachers.
2. The students may participate in those parts of the regular school program where success is possible.
3. Intensive small-group and one-to-one services are available in those areas where special instruction is needed.
4. There is a readily identifiable location in the school where students can be found when it is necessary to provide additional diagnostic or follow-up services.
5. The special classroom teachers are able to help the students with preparation for their regular classes.

The disadvantages of part-time special class attendance include the following:

1. The students are segregated from their age mates for a portion of each day.
2. The students cannot benefit from the instruction occurring in the regular classroom program while they are in the special classroom.
3. The students spend part of each day in a program that is easily recognized by their peers as being different.
4. Problems are often encountered in gaining teacher and peer acceptance of special class students when attempts are made to integrate them into the regular school program.

FULL-TIME SPECIAL CLASSES

Those students whose learning and/or behavior problems are so severe that they are not able to benefit significantly from regular classroom instruction need self-contained, full-time special class programs. These students receive their academic instruction from specially trained teachers. Theoretically, most full-time special classes serve one type of exceptional child.

Students who are enrolled in full-time special classes usually participate with students from the regular school programs in nonacademic, out-of-the-classroom activities such as athletics, playground, assembly programs, and lunch. Many also receive part-time instruction from specialists in music, art, physical education, and speech correction. Full-time special class attendance is more appropriate for those with severe and moderate problems than it is for those with mild or borderline problems.

Among the advantages of full-time special class attendance are the following:

1. The students can be provided with intensive day-long instruction in a structured environment.
2. A specially trained and certified teacher is available to provide instruction for the students throughout the entire school day.
3. A totally individualized instructional program can be designed for individual students when their specific needs differ significantly from those of their age mates or classmates.
4. Students who are highly vulnerable to ridicule and isolation in regular classrooms are provided with shelter and the possible support of an accepting peer group.

Among the disadvantages are the following:

1. Those who are enrolled in special class programs tend to become segregated from their age mates who are enrolled in the regular school program.
2. Placement in a special class tends to foster the creation of a self-fulfilling prophecy that uses the student's history of failure as a basis for predicting and/or justifying future failure.
3. Full-time special class placement creates the need for eventual re-entry into the mainstream of the school or society.
4. The student's membership in a group that can be identified as different may result in ridicule and rejection.
5. The absence of a peer group that does not have apparent problems means students do not have appropriate models on whom they can pattern behavior change.

SPECIAL DAY SCHOOLS

Some students with learning problems find it necessary to attend special day schools. This occurs most frequently when the student has a problem not generally found in the school-age population. Special day schools are usually found in large cities, where it is easier to gather students with similar severe problems together for specialized instruction.

Some special day schools are part of the comprehensive program of services offered by a public school system. Others are private agencies that support themselves through tuition paid by the students' home school districts. Special day schools are usually staffed with specially trained teachers and a number of full- or part-time support personnel such as speech therapists, audiologists, psychologists, and adaptive physical educators.

The advantages of special day schools include the following:

1. The school's physical facilities can be designed specifically to meet the needs of the students being served.
2. The teachers are able to benefit from their association with other specialists who have similar backgrounds and responsibilities.
3. Teachers who are part of a professional group are much less likely to experience the feelings of isolation that are often experienced by specialists who work mostly with general educators.
4. Comprehensive medical, social, psychological, speech-correction, physical or recreation therapy, and other ancillary services can be provided by specialists who have in-depth knowledge of the specific types of problems being served.

The disadvantages of special day schools include the following:

1. The students may be isolated for long periods of time from students who do not have problems.
2. The students are isolated from other children in their neighborhoods, who usually attend schools located near their homes.
3. The amount of time students must spend traveling to and from special day schools is often excessive.
4. The extra transportation that may be required to take students to and from special day schools can add significantly to the cost of educating students.
5. The absence of students in the special day school population who do not have problems means that students do not have appropriate models on whom to pattern behavior change.
6. Teachers who have taught in a special day school for several years often tend to start accepting the below-average performance of the students as normal.

RESIDENTIAL SCHOOLS

That small proportion of the population with severe and profound learning and/or behavior problems needs the services of residential or institutional facilities. These facilities which may be privately or publicly supported and administered, provide twenty-four-hour-a-day care, including lodging, food, medical and educational services, and sometimes custodial services.

Some residential facilities specialize in the care and treatment of individuals who have one type of problem; others serve individuals who have a number of different types of problems. Children who may require the services of a residential facility and school usually include those with severely or profoundly limited intelligence, vision, hearing, or mobility. Sometimes children with severe social and emotional problems must also be placed in residential facilities.

The educational services provided in a residential school may extend beyond the classroom to include specialized treatment and stimulation during meals or in the dormitory. Twenty-four-hour-a-day placement means that intensive services can be provided for residents most of the time they are awake.

The advantages of residential placement and instruction in a residential setting include the following:

1. Specially trained personnel are available on a twenty-four-hour-a-day basis to care for and train the residents.
2. Medical services are available on a twenty-four-hour-a-day basis in most instances.
3. Residential placement tends to remove some of the pressure that highly or totally dependent children often place on their parents and siblings.
4. A sheltered environment is provided that protects the rights of those members of society who may be highly vulnerable to abuse or misuse by others.
5. Society is protected from those whose severe social or emotional problems may prompt behavior that infringes on the rights of others.

The disadvantages of residential facilities and schools include the following:

1. Placement in a residential facility makes it necessary to remove the child from the home and neighborhood and is the most restrictive of all the program alternatives.
2. The children's problems tend to be emphasized more than their strengths.
3. Children tend to become dependent on the rigidity of institutional life, which makes it hard for them to leave the facility.
4. Twenty-four-hour-a-day care and training programs are much more expensive than community-based day school programs.
5. Those who are placed in residential programs tend to be forgotten by other members of society.
6. Inadequate funding often results in inadequate services and overcrowded facilities that are sometimes dehumanizing.

HOSPITAL SCHOOLS, TREATMENT CENTERS, AND HOMEBOUND INSTRUCTION

Students with severe emotional and/or health problems may require hospital school, treatment center, or homebound instruction services. These services consist of intensive psychotherapy, corrective surgery, diet management, observation, rehabilitation, and/or academic instruction. This group of students also includes accident victims who must be hospitalized because of their need for heavy body casts, traction, or rehabilitation. The instructional services for the homebound and hospitalized permit these students to continue to make academic progress while they are unable to attend school. Instruction may be provided on a one-to-one tutorial basis, by a home-school or hospital-school telephone connection, or in a special school operated as part of the hospital.

The advantages of providing instruction in a hospital or treatment center or the student's home include the following:

1. Students continue to receive instruction even though they are unable to attend school.
2. An accident, an illness, or corrective surgery that requires several weeks' hospitalization or convalescence does not make it necessary for the student to repeat an entire semester or year of school.
3. Academic success can boost the morale of students who are waiting for a broken bone or incision to heal.

Problems that are often encountered during attempts to provide instruction in students' homes or in hospitals include the following:

1. Students often fall behind their classmates between the time they are admitted to the hospital and the time when it is decided that the length of stay will be long enough to justify initiation of special instructional services.
2. Attempts to correlate the instruction provided in the hospital or the student's home with that provided in the school often encounter difficulty.
3. Students often find it hard to maintain social contact with their classmates and age-level peer group.

OTHER CONSIDERATIONS

During their efforts to select the least restrictive, most appropriate placements and services for students, placement committees should also consider these major factors (adapted from Dunn, 1963, 1973): the student's abilities and disabilities; the number and severity of the student's problems; the student's age at the onset of the problem and his or her current age; the student's scholastic aptitudes, behavioral characteristics, social maturity, and wishes and goals; the special competencies of the different teachers; travel distances and times that will be involved; parental attitudes and wishes; home and neighborhood conditions; and pressures on the student's parents, family, and teachers.

SUMMARY

1. Reynolds described the different approaches to providing services for the handicapped as a hierarchy ranging from handling problems in the regular classroom to highly restrictive hospital and treatment center programs.

2. Mainstreaming emphasizes the movement of students from restrictive environments toward participation in regular classroom programs.
3. The selection of appropriate educational placements for students must emphasize the least restrictive, most productive educational environments.
4. Each student should show progress within ten weeks after placement in a new program.
5. Each service delivery model has advantages and disadvantages that should be considered by those selecting a placement for students.

REFERENCES

Adamson, G., and G. Van Etten. 1972. "Zero Reject Model Revisited: A Workable Alternative." *Exceptional Children*, 38 (May), 735–738.

Dunn, L. M. 1963, 1973. *Exceptional Children in the Schools*. New York: Holt, Rinehart and Winston, Inc.

Reynolds, M. C. 1962. "A Framework for Considering Some Issues in Special Education." *Exceptional Children*, 7 (March), 367–370.

PART TWO

*Diagnosis and Remediation of
Social, Behavioral, Perceptual,
and Language Problems*

SIX

Diagnosis and Remediation of
Social and Behavioral Problems

Students who have difficulty learning often experience problems adjusting to the school, classroom routines, and the pressures of daily life. In many cases it is difficult to determine if their adjustment problems are the cause of their learning problems or the result. Often a teacher must engage the student in a one-to-one clinical teaching experience before determining which is the cause and which the effect. The social and behavioral problems discussed in this chapter include hyperactivity, hypoactivity, distractibility and short attention span, impulsivity, perseveration, disorganization, social imperception, and the dyslogic syndrome.

HYPERACTIVITY

Hyperactive students are characterized by excessive movement and motor activity. They seem to be constantly in motion: tapping their feet or pencils, opening and closing their desk tops, or shuffling papers. They are often referred to by their teachers as being in the process of "climbing the walls." Hyperactive behavior also tends to involve distractibility, impulsiveness, short attention span, clumsiness, emotional liability, poor peer relationships, low self-esteem, and irritability.

Longhorne and Loney (1976) estimate that approximately 50 percent of all childhood behavior disorder referrals are for hyperactivity. Strauss and Lehtinen (1947) list hyperactivity as one of the characteristics of the brain-injured children they studied. Johnson and Myklebust (1967) describe hyperactivity as a *nonverbal disorder* of learning that often accompanies brain dysfunction.

Feingold (1975) indicates that more than five million children in the United States are hyperactive. Although they are bright and physically sound, they are psychologically disturbed. He reports, "They cannot sit still or concentrate; they disrupt their classrooms, burst into fits, create chaos, or at times injure them-selves.'' Feingold believes that many times hyperactivity is caused by synthetic food colorings and flavorings. He advocates removing these substances from hyperactive children's diets as an alternative to using medication to control their activity levels.

Wunderlich (1973) frequently observed hyperactivity in children with what he called the *neuro-allergic syndrome* (NAS). Wunderlich described NAS as a series of related problems caused in part by a combination of minimal brain dysfunction and allergy. He indicated that NAS children are much more likely than their age mates to be hyperactive, overaggressive, tense, irritable, fatigued, or destructive. Wunderlich suggests that the learning and behavioral problems of NAS children may be complicated by hypoglycemia (low blood sugar) and diets that contain excessive amounts of sugar. He also believes that the congestion of the eustachian tubes that often accompanies allergies may be a major cause of auditorily based learning problems. He advocates a variety of different therapeu-tic approaches, including medication, megavitamin therapy, and proper nutrition.

Photobiologist John Ott (1973) suggests that hyperactive children's excessive motor activity may be caused by exposure to minute levels of radiation given off by color television sets and fluorescent lights. He reports that encouraging decreases in the activity levels of hyperactive students were observed in classrooms where the standard cool white fluorescent light bulbs were replaced with bulbs that emitted long-wavelength ultraviolet light rated at 2,400 to 4,000 angstroms. The ends of these light fixtures were also shielded with lead to prevent the emittance of radiation during this preliminary research study.

Ott also believes that many hyperactive children may be having problems because of chemical imbalances in their bodies. Artificial lighting, for example, lacks the wavelengths necessary for bodily health. Further, eyeglasses, window glass, and automobile windshields may be screening out the life-giving rays needed for proper operation of the body's endocrine system, which in turn con-trols the body's chemistry.

Whalen and Henker (1976) state that the issue is one of quality rather than quantity of movement. They report that children who exhibit inordinately high levels of motor restlessness when asked to perform a specific structured task are frequently no more active than other children during unstructured activities. They conclude that hyperactive children's behavior problems are due to their inability to respond appropriately to the social demands and to the structure required in certain situations.

The lack of a generally accepted cause and an exact description of hyperactiv-ity makes it difficult to prescribe specific techniques and methods for working with these students. However, the following methods and procedures are often effective:

Structure the classroom and lessons so that the source of stimuli is limited and the work area is free from distractions.

Use carpeting and other sound-absorbing surfaces to reduce distracting noises.

Provide carrels to which students can retreat when they are having trouble controlling their activity level or when they need to get away from classroom distractions.

Use bulletin boards that fold out of sight like pages in a book to display students' written work and artwork so that the material being displayed will not serve as a constant source of stimulation for students.

Structure the students' daily schedule so that they will be able to plan and prepare for each event without needing to cope with last-minute changes and surprises.

Structure each lesson so that the students can master the material within a time period that is compatible with their attention span.

Ask the students to perform tasks and errands that permit them to move about the classroom and school building. These opportunities can be saved for those times when a student needs a break or a change of pace.

Gradually increase the length and difficulty of tasks as students demonstrate their ability to handle shorter, less difficult tasks.

Prepare a number of low-pressure, fun activities for when students need to spend a few minutes regaining control or relaxing.

Reduce the students' exposure to food additives and colorings.

Help the students to remember to take their medication.

Guard against permitting the students to become overly tired. Students often find it harder to control their hyperactivity when they are tired.

Reinforce appropriate behavior with free time or time to participate in preferred activities.

HYPOACTIVITY

The behavior of *hypoactive* students is characterized by underactivity or failure to respond when a response should be made. Kronick (1973) indicates that it takes a long time for the hypoactive child to dress, walk to school, make his or her bed, and perform most other activities. She describes the typical adult's reaction to the hypoactive student as being "If only I could light a fire under him!" She believes that the hypoactive child "may be expending as much energy as his hyperactive counterpart, because though his body remains in one place, his mind flits from thought to thought, and his attention is easily distracted" (p. 147).

Some of the following techniques may be useful in helping hypoactive students:

Give them specific tasks to perform and specific lengths of time to complete these tasks.

Use an egg timer to indicate when the time they have been given to complete a task has expired.

student for completing tasks and for completing them within the
∙d length of time.
∙rmine if the prescribed task has actually been completed.

DISTRACTIBILITY AND
SHORT ATTENTION SPAN

Many students who have learning problems are easily distracted. Their attention may be led away from the assigned task by any noise, motion, light, or color in the classroom. They may pay attention to everything going on in the classroom but the assigned task. Often they will work on the assigned task for a brief period of time but not long enough to complete it. Many hyperactive students have short attention spans and are highly distractible.

Procedures that are often effective when used with these students include the following:

Use carrels to isolate them when they are unable to handle the level of visual stimuli they are encountering.

Remove background noises, bulletin board displays, and other sources of potentially distracting visual and auditory stimuli.

Create an environment that has neutral colors and sound-absorbing floor, wall, and ceiling surfaces.

Remove all materials that are not required for completing the assigned lesson from students' desk tops.

Provide students with a specific time for completing each assigned task.

Place stereo headsets on students without plugging them into a sound source to reduce the reception of distracting sounds.

Use a card with a window cut in it or a frame to focus the students' attention on a specific area, problem, line of print, or paragraph.

Use a colored placemat as the background for assigned tasks. Use the student's favorite color to restrict his or her tendency to be distracted by other visual stimuli.

Organize the various events of the day so that activities that tend to stimulate or excite students come after, rather than before, activities that require extended periods of concentration.

Provide a "study booth" made out of a large, well-lighted, and ventilated box that has been carpeted on the inside for comfort. Permit students to retreat to this quiet box to get away from distracting auditory or visual stimuli. (Do not, however, use this same box as a place for punishment.)

Seat these students so that they are facing a wall with their backs to the other students.

IMPULSIVITY

Students who are impulsive tend to act or talk before thinking about what they are doing or saying. These students seem unable to anticipate effectively the consequences of their behavior before responding. As a result, they tend to find themselves in trouble with others and their environment much more frequently than do their peers. Impulsive behavior is characterized by talking out of turn, expecting to be answered immediately, rushing out in front of an oncoming car without stopping to look both ways, quickly completing and handing in assignments without checking them over, commenting on how someone else looks without stopping to think about how the comment will affect this person's feelings, or repeatedly jumping out of one's seat without permission.

Procedures that are often effective with impulsive students include the following:

Involve students in purposeful structured activities that follow a predictable sequence.
Have students practice pausing a few moments before acting or speaking so they will have time to preview the planned response.
Have students outline planned responses in writing before acting or speaking.
Tape-record students' oral responses so they can be reviewed and discussed later.
Assure students that it is not necessary to be the first one to speak or hand in assignments.
Set definite limits that students know will be consistently and fairly enforced.
Be as accepting and understanding as possible.
Permit students to earn the opportunity to participate in desired activities by demonstrating self-control.
Impose the external controls needed to protect students from danger and injury until they develop the control needed to handle activities like crossing streets and using knives and matches.
Help students develop self-control and responsibility for their own behavior.
Systematically reward students for progress they make in learning to control their own impulsivity.
Remove pressures that students may interpret as signals that immediate responses are required.

PERSEVERATION

Students who *perseverate* tend to be unable to discontinue a response pattern once it is started. They may produce an unending series of identical motoric responses long after the response is called for. For example, the student who has been asked to print one row of a particular letter may continue until the entire page is full. Or the student may continue to talk about a certain topic long after the others in the group have gone on to another topic.

Johnson and Myklebust (1967) indicate that students may also perseverate auditorily. These students are apt to attend to sounds they have heard in the recent past rather than to new environmental sounds being heard. This inability to shift to new auditory stimuli and motoric and verbal responses may interfere with their interpersonal relationships and academic success. Students tend to perseverate more when they are tired than when they are well rested.

The following procedures may help students who tend to perseverate:

Remove toys or objects with which they tend to perseverate.

Place a red check mark or X at the point on the line or page where the students should end a written activity.

Verbally tell the students to stop when the task is completed.

Change the type of task so that a different type of response (for example, from verbal to motor or motor to verbal) will be required when the level of perseveration becomes excessive.

Avoid assignments that involve repetitious acts.

Develop a clue that you use to let students know they are perseverating, for example, holding up one finger the first time a topic or task has been repeated, two fingers the second time, and so on (Kronick, 1973).

Have students practice varying their responses to certain social situations, for example, using various greetings.

Have students switch to a distinctly different activity or topic.

Have one student alternate making responses with a companion.

Let students know a few minutes or a minute before a task is to be completed so they can anticipate when a change of activity will occur.

Have students participate in games that require stopping and starting.

Have students stop and stand up or move to a different chair or desk when changing tasks.

Have students participate in choral reading or oral reading with a good companion reader (Blackwell and Joynt, 1972).

Force movement with a controlled reading device* (Blackwell and Joynt, 1972).

As Kronick (1973) points out, "Allowing the child to continue using inappropriate behavior is poor training for the future" (p. 147).

DISORGANIZATION

Disorganized students are frequently unable to complete their assigned class work successfully. They may spend most of their time producing scattered, mean-

Controlled reading devices project words onto a screen at a controlled rate. They are used to help students increase their rate of work perception.

ingless responses that have little to do with the assigned material. Disorganized persons tend to be unable to set priorities and coordinate their efforts so that their behavior contributes to reaching their goals.

Procedures that are often effective with students who are disorganized include the following:

Structure the classroom and instructional activities so that the students know what they are expected to do.

Help students develop routines they can use to structure their own activities.

Organize instructional tasks so they follow a logical, predictable, sequential pattern that can be followed step by step.

Organize instructional tasks around topics that are of interest to the students.

Use self-correcting materials that give immediate feedback to students and that direct them on to the next activity.

Reduce or remove visual or auditory stimuli that may distract students from the procedures they should be following.

Teach students the importance of making outlines, arranging notebooks carefully, and lining up figures neatly (Blanco, 1972).

SOCIAL IMPERCEPTION

Social imperception is described by Johnson and Myklebust (1967) as a nonverbal learning disorder that involves an inability to perceive oneself in relation to the behavior of others as well as to events and circumstances that involve others. This failure is closely related to the failure to observe and interpret correctly the meanings conveyed by other people's facial expressions, actions, tone of voice, gestures, and touch.

Students who suffer from social imperception should not be confused with those who are emotionally disturbed or have disciplinary problems (Johnson and Myklebust, 1967). Social perception problems are among the most debilitating of learning disabilities because they interfere with the acquisition of basic behavior patterns and controls. Students who experience social perception problems must be taught those social skills and understandings that most people acquire incidentally while they are maturing.

The following activities are described by Johnson and Myklebust as helpful with students who are having social perception problems:

Verbalize interpretations of the nonverbal world for the students.

Give students practice in observing other people, with particular attention to signs that indicate their feelings, (such as upturned mouths meaning happiness, raised eyebrows indicating surprise, and so on).

Have students examine selected pictures for signs of feelings. Discuss each picture with the students.

Use a Polaroid camera to record expressions of people, and discuss these photos.

Have students analyze and describe the people in pictures that appear in newspapers, magazines, and films.

Have students practice manners and conversations that are appropriate for use in different situations.

Organize games, such as charades, that require students both to pretend and to interpret the actions of others.

The activities in the DUSO (Developing Understanding of Self and Others) kits (Dinkmeyer, 1970) are helpful when used with students who have social maturity and social perception problems.

DYSLOGIC SYNDROME

Some students who have learning problems exhibit a pattern of "deviant" behavior referred to as the *dyslogic syndrome* (Wacker, 1975). Their behavior is characterized by frequent use of faulty logic in thinking and responding to real-life situations. They have readily available reasons for everything they have done. Unfortunately, in most cases these explanations involve unacceptable logic. For example, they may justify cheating or stealing because they feel they have been rejected. They may justify or explain away responsibility for their hyperactivity by blaming it on a brain injury they can do nothing about. They may contradict themselves without being aware of the discrepancy in what they have said.

Anderson (1963) describes dyslogic syndrome students as restless, driven youngsters who are distractible and immature and who do not get along well with others. She indicates that their frustration tolerance is low and they do not display the usual sense of pity, remorse, or sympathy in situations that call for it. Wacker (1975) indicates that they frequently become irritated or depressed without any apparent reason. Their social perception problems impair their ability to monitor their own behavior and that of others. As a result, they tend to respond with inappropriate emphasis to situations that logically should be regarded as trivial.

Wacker (1974) indicates that between 70 and 90 percent of juvenile delinquents have learning disabilities. He describes dyslogic syndrome students as prime candidates for delinquency unless their problems can be diagnosed and treated early. These problems are most pronounced when the students are placed under pressure or are "crossed" by a parent, teacher, examiner, or peer.

Explanations of the cause of the dyslogic syndrome range from minimal brain dysfunction (Wacker, 1975) to a biochemical imbalance that causes cerebral dysfunction (Rimland, 1972). Unfortunately, the failure of dyslogic syndrome students to comprehend the logical aspects of interpersonal relationships and communication makes them poor candidates for psychotherapy (Anderson, 1972).

Following are some suggestions for helping dyslogic syndrome students:

Begin habit training early in life (Anderson, 1972).

Shift from abstract to concrete communication (Anderson, 1963).

Try not to overreact (Wacker, 1975).

Give the students time for the logic in your argument to sink in (Wacker, 1975).

Increase your tolerance level for the student's behavior (Wacker, 1975).

Use operant conditioning with severe cases (Rimland, 1972).

Use medically prescribed medication to help quiet the student down (Wender, 1971; Bogoch, 1970).

Test and treat for vitamin/mineral/diet deficiencies and/or allergies (Cott, 1972; Hawkins and Pauling, 1973; Rimland, 1972; Crook, 1975; Wunderlich, 1973).

SUMMARY

1. Students who have difficulty learning often experience difficulty adjusting to school, classroom routines, and the pressures of daily life as well.

2. The excess movement and motor activity of hyperactive students accounts for approximately 50 percent of all childhood behavior disorder referrals.

3. A number of environmental factors such as allergies, fluorescent lights, low blood sugar, and food additives have been mentioned as possible causes or contributors to hyperactivity.

4. The hypoactive child's behavior is characterized by underactivity or failure to respond when a response should be made.

5. Procedures such as the use of carrels and sound-absorbing wall, floor, and ceiling surfaces can help reduce stimuli that may distract the student who has a short attention span.

6. Activities such as consciously stopping to think through responses or writing out what is to be said before saying it can help the impulsive student stay out of trouble.

7. Perseveration involves the inability to discontinue a motor or vocal response pattern once it is started.

8. Disorganized students need help in learning to structure their priorities and to coordinate their efforts so that their behavior contributes to reaching their goals.

9. The use of faulty logic in thinking and responding to real-life situations is characteristic of the dyslogic syndrome.

REFERENCES

Anderson, C. M. 1963. *Jan, My Brain-Damaged Daughter.* Storrs, Conn.: Durham Press.

Anderson, C. M. 1972. *Society Pays.* Louisville, Ky.: Walker and Company.

Blackwell, R. B., and R. R. Joynt. 1972. *Learning Disabilities Handbook for Teachers*. Springfield, Ill.: Charles C Thomas.

Blanco, R. F. 1972. *Prescriptions for Children with Learning Problems*. Springfield, Ill.: Charles C Thomas.

Bogoch, S. 1970. *The Broad Range of Use of Diphenylhydantoin*. New York: Dreyfus Medical Foundation.

Cott, A. 1972. "Megavitamins: The Orthomolecular Approach to Behavioral Disorders and Learning Disabilities." *Academic Therapy*, 3 (Spring), 245–258.

Crook, W. G. 1975. *Can Your Child Read? Is He Hyperactive?* Jackson, Tenn.: Pedicenter Press.

Dinkmeyer, D. D. 1970. *Developing Understanding of Self and Others*. Circle Pines, Minn.: American Guidance Service.

Feingold, B. F. 1975. *Why Your Child Is Hyperactive*. New York: Random House.

Hawkins, D., and L. E. Pauling, eds. 1973. *Orthomolecular Psychiatry*, San Francisco: Freeman.

Johnson, D. J., and H. R. Myklebust. 1967. *Learning Disabilities: Educational Principles and Practices*. New York: Grune and Stratton.

Kronick, D. 1973. *A Word or Two About Learning Disabilities*. San Rafael, Calif.: Academic Therapy Publications.

Longhorne, J. E., and J. Loney. 1976. "Childhood Hyperkinesis: A Return to the Source." *Journal of Abnormal Psychology*, 85, 201–209.

Ott, J. N. 1973. *Health and Light: The Effects of Natural and Artificial Light on Man and Other Living Things*. Old Greenwich, Conn.: Devin-Adair.

Rimland, B. 1972. "Operant Conditioning: Breakthrough in the Treatment of Mentally Ill Children." In *Readings on the Exceptional Child*. Ed. E. P. Trapp and P. Himelstein. New York: Appleton-Century-Crofts.

Strauss, A. A., and L. Lehtinen. 1947. *Psychopathology of the Brain-Injured Child*. New York: Grune and Stratton.

Wacker, J. A. 1974. *The Reduction of Crime through the Prevention and Treatment of Learning Disabilities: A Report to the Law Enforcement Assistance Administration*. Washington, D. C.: U. S. Government Printing Office.

Wacker, J. A. 1975. "The Dyslogic Syndrome." *Texas Key*. Austin, Tex.: Texas Association for Children with Learning Disabilities.

Wender, P. H. 1971. *Minimal Brain Dysfunction in Children*. New York: Wiley-Interscience.

Whalen, C. H., and B. Henker. 1976. "Psychostimulants and Children: A Review and Analysis." *Psychological Bulletin*, 83 (November), 1113–1130.

Wunderlich, R. C. 1973. *Allergy, Brains and Children Coping*. St. Petersburg, Fla.: Johnny Reads, Inc.

SEVEN

Diagnosis and Remediation of
Perceptual Motor Problems

Students who experience *perceptual motor* problems exhibit a number of different types and degrees of difficulty processing tactual-kinesthetic, visual, and auditory stimuli. The specific problem areas discussed in this chapter include gross motor coordination, fine motor coordination, body image, laterality and directionality, tactual defensiveness, inappropriate gestures, and proxemic perception. Visual perceptual/processing problems are discussed in Chapter 8, and auditory perceptual/processing problems in Chapter 9.

GROSS MOTOR COORDINATION

Students who have *gross motor coordination* problems appear clumsy, uncoordinated, and awkward. They are often unable to compete with their age mates in athletic activities. At times they may appear to be at war with their environment. They may collide frequently with tables, chairs, and other equipment found in their classrooms. They may fall downstairs or upstairs or off playground equipment much more frequently than others their age. When teams are being organized for ball games during recess time, these students will usually be the last ones chosen. They will probably also be the last ones to finish when their physical education class is asked to run the length of the playground or around the track. Problems in this area are often accompanied by self-concept problems and feelings of inadequacy.

The procedures that Valett (1969) suggests for use with students who have gross motor coordination problems include activities in each of the following areas:

rolling one's body in a controlled manner
sitting in a normal erect position without support or constant reminders

crawling on hands and knees in a smooth, coordinated way
walking erect in a coordinated fashion without support
running on a track or obstacle course without a change of pace
throwing a ball or beanbag with a reasonable degree of accuracy
jumping over simple obstacles without falling
skipping in normal play
dancing in a coordinated response to music
using muscular strength to perform physical tasks.

FINE MOTOR COORDINATION

Students who have *fine motor coordination* problems frequently have difficulty manipulating objects or performing tasks with their fingers. These problems often appear in activities such as coloring, writing, lacing shoes, buttoning clothes, fitting objects together, or using scissors. The results of these students' efforts to use fine motor skills will often look like those of much younger students.

Activities and procedures that are often helpful in developing fine motor coordination include the following:

stacking blocks and fitting objects together
strengthening finger muscles by molding or pinching off pieces of clay or playdough and squeezing sponges and soft rubber balls
drawing and coloring
stringing beads or macaroni
sorting objects that vary in size, color, and shape
folding paper
reproducing block designs or patterns of beads
tracing geometric figures, numbers, and letters
sewing and lacing
completing dot-to-dot pictures
snapping snaps, buttoning small and large buttons, tying shoes, and zipping zippers
reproducing peg-board designs
assembling puzzles
coloring within the lines
playing marbles, checkers, tic-tac-toe, and jacks

BODY IMAGE

Body image refers to a person's awareness of his or her body and its capabilities. Chaney and Kephart (1968) state that the definition of body image involves answers to four major questions: "What are the parts of the body? What do they each do? How do you make them do it? and Where is the body and its parts in space while they are doing it?" (p. 15)

Johnson and Myklebust (1967) indicate that some children who have body image problems may be unable to identify the parts of their own body on command. They may be unable to recognize their own faces in a mirror or to make the spatial judgments needed to organize and produce drawings of human figures. Educators should make sure that students' failures in these areas are not due to other problems. The students may not be hearing or understanding the requests, or they may lack the visual acuity needed to see whatever is to be identified.

The following activities and techniques are often helpful when used with students who have body image problems:

Have students make a life-size tracing of a classmate's body and then of their own body.

Have students draw in the face, fingernails, and other details on a sheet of paper containing an outline of their body.

Have students crawl under, over, and through an obstacle course. Ask them to describe what they are doing while moving through the course.

Have students practice moving and touching various parts of their own bodies while facing a full-length mirror.

Cut pictures of the body into two pieces and then into several pieces and have students reassemble them into a whole.

Give students partially completed drawings and ask them to draw in the missing parts.

Have students imitate the body movements of another person.

LATERALITY AND DIRECTIONALITY

Students who have *laterality* problems lack internal awareness of the space located to the left or right of the midline of their bodies. These students are sometimes observed holding their free arm tightly to the side of their body or moving it in a mirror image of the arm being used to write. They may position their work to one side of their midline to avoid crossing it with their eyes while reading and with their eyes and hands while writing.

Students who have *directionality* problems experience difficulty projecting the internal awareness of left and right that is involved in laterality into the space located beyond their fingertips. Directionality is the spatial concept that permits students to locate and describe objects located to the right and left of their midlines.

Procedures and activities that are often helpful with students who have laterality and directionality problems include the following:

Put nail polish on the little finger of the students' left hands. Teach them that
reading and writing both start at the far left-hand side (Kronick, 1969).

Make a green check mark or dot on the left side of the paper where the student
should start.

Trace hands on paper and then label them as left or right. Ask students to sort
tracings of left and right hands into separate piles.

Have students identify left and right parts of their bodies, the bodies of others, and
bodies of people in pictures (for example, left ear and right foot).

Organize a series of pictures into a left-to-right sequence so they tell a story.

Cut pictures of people into parts and then have students reassemble them.

Play games that emphasize movement of the left and right sides of the body.

TACTUAL DEFENSIVENESS

Students who are *tactually defensive* frequently are uncomfortable when they are
touched. This is particularly so when the point of contact is on the back, where
the student cannot see what is happening. Ayres (1972) indicates that the major
problems faced by tactually defensive students are likely to be behavioral rather
than academic. Tactual defensiveness in students can sometimes be reduced by
seating them so that their backs are next to a wall or in such a way that other
classmates do not frequently pass by their desks.

GESTURES

Johnson and Myklebust (1967) describe *gestures* as a form of communication that
has both receptive and expressive components. Each gesture conveys a feeling,
attitude, expectation, or request. Some gestures have universal meaning while
others are unique to a particular culture.

Students who fail to receive and comprehend the messages conveyed by
gestures may fail to respond or may respond inappropriately. As a result, they may
be viewed as disobedient, defiant, or rude. Some students may comprehend the
meaning of others' gestures but be unable to initiate the motoric movements
needed to produce the responses they want to make. Their difficulties may be due
to poor timing, use of the wrong gestures, or use of gestures that are regarded by
others to be vulgar.

The following procedures are recommended for use in teaching students to
correctly read and produce appropriate gestures:

Explain the importance of responding appropriately to others' gestures.

Explain the importance of using appropriate gestures when communicating with
others.

Have students practice making appropriate responses to various gestures (for
 example, moving toward a person who signals them to come).

Help students learn to associate the proper movement with the experience it
 represents.

Help students learn to look and imitate by placing their hands in the appropriate
 position and guiding them through the sequence of movements (Johnson and
 Myklebust, 1967).

Have the students close their eyes so they can concentrate on the feel of the
 movement (Johnson and Myklebust, 1967).

Have the students watch themselves in a mirror while they imitate the teacher's
 gestures.

PROXEMIC PERCEPTION

Students who have *proxemic perception* difficulties tend to experience problems
because they fail to position their bodies an appropriate distance from the bodies
of others while they are communicating with them. They may stand or sit so
close to others that they violate or infringe on the territory these people regard as
theirs. This infringement may involve bumping, stepping on toes or heels, touching, or just being closer to the other person than the communication justifies. As a
result, they may be viewed by others as pushy, inept, or unduly friendly. Some
students tend to stand farther away from the person they are communicating with
than necessary. These students are likely to be viewed by others as cold, unin-
terested, or unwilling to become involved. Proxemic perception problems are a
form of spatial orientation problem.

Hall (1963) describes proxemic study as "the study of how man uncon-
sciously structures microspace—the distance between men in conduct of daily
transactions, the organization of space in his houses and buildings and ultimately
the layout of his towns" (p. 1003). Hall suggests that four proxemic zones are
observable in middle-class adults who are natives of the northeastern seaboard of
the United States. Each zone is characterized by an approximate distance between
those who are communicating and by a type of conversation that tends to occur.
The four zones are as follows:

1. *The intimate zone.* In the intimate zone (0–18 inches), the other person's
   presence is overwhelming. People converse intimately with each other at this
   distance.
2. *The personal zone.* The physical features of the other person are very apparent
   in the near personal zone (1½–2½ feet). Holding hands is done in this zone.
   In the far personal zone (2½–4 feet), one's vision of the other person remains
   clear while physical contact becomes difficult. People might discuss personal
   problems and feelings in this zone.

3. *The social zone.* Touching is not possible in the near phase of the social zone (4–7 feet). Personal business and conversation is characteristic of this zone. The far social zone (7–12 feet) makes viewing of the other person's entire body possible. Formal business is typical of the communication that occurs in this zone.
4. *The public zone.* The other person is visible but not the details of his or her face in the near phase of the public zone (12–25 feet). The speaker addressing a small audience is characteristic of the type of communication that occurs at this distance. The details of facial and bodily movement also become difficult to see in the far phase of the public zone (over 25 feet). The speaker addressing a large audience (for example, a political candidate speaking in a large auditorium full of people) is characteristic of this type of communication.

Wood (1976) reports that children seem to learn the "rules" of the zones of territory in a step-by-step fashion. Her research regarding the tentative ages at which children acquire an understanding of various territorial zones is summarized in Table 7.1.

TABLE 7.1 *Children's Acquisition of Territorial Zones**

Age	Zone	Explanation
Birth to 3 years	Intimate	Children learn the closeness of communication with their mothers, other members of their family, and caretakers. They engage in touch, desire hugging, and profit from "close" communication.
3 to 7 years	Personal	With their acquisition of language, children become full-fledged communicators. They talk to others, usually on a personal basis. Much of their activity is self-centered (egocentric), and they have not acquired an understanding of socialization to any great extent.
7 years and older	Social	When children become more social, as opposed to egocentric, they form strong social relationships. They learn how to behave in social settings, and they can understand social relationships.
7 years and older	Public	Older children acquire an awareness of a "public" type of communication, particularly if the school setting offers the opportunity for performing in a public situation.

SOURCE: Barbara S. Wood, *Children and Communication: Verbal and Nonverbal Language Development.* © 1976, p. 239. Reprinted by permission of Prentice-Hall, Inc., Englewood Cliffs, N.J.

*If proxemic zones are acquired in a zone-by-zone fashion, then we might assume that the zones learned first are retained while further learning takes place.

Students aged 7 or 8 who have failed to acquire adequate proxemic perception skills should be provided with instruction designed to help them learn these skills. These students may be helped by such activities as role playing and photographing and analyzing appropriate and inappropriate proxemic relationships. Teachers and other adults should also accept the fact that children naturally tend to stand closer to adults than adults do to others.

EVALUATING PERCEPTUAL MOTOR SKILLS

The following instruments are among those frequently used to evaluate students' perceptual motor skills:

Ayres, A. J. *Southern California Test Battery for Assessment of Dysfunction (Southern California Perceptual Motor Test; Southern California Figure-Ground Visual Perception Test; Southern California Kinesthesia and Tactual Perception Tests; Ayres Space Test).* Los Angeles: Western Psychological Services, 1969. The separate tests included in this test battery are used to assess a wide range of specific perceptual motor functions of students aged 3 to 10.

Bruinicks, R. *Bruinicks-Oseretsky Test of Motor Proficiency.* Circle Pines, Minn.: American Guidance Service, 1978. A test battery for the individual assessment of eight aspects of gross and fine motor development of children aged 4½ to 14½.

Harris, A. J. *Harris Tests of Lateral Dominance.* New York: Psychological Corporation, 1947–1958. Tests that are used with those aged 7 to adult to determine right or left eye, hand, and foot preference.

Roach, C., and N. C. Kephart. *The Purdue Perceptual Motor Survey Test.* Columbus, Ohio: Charles E. Merrill, 1966. An observational device for use in assessing the balance and posture, body image and differentiation, perceptual motor match, ocular control, and form perception of children aged 6 to 10.

Valett, R. E. *A Psychoeducation Inventory of Basic Learning Abilities.* Belmont, Calif.: Fearon Publishers, 1968. A survey of skill development that includes sections on gross motor development, sensory motor integration, perceptual motor skills, language development, and conceptual skills of children aged 2 to 7.

EFFECTIVENESS OF PERCEPTUAL MOTOR TRAINING

Many educators incorrectly assume that perceptual motor training is a recommended technique for remediating reading problems. Those who have attempted to remediate reading problems by using perceptual motor techniques, however, report significant gains in their students' perceptual motor skills but no significant change in their reading performance.

Perceptual motor training is designed to help develop balance, posture, flexibility and accuracy of movement, coordination, rhythm, and awareness of one's own body and its relationship to objects in space. Properly used training procedures can lead to development of basic perceptual motor competency. These competencies would appear to play an important role in the development of the ego skills that are basic to a positive self-concept and confidence.

SUMMARY

1. Students with perceptual motor problems exhibit a number of different types and degrees of difficulty processing tactual-kinesthetic, visual, and auditory stimuli.
2. A variety of remedial suggestions and procedures exist for encouraging the development of skills in each area.
3. Several diagnostic tests and surveys are available for use in assessing perceptual motor performance.
4. Perceptual motor training should emphasize the development of perceptual motor proficiency rather than reading.
5. Little evidence exists in support of the belief that mastery of visual perceptual skills transfers directly to the development of academic skills.

REFERENCES

Ayres, A. J. 1972. *Southern California Sensory Integration Tests.* Los Angeles: Western Psychological Services.

Benton, A. 1959. *Right-Left Discrimination and Finger Localization.* New York: Paul B. Hoeber.

Chaney, C. M., and N. C. Kephart. 1968. *Motoric Aids to Perceptual Training.* Columbus, Ohio: Charles E. Merrill.

Hall, E. T. 1963. "A System for the Notation of Proxemic Behavior." *American Anthropologist,* 65, 1003–1026.

Johnson, D. J., and H. R. Myklebust. 1967. *Learning Disabilities: Educational Principles and Practices.* New York: Grune and Stratton.

Kronick, D. 1969. *They Too Can Succeed: A Practical Guide for Parents of Learning Disabled Children.* San Rafael, Calif.: Academic Therapy Publications.

Lerner, J. W. 1976. *Children with Learning Disabilities.* 2nd ed. Boston: Houghton Mifflin Company.

Valett, R. A. 1969. *Programming Learning Disabilities.* Belmont, Calif.: Fearon Publishers.

Wood, B. S. 1976. *Children and Communication: Verbal and Nonverbal Language Development.* Englewood Cliffs, N. J.: Prentice-Hall.

EIGHT

Diagnosis and Remediation of
Visual Perceptual Problems

Visual processing consists of a number of visual perceptual tasks that are involved in receiving, organizing, and interpreting visual stimuli. These tasks consist of visual reception, visual discrimination (prominent feature discrimination, figure-ground discrimination, and visual closure), visual association, visual memory (revisualization and visual sequential memory), eye-hand coordination/visual motor integration, visual form constancy, perception of position in space, and perception of spatial relations.

Students who have learning problems may have difficulty with one or more of the above visual perceptual tasks. The presence of a visual perceptual problem does not automatically mean the student will have trouble learning to read, nor does the presence of a reading problem mean that the student will also have a visual perceptual problem. Tests selected from the following instruments can be used to determine if the student has strengths or deficits in these task areas:

Illinois Test of Psycholinguistic Abilities, Kirk, McCarthy, and Kirk (1968), for visual reception, visual association, visual sequential memory, and visual closure subtests

Developmental Test of Visual Perception, Frostig et al. (1964), for eye motor/hand coordination, figure-ground discrimination, constancy of shape, position in space, and spatial relations subtests

Developmental Test of Visual Motor Integration, Beery and Buktenica (1967)

Mertens Visual Perception Test, Mertens (1969)

Ayres Space Test, Ayres (1962)

Southern California Figure-Ground Visual Perception Test, Ayres (1966)

Detroit Tests of Learning Aptitude, Baker and Leland (1967), for visual attention span for letters and visual attention span for objects

Students who have difficulty processing visual perceptual materials should receive special instruction designed to facilitate improvement of their skills in these areas. Visual perceptual training should accompany and complement instruction in the academic areas, not replace it. Teachers who replace a student's reading instruction with visual perception training should not expect the student to make significant gains in reading performance.

VISUAL RECEPTION

Kirk and Kirk (1971) describe *visual reception* as the "ability to gain meaning from visual symbols" (p. 23). Visual reception occurs when visual input enters the perceptual system. Students who have visual reception problems may have trouble selecting essential clues, scanning the perceptual field in search of information, organizing what is received into a recognizable whole, and attaching meaning to the visual symbols that are seen.

Remedial activities and experiences that are useful in developing visual reception skills include the following:

identifying shapes, colors, letters, and numbers
matching shapes, colors, and numbers
matching pictures to actual objects
tracing the outlines of figures and geometric forms
identifying items appearing in pictures in magazines and catalogs
identifying missing parts
matching words and sentences to pictures

Other activities are described in Minskoff, Wiseman, and Minskoff (1972) and Karnes (1972).

VISUAL DISCRIMINATION

Visual discrimination involves the ability to recognize the similarities and differences among items. Recognition and differentiation of the shapes and sizes of letters, words, and numbers; figure-ground discrimination; and visual closure are the three main types of visual discrimination involved in academic tasks.

Recognition and Differentiation   Geake (1970) and Smith (1967) provide activities designed to help students discriminate visually among letters and among words. Numerous workbooks that contain exercises for use in learning to recognize letters, geometric figures, and numbers are available from publishers of educational materials. Teacher-designed sorting and classification activities, such as sorting buttons by size and color and sorting and matching coins, can be used to develop recognition and differentiation skills.

Figure-Ground Discrimination   Students with visual figure-ground discrimination problems may lose their place frequently while reading. They may also have trouble locating a word in the dictionary, an index, or a sentence; scanning for specific information; and interpreting stories or social situations. Activities that may help them in these areas include the following:

finding hidden figures, letters, words, or numbers in pictures
using the dictionary, tables of contents, book indexes, and telephone books
scanning for a specific letter, word, or fact
isolating words that are against a confused background or that are run together
     with no spaces left between

Other helpful activities are contained in Frostig et al. (1964) and Minskoff, Wiseman, and Minskoff (1972). Finally, figure-ground discrimination activities that require the student to differentiate letters of the alphabet or words from background material should be used whenever possible.

Visual Closure   Students who have visual closure problems experience difficulty identifying a visual stimulus when part of it is missing. For example, they tend to have trouble completing incomplete figures; identifying missing parts of pictures, letters, numbers, or words; identifying complete forms of partially exposed pictures, letters, numbers, or words; completing words by closing spaces between letters (for example, *rab-bit, h-at*); and supplying the missing word when a blank appears in a sentence in place of a word. In addition to the activities contained in Minskoff, Wiseman, and Minskoff (1972) and Karnes (1972), the following may be useful in developing visual closure:

matching incomplete pictures of objects, geometric figures, letters, or numbers
     with complete pictures of these items
completing dot-to-dot, number-to-number, and letter-to-letter pictures
naming the missing part of a picture
assembling puzzles containing known objects
finding hidden objects, letters, or numbers in pictures
naming objects from their shadows
completing words by supplying the missing letters
completing sentences by supplying the missing words
practicing perceiving a whole when there are conflicting visual stimuli present
     (Lombardi and Lombardi, 1977)

VISUAL ASSOCIATION

Visual association is described by Kirk and Kirk (1971) as the organizing process by which one relates concepts presented visually. Students who find it difficult to make visual associations may have trouble connecting a name, size, shape, or color with the object, figure, number, letter, or word it describes; identifying opposites, similarities, and differences among visual stimuli; identifying the item in a group that is not related to the other items in the group (for example, 1, 2, A, 4); relating the parts of an object to the whole object; predicting possible outcomes of visually presented material; grouping and classifying items according to common properties and uses; finding and evaluating alternative solutions to problems; and understanding money concepts. They may be helped in these areas by the exercises contained in Minskoff, Wiseman, and Minskoff (1972) and Karnes (1972) as well as by the following activities and experiences:

sorting and classifying objects
matching objects of the same size, shape, color, or number
identifying opposites
identifying objects in a group that are not related to any other objects in the group
matching pictures of people to their work, furniture to the room of the house
    where it belongs, and animals to their young
matching words to pictures and sentences
indicating verbally why objects are or are not included in groups
predicting possible outcomes in visually presented material (Lombardi and
    Lombardi, 1977)

VISUAL MEMORY

Students who have visual memory problems may have trouble retaining or recalling visual experiences. Some of these students are unable to recognize visual stimuli they have previously viewed. Others are able to recognize previously viewed visual stimuli but are unable to reproduce them. The two most frequently encountered forms of visual memory problems are *revisualization* and *visual sequential memory problems*.

Revisualization   Johnson and Myklebust (1967) describe revisualization as a process involving the visual memory and production of letters and words. Students who have revisualization problems are not able to retrieve the visual image of the requested letter, number, or symbol from memory. They may be able to read words they cannot recall. They can copy as long as the material being copied remains visible.

Johnson and Myklebust (1967) propose the following remedial suggestions and procedures for use in developing revisualization skills:

Select material that has large print and clear, well-defined lines that present sharp
    visual images.
Structure the learning environment to attract and maintain students' attention.

Use auditory and tactual kinesthetic modalities to prompt visual recall.

Give students practice in recognizing pictures, letters, numbers, and symbols after a few seconds' exposure.

Give students practice in revisualizing part of the visual image by filling in the missing letters in partially completed words.

Visual Sequential Memory   Students who have visual sequential memory problems find it difficult to remember and reproduce sequences of items they have seen. They may have difficulty organizing a series of letters, numbers, words, phrases, or sentences in the same order as they were last seen; reordering a series of pictures, words, phrases, or sentences so that they show the order in which certain events occurred; remembering what events in a series have already been seen and which ones come next; and remembering the order of the letters in a word while trying to spell it.

Encourage these students to develop a system that will help them remember a visual sequence. Have them note which items are different from the predominant item, or find a key number, word, or phrase that will make the sequence easier to recall. They may wish to use tactile or kinesthetic sensation as reminders, as well as any gimmicks and crutches they might find helpful.

Remedial activities and experiences recommended for developing visual sequential memory can be found in Minskoff, Wiseman, and Minskoff (1972) and Karnes (1972). Others include the following:

Have students reproduce a series of beads, parquetry blocks, or colors from memory.

Have students reproduce a pegboard pattern or block design from memory.

Teach students standard visual sequences such as the alphabet, number system, days of the week, or months of the year.

Give students practice in identifying letters, numbers, or words that are out of sequence.

Give students practice in remembering room numbers, street addresses, telephone numbers, and zip codes.

Give students practice in remembering sequences of letters in words and of words in sentences.

Use white magnetic letters on a black background. This provides an eye-catching contrast for the student who is not in the habit of attending to the detail involved in the letters.

Perform activities that foster development of visual imagery:

Write on the student's back and have him or her match it.

Write on the table top and have the student match it.

Write on the student's back or table top and have the student reproduce it in writing or label it verbally.

Show a series of letters as real words not in the student's vocabulary and have him or her reproduce the words in writing.

Show students words briefly on flash cards and have them reproduce the words in writing.

EYE-HAND COORDINATION/VISUAL MOTOR INTEGRATION

The coordination or integration of the movements of the eyes with the movements of the hands is called *eye-hand coordination.* Children first learn to match the movements of their eyes with the movements of their hands; they then learn to use the eyes to direct the movements of the hands. Eye-hand coordination is also called *perceptual motor match* and *visual motor integration.*

Students with eye-hand coordination problems may have trouble catching balls; drawing straight lines and slanted or curved lines; stopping and starting at a given point; placing objects in specified positions; threading a needle; tracing numerals, letters, or pictures; writing numerals or letters that are consistent in size; writing on the line; using tools; assembling objects; and performing the eye-tracking movements involved in reading. They may be helped by the following activities and exercises:

stacking blocks
stringing beads
placing pegs into peg boards
hammering nails into boards
playing games that involve throwing and catching balls
tracing and coloring pictures
playing dominoes, marbles, or checkers
performing eye-tracking exercises (Geake, 1970; Smith, 1967)

VISUAL FORM CONSTANCY

The ability to recognize figures, letters, and numerals even when their size, color, shading, texture, or position in space is changed is called *visual form constancy.* This visual perceptual skill involves the ability to recognize that an object or symbol has unchanging properties. For example, students who have difficulty with the perception of visual form constancy find it hard to recognize familiar letters or words when the type style has been changed; identify objects or drawings when they are viewed at different angles or distances, recognize figures, letters, or numerals when their size, color, or position in space is changed; recognize a word when it appears again later in the same sentence or paragraph; and visualize what is read silently or orally. In addition to those contained in Frostig and Horne (1964), remedial activities and experiences that are often helpful in developing an understanding of visual form constancy are the following:

locating all the objects of a certain shape, size, or color in a room
identifying objects or drawings at different distances and angles
sorting objects into groups of the same size, shape, or color
identifying how objects and symbols are different
drawing diagrams of three-dimensional objects
finding words that are printed in various type styles
distinguishing between whole and incomplete objects or symbols

POSITION IN SPACE

Perception of the relationship of single objects in space to one's own body is called *perception in space* (Frostig, 1961). This perceptual skill consists of the ability to locate forms that are reversed, inverted, or rotated; to recognize likenesses and differences in forms; and to discriminate the position of figures, objects, letters, and numerals in space. Students who have problems in this area often find it difficult to determine the relationship between their bodies and the objects or symbols located in the space around them, move specific parts of their bodies when they are asked to move them to prescribed positions in space, distinguish between directions involving the location of objects in space, differentiate between positions of symbols (for example, b-d-p-q, m-w, f-t, 6-9, 24-42), read maps, and locate objects from verbal or written directions. Remedial suggestions and procedures that may help them develop an understanding of position in space include the following:

identifying geometric figures, letters, or numerals on a page containing a variety
     of inverted, reversed, and rotated symbols
locating the direction of objects from oneself
practicing physical exercises and movement experiences that develop an aware-
     ness of body parts
locating objects from verbal or written directions
imitating body positions
reading maps and blueprints
differentiating left from right

Also helpful are the exercises contained in Frostig and Horne (1964).

SPATIAL RELATIONS

The ability to see the relationships between two or more objects and to relate this group of objects to oneself is called perception of *spatial relations*. Students who have spatial relations problems may have trouble judging the distance between objects; copying groups of figures, pictures, letters, numerals, words, or sentences; placing numbers in rows and columns so they can be dealt with mathematically; remembering visual sequences; and understanding the quantitative relationships involved in mathematics. Activities and procedures recommended for their use, in addition to those in Frostig and Horne (1964), include the following:

copying cube and block designs
copying bead designs
duplicating peg board designs
describing the relationships between objects that vary in terms of shape, size,
    weight, quantity, and distance
following directions in locating objects or places
reading blueprints and maps
practicing writing and spelling

EFFECTIVENESS OF VISUAL PERCEPTUAL TRAINING

Some educators mistakenly attempt to use visual perceptual training to improve students' reading performance. These attempts usually result in significantly improved visual perceptual skills but little or no improvement in reading performance. Those who seek to improve students' reading skills should concentrate on providing basic reading instruction. There is little evidence that mastery of visual perceptual skills transfers directly to development of reading skills. A strong instructional program in reading combined with a supplemental perceptual training program is suggested for students who have deficits in both areas.

SUMMARY

1. Visual processing consists of a number of visual perceptual tasks that are involved in receiving, organizing, and interpreting visual stimuli.
2. The presence of a visual perceptual problem does not automatically mean that the student will also have a reading problem.

3. A large number of tests contain subtests that can be used to assess visual perceptual skills.
4. Visual perceptual training should complement, not replace, academic instruction.
5. Visual perceptual training should be used to develop visual perceptual skills, not as a remedial reading technique.
6. There is little evidence that mastery of visual perceptual skills transfers directly to the development of academic skills.

REFERENCES

Ayres, A. J. 1966. *Southern California Figure-Ground Visual Perception Test.* Los Angeles: Western Psychological Services.

Ayres, A. J. 1962. *Ayres Space Test.* Los Angeles: Western Psychological Services.

Baker, H. J., and B. Leland. 1967. *Detroit Test of Learning Aptitude.* Indianapolis: Bobbs-Merrill.

Beery, K. E., and N. A. Buktenica. 1967. *Developmental Test of Visual Motor Integration.* Chicago: Follett.

Frostig, M., and D. Horne. 1964. *Frostig Program for Development of Visual Perception.* Chicago: Follett.

Frostig, M., P. Maslow, D. W. Lefener, and J. R. B. Whittlesey. 1964. *Frostig Developmental Test of Visual Perception.* 1963 Standardization. Palo Alto, Calif.: Consulting Psychologists Press.

Geake, R. R. 1970. *Primary Alphabet Tracking.* Worthington, Ohio: Ann Arbor Publishers.

Johnson, D. J., and H. R. Myklebust. 1967. *Learning Disabilities: Educational Principles and Practices.* New York: Grune and Stratton.

Karnes, M. B. 1972. *GOAL (Game Oriented Activities for Learning).* Springfield, Mass.: Milton Bradley.

Kirk, S. A., and W. D. Kirk. 1971. *Psycholinguistic Learning Disabilities: Diagnosis and Remediation.* Urbana: University of Illinois Press.

Kirk, S. A., J. J. McCarthy, and W. D. Kirk. 1968. *Illinois Test of Psycholinguistic Abilities.* Urbana: University of Illinois Press.

Lombardi, T. P., and E. J. Lombardi. 1977. *ITPA: Clinical Interpretation and Remediation.* Seattle: Special Child Publications.

Mertens, M. K. 1969. *Mertens Visual Perception Test.* Los Angeles: Western Psychological Services.

Minskoff, E. H., D. E. Wiseman, and J. G. Minskoff. 1972. *MWM Program for Developing Language Abilities.* Ridgefield, N. J.: Educational Performance Associates.

Smith, D. E. P. 1967. *Word Tracking.* Worthington, Ohio: Ann Arbor Publishers.

NINE

Diagnosis and Remediation of
Auditory Language Problems

The understanding of auditory language and the production of speech are two of the most important human accomplishments (Lerner, 1976). Children who fail to understand the auditory stimuli they receive are unlikely to remember or use what they hear, leaving them with nothing on which to base their speech. Chomsky (1965) indicates that the acquisition of our *auditory-vocal communication system* is based on the language code used in the sounds we hear. Bloom and Lahey (1978) point out that "language is a code whereby ideas about the world are represented through a conventional system of arbitrary signals for communication" (p. 4).

TYPES OF AUDITORY LANGUAGE PROBLEMS

Kirk and Gallagher (1979) describe three general deviations in language processes: language disorders, delayed speech and language, and aphasia.

Language Disorders

Students with language disorders may have difficulty discriminating among sounds and learning the sound/symbol relationships needed to hear words, parts of words, and inflections. They may also experience problems integrating and using the sound and word patterns needed to organize words and phrases into syntactically correct sentences. Language disorders may interfere with the development of correct grammar and meaning.

Bloom and Lahey (1978) describe language as the product of an interaction of *content, form,* and *use.* Normal language results from the successful interaction of content, form, and use whereas disordered language occurs when there is a disruption of any one of these components or in the interaction among them. Language *content* consists of what individuals talk about or understand in messages. Included are object knowledge, object relations, and event relations. Language *form* refers to the shape or sound of messages in terms of their acoustic and phonetic qualities, functions, and syntax. The function of a word can be described in terms of its part of speech, whereas the form of a sentence can be described as being declarative or a question. The syntax is reflected in the word order. Language *use* involves the form the speaker chooses from the available alternatives.

Delayed Language Development

Bangs (1968) describes delayed language development as language development that is progressing in an orderly but significantly slower than normal fashion. Whereas disordered or deficient language represents a departure from the usual orderly pattern of learning the language code, delayed language is characterized by its adherence to a normal developmental pattern. Delayed language development may also be related to factors such as mental retardation, deafness, and emotional disturbance.

Aphasia

Myklebust (1957) uses the term *auditory aphasia* to describe the ability to hear and gain meaning from all the sounds in the environment except speech. He uses the term *auditory agnosia* to describe the failure to gain meaning from environmental and speech sounds one hears.

Children who are partially or totally unable to gain meaning from and/or repeat the auditory stimuli they hear should be distinguished from those who lack the auditory acuity needed to hear. Children with a partial hearing loss are referred to as hard of hearing. Children with auditory perceptual problems, on the other hand, can hear sounds even though they are unable to recognize these sounds (Berry and Eisenson, 1956).

It should be noted that the term *aphasia* is commonly used to refer to both partial and total failure to gain meaning from speech. This use is a departure from the general rule of thumb, which is that a term beginning with *a* refers to a total inability to perform whereas the prefix *dys* indicates partial inability. Technically, the term *dysphasia* should be used to refer to those who have a partial inability to gain meaning from the speech they hear.

The term aphasia is usually applied to adults who have lost part or all of their speech as the result of a stroke or severe blow to the head. The number of children who are actually diagnosed as being aphasic is quite small. Many more exhibit some of the same types of receptive and expressive auditory language problems as are experienced by aphasics. Kirk and Gallagher (1979) observe that considerable difficulty is involved in differentiating between delayed speech and aphasia, and that the terms are often misapplied. They advise evaluators and teachers to focus on children's problems as they relate to *auditory-vocal disorders.* This approach to problems of perception, speech, and language produces information that can lead to remediation programs.

Auditory Processing Dysfunctions

Chalfant and Scheffelin (1969) call auditory perceptual problems *auditory processing dysfunctions.* They suggest that children who do not process auditory stimuli effectively may have trouble identifying the source of sounds; discriminating among sounds or words; reproducing pitch, rhythm, and melody; differentiating significant from insignificant stimuli; combining speech sounds into words; and understanding the meaning of sounds.

STEPS IN LANGUAGE ACQUISITION

According to Myklebust (1960), three steps are involved in the acquisition of language: the development of inner language or meaningfulness, the development of auditory receptive language, and the development of auditory expressive language.

Development of Inner Language

Inner language is described by Goldstein (1948) as the language we use to communicate with ourselves; Johnson and Myklebust (1967) refer to it as the language we use to think. Wallace and Kauffman (1978) suggest that "Inner language development is dependent upon the child's ability to: (1) Establish verbal imagery for sounds, words, concepts, etc. (2) Use the complex maze of skills needed in the logical thinking process" (p. 151).

Students with an inner language disorder may have difficulty acquiring meaning from verbal symbols, be unable to transform experience into verbal symbols, be able to read but fail to grasp the meaning of paragraphs, exhibit a wide discrepancy between verbal and nonverbal mental test scores (with the verbal scores being superior), and show peculiar learning patterns that reflect their failure to develop a consistent norm of experience (Johnson and Myklebust, 1967).

Students with inner language problems involving difficulty with verbal imagery may benefit from the following activities:

listening to sounds on a prerecorded tape or record and selecting objects or pictures showing the sources of these sounds

naming specific objects as the teacher points to them (Wallace and Kauffman, 1978)

pointing to those objects in a group that have the same use (for example, a cup and glass)

pointing out how pairs of objects are the same and different (for example, a guitar and violin) (Wallace and Kauffman, 1978)

drawing pictures of objects that have been described verbally

Students with inner language problems involving difficulty with thinking skills may benefit from the following activities:

classifying items according to size, color, shape, or number

answering questions that require explanation of logical relationships (for example, "Do birds have wings?" "Do you lick an ice cream cone with your knees?") (Bush and Giles, 1977)

answering questions that ask students to list things, such as things that have wheels, that are smaller than an ant, or that have hair (Smith, 1974)

explaining the inconsistencies involved in questions such as those proposed by Bush and Giles (1977): "Would a dress made of flowers last a month?" "Can you fish in a swimming pool?" "If you are tired, are you ready to play?"

identifying the two words in a series that are related (for example, dog-cat-apple, chair-table-knife, milk-stone-water) (Wallace and Kauffman, 1978)

Development of Auditory Receptive Language

Wallace and Kauffman (1978) describe auditory receptive language as the comprehension of the spoken language of others. The inability to understand the spoken language one hears is called *auditory receptive aphasia.*

Chalfant and Scheffelin (1969) describe four developmental tasks involved in the successful acquisition of auditory receptive language: *attention* to noises, speech sounds, words, phrases, and sentences; *discrimination* between the auditory-vocal sound units; *establishment of correspondence* between sound units and their corresponding objects or events; and automatic *auditory-vocal reception* of language signals.

Development of Auditory Expressive Language

Johnson and Myklebust (1967) describe students who are unable to produce spoken language as *auditory expressive aphasics.* These students are unable to express themselves verbally even though they understand speech and language and have no muscular paralysis that prevents them from speaking (Lerner, 1976). In extreme cases they may substitute pointing and gestures for the use of oral language in making their needs known.

The term *dysnomia* means difficulty in remembering and expressing words. Students with dysnomia frequently substitute words or use a word such as "thing" whenever they cannot think of the name of something (Lerner, 1976). At other times they may talk around an object, saying everything possible about it except the name they are trying to remember.

Chalfant and Scheffelin (1969) describe four developmental tasks required for the successful production of expressive auditory language: *intention* to respond and the decision to send a vocal message, *retrieval* and *formulation* of signals needed to respond, *organization* in one's mind of the *vocal-motor sequences* needed to express ideas, and automatic *auditory-vocal expression*.

Three types of *expressive aphasia* are described by Johnson and Myklebust (1967): faulty reauditorization, vocal-motor production difficulties, and defective formulation and syntax. *Reauditorization* problems involve the inability to remember and retrieve words for spontaneous usage. These students can usually understand and recognize the words even though they are not able to recall them. Suggested activities for use in developing reauditorization are discussed as part of the auditory memory section later in this chapter.

Students who are unable to remember the vocal-motor movements needed to produce oral language are referred to as *vocal-motor aphasics.* Their inability to voluntarily initiate the tongue and lip movements needed to speak is not due to paralysis. Chalfant and Scheffelin (1969) identified the six tasks involved in vocal-motor language production. They include (1) *motion* of the vocal-motor apparatus and the random production of vocal sound units, (2) *attention* to the kinesthetic sensations experienced while producing random sounds, (3) *repetition* of the vocal-motor movements and the resulting vocal sound units, (4) *discrimination* between the kinesthetic sensations and vocal sound units produced by each movement, (5) *establishment of correspondence* between vocal-motor movements and the sounds produced when each movement is repeated, and (6) *automatic vocal-motor production* of the vocal-motor and sound units needed to produce oral language. A speech therapist trained to provide basic instruction in language development can be of assistance when the student has a severe language problem.

Students with formulation and syntax problems experience difficulty in stringing words together to form syntactically correct sentences (Lerner, 1976). They may be able to use single words or simple phrases but be unable to organize these words into sentences to express their ideas. This form of expressive language problem is referred to as *formulation aphasia* or *syntactical aphasia* (Johnson and Myklebust, 1967). The characteristics, diagnosis, and remediation of formulation and syntax problems are discussed in detail later in this chapter.

DIAGNOSTIC AND REMEDIAL PROCEDURES

The auditory-vocal communication difficulties of students may include one or a combination of problems in areas such as auditory acuity, auditory attention, auditory discrimination, speech articulation, auditory reception and verbal comprehension, auditory association, auditory memory, sound blending and auditory closure, vocabulary development and verbal expression, production of syntactically correct language and grammatic closure, and auditory analysis and judgment.

Auditory Acuity

The ability to hear is a major prerequisite to the acquisition of language. Any attempt to determine why a student is not hearing should begin with *puretone audiometric* testing, which indicates the extent to which the student can or cannot hear with each ear and enables one to determine if the student's problem is due to an inability to hear or an inability to process effectively what is heard. Informal diagnostic procedures using "watch-tick" and "whisper" tests are not sophisticated enough to answer questions about auditory acuity.

Behaviors that suggest a student's hearing may need to be tested include failure to respond to sound, inconsistent response to sound, turning head toward sound when listening, cupping hand over ear to listen, daydreaming, frequent earaches, frequent runny ears, excessive dependence on visual stimuli, frequent requests to have words or questions repeated, speech and sound distortions, and deficient vocabulary development.

Auditory Attention

Failure to listen for possible auditory stimuli and to attend to the sounds produced may result in incomplete language development. Behaviors that indicate students may not be attending to auditory stimuli include failing to turn their heads toward the sound source, failing to maintain eye contact with the sound source or speaker, exhibiting a short attention span, being easily distracted from the sound source, failing to complete assignments involving listening, appearing to listen but not comprehending what is said, letting the mind wander from the discussion, and failing to follow oral directions. Counts of students' attending behaviors during specific time intervals can be used to determine the extent of their attention or lack of attention to auditory stimuli. Instructional procedures can then be designed to modify their behavior so that the ratio of attending behaviors to nonattending behaviors will increase.

Some procedures that are helpful in teaching students to attend to auditory stimuli are the following:

amplifying the auditory stimuli to increase the difference between sound and no sound

using visible sound sources such as manipulative toys, musical instruments, pots and pans, or Halloween noise makers

repeatedly turning the student's head toward the source of the sound

turning the student's head to make the sound source visible

selectively reinforcing responses that are the result of attention to auditory stimuli.

Auditory Discrimination

The ability to discriminate among sounds or words enables the student to detect differences that exist in the oral language he or she hears. Students who are having trouble discriminating among auditory stimuli tend to have difficulty determining the location of the sound source in relation to themselves, identifying gross sound differences, distinguishing among environmental sounds, identifying changes in pitch and loudness, distinguishing among consonant sounds, distinguishing among vowel sounds, determining if pairs of words are the same or different, determining if two sequences of sounds are the same or different, determining if pairs of words rhyme, and distinguishing between auditory figure and auditory ground.

There are several formal tests that are frequently used to assess auditory discrimination. The Goldman-Fristoe-Woodcock Test of Auditory Discrimination (1970) includes auditory discrimination tasks with and without background noise. The Goldman-Fristoe-Woodcock Auditory Selective Attention Test (1974) requires the student to discriminate among auditory stimuli that are presented in the presence of background noises that gradually increase in intensity. The three types of background noises used are fanlike noise, cafeteria noise, and voice noises. The Wepman Test of Auditory Discrimination (1958) includes forty pairs of words. The student responds by indicating if the two words spoken by the examiner are the same or different.

Teachers can informally assess other aspects of auditory discrimination relatively easily. Tasks involving differences in environmental sounds can be created by using the prerecorded cards that accompany recording devices like the Language Master. Various types of noise makers can be used to assess ability to locate the sources of sounds and determine the differences among environmental sounds. The ability to discriminate among variations in the pitch and loudness of sounds can be assessed through striking notes on a piano, using a pitch pipe, or humming sounds of different pitches and volumes. Rhythmic patterns can be beat on a drum, piano, tambourine, or table top to determine if the student can identify rhythmic differences. Students should not be able to watch the production of the sounds or rhythms. Those with strong visual skills may be able to determine if the same motor pattern or differing motor patterns are being used to create the sound or rhythms.

Three main activities are involved in auditory discrimination: distinguishing among sounds that vary on a single acoustic dimension, discriminating among sequences of sounds varying on several dimensions, and discriminating between auditory figure and auditory ground. A discussion of each of these auditory discrimination activities follows.

Single Dimension Discrimination   The distinction among auditory stimuli that vary on one dimension may be based on frequency (pitch), decibel level (loudness), or number, rate of presentation, duration, kind, and location of the sounds. The auditory stimuli being received may be speech or nonspeech sounds.

Students who are unable to determine the differences and similarities among initial or final sounds of words, consonant blends, or vowels usually have difficulty acquiring understanding, and using spoken language. Those who have trouble analyzing and synthesizing a series of sounds into meaningful language often experience problems in auditory memory, speech, and reading. Some general principles that should be remembered when developing auditory discrimination training activities include the following:

Begin with two sounds that are clearly different (for example, *h, k, s*).
Introduce familiar sounds first.
Remember that younger children usually need a longer time to absorb sound.
Follow discrimination among single sounds with discrimination among words.
Move from discrimination among gross differences (for example, a telephone ring
  and a knock on the door) to finer discriminations (for example, a telephone
  ring and a door bell).

Multiple Dimension Discrimination   Some students who successfully discriminate among sounds varying on one dimension are unable to discriminate among sounds varying on several dimensions. These students are likely to be unable to reproduce groups or sequences of auditory stimuli.

Chalfant and Scheffelin (1969) point out that processing auditory stimuli that vary on several acoustic dimensions is an important factor in the acquisition of spoken language. Reproducing patterns or groups of auditory stimuli sequentially creates rhythm. Therefore, tapping tasks are frequently used in the evaluation of students' rhythmic abilities. The examiner usually presents a series of taps that vary in loudness or frequency; the examiner also varies the grouping of the taps and the size of the intervals between taps. The student responds by reproducing the auditory stimuli demonstrated by the examiner.

Auditory Figure-Ground Discrimination   The ability to discriminate between auditory figure and auditory ground involves differentiating relevant auditory stimuli from irrelevant stimuli. The relevant stimuli become the recognizable auditory figure, whereas the irrelevant stimuli are tuned out or pushed into the background. Figure-ground discrimination problems may take the form of an inability to differentiate between relevant and irrelevant speech sounds, between speech and nonspeech sounds, or both. Sounds made on the other side of the classroom may appear as loud to the student as those made next to his or her desk. The extra effort required to discriminate between auditory figure and ground is often fatiguing for these students.

The effect of auditory figure-ground discrimination problems on students can often be reduced by installing carpeting, acoustical tile, or other surfaces that reduce classroom noise; having the student wear the type of ear muffs worn by target shooters when they are practicing, or a stereo head set that is not plugged into a sound source; and removing as much of the distracting and irrelevant auditory stimuli from the environment as possible.

Speech Articulation

Learning to vocalize the individual speech sounds is an important step in the development of expressive auditory language. Children with articulation problems frequently fail to pronounce individual speech sounds correctly, omit certain sounds while speaking, substitute sounds for others, add sounds to words, and distort speech sounds.

The *Templin-Darley Test of Articulation* (1964) and the *Goldman-Fristoe Test of Articulation* (1972) are two of the most frequently used tests of articulation. The assistance of a speech therapist should be sought whenever it is suspected that a student is having an articulation problem.

Auditory Reception and Verbal Comprehension

The reception and comprehension of auditory stimuli are prerequisites to the development of oral language. Kirk and Kirk (1971) describe auditory reception as the "ability to understand auditory symbols" (p. 23). Auditory reception is the sensory act that occurs when auditory input is introduced into the perceptual system.

Students with auditory reception problems may have trouble listening or attending to auditory stimuli; comprehending the meaning of abstract words; answering yes and no questions containing one concept; answering comprehension questions about material they have read; understanding what they hear on a phonograph, tape recorder, or radio; following verbal directions; identifying objects from verbal descriptions; attaching meaning to words; and discriminating among auditory stimuli.

Subtests and tests for assessing the ability to receive and comprehend oral language include the Auditory Reception subtests of the *Illinois Test of Psycholinguistic Abilities* (Kirk, McCarthy, and Kirk, 1968); the *Peabody Picture Vocabulary Test* (Dunn, 1965); the Picture Vocabulary subtest of the *Test of Language Development* (Newcomer and Hammill, 1977); the Comprehension subtest from the *Wechsler Intelligence Scale for Children–Revised* (Wechsler, 1974); the *Test for Auditory Comprehension of Language* (Carrow, 1973a); the Receptive Language subtest of the *Northwestern Syntax Test* (Lee, 1969); the *Boehm Test of Basic Concepts* (Boehm, 1971); and the Inventory of Language Abilities in the *MWM Program for Developing Language Abilities* (Minskoff, Wiseman, and Minskoff, 1972).

Remedial activities and suggestions to use in developing auditory reception skills include practice in the following areas:

repeating rhythms
using the Language Master
listening for specific sounds or words
recognizing environmental and speech sounds
following verbal directions
verbally describing the likenesses and differences between sounds (number, volume, pitch)
answering questions that require yes or no responses
repeating sentences of increasing length and complexity

Dunn, Horton, and Smith (1965, 1966, 1967, 1968) and Minskoff, Wiseman, and Minskoff (1972) also offer useful exercises and activities.

Some students who are able to grasp the meaning of words presented in isolation are unable to understand sentences. This may be due to their failure to remember all of the words heard or to an inability to relate the meanings of the words to each other. Suggested activities for these students include the following:

responding yes or no to questions such as "Do dogs fly?" "Is water wet?" and "Can an airplane walk?" (Bush and Giles, 1977)
indicating comprehension of two-word noun-verb combinations (for example, "John runs") and adjective-noun combinations (for example, "Big dog") by acting out the sentence and pointing to a picture that describes it (Eisenson, 1972)
answering questions that require comparisons, such as "Who barks, a rabbit or a dog?" (Wallace and Kauffman, 1978)
listening to a sentence and supplying the correct word, for example, "I am thinking of a word that tells us what to eat soup with" (Lerner, 1976)
filling in the blanks in short stories and poems

Auditory Association

The ability to relate spoken words and concepts to each other in a meaningful way is known as *auditory association.* Auditory association is an organizing process that enables people to manipulate language in a meaningful way. Students who have auditory association problems may be unable to explain the likenesses and differences among sounds, organize words into categories, verbally classify objects and sounds, hold two or more concepts in mind and consider them in relationship to each other (Kirk and Kirk, 1971), verbalize what is absurd or foolish about nonsense statements, explain what they hear using different words or terminology, associate a story that is heard to their own life experiences (Minskoff, Wiseman, and Minskoff, 1972), or find and evaluate alternative solutions to a problem (Kirk and Kirk, 1971).

The following tests and subtests are used in the assessment of auditory association ability: The Auditory Association subject of the *Illinois Test of Psycholinguistic Abilities* (Kirk, McCarthy, and Kirk, 1968); the Similarities subtest of the *Wechsler Intelligence Scale for Children–Revised* (Wechsler, 1974); the Verbal Opposites, Verbal Absurdities, and Likenesses and Differences subtests of the *Detroit Tests of Learning Aptitude* (Baker and Leland, 1967); and the Inventory of Language Abilities in the *MWM Program for Developing Language Abilities* (Minskoff, Wiseman, and Minskoff, 1972).

Bush and Giles (1977) recommend the following remedial activities and experiences for use in developing auditory association skills:

classifying objects after hearing their names

verbalizing opposites of words, such as open—shut

explaining what they would do if "mother gave you some ice cream", or "the
   telephone rang"

building concepts of likeness and difference by explaining how a group of things
   are alike (for example, an apple, orange, pear, carrot)

identifying sounds made in various situations such as when a person eats, or
   sneezes

identifying the main idea of an analogy

predicting the outcome of incomplete sentences or stories

Auditory Memory Problems

Students who have auditory memory problems may have trouble retaining or recalling what they have heard. Some find it hard to recognize sounds they have heard; others are able to recognize previously heard auditory stimuli but are unable to retrieve the auditory signals needed to produce the desired sounds. Reauditorization and auditory sequential memory problems are the two most frequently encountered auditory memory problems.

Reauditorization Johnson and Myklebust (1967) describe reauditorization as an auditory process that involves the memory and retrieval of auditory impressions for spontaneous use. Those who have a reauditorization problem know what they want to say but are unable to recall the auditory impressions needed to vocalize the sounds or words they want to produce.

Johnson and Myklebust (1967) indicate that students with reauditorization problems often make the following adaptations in their language: using gestures, pantomime, or pictures they have drawn to express themselves; waiting several seconds before responding; substituting a sound made by the object for its name ("barking" for the word "dog"); substituting a word from within the same general category or one with a similar meaning ("pie" for "cake" or "car" for "automobile"); describing the use of an object rather than giving its name ("eat" for "fork"); and substituting a word as a means of communicating. They suggest the following remedial activities for use with these students:

using extensive auditory stimulation that emphasizes repetition of words in a meaningful setting

organizing inputs so they are presented in context, in pairs, in association, and by category

using visual clues, partially completed sentences, an associated word, or the first sound of a word to facilitate recall

using word associations (for example, salt and pepper, bread and butter, table and chair) to facilitate recall

using a series that occurs in logical order to prompt recall (for example, clothing listed in order from head to foot—hat, shirt, pants, socks, shoes)

using rapid naming drills to practice responding as quickly as possible

having the student remain silent for a few seconds so he or she can hear the word "internally" before saying it

Auditory Sequential Memory Auditory sequential memory is the auditory process that enables a student to recall, retrieve, and reproduce sequences of auditory impressions from memory. Students who have auditory sequential memory problems may have trouble remembering oral directions; attending to the details of auditory stimuli (Kirk and Kirk, 1971); reproducing a series of auditory impressions after hearing them; recalling the events of a previous day or week in correct order (Minskoff, Wiseman, and Minskoff, 1972); remembering the sequence of events in a story, poem, song, or radio program that has been heard; storing and retrieving information (Kirk and Kirk, 1971); recalling the order in which the days of the week, seasons, or months of the year occur; and recalling the oral spelling of words, telephone numbers, and addresses (Minskoff, Wiseman, and Minskoff, 1972).

Tests and subtests of tests that are used in the assessment of auditory sequential memory include the Auditory Sequential Memory subtests of the *Illinois Test of Psycholinguistic Abilities* (Kirk, McCarthy, and Kirk, 1968), which assess short-term memory of sequences of nonmeaningful digits; the Digit Span subtest of the *Wechsler Intelligence Scale for Children — Revised* (Wechsler, 1974), which assesses short-term memory of nonmeaningful digits; the Auditory Attention Span for Unrelated Words (short-term memory of sequences of nonmeaningful words), the Auditory Attention Span for Related Syllables (short-term memory of sequences of meaningful words), and the Oral Commissions and Oral Directions subtests of the *Detroit Tests of Learning Aptitude* (Baker and Leland, 1967); and the Inventory of Language Abilities in the *MWM Program for Developing Language Abilities* (Minskoff, Wiseman, and Minskoff, 1972).

In addition to those contained in Minskoff, Wiseman, and Minskoff (1972), remedial activities that will help students improve their auditory sequential memory skills include the following:

repeating directions that they have received before attempting to follow them
taking notes while trying to memorize material so that the visual and kinesthetic feedback will help facilitate memory
explaining the sequential nature of the auditory symbols
listening to auditory sequences with closed eyes to see if the visual stimuli they have been receiving are interfering with their listening
practicing attending to auditory stimuli
practicing following directions that involve several steps
practicing recalling meaningful number sequences such as telephone numbers, social security numbers, and addresses
memorizing songs, stories, and rhymes such as "The Twelve Days of Christmas" or "The Three Bears" (Bush and Giles, 1977)
listening to entire sequences before repeating them (Lombardi and Lombardi, 1977)
using clues such as rhythmic presentation to prompt recall (Kirk and Kirk, 1971)

Sound Blending and Auditory Closure

Sound Blending Sound blending consists of synthesizing and integrating isolated sounds into syllables and words. The ability to discriminate among sounds is a prerequisite to the development of proficiency in sound blending. Those who are unable to discriminate among sounds cannot be expected to blend these sounds together. These students tend to experience difficulty with tasks in which they are required to combine isolated sounds to form whole words, hear and perceive isolated sounds as part of a word, benefit from phonetically based instruction in reading, and pronounce new words.

The Sound Blending subtests of the *Illinois Test of Psycholinguistic Abilities* (Kirk, McCarthy, and Kirk, 1968) are used in the formal assessment of sound-blending ability. The *Spache Diagnostic Reading Scales* (Spache, 1972) contain a supplemental phonics test that can be used to informally assess the ability to blend nonsense syllables together. The Inventory of Language Abilities in the *MWM Program for Developing Language Abilities* (Minskoff, Wiseman, and Minskoff, 1972) contains a check list for use in the informal assessment of auditory closure and sound blending abilities.

Remedial activities and experiences that are often used in improving sound-blending skills include practice in identifying words containing whole words that have been blended together (for example, water + melon = watermelon); in producing the individual sounds in a word and "saying them fast" so that they are said as a word; and in blending parts of words into meaningful wholes (Lombardi and Lombardi, 1977). Also useful are the exercises contained in Minskoff, Wiseman, and Minskoff (1972).

Auditory Closure Auditory closure is a related language ability that enables a student to complete a word when part of it is not pronounced. Those who lack auditory closure skills find it hard to discriminate among sounds, attend to auditory stimuli, or fill in the gaps when they miss parts of a word or conversation.

The Auditory Closure subtest of the *Illinois Test of Psycholinguistic Abilities* (Kirk, McCarthy, and Kirk, 1968) is used to formally evaluate this skill. Remedial activities and experiences that are often helpful in the development of auditory closure include the following, as well as those described in Minskoff, Wiseman, and Minskoff (1972):

filling in the missing letter in orally presented words
filling in the missing word in an orally presented sentence
identifying the missing element in a series
completing an established rhythm pattern
relating the sound-symbol sequence with the corresponding visual-symbol
   sequence

Vocabulary Development and Verbal Expression

A well-developed oral vocabulary is needed to interpret ideas and produce meaningful vocal-motor expression. This facility makes it possible to communicate with others, speak in front of groups, act in dramatic productions, and give oral reports.

Instruments that can be used to assess the student's expressive language development include the Vocabulary subtest of the *Wechsler Intelligence Scale for Children–Revised* (Wechsler, 1974); the Verbal Expression subtest of the *Illinois Test of Psycholinguistic Abilities* (Kirk, McCarthy, and Kirk, 1968); the vocabulary items on the *Stanford-Binet Intelligence Scale* (Terman and Merrill, 1960); and the Free Association and Picture Absurdities subtests of the *Detroit Tests of Learning Abilities* (Baker and Leland, 1967).

The development of oral vocabulary and verbal expression skills usually begins with activities designed to facilitate the understanding and use of naming words (nouns). These activities continue with the systematic introduction of other parts of speech and the use of these words with those previously learned. The complexity of the sentences that can be built gradually increases as additional parts of speech and more words are learned. Following are descriptions of activities that can be used to assist students in learning to understand and use the various parts of speech.

Understanding and Using Nouns   Words that *name* people or objects are the most basic and the easiest to comprehend. Students who have trouble using naming words should receive instruction that begins with simple, concrete names of body parts, toys, furniture, pets, and people. The words selected should gradually become more abstract as the student progresses.

Play sessions are helpful in teaching language to younger children. A doll house and furniture can be used to teach concepts of things that are used around the house. Airplanes, cars, boats, and trains can be used to teach concepts related to transportation, speed, and distance. A classroom store can be used to teach the names of foods, tools, and so on. Dolls and stuffed animals can be used to teach body parts and the names of clothing.

Use parallel play to describe what you and the student are discussing. Gradually ask the child to hand items to you as you name them. Discuss the names and functions of each item. Have the student indicate his or her understanding of concepts by identifying specific items as they are named. Follow parallel play with combined play that emphasizes the development of meaningful language concepts.

Understanding and Using Verbs   According to Johnson and Myklebust (1967), "The basic goal in teaching verbs calls for the child to learn that the word represents an action, not the name of an object" (p. 91). As a result, these words tend to be difficult to comprehend. When teaching these words, encourage the student to act out the action described by the word. For example, actual running might be associated with the introduction of the word *running*. Johnson and Myklebust recommend the use of pictures showing the word being acted out. The pictures may also contain examples of not acting out the word (for example, a picture of a person who is standing still).

Understanding and Using Adjectives   Adjectives are words that modify nouns by describing their *qualities*. They describe the nouns they appear with by answering the questions, "Which one?" "What kind?" and "How many?" They are always taught in combination with nouns—never in isolation. Johnson and Myklebust (1967) indicate that instruction designed to teach students that adjectives describe the qualities of nouns must be accompanied by instruction that teaches them that adjectives are not names of objects, do not describe actions, and cannot be used to describe more than one object or experience.

The following instructional sequence can help students learn to comprehend and use adjectives.

1. Use real experiences involving the same single noun and a pair of adjectives that are opposites (for example, hot water and cold water or rough wood and smooth wood).
2. Use one adjective with several nouns (for example, hot water, hot milk, and hot cookies or rough wood, rough paper, and rough cloth or red ball, red balloon, red crayon, red paper, and red ribbon).
3. First *state the condition* and then ask the student a question that requires a response in the form of a complete sentence describing the condition.

   Example 1:
   Teacher: "This wood feels rough. How does this wood feel?"
   Student: "It feels rough."
   Teacher: "Yes, it feels rough."

   Example 2:
   Teacher: "This wood feels smooth. How does this wood feel?"
   Student: "It feels smooth."
   Teacher: "Yes, it feels smooth."

   If necessary, assist the student by saying "It feels," and then pause so that the student can complete the statement with the appropriate adjective.
4. Talk with the student about characteristics of the concepts rough and smooth, such as being "bumpy" or "not bumpy." Then repeat, "This wood feels rough," "This wood feels smooth."
5. Compare rough and smooth in the same way using other objects such as cloth or paper.
6. Ask the student to hand you the rough one or to hand you the rough paper. Follow with a request to hand you the wood that feels smooth.
7. Hold one of the objects or items up and ask, "Is this rough?" The item held up should possess the characteristics described in the teacher's question. The student should answer, "Yes, it is rough." Repeat using other objects.
8. Hold one of the objects or items up and ask, "Is this rough or smooth?" The student should respond, "Yes, it is rough" or "Yes, it is smooth" or "No, it is not rough" or "No, it is not smooth."
9. Ask the student, "How does this feel?"

Other suggestions for use in learning to comprehend and use adjectives include:

Adjective brainstorming—give the student a noun and one minute to write or give as many applicable adjectives or descriptive words as possible (for example, for the noun *summer:* hot, humid, sticky, warm, green, bright, extended, dry, long, short, dragging, expected, late, last, next, brown, flowering) (Bailey, 1975).

Have the student label different objects with noun-adjective combinations. Students like to use stick-on labels on which the words have been typed.

Have students match adjectives to pictures of objects they describe.

Teach words that describe feelings, such as *happy* and *sad.*

With older students, use work sheets that require selecting the correct adjective from several choices or filling adjectives in blanks that have been left in sentences.

Understanding and Using Prepositions   Prepositions are words that indicate the location of objects in space and time. Prepositions such as *on, behind, in, over,* and *under* help us identify the exact point in space where the object being described is located.

The following instructional sequence can be used to help students learn to comprehend and use prepositions.

1. Start by having the student move to different locations in the room. For example, say to the student: "John, stand in front of the table," "John, stand on top of the table," "John, stand beside the table." Use the same verb each time. Follow each response by asking the student where he or she is standing.

2. Move an object from one location to several other locations that are all related to a stationary object. For example, start by putting a book on top of a box, then put it under the box, beside the box, and so on. Ask the student where the book is located each time it is moved. Demand an answer that consists of a complete sentence (for example, "The book is under the box."). Make sure that the same initial words are used in each verbal request (for example "Put the book in the box," "Put the book behind the box.").

3. Move one object to different locations related to two objects that remain stationary. For example, ask the student to (1) put the book under the box, (2) put the book under the block, (3) put the book behind the block, (4) put the book between the box and the block. Follow with questions requiring complete-sentence responses.

4. Ask recognition questions that require the student to distinguish between obvious differences. For example, ask "Is the book under the box or on top of the box?" not "Is the book beside or behind the box?"

5. Move to a two-dimensional presentation on the vertical surface of a chalkboard. A chalkboard that can be gradually adjusted so that it becomes a horizontal writing surface will help the student bridge the gap that exists between writing on a chalkboard and on the desk top.

6. Move on to matching, multiple-choice, and reading activities that involve the use of prepositions.

Understanding and Using Adverbs   Adverbs are words that modify the meaning of verbs, adjectives, or other adverbs. They answer the questions "How?" "Where?" "Why?" "How much?" and "To what extent?" For example, in the sentence "He walked slowly," the adverb "slowly" modifies the verb "walked" by stating how he walked. The adverb "very" in the sentence "She was very pretty" modifies the adjective "pretty" and tells to what extent she was pretty. In the sentence "He rode very slowly," the adverb "very" modifies the adverb "slowly" to indicate how slowly he rode.

The instructional sequence suggested for use in teaching adjectives can also be used to teach the comprehension and use of adverbs. For example, toy cars and airplanes can be used to demonstrate the adverbs "fast" or "slow."

Understanding and Using Pronouns   Pronouns are words used in place of people's names (for example, *he, she, they*), in place of previously named people, or in place of objects or items (*it, they*). In some cases a pronoun such as *you* may be understood from the text even though it is not actually stated. Students who have learned to understand the more basic receptive auditory language skills may require practice in the appropriate substitution of pronouns for some of the nouns in their language.

If possible, teach pronouns to several students at one time so that members of the group can practice using the pronouns with each other as they are introduced. Sign language is sometimes helpful to those who are having trouble learning to use oral language. Reviewing elementary reading materials that introduce pronouns can sometimes be helpful to older students who do not understand the relationship between nouns and pronouns.

Syntactically Correct Language and Grammatic Closure

The production of grammatically correct oral language depends on the following factors: memory of the words and concepts needed to express one's ideas; memory of the language patterns needed to express thoughts and ideas; selection of nouns, verbs, adjectives, adverbs, and pronouns needed to organize (formulate) a grammatically correct sentence; and production of vocal-motor movements needed to express the syntactically correct sentence that has been formulated. Students who have not learned to formulate and produce syntactically correct oral language automatically tend to use incorrect verb tenses, use incorrect word order when speaking, and experience difficulty expressing ideas vocally.

Grammatic closure is the auditory skill that enables people to produce grammatically and syntactically correct language automatically. A student who has poor grammatic closure may have difficulty discriminating among sounds; remembering auditory sequences; understanding and applying verb tenses, plurals, and idioms in an acceptable manner; producing syntactically correct language; and identifying grammatical or syntactical errors in his or her own language or that of others.

Tests and subtests that are frequently used in the formal assessment of grammatic closure and syntax include the Grammatic Closure subtest of the *Illinois Test of Psycholinguistic Abilities* (Kirk, McCarthy, and Kirk, 1968); the Sentence Imitation and Grammatic Completion subtests of the *Test of Language Development* (Newcomer and Hammill, 1977); the *Northwestern Syntax Screening Test* (Lee, 1969); and the *Carrow Elicited Language Inventory* (Carrow, 1973b). Methods of informal assessment include the following:

Present an object or picture of an object to the student and ask "What is this?" The structure of the student's response will give an indication of the sophistication of his or her language development.

Show the student a picture of a dog that is running and ask "What is the dog doing?"

Have the student complete sentences by filling in an omitted word or words. The word or words omitted can be varied to assess the student's ability to use various parts of speech correctly.

Have the student unscramble sentences so that they appear in syntactically correct order.

Teachers should provide a syntactically correct oral language model that students can imitate. In addition, procedures and activities that are often helpful for students who require assistance with grammatic closure and the production of syntactically correct language include the following:

Build two- or three-word sentences by rearranging scrambled word cards.

Combine single words to produce two-word phrases and sentences consisting of a noun and verb. For example, asked "What do dogs do?" the student responds, "Dogs run." This is repeated several times before moving on to the next combination.

Build two- and three-word sentences about meaningful activities or pictures.

Complete sentences by filling in blanks created by omitting a word or words. Certain words can be omitted to provide practice in using various parts of speech correctly, (for example, subject-verb agreement, adjectives, prepositions, and so on) (Johnson and Myklebust, 1967).

Unscramble a series of words and write them in a syntactically correct sentence.

Transform the word order of sentences without changing the meaning. For example, change "The dog is chasing a car" to "The car is being chased by the dog."

Transform sentences that make statements into sentences that ask questions. For example, change the statement, "The dog is chasing the car" into the question, "Is the dog chasing the car?"

Distinguish between syntactically correct sentences and incorrect sentences.

Formulate a series of related syntactically correct sentences to form a paragraph or short story.

Teachers can also use the *Fitzgerald Key* to teach sentence structure. The Fitzgerald Key is an instructional device originally designed for use in teaching language to the deaf. Figure 9.1 contains an example of Ruth Edgington's (1969) simplified form of Fitzgerald's (1954) key. The Fitzgerald Key is used to teach language structure by clarifying word order. This approach should not be confused with sentence diagramming, which usually involves rearrangement of the word order of the sentence.

FIGURE 9.1 *Simplified Fitzgerald Key*

	Who	**Verb**	**What**	**Where**	**When**
1.	John	was absent			yesterday.
2.	I	went		to Scouts.	after school.
3.	Roger	walked		to my desk.	
4.	Bob and I	rode	our bicycle	downtown	Saturday.

SOURCE: R. Edgington. "Teaching Language Patterns." *Academic Therapy Quarterly*, 4 (1969), 139–145. Reprinted by permission of Academic Therapy Publications, San Rafael, Calif.

Auditory Analysis and Judgment

The ability to listen critically and make judgments about what is heard indicates that the student is able to receive and express auditory concepts effectively. This ability is acquired through repeated language experiences that require listening to language, evaluating what is heard, and formulating responses. Wallace and Kauffman (1978) indicate that the ability to listen and make critical judgments about the oral language one hears includes the ability to

decide if a statement is true or false
decide if a statement is fact or opinion
select different words that have the same meanings from a paragraph or story
locate obvious errors placed in a story that has been read to the student
predict what will happen when periodic stops are made while someone is reading
    or telling a story

Auditory Language Evaluation Summary

The form for the Auditory Language Evaluation Summary on pages 116–118 has been prepared for use in organizing data relating to the material covered in this chapter. A number of different instruments may be selected for use in answering most of the questions listed on the form. It is not usually necessary to administer all of these tests.

PARENT-DIRECTED LANGUAGE DEVELOPMENT ACTIVITIES

Parents and older siblings can play a major role in helping children who have language development problems. Activities and procedures that can be used in the home to encourage language development include the following:

talking to other family members in the presence of the student

verbalizing what is being done and then asking the child to repeat what was said

involving children in various activities by describing what is being done (for example, while using a tool, baking a cake, sewing, working on a car, or building something)

placing labels on objects in the home and discussing them as they are used

discussing body parts while the child is being bathed or dressed

talking with the child as meals are being prepared

conversing while traveling in a car

using picture books or catalogs containing pictures that can be discussed

having older students use a catalog to prepare a $100 list of toys

conducting formal lessons on the spot when they are needed

insuring that facial expressions and gestures do not give confusing meaning to the child

Other useful activities are provided in Karnes (1977).

LANGUAGE DEVELOPMENT PROGRAMS

A large number of commercially published language development programs are available for use with students who have oral language, reception, and expression problems. Among the most widely used are *DISTAR Language* (Engelmann, Osborne, and Engelmann, 1969); *GOAL (Game Oriented Activities for Learning)* (Karnes, 1972); *Goldman-Lynch Sounds and Symbols Development Kit* (Goldman and Lynch, 1971); *Learning Language at Home* (Karnes, 1977); the *MWM Program for Developing Language Abilities* (Minskoff, Wiseman, and Minskoff, 1973); the *Peabody Early Experience Kits* (Dunn et al., 1976); and the *Peabody Language Development Kits* (Dunn, Horton, and Smith, 1968).

AUDITORY LANGUAGE EVALUATION SUMMARY

Name_____   Birth Date_____

School_____   Teacher_____

1. AUDITORY ACUITY: Can the student hear? (Distinguish between sound and no sound)

Puretone Audiometric Exam	Left Ear		Right Ear
Date_____	Normal		Normal
	Mild Loss	(20--40 db)	Mild Loss
Thresholds:	Moderate	(40--60 db)	Moderate
Left Ear_____(db)_____(cps)	Severe	(60--75 db)	Severe
Right Ear_____(db)_____(cps)	Profound	(75-100 db)	Profound

2. AUDITORY ATTENTION: Does the student listen (attend) to auditory stimuli?

Displays short attention span.	Regularly	- Occasionally	- Rarely
Easily distracted from assigned task.	Regularly	- Occasionally	- Rarely
Fails to turn head toward sound source.	Regularly	- Occasionally	- Rarely
Fails to maintain eye contact with speaker.	Regularly	- Occasionally	- Rarely
Fails to keep mind on topic being discussed.	Regularly	- Occasionally	- Rarely
Fails to follow oral directions.	Regularly	- Occasionally	- Rarely

3. AUDITORY DISCRIMINATION: Can the student distinguish (discriminate) between auditory stimuli?

Wepman Auditory Discrimination:Form I _____ of 30 Diff. _____ of 10 Same

Form II _____ of 30 Diff. _____ of 10 Same

G-F-W Auditory Discrimination: Quiet Subtest: Total Errors____%tile____Pauses_____

Noise Subtest: Total Errors____%tile____Pauses_____

G-F-W Selective Attention	Quiet	_____ of 11	_____%tile	_____Age Equiv.
	Fan-like Noise	_____ of 33	_____%tile	_____Age Equiv.
	Cafeteria Noise	_____ of 33	_____%tile	_____Age Equiv.
	Voice	_____ of 33	_____%tile	_____Age Equiv.
	Total	_____ of 100	_____%tile	_____Age Equiv.

TOLD Word Discrimination   Lang. Age. _____   Scaled Score _____

4. SPEECH ARTICULATION: Can the student produce (articulate) speech sounds?

Goldman-Fristoe Test of Articulation

	No. of Errors	Percentile Rank
Sounds in Words		
Syllable Stimulability		

Sounds Needing Attention (Indicate if sound is produced incorrectly when it appears in the initial, medial or final position.) _____

_____

5. SOUND BLENDING/AUDITORY CLOSURE: Can the student blend sounds together and fill in missing sounds?

ITPA Sound Blending   PLA_____ Scaled Score_____

ITPA Auditory Closure   PLA_____ Scaled Score_____

6. VERBAL COMPREHENSION/AUDITORY RECEPTION: Does the student (understand) verbal stimuli?

ITPA Auditory Reception   PLA_____ SS_____

PEABODY PICTURE VOCABULARY   Lang. Age_____ SS_____

TOLD Picture Vocabulary   Lang. Age_____ SS_____
TACL (Carrow)   Raw Score_____ % tile_____

7. AUDITORY ASSOCIATION: Can the student relate (associate) words or ideas which are received auditorily?

ITPA Auditory Association   PLA_____ SS_____

WISC Similarities   MA_____ SS_____

Detroit Verbal Opposites   MA_____

Detroit Verbal Absurdities   MA_____

Detroit Likenesses and Differences   MA_____

8. AUDITORY SEQUENTIAL MEMORY: Can the student remember auditory sequences?

ITPA Auditory Sequential Memory   PLA_____ SS_____

WISC Digit Span   MA_____ SS_____

Detroit Aud. Attn. Span for Unrelated Words   MA_____

Detroit Aud. Attn. Span for Related Words   MA_____

Detroit Oral Commissions   MA_____

Detroit Oral Directions   MA_____

9. VOCABULARY DEVELOPMENT/VERBAL EXPRESSION: Does the student have the vocabulary and verbal expression skills needed to make meaningful oral responses?

WISC Vocabulary   MA_____

ITPA Verbal Expression   PLA_____

Detroit Free Association   MA_____

Detroit Picture Absurdities   MA_____

10. SYNTACTICALLY CORRECT LANGUAGE/GRAMMATIC CLOSURE: Does the student formulate and produce syntactically (grammatically) correct oral language?

ITPA Grammatic Closure   PLA_____ SS_____

TOLD Sentence Imitation   Lang. Age_____ SS_____

TOLD Grammatic Completion   Lang. Age_____ SS_____

Northwestern Syntax Screening Test   Reception_____ of 20 Correct_____ % tile

                                     Expression_____ of 20 Correct_____ % tile

11. AUDITORY ANALYSIS AND JUDGMENT: Can the student analyze and discuss ideas and concepts
received auditorily?

Correctly decides if a statement is true or false.	Regularly	Occasionally	Rarely
Correctly decides if a statement is fact or opinion.	Regularly	Occasionally	Rarely
Identifies different words in a passage which have the same meaning.	Regularly	Occasionally	Rarely
Locates errors which have been placed in a story that has been read to the student.	Regularly	Occasionally	Rarely
Predicts what will happen next when the person who is reading or telling a story stops.	Regularly	Occasionally	Rarely

SUMMARY

1. Kirk and Gallagher divide language problems into language disorders, delayed speech and language, and aphasia.
2. Bloom and Lahey describe language as the product of an interaction of content, form, and use.
3. Language disorders involve problems such as difficulty discriminating among sounds and learning the sound/symbol relations needed to hear words, parts of words, and inflections.
4. Students with delayed language development follow the normal developmental pattern but at a slower than normal rate.
5. Aphasic students hear speech but fail to gain meaning from what is heard.
6. Students with auditory processing problems tend to experience difficulty receiving, storing and associating, retrieving, and expressing auditory-vocal material.
7. Inner language is the language we use to think and communicate with ourselves.
8. Receptive auditory language involves the ability to receive and understand the spoken language that is heard.

9. Expressive auditory language involves the retrieval and oral expression of auditory concepts.
10. Auditory perception and processing involve a number of identifiable tasks that can be used to diagnose and remediate auditory-vocal language communication problems.
11. Parent-directed language development activities can play a major role in helping children who have language development problems.

REFERENCES

Baily, E. J. 1975. *Academic Activities for Adolescents with Learning Disabilities.* Evergreen, Colo.: Learning Pathways Inc.

Baker, H., and B. Leland. 1967. *Detroit Tests of Learning Abilities.* Indianapolis: Bobbs-Merrill.

Bangs, T. E. 1968. *Language and Learning Disorders of the Pre-Academic Child.* New York: Appleton-Century-Crofts.

Berry, M. F., and J. Eisenson. 1956. *Speech Disorders: Principles and Practices of Therapy.* New York: Appleton-Century-Crofts.

Bloom, L., and M. Lahey. 1978. *Language Development and Language Disorders.* New York: John Wiley and Sons.

Boehm, A. 1971. *Boehm Test of Basic Concepts.* New York: The Psychological Corporation.

Bush, W. J., and M. T. Giles. 1977. *Aids to Psycholinguistic Teaching.* 2nd ed. Columbus, Ohio: Charles E. Merrill.

Carrow, E. 1973a. *Test for Auditory Comprehension of Language.* Austin, Tex.: Learning Concepts.

Carrow, E. 1973b. *The Carrow Elicited Language Inventory.* Austin, Tex.: Learning Concepts.

Chalfant, J. C., and M. A. Scheffelin. 1969. *Central Processing Dysfunctions in Children: A Review of Research.* Washington, D. C.: U. S. Government Printing Office.

Chomsky, N. A. 1965. *Aspects of the Theory of Syntax.* Cambridge, Mass.: MIT Press.

Dunn, L. M. 1965. *Peabody Picture Vocabulary Test.* Circle Pines, Minn.: American Guidance Service.

Dunn, L. M., K. B. Horton, and J. O. Smith (1968). *Peabody Language Development Kits.* Circle Pines, Minn.: American Guidance Service.

Dunn, L. M. et al. 1976. *Peabody Early Experiences Kit.* Circle Pines, Minn.: American Guidance Service.

Edgington, R. 1969. "Teaching Language Patterns." *Academic Therapy Quarterly,* 4, 130–145.

Eisenson, J. 1972. *Aphasia in Children.* New York: Harper & Row.

Engelmann, S., S. J. Osborne, and T. Engelmann. 1969. *DISTAR Language.* Chicago: Science Research Associates.

Fitzgerald, E. 1954. *Straight Language for the Deaf.* Washington, D. C.: Volta Bureau.

Goldman, R., and M. Fristoe. 1972. *Goldman-Fristoe Test of Articulation.* Circle Pines, Minn.: American Guidance Service. 1972.

Goldman, R., M. Fristoe, and R. Woodcock. 1970. *Goldman-Fristoe-Woodcock Test of Auditory Discrimination.* Circle Pines, Minn.: American Guidance Service.

Goldman, R., M. Fristoe, and R. Woodcock. 1974. *Goldman-Fristoe-Woodcock Auditory Selective Attention Test.* Circle Pines, Minn.: American Guidance Service.

Goldman, R., and M. E. Lynch. 1971. *Goldman-Lynch Sounds and Symbols Development Kit.* Circle Pines, Minn.: American Guidance Service.

Goldstein, K. 1948. *Language and Language Disturbances.* New York: Grune and Stratton.

Johnson, D. J., and H. R. Myklebust. 1967. *Learning Disabilities: Educational Principles and Practices.* New York: Grune and Stratton.

Karnes, M. B. 1972. *GOAL (Game Oriented Activities for Learning).* Springfield, Mass.: Milton Bradley.

Karnes, M. B. 1977. *Learning Language at Home.* Reston, Va.: Council for Exceptional Children.

Kirk, S. A., and J. J. Gallagher. 1979. *Educating Exceptional Children.* 3rd ed. Boston: Houghton Mifflin Company.

Kirk, S. A., J. J. McCarthy, and W. D. Kirk. 1968. *Illinois Test of Psycholinguistic Abilities.* Urbana: University of Illinois Press.

Kirk, S. A., and W. D. Kirk. 1971. *Psycholinguistic Learning Disabilities: Diagnosis and Remediation.* Urbana: University of Illinois Press.

Lee, L. 1969. *Northwestern Syntax Screening Test.* Evanston, Ill.: Northwestern University.

Lerner, J. 1976. *Children with Learning Disabilities.* 2nd ed. Boston: Houghton Mifflin Company.

Lombardi, T. P., and E. J. Lombardi. 1977. *ITPA: Clinical Interpretation and Remediation.* Seattle, Wash.: Special Child Publications.

Minskoff, E. H., D. E. Wiseman, and J. G. Minskoff. 1972. *MWM Program for Developing Language Abilities.* Ridgefield, N. J.: Educational Performance Association.

Myklebust, H. R. 1957. "Aphasia in Children." In *Handbook of Speech Pathology,* ed. L. Travis. New York: Appleton-Century-Crofts.

Myklebust, H. R. 1960. *The Psychology of Deafness.* New York: Grune and Stratton.

Newcomer, P. L., and D. D. Hammill. 1977. *Test of Language Development.* Austin, Tex.: Empiric Press.

Spache, G. 1972. *Spache Diagnostic Reading Scales.* Monterey, Calif.: McGraw-Hill.

Templin, M., and F. Darley. 1964. *Templin-Darley Tests of Articulation.* Iowa City: Division of Extension and University Services, the University of Iowa.

Terman, L., and M. Merrill. 1960. *Stanford-Binet Intelligence Scale.* Rev. ed. Boston: Houghton Mifflin Company.

Wagner, G., M. Hosier, and M. Blackman. 1970. *Listening Games: Building Listening Skills with Instructional Games.* New York: Teachers Publishing.

Wallace, G., and J. M. Kauffman. 1978. *Teaching Children with Learning Problems.* Columbus, Ohio: Charles E. Merrill.

Wepman, J. 1958. *Auditory Discrimination Test.* Los Angeles: Western Psychological Associates.

Wechsler, D. 1974. *Wechsler Intelligence Scale for Children–Revised.* New York: The Psychological Corporation.

PART THREE

Diagnosis and Remediation
of Reading Problems

TEN

Diagnosis of Reading Problems

Reading problems are among the best known and most debilitating of all learning problems. When they continue uncorrected, they often contribute to the development of learning problems in other academic areas. The inability to read forces people to depend on others to read material they would normally read for themselves.

Johnson and Myklebust (1967) indicate how dependent we are on reading by pointing out that the person who is unable to read cannot read danger signs, the timetables involved in the use of public transportation, or the menu when eating in a restaurant; look up a telephone number in case of an emergency; or complete application forms for employment or a driver's license.

SYMPTOMS OF READING DISABILITY

Brueckner and Lewis (1947) list the following symptoms of reading disabilities:

1. slow rate of oral or silent reading
2. inability to answer questions about what is read, showing lack of comprehension
3. inability to state the main topic of a simple paragraph or story
4. inability to remember what is read
5. faulty study habits, such as failure to reread, summarize or outline
6. lack of skill in using tools to locate information such as index and table of contents
7. inability to follow simple printed or written instructions

8. reading word by word rather than in groups, indicating short perception span
9. lack of expression in oral reading
10. excessive lip movement in silent reading
11. vocalization in silent reading, whispering
12. lack of interest in reading in or out of school
13. excessive physical activity while reading, such as squirming, head movements
14. mispronunciation of words
    a. gross mispronunciation, showing lack of phonetic ability
    b. minor mispronunciation, due to failure to discriminate beginnings and endings
    c. guessing and random substitutes
    d. stumbling over long, unfamiliar words, showing inability to attack unfamiliar words
15. omission of words and letters
16. insertion of words and letters
    a. that spoil meaning
    b. that do not spoil the meaning
17. substitution of words in oral reading
    a. meaningful
    b. meaningless
18. reversals of whole words or parts of words, largely faulty perception
19. repetition of words or groups of words
20. character of eye movements
    a. excessive number of regressive eye movements
    b. faulty return sweep to the beginning of the next line
    c. short-eye voice span
    d. excessive number of eye fixations per line

Kaluger and Kolson (1978) report that the following reading skills are the ones most frequently evaluated in reading clinics:

1. basic word attack skills
    a. structural analysis
    b. phonetic analysis
        1. blendings
        2. sound-symbol relationships
    c. contextual clue
    d. prefixes and suffixes
    e. syllabication
2. level of comprehension and recall
3. level of vocabulary development
4. rate of reading

5. directional habit
6. study skills
7. location and reference skills
8. reading tastes and interests
9. needs of content fields
10. rate of learning (p. 44)

DIAGNOSIS

Diagnosis is the first step in the evaluation-teaching cycle described by Kirk, Kliebhan, and Lerner (1978). They view this cycle as a process involving five steps in all: diagnosis; planning of the teaching task; implementation of the teaching plan; evaluation of student performance; and modification of the diagnosis, formulation of new plans, and implementation of new teaching strategies.

The procedures teachers use in reading diagnosis depend on the amount of experience they have and the types of questions that must be answered. Teachers with extensive experience in reading diagnosis and instruction tend to use informal procedures much more often than inexperienced teachers, who tend to rely on formalized assessment procedures. Teachers who must answer specific questions about the grade level at which students are reading must use standardized tests that produce the data needed to answer these questions. Each question requires procedures that will produce specific types of information. For example, those who need to know which reading skills have been successfully mastered and which ones should be taught next often prefer criterion-referenced tests.

Informal Reading Diagnosis

Experienced teachers frequently find informal diagnostic questions helpful in determining the type of assistance needed by students who are having trouble learning to read. These same questions are helpful to inexperienced teachers who are trying to decide if a student should be referred to a reading or learning disabilities specialist for diagnostic services.

Kottmeyer's (1959) *Diagnostic Inventory of Reading Skills* contains fourteen informal diagnostic questions:

1. How much sight word vocabulary has he? (Dolch words)
2. Does he try to use context clues?
3. Does he know the names of letters?
4. Does he know the consonant sounds?
5. Can he substitute beginning consonant sounds?
6. Can he hear the short vowel sounds in words?
7. Can he tell when vowel sounds are long in words?

8. Does he know the common vowel digraphs?
9. Can he blend letter sounds to form words?
10. Does he make reversals?
11. Does he see common prefixes as units?
12. Does he see common suffixes as units?
13. Does he see compound words as units?
14. Can he divide long words into parts? (pp. 91–97)

Miscue Analysis

Miscue analysis is a systematic method of recording and analyzing oral reading errors or miscues (K. Goodman, 1965, 1969; Y. Goodman, 1972). The Goodmans describe this approach as a psycholinguistic approach that provides information about the student's language, reasoning skills, and reading process.

Error analysis procedures have traditionally been limited to counting the discrepancies between what the student reads orally and what appears in print. Miscue analysis views these discrepancies as miscues and examines them in terms of their remedial implications. The errors are analyzed to see if they are due to phonic, grammatical, semantic, dialect, or other types of problems such as the student's own faulty language patterns. The Goodmans believe that the student who looks at the sentence "I am going" and says "I be going" may actually be demonstrating a faulty pattern rather than a reading problem. The method is described in detail in Burke and Goodman (1972).

Criterion-Referenced Reading Tests

Criterion-referenced reading tests are useful in determining which reading skills have been mastered and which skills should be taught next. They produce the type of information about student performance that is needed to plan instruction on a day-to-day basis.

The lack of agreement regarding the exact sequence of skills each student must master in order to learn to read greatly complicates the development of criterion-referenced reading tests. Lists of objectives for the items contained in standardized reading tests are now being made available by many publishers for those who wish to use these instruments as criterion-referenced tests. However, many teachers are still finding it necessary to design their own criterion-referenced reading tests.

The following criterion-referenced tests are designed to assess many of those basic reading skills that are not usually covered in the norm- and criterion-referenced reading tests now on the market.

The CRD Basic Reading Skills Tests and
Word Recognition Lists

The *CRD (Criterion-Referenced Diagnostic) Basic Reading Skills Tests* on pages 132–139 are designed for use by classroom teachers and psychoeducational diagnosticians in the assessment of beginning reading skills. Tests should be selected from this series that assess those specific skills in which the student may lack proficiency. It will not be necessary to administer all twenty-two tests in most cases.

The examiner should give the student a copy of the tests to read from while the student's successes and errors are recorded on a second copy. This second copy should be used by the student when tests requiring written responses are being administered.

Students who fail to respond correctly to the items in tests 1 and 2 should be questioned to determine if they understand the concepts of "same" or "matching" and "different." Help the student develop these basic concepts before attempting to re-evaluate the student's basic reading skills.

The following list of key words is provided for examiners who find it necessary to review the pronunciation of the various short and long forms of the letters in the alphabet.

Sound	Key word	Sound	Key word
ă	pat	ā	pay
âr	care	ä	father
b	bib	ch	church
d	deed	ĕ	pet
ē	bee	f	fife
g	gang	h	hat
wh	which	ĭ	pit
ī	pie	îr	pier
j	judge	k	kick
l	lid	m	mum
n	no	ng	thing
ŏ	pot	ō	toe
ôr	for	oe	noise
ŏŏ	took	ōō	boot
ou	out	p	pop
r	roar	s	sauce
sh	ship	t	tight
th	thin	ŭ	cut
ûr	urge	v	value
w	with	y	yes
z	zebra		

The *CRD Reading Summary* form on page 131 provides space for each basic test and word recognition list. A predetermined, set criterion of acceptable performance is not listed for each basic test and word recognition list. This determination should be established by the student's teacher so that it will be compatible with the instructional situation and goals. The *CRD Reading Summary* form also provides space for recording the length of time required for the student to complete each basic test and word recognition list. This optional information should be collected when concern exists regarding the student's rate of response.

A series of six 25-word *Word Recognition Lists* are provided on pages 140–143 for use in those situations when it is necessary to determine the approximate level at which students should begin in basal readers. Those desiring information regarding the grade level at which the student is reading should use one of the many standardized reading tests available. The levels at which the words in the *CRD Word Recognition Lists* are placed is based on Harris and Jacobson's (1972) computer analysis of the levels where various words appear in the major reading series.

Major credit is extended to Christine Rucker, learning disabilities specialist, Roosevelt Elementary School District, Phoenix, Arizona, and Madlyn Constantino, master's degree candidate in special education at Arizona State University. Their assistance in developing this instrument is greatly appreciated.

CRD Reading Summary

Experimental Edition

© 1979 by Larry A. Faas

NAME _____

GRADE _____ CA _____ SCHOOL _____

TEACHER _____ DATE _____

Basic Skills # Skill	Number Correct	CAP*	Time	Remarks
1. VISUAL DISCRIMINATION I: Letter Matching	of 9	of 9		
2. VISUAL DISCRIMINATION II: Different Letters	of 12	of 12		
3. VISUAL DISCRIMINATION III: Word Matching	of 8	of 8		
4. VISUAL DISCRIMINATION IV: Different Words	of 15	of 15		
5. RECOGNITION OF LETTERS I: By Their Names	of 26	of 26		
6. NAMING UPPER CASE LETTERS	of 52	of 52		
7. NAMING LOWER CASE LETTERS	of 52	of 52		
8. ALPHABET SEQUENCE (# in correct order)	of 24	of 24		
9. WRITING ALPHABET	of 26	of 26		
10. VOWEL RECOGNITION	of 15	of 15		
11. JOINED CURSIVE ALPHABET	of 22	of 22		
12. AUDITORY DISCRIMINATION I: Single Consonant Sounds	of 15	of 15		
13. RECOGNITION OF LETTERS II: By Their Sounds	of 24	of 24		
14. AUDITORY DISCRIMINATION II: Single Vowel Sounds	of 15	of 15		
15. VOWEL-CONSONANT (V-C) BLENDING-Long Vowel	of 10	of 10		
Short Vowel	of 10	of 10		
16. CONSONANT DIGRAPHS	of 7	of 7		
17. CONSONANT-VOWEL (C-V) BLENDING-Long Vowel	of 10	of 10		
Short Vowel	of 10	of 10		
18. C-V-C BLENDING ---Long Vowel	of 10	of 10		
Short Vowel	of 10	of 10		
19. CONSONANT BLENDING (C-C and C-C-C)	of 15	of 15		
20. AUDITORY BLENDING	of 15	of 15		
21. VOWEL DIGRAPHS	of 6	of 6		
VOWEL DIPHTHONGS	of 4	of 4		
22. AUDITORY DISCRIMINATION III: Word Discrimination	of 15	of 15		

Word Recognition	Number Correct	CAP	Time	Remarks
LEVEL PP	of 25	of 25		
P	of 25	of 25		
1	of 25	of 25		
2	of 25	of 25		
3	of 25	of 25		
4	of 25	of 25		
5	of 25	of 25		
6	of 25	of 25		

*Criterion of Acceptable Performance

CRD* Basic Reading Skills Tests

Experimental Edition

© 1979 by: Larry A. Faas

Name_____

Grade_____ CA____ School_____

Teacher_____ Date _____

1. VISUAL DISCRIMINATION I: LETTER MATCHING *Directions:* Read to the student-- DRAW A CIRCLE AROUND EACH LETTER IN THE ROW WHICH IS THE SAME AS (MATCHES) THE LETTER IN THE BOX. *Scoring:* Count the number of correct responses.

Example								
b	d	q	(b)	p	d	(b)	q
G	C	G	O	ɔ	ꟼ	G	C
K	R	Ʞ	К	Я	H	R	K
n	u	m	h	n	u	n	m
t	t	f	f	t	ɟ	t	f

_____ marked incorrectly _____ of 9 Correct   Time _____

2. VISUAL DISCRIMINATION II: DIFFERENT LETTERS *Directions:* Read to the student-- DRAW A CIRCLE AROUND EACH LETTER IN THE ROW WHICH IS DIFFERENT FROM (NOT THE SAME AS) THE LETTER IN THE BOX. *Scoring:* Count the number of correct responses.

M	M	M	W	M	N	M	M
p	p	b	q	p	d	p	q
c	c	c	e	e	c	e	o
h	h	n	h	h	k	h	h

_____ marked incorrectly _____ of 12 Correct   Time _____

*Criterion-Referenced Diagnostic

Name_____ Date_____

---

3. VISUAL DISCRIMINATION III: WORD MATCHING *Directions:* Read to the student---DRAW A CIRCLE AROUND EACH WORD IN THE ROW WHICH IS THE SAME AS (MATCHES) THE WORD IN THE BOX. *Scoring:* Count the number of correct responses.

me	ne	me	em	me	we
pod	pob	pop	pad	bop	pod
kit	kif	hit	kit	tik	kit
saw	sam	was	mas	saw	was
bed	deb	bed	ped	bep	bed

_____ marked incorrectly   _____ of 8 Correct   Time _____

---

4. VISUAL DISCRIMINATION IV: DIFFERENT WORDS *Directions:* Read to the student---DRAW A CIRCLE AROUND EACH WORD IN THE ROW WHICH IS DIFFERENT FROM (NOT THE SAME AS) THE WORD IN THE BOX. *Scoring:* Count the # of correct responses.

on	ou	on	no	uo	on
top	top	pot	fop	top	tod
man	won	mon	man	mau	man
nit	nit	hit	tin	mit	nit
run	run	nur	run	rnu	ran

_____ marked incorrectly   _____ of 15 Correct   Time _____

Name_____ Date_____

5. RECOGNITION OF LETTERS I: NAMING   *Directions:* Direct the student's attention to the alphabet printed at the bottom of this page and say---POINT TO LETTER WHICH I NAME AS SOON AS I SAY IT. IF YOU DON'T KNOW THE LETTER, JUST SAY "I DON'T KNOW" AND WE WILL GO ON TO THE NEXT LETTER. *Scoring:* Circle all errors. Make X's on letters not attempted. Letters missed should be added to the end of the series so they can be repeated.

M   H   C   F   O   V   I   A   N   R   D   X   Z

J   P   W   S   E   K   T   Y   U   G   Q   B   L

_____ of 26 Correct   Time_____

6. NAMING UPPER CASE LETTERS   *Directions:* Give the student a copy of this page and say---TELL ME THE NAMES OF THE FOLLOWING LETTERS WHEN I POINT TO THEM. *Scoring:* Use the same procedure as used for # 5.

C   W   S   E   K   T   Y   G   Q   U   M   V   A   B   N   D   H   M

F   O   V   I   A   N   R   D   X   P   S   C   F   L   Z   J   P   T

U   E   L   Q   W   J   X   K   Z   G   H   B   O   I   R   X

_____ of 52 Correct _____Time _____

7. NAMING LOWER CASE LETTERS   *Directions/Scoring:* Same as for # 5.

t   e   g   u   l   q   w   j   x   p   s   z   k   y   u   h   o   b

c   r   i   w   s   e   k   y   g   b   q   m   f   v   a   n   d   h

m   c   f   o   v   a   i   n   d   r   x   p   l   z   j   t

_____ of 52 Correct   Time _____

a   b   c   d   e   f   g   h   i   j   k   l   m

n   o   p   q   r   s   t   u   v   w   x   y   z

© 1979 by Larry A. Faas   Name_____ Date_____

8. ALPHABET SEQUENCE *Directions*: Read to the student --COMPLETE EACH SET OF LETTERS BY WRITING THE MISSING LETTER/S IN THE BLANK/S. Oral responses can be used when the student doesn't know how to write.

a b ___   h i ___   u v ___   f g ___   d e ___   k l ___

b ___ d   l ___ n   k ___ m   p ___ r   c ___ e   n ___ p

___ e ___   ___ o ___   ___ l ___   ___ s ___   ___ q ___   ___ i ___

_____ of 24 correct   Time_____

9. WRITING THE ALPHABET *Directions*: Read to the student---WRITE THE ALPHABET IN THE FOLLOWING SPACE. The student may use manuscript or cursive letters. *Scoring*: Count the number of correct letters.

_____ letters formed correctly _____ of 26 in correct order   Time _____

10. VOWEL RECOGNITION *Directions*: Read to the student---DRAW A CIRCLE AROUND ALL OF THE VOWELS *Scoring*: Count the number of correct responses.

b i a s e l c r q u g d f d i k a m

g z o m t s a v t p h e g u l c n o

e h r u p n f z i t x r q n p k a h

_____ of 15 correct   Time_____

11. JOINED CURSIVE ALPHABET *Directions*: Read to the student--- WRITE THE ALPHABET IN JOINED CURSIVE LETTERS. COMPLETE THE SERIES OF LETTERS THAT HAS BEEN STARTED. *Scoring*: Count the # of correct letters.

abcd

_____ Of 22 correct   Time_____

Name_____ Date_____

12. AUDITORY DISCRIMINATION I: SINGLE CONSONANT SOUNDS *Directions*: Read to the student---I WILL SAY TWO LETTER SOUNDS. LISTEN CAREFULLY AND TELL ME IF I SAY THE SAME SOUND TWICE OR IF I SAY TWO DIFFERENT SOUNDS. Shield your mouth while saying the sounds. *Scoring*: Count # correct.

p – p ____	h – w ____	m – m ____
t – d ____	b – b ____	z – s ____
f – th ____	sh –sh ____	g – k ____
s – s ____	l – l ____	g – d ____
v – th ____	ch – j ____	f – s ____

____ of 15 Correct   Time ____

13. RECOGNITION OF LETTERS II: SOUNDS *Directions*: Read to the student---Direct the student's attention to the alphabet printed at the bottom of this page and say---POINT TO THE LETTER AS I MAKE IT'S SOUND. *Scoring*: Count the number of correct responses.

m h c f o v i a n r d g z l j p w s e
k t y u b

____ of 24 Correct   Time ____

14. AUDITORY DISCRIMINATION II: SINGLE VOWEL SOUNDS *Directions*: Read to the student---I WILL SAY TWO LETTER SOUNDS. LISTEN CAREFULLY AND TELL ME IF THESE SOUNDS ARE THE SAME OR DIFFERENT. Shield your mouth while saying the sounds. *Scoring*: Count the number of correct responses.

ā – ē ____	ĕ – ĭ ____	ŭ – ĭ ____
ĭ – ŏ ____	ā – ĭ ____	ō – ō ____
ă – ă ____	ī – ī ____	ā – ŭ ____
ū – ē ____	ŏ – ā ____	ĕ – ĕ ____
ŏ – ŭ ____	ŭ – ă ____	ī – e ____

____ of 15 Correct   Time ____

a b c d e f g h i j k l m

n o p q r s t u v w x y z

Name _____ Date _____

15. VOWEL-CONSONANT (V-C) BLENDING *Directions*: Read to the student--- MAKE THE SOUND OF EACH OF THE FOLLOWING LETTERS. THEN COMBINE THE SOUNDS AND SAY THEM TOGETHER. eg. a — m = am. *Scoring*: Count the number of correct responses.

LONG VOWELS	SHORT VOWELS
ē – v ____	ă – t ____
ā – k ____	ĭ – f ____
ī – g ____	ŏ – p ____
ō – b ____	ĕ – k ____
ū – z ____	ŭ – n ____
ā – d ____	ă – b ____
ū – s ____	ŏ – v ____
ō – t ____	ŭ – z ____
ī – m ____	ĕ – t ____
ē – z ____	ĭ – n ____

____ of 10 Correct   Time ____   ____ of 10 Correct   Time ____

16. CONSONANT DIGRAPHS *Directions*: Read to the student---SAY THE SOUND MADE BY EACH OF THE FOLLOWING PAIRS OF LETTERS *Scoring*: Count the # of correct responses.

sh ____   th ____

ck ____   ch ____

ng ____

ph ____

wh ____

____ of 7 Correct   Time ____

© 1979 by Larry A. Faas

© 1979 by Larry A. Faas   Name _____ Date _____

---

17. CONSONANT-VOWEL (C-V) BLENDING *Directions*: Read to the student---MAKE THE SOUND OF EACH OF THE FOLLOWING LETTERS. THEN COMBINE THE SOUNDS AND SAY THEM TOGETHER. eg. S — O = SO. *Scoring*: Count the number of correct responses.

LONG VOWELS	SHORT VOWELS
b – ō ____	j – ĭ ____
f – ī ____	m – ŏ ____
s – ō ____	p – ĕ ____
t – ē ____	n – ŭ ____
k – ū ____	s – ĕ ____
h – ō ____	r – ă ____
l – ī ____	c – ŭ ____
z – ā ____	t – ĭ ____
d – ū ____	v – ŏ ____
b – ē ____	z – ă ____

____ of 10 Correct   Time _____   ____ of 10 Correct Time _____

---

18. CONSONANT-VOWEL-CONSONANT (C-V-C) BLENDNG *Directions*: Read to the student---MAKE THE SOUND OF EACH OF THE FOLLOWING LETTERS. THEN COMBINE THE SOUNDS AND SAY THEM TOGETHER. eg. s a m = sam. *Scoring*: Count the number of correct responses.

LONG VOWELS	SHORT VOWELS
b – ā – n ____	b – ŭ – t ____
f – ī – b ____	s – ŏ – p ____
l – ū – t ____	l – ĭ – m ____
h – ō – m ____	d – ĕ – k ____
d – ē – n ____	n – ă – d ____
g – ī – z ____	k – ŭ – f ____
k – ū – p ____	g – ŏ – m ____
h – ō – j ____	r – ĭ – s ____
r – ā – v ____	z – ĕ – b ____
m – ē – f ____	p – ă – n ____

____ of 10 Correct   Time _____   ____ of 10 Correct Time _____

19. CONSONANT BLENDING (C-C AND C-C-C) *Directions:* Read to the student—MAKE THE SOUND OF EACH OF THE FOLLOWING LETTERS. THEN COMBINE THE SOUNDS AND SAY THEM TOGETHER. *Scoring:* Count the # correct.

b – l ___	n – d ___	g – l ___
t – r ___	b – r ___	s – p – r ___
s – t ___	p – l ___	s – p – l ___
b – r ___	d – r ___	s – c – r ___
c – r ___	f – r ___	s – t – r ___

_____ of 15 Correct   Time _____

20. AUDITORY BLENDING *Directions:* Read to the student—SAY THE WORD I AM SOUNDING OUT. A one-half second pause should be made between each sound. *Scoring:* # Correct

o-n ___	l-a-n-d ___	ch-a-m-p ___
m-ay ___	c-l-i-p ___	p-l-a-n-t ___
m-e-t ___	s-t-o-ne ___	th-u-n-d-er ___
g-o-t ___	n-e-v-er ___	t-r-a-ff-i-c ___
t-u-b ___	a-f-t-er ___	v-a-l-e-n-t-i-ne ___

_____ of 15 Correct   Time _____

21. VOWEL DIGRAPHS AND DIPHTHONGS *Directions and Scoring:* Same as # 16.

DIGRAPHS

ea ___	ai ___
oa ___	ay ___
ei ___	
ee ___	

DIPHTHONGS

oi ___
ou ___
oy ___
ow ___

_____ of 6 Correct Time ____   _____ of 4 Correct Time _____

22. AUDITORY DISCRIMINATION III: WORD DISCRIMINATION *Directions:* Read to the student—TELL ME IF THE TWO WORDS I SAY ARE THE SAME OR DIFFERENT. Shield your mouth while saying the words. *Scoring:* Count the # of correct responses.

fat - vat ___	set - sit ___	shall - shell ___
dim - din ___	vow - thou ___	pin - pen ___
tab - tab ___	bay - bay ___	hat - had ___
time - dime ___	tap - tap ___	far - far ___
pit - bit ___	when - wren ___	boy - toy ___

_____ of 15 Correct   Time _____

CRD WORD RECOGNITION

Experimental Edition
© 1979 by: Larry A. Faas

Name_____
Grade_____ CA_____ School_____
Teacher_____ Date_____

LEVEL PP	LEVEL P
1. a	1. of
2. I	2. so
3. go	3. ask
4. at	4. pet
5. we	5. new
6. it	6. two
7. no	7. man
8. is	8. she
9. to	9. eat
10. me	10. his
11. he	11. yes
12. are	12. fish
13. red	13. cake
14. dog	14. boat
15. the	15. good
16. can	16. then
17. big	17. away
18. see	18. into
19. ran	19. tree
20. did	20. went
21. for	21. show
22. get	22. about
23. who	23. paint
24. you	24. father
25. stop	25. birthday

_____ of 25 Correct   _____ of 25 Correct

CAP _____ of 25 Time_____   CAP _____ of 25 Time_____

CRD WORD RECOGNITION

Experimental Edition

© 1979 by: Larry A. Faas

Name_____

Grade_____ CA____ School_____

Teacher_____ Date_____

LEVEL 1	LEVEL 2
1. pan	1. rag
2. off	2. I've
3. how	3. bell
4. try	4. open
5. far	5. year
6. miss	6. ugly
7. fall	7. land
8. lost	8. rope
9. bark	9. chair
10. more	10. heavy
11. than	11. fruit
12. dark	12. shook
13. game	13. field
14. farm	14. lunch
15. build	15. alone
16. first	16. slide
17. after	17. stone
18. three	18. swish
19. right	19. empty
20. pocket	20. cowboy
21. should	21. winter
22. behind	22. dollar
23. stopped	23. nearby
24. kitten	24. tonight
25. another	25. breakfast

_____of 25 Correct   _____of 25 Correct

CAP _____of 25 Time_____   CAP _____of 25 Time_____

CRD WORD RECOGNITION

Experimental Edition

© 1979 by: Larry A. Faas

Name_____

Grade_____ CA_____ School_____

Teacher_____Date_____

LEVEL 3	LEVEL 4
1. jet	1. mist
2. curl	2. rider
3. main	3. hawk
4. bath	4. porch
5. drag	5. birch
6. fancy	6. zebra
7. child	7. clank
8. grasp	8. tempt
9. cheese	9. speed
10. broom	10. limit
11. united	11. sixty
12. ribbon	12. unlike
13. needle	13. fallen
14. person	14. canary
15. hidden	15. adjust
16. juggle	16. former
17. comfort	17. control
18. promise	18. hunter
19. instant	19. glitter
20. shadow	20. rancher
21. workman	21. setting
22. stomach	22. painter
23. sparkle	23. student
24. thunder	24. drugstore
25. yesterday	25. astronaut

_____of 25 Correct   _____of 25 Correct

CAP _____of 25 Time_____   CAP _____of 25 Time_____

CRD WORD RECOGNITION

Experimental Edition

© 1979 by: Larry A. Faas

Name_____

Grade_____ CA_____ School_____

Teacher_____Date_____

LEVEL 5	LEVEL 6
1. loft	1. famine
2. gleam	2. woolen
3. anvil	3. barren
4. title	4. phrase
5. range	5. villain
6. fever	6. summit
7. poise	7. offense
8. magnet	8. academy
9. robber	9. senator
10. corral	10. rainbow
11. thrash	11. trooper
12. buckle	12. crimson
13. beckon	13. positive
14. orphan	14. campaign
15. yonder	15. judgment
16. involve	16. reminder
17. horizon	17. memorial
18. spaniel	18. quotation
19. wistful	19. elaborate
20. straddle	20. gangplank
21. sympathy	21. vegetation
22. emergency	22. artificial
23. childhood	23. misfortune
24. determine	24. impression
25. mechanical	25. disturbance

_____of 25 Correct   _____of 25 Correct

CAP _____of 25 Time_____   CAP _____of 25 Time_____

Standardized Oral Reading Tests

Standardized oral reading tests are an important tool for those who work with students who have learning problems. They provide the examiner with an opportunity to observe, record, and analyze the reading errors that are being made, and are particularly useful in answering questions regarding the grade level at which students are reading.

Oral reading tests must be administered individually and require 30 to 90 minutes for administration plus time for scoring and interpretation. Practice is required to become proficient in their use. They are usually designed for use in accuracy checks on errors such as omissions, insertions, mispronunciations, reversals, substitutions, hesitations, inversions, regressions, repetitions, and punctuation errors. Analysis of these errors provides information on the student's strengths and needs for specific types of remediation.

A large number of standardized reading tests are available and widely used. Among them are the following:

Botel Reading Inventory. Follett, Inc. A group test containing several subtests that are used to determine the reading instruction levels of students in grades 1 through 12. Tests of phonics, word recognition, word opposites, and listening are included.

Durrell Analysis of Reading Difficulty. Harcourt Brace Jovanovich, Inc. A battery of diagnostic tests for discovering weakness and faulty habits in reading that may be corrected in a remedial program. For use with nonreaders to students in grade 6 and older who are performing substantially below grade level.

Gates-MacGinitie Reading Tests. Teachers College Press. A general group test of silent reading containing five forms for students in grades 1 through 12. Each form contains vocabulary, comprehension, speed, and accuracy subtests.

Gilmore Oral Reading Test. Harcourt Brace Jovanovich, Inc. An individually administered oral reading test for grades 1 through 8. Provides information about word accuracy.

Gray Oral Reading Tests. Bobbs-Merrill. An individual test consisting of thirteen oral reading passages.

Spache Diagnostic Reading Scales. California Test Bureau/McGraw-Hill. A battery of tests that includes three word lists, twenty-two graded reading passages, and eight supplementary phonics tests. Administered individually by reading specialists to students in grades 1.5 through 8 and disabled readers in grades 9 through 12.

Woodcock Reading Mastery Tests. American Guidance Service. Consists of letter identification, word identification, word attack, word comprehension, and passage comprehension subtests. Individually administered for grades K through 12.

Assessing Reading Comprehension

Educators usually place so much emphasis on assessing students' word-attack skills that they often forget to evaluate their reading comprehension abilities. Reading comprehension involves grasping and understanding, or knowing the meaning of, the words or passages being read.

Smith (1969) identifies four levels of comprehension: (1) *literal comprehension*, which involves direct and obvious meaning; (2) *interpretation*, which uses the content as a base for deductive reasoning; (3) *critical reading*, involving the analysis and evaluation of the material; and (4) *specific word meanings*, gained through recognizing the implications of the multiple meanings of words. Ekwall (1976) lists other categories, such as the ability to see main ideas, important details, the author's purpose and organization, developmental images, and sequences of ideas. He also describes the close relationship between reading comprehension and study skills.

The assessment of reading comprehension usually involves some form of passage that is read either by the student or to the student, followed by a series of questions regarding the message contained in the passage. The student's comprehension is determined by computing the percentage of items that are answered correctly. For example, the student who correctly answers three of the four questions about a passage would be assumed to have comprehended 75 percent of the material read.

Most standardized diagnostic reading tests contain a series of comprehension questions on each of the graded passages. Teachers can informally diagnose a student's reading comprehension by preparing a series of comprehension questions on a passage of known difficulty level.

The *cloze* procedure described by Kirk, Kliebhan, and Lerner (1978) is another informal method for obtaining diagnostic information about a student's reading comprehension. Passages from the student's classroom reading material are retyped, minus every fifth word (Rankin and Culhane, 1969) or every tenth word (Karlin, 1973). The student is then asked to fill in the missing words while reading the passage. Miller (1974) indicates that a student's average level of comprehension can be determined by multiplying the percentage of the blanks successfully completed by 1.67. The cloze procedure is discussed in greater depth in Chapter 12.

SUMMARY

1. Reading problems are among the best known and most debilitating of all learning problems.
2. Kirk, Kliebhan, and Lerner describe reading diagnosis as a five-step procedure that extends from estimating the student's reading potential to recommending remedial procedures.
3. Teachers who have had extensive experience in reading diagnosis tend to use

informal procedures much more often than do inexperienced teachers, who must rely on formalized assessment procedures.

4. Miscue analysis is a systematic method for recording and analyzing oral reading errors.
5. Criterion-referenced reading tests are designed for use in determining which reading skills have been mastered and what skills should be taught next.
6. Standardized reading tests provide information that can be used in answering questions about the grade level at which the student is reading.
7. The assessment of reading comprehension is an important but often neglected dimension of reading diagnosis.

REFERENCES

Bruckner, L. J., and W. D. Lewis. 1947. *Diagnostic Test and Remedial Exercises in Reading.* New York: Holt, Rinehart and Winston.

Burke, C., and Y. Goodman. 1972. *Reading Miscue Inventory: Manual Procedure for Diagnosis and Evaluation.* New York: Collier-Macmillan.

Ekwall, E. E. 1976. *Diagnosis and Remediation of the Disabled Reader.* Boston: Allyn and Bacon, Inc.

Goodman, K. 1965. "A Linguistic Study of Cues and Miscues in Reading." *Elementary English Review*, 42, 639–643.

Goodman, K. 1969. "Analysis of Oral Reading Miscues." *Reading Research Quarterly*, 5 (Fall), 9–30.

Goodman, Y. 1972. "Reading Diagnosis—Qualitative and Quantitative." *The Reading Teacher*, 25, 32–37.

Harris, A. J., and M. D. Jacobsen. 1972. *Basic Elementary Reading Vocabularies.* New York: Macmillan Company.

Johnson, D. J., and H. R. Myklebust. 1967. *Learning Disabilities: Educational Principles and Practices.* New York: Grune and Stratton.

Kaluger, G., and C. J. Kolson. 1978. *Reading and Learning Disabilities.* Columbus, Ohio: Charles E. Merrill.

Karlin, R. 1973. "Evaluation for Diagnostic Teaching" In *Assessment Problems in Reading.* Ed. W. MacGinitie. Newark, Del.: International Reading Associa-

Kirk, S. A., J. M. Kliebhan, and J. W. Lerner. 1978. *Teaching Reading to Slow and Disabled Learners.* Boston: Houghton Mifflin Company.

Kottmeyer, W. 1959. *Teacher's Guide for Remedial Reading.* New York: McGraw-Hill, Inc.

Miller, W. H. 1974. *Reading Diagnosis Kit.* New York: Center for Applied Research in Education, Inc.

Rankin, E. F., and J. W. Culhane. 1969. "Comparable Cloze and Multiple-Choice Comprehension Test Scores." *Journal of Education*, 13 (December), 193–198.

Smith, N. B. 1969. "The Many Faces of Reading Comprehension." *Reading Teacher*, 23, No. 3, 249–259.

ELEVEN

Instructional Approaches for Various Patterns of Strengths and Deficits

Students who have a history of reading problems usually need remedial assistance that will enable them to catch up with other class members. Teachers need to select the reading method that will be most effective in producing the desired skill development. Instructional methods that capitalize on the student's learning strengths are much more likely to produce the desired results than methods that do not reflect sensitivity to these factors.

Process analysis makes it possible to identify the students' learning strengths and deficits and provides teachers with information on how students should be taught. Task analysis indicates what skill should be taught next. This chapter offers specific suggestions for selecting those instructional approaches that will be most helpful to students who exhibit various patterns of strengths and deficits. The combinations of learning strengths and deficits and the types of instructional problems and settings discussed include auditory channel strengths accompanied by visual channel deficits, visual channel strengths accompanied by auditory channel deficits, combined visual and auditory channel deficits, automatic level response development, older students reading at the primary level, and better silent than oral reading.

INSTRUCTIONAL APPROACHES FOR VISUAL DEFICITS AND AUDITORY STRENGTHS

Students who have visual channel deficits often experience mild to moderate difficulty in reading. These deficits may include problems with visual form discrimination, visual closure, speed of visual perception, perception of position in

This chapter is based on an outline prepared by Dorothy Tuch and Christine Rucker. Christine Rucker assisted with the writing and editing of this material.

space, perception of spatial relations, visual figure-ground discrimination, ocular control, or visual sequential memory. Some students fail to perform the tasks involved in these areas at an automatic response level, and tend to require extra time to reason out answers to questions. These deficits or inefficiencies in visual processing may contribute to their lack of progress in reading.

Alphabetic or Phonetic Approach

Students who experience difficulty in learning and remembering the shapes of letters are called *visual dyslexics* (Johnson and Myklebust, 1967). The degree of reading impairment ranges from mild to very severe. Visual dyslexic students tend to reverse letters and symbols (for example, *p* for *q* or *b* for *d*), reverse words (for example, *stop* for *pots* or *was* for *saw*) and invert letters (for example, *u* for *n* or *d* for *p*). In addition, they have trouble retrieving the visual image of a letter or word from their memory when they hear it, remembering the order in which visual stimuli were presented, identifying similarities and differences among visual stimuli, perceiving visual stimuli, doing readiness tasks involving visual memory or form comparison, keeping their places while reading, and breaking words down into parts or combining the parts into whole words.

According to Johnson and Myklebust (1967), the alphabetic approach has proven most effective with visual dyslexics who have auditory strengths. This approach, which emphasizes the teaching of letter sounds and letter sound groups (*th, sh, ch*) and the blending of these sounds into meaningful words, is used in the instructional procedures developed by Gillingham and Stillman (1975), Hegge, Kirk, and Kirk, (1936), and Englemann and Bruner (1969). These procedures are discussed in Chapter 13. Commercially published reading programs following an alphabetic or phonetic approach include *Action Reading: A Participatory Approach* (Cureton, 1974), *Phonetic Keys to Reading* (Harris and Creekmore, 1972), and *Alpha I* and *Alpha Time* (Reiss and Friedman, 1969, 1972).

Linguistic Approach

A linguistic reading approach in which students are asked to learn word patterns is recommended for use with the students who have auditory channel strengths and visual channel deficits. The students' auditory strengths can be utilized to help them master the auditory-vocal attributes of words, which will provide them with valuable assistance in learning to utilize the related, recurring visual patterns found in linguistic reading material. *Let's Read: A Linguistic Approach* by Bloomfield and Barnhart (1961) contains a thorough discussion of this approach and a sequence of 245 lessons. Other commercially published reading programs following a linguistic approach include *McGraw Hill's Programmed Reading*

(Buchanan, 1973), *Merrill Linguistic Reading Program* (Fries et al., 1973), *Lippincott Basic Reading* (McCracken and Walcutt, 1970), *SRA Basic Reading Series* (Rasmussen and Goldberg, 1965), and the *Sullivan Reading Series* (Sullivan, 1966).

Sight-Word Approach

The sight-word or whole-word approach is not recommended for use with students who are experiencing difficulty processing visual information. The only exception to this rule occurs when it is necessary to teach nonphonetic words that the student needs to read, such as *was, the, you,* and *were.* Drills, exercises stressing the beginning sound of each word, and context clues should all be used, and, when necessary, the Fernald method of tracing and saying new words (see Chapter 12).

Teachers in regular classrooms where the reading material is limited to a basal reading series that follows a sight-word approach often experience difficulty in teaching reading to students who have mild to moderate visual channel deficits. The following suggestions are offered for use by teachers locked into this type of situation:

1. As much as possible, provide supplemental instruction that emphasizes:
   a. visual discrimination activities using sight words
   b. tracing of specific words
   c. use of word tracking tasks based on vocabulary from the basal series
   d. use of individual flash cards
   e. use of phrase cards
   f. playing "concentration" using the sight words from the basal series
   g. use of the Fernald approach (see Chapter 12)
   h. use of dictated sentences to teach left-to-right movement
2. The use of phonetic crutches should be taught as soon as possible:
   a. start by teaching the beginning letter sounds
   b. follow with word families or blending
   c. do not confuse the student by attempting to teach the distinction among beginning, middle, and final sounds
3. Teach the student to use compensating mechanisms, such as:
   a. using a finger to keep from getting lost
   b. placing a card below the line being read
   c. cutting a window in a card that permits the student to cover all of the page with the exception of the phrase or line being read
   d. organizing oneself to attempt independent activity

The classroom teacher should watch carefully to be sure that the student is actually reading. Some students with strong auditory memory skills are able to listen to other children read and then give the appearance of reading when they are actually repeating what they heard.

Other Approaches

Increasing Speed of Perception Tachistoscopic presentation of letters, groups of letters, and words often helps students who are slow to respond. Stop watches, egg timers, and other timing devices can be used to determine the students' rates of response, which can then be plotted on a graph.

Correcting Ocular Control Problems Students who have ocular control problems frequently jump from the line they are reading to the line below or above it. They also tend to get lost while making the backsweep from the end of the line they have just read to the beginning of the next line.

   Primary Alphabet Tracking by Geake (1967) and *Word Tracking* by Smith (1970) both contain exercises that are helpful with students who are having these types of problems. The *Slingerland Screening Tests* (1964, 1970, 1974) contain a subtest designed to measure the student's far-point/near-point copying ability. This subtest requires students to focus on a wall chart (far-point) and then reproduce what they see on the test booklet (near-point). This type of activity gives students the opportunity to become more proficient at making the visual adjustments required to perceive stimuli at these widely differing distances. It closely resembles the copying activities that are required nearly every day in most regular classrooms.

   Students with severe ocular control problems may be instructed to cross out the first letter of each word as it is read. They may also be asked to draw a line under the line of print as it is read. The backsweep from the end of the line to the beginning of the next line should be as fast as possible. Students with ocular control and figure-ground discrimination problems should be encouraged to use a finger to follow along as they read. Most students will stop using their fingers on their own when they no longer need them.

Eliminating Crossing the Midline Problems Students with midline problems tend to avoid crossing the midline of their bodies with their eyes when reading and with their hands when writing. They will place the book or writing paper entirely to one side of their midline so that crossing it will not be necessary. In severe cases, students may even tilt their heads so that only one eye is used to read or direct their handwriting.

   The "belly button technique" may be helpful for students who avoid crossing their midlines. The teacher draws a 2-inch vertical arrow in the middle of the bottom of a sheet of graph paper containing ½-inch squares. This paper is placed directly in front of the student so it is square with the student's shoulders and the arrow points directly at his or her belly button. The teacher then instructs the student to print a lower-case letter *b* in each of the first three squares in the top row, starting at the left-hand margin. As soon as this is done, the student is asked to move down the page to the second row. Another set of three lower case *b*'s is printed. This time the first of the three letters is written in the second square on the line. This procedure is repeated with the three letters being moved one space to the right on each new line. Right-handed students must reach across their midline to print the first set of letters. Each new line requires them to move their hands and eyes farther to the right until they cross the midline. Left-handed students gradually move to the right on each new line until they cross the midline with the writing hands and eyes. The letter *b* is used because it is necessary to pull from left to right as the lower part is printed. See Figure 11.1.

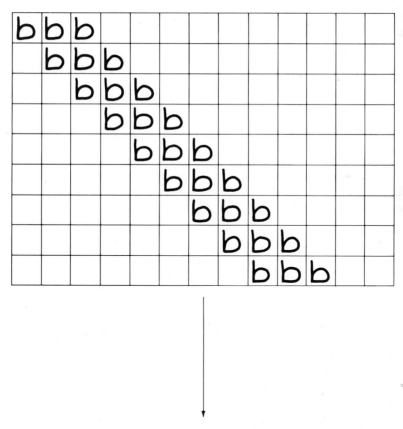

FIGURE 11.1   *Example of the Belly Button Technique*

Distinguishing Between b, d and p, q   Students who have visual perceptual problems frequently confuse the printed lower-case forms of *b, d* and *p, q.* The "thumbs up" procedure is suggested as an aid to distinguishing between *b* and *d.* The student closes the fingers of both hands while the thumbs are pointed upward and the hands are held a few inches apart. Viewed thus, the left hand represents the correct form of the letter *b,* which comes before *d* in the alphabet. The student's right hand represents the letter *d.*

The "thumbs down" procedure, which is the same as the above procedure but with the thumbs pointing down, is used to distinguish between *p* and *q.* The student is again advised to read the letters from left to right.

Questions students can be taught to ask themselves to help them distinguish between *b* and *d* include the following: Can you make a capital *b* by adding a bump at the top? If you draw a *c* beside the up-and-down line, will you have a *d*? Could you lay a board on the letters and make a bed out of letters in the order you are using them?

INSTRUCTIONAL APPROACHES FOR AUDITORY DEFICITS AND VISUAL STRENGTHS

Students who have auditory channel deficits often experience mild to moderate difficulty in reading. These deficits may include problems in one or more areas. At the automatic level the student may have difficulty with auditory discrimination, auditory sequential memory, sound blending, auditory closure, or grammatic closure and syntax. At the representational level the student may have difficulty with the development of basic concepts, reception of auditory stimuli, auditory association, or verbal fluency.

Sight-Word Approach

Students who experience difficulty learning and retaining the sounds of letters and words are called *auditory dyslexics* (Johnson and Myklebust, 1967). The degree of reading impairment ranges from mild to very severe. Auditory dyslexic students often find it hard to discriminate between similar sounds and words; sound out unfamiliar words; understand sound-letter correspondence; break words into syllables and letters; blend sounds into words; retrieve the sound of a letter, a familiar musical selection, or the sound made by something in the environment; or remember the order in which a sequence of auditory stimuli was received.

Johnson and Myklebust (1967) suggest using a sight-word approach with auditory dyslexics during the initial stages of reading instruction. This approach permits students who lack the auditory processing skills needed to learn to read phonetically to develop sight-word vocabularies.

The Fernald approach, the language experience approach, the neurological impress method, the cloze procedure, nonvisual AKT, and kinetic patterning techniques all use the sight-word approach (see Chapter 12). Two commercially published reading programs that follow a sight-word approach are the *Ginn Basic Reading Program* (Gunn, 1967) and the *Macmillan Reading Program* (Harris et al., 1970).

Teachers should present all new words in a meaningful context, stressing comprehension from the very beginning. They should spend time repeating and overteaching the sight-word vocabulary so that students will be able to respond automatically without needing to stop to analyze the word when they see it. This is especially important in the case of structural words such as *are, am, were,* and *they.*

Phrase Reading

Teachers should introduce phrase reading as early as possible, starting with two-word phrases and following with three- and then four-word phrases. A group of three or four cards should be prepared with each card containing a different phrase in which the word being taught appears. This new "target" word should be the only word on each of the cards that is not already known to the students.

The following activities are useful for teachers who are using phrase cards to teach students to pronounce "target" words automatically each time they are seen:

Change the position where the word appears in the various phrases.
Change the phrases so that various intonation patterns are required to read them.
Gradually increase the reading speed as the phrases are reread.
Immediately correct errors. Do not ask the student to correct the error. Do not say "no." Do not ask the student to give the beginning sound.
When the student's performance approaches the automatic response level, introduce distracting activities such as the following: (1) Have the student tap the table top, pat stomach, or scratch while reading; (2) Tap a rhythm as the student reads; or (3) Time the student with a stop watch while the phrases are being read.
Include a selection of previously learned phrases for the purpose of review and to add to the complexity of the activity.

The ability to produce sounds, read words, or read phrases becomes a response at the automatic level through *repetition* and *overlearning under pressure.*

Teaching Sound-Symbol Relationships

The use of a whole-word approach to help students develop a sight-word vocabulary should be accompanied by assistance in the word-attack skills students need to extend their range of reading beyond the confines of a sight-word vocabulary. Students must eventually develop the ability to sound out and read words they have not previously encountered.

The development of phonetic skills should begin with study of beginning-position consonants, short vowels, and digraph sounds. Students' visual channel strengths should be used when teaching sound-symbol relationships whenever possible. The inflatable, huggable letters of the alphabet included in *Alpha I* (Reiss and Friedman, 1969) are an example of the type of visual aids that can be used to help students learn sound-symbol relationships. Word cards containing key words chosen by the student are another example. Cards that contain a picture of an item, the word that names an item, and the first letter of the word are often used to prompt students' memory of a letter sound.

Commercially published reading programs containing sections that emphasize learning beginning sounds include *Houghton Mifflin Reading Series: Getting Ready to Read* (Durr et al., 1976), the *Merrill Linguistic Reading Program* (Fries et al., 1973), *Phonovisual Charts* (Schoolfield and Timberlake, 1966), and *Alpha I* (Reiss and Friedman, 1969).

Teachers should not introduce new sounds too rapidly. Students should learn a few sounds so well that they automatically produce them when they see the corresponding letter. When they have mastered these sounds, other letter sounds can be presented.

Sounds should be emphasized in reading sight words as soon as the student knows a few letter sounds. Using newly learned sounds as keys to facilitate the recall of printed words will help motivate the student to learn the sounds of the other letters. It will also show the student the importance of sound-symbol relationships. The following techniques are helpful when a student needs assistance in this area:

Use rapid drill in the presence of interfering activities.
Immediately tell the student the correct answer when an error is made.
Have the student who is experiencing difficulty with a specific sound (1) try
   yelling it several times, (2) try saying the sound while tracing it, or (3) try
   saying it while writing it. Or discontinue using the sound for two or three
   weeks and then reintroduce it as a new sound.

When students have mastered several beginning consonants and the short *a* and *i,* they should learn to combine these letters into meaningful three-letter words. A linguistic approach using word families is effective at this point. First introduce the CVC (consonant, verb, consonant) letter order. If this doesn't work, use rhyming word families. Ask the student to pronounce the word, explain its meaning, and use it in a sentence. Avoid blending the individual sounds into words and using nonsense words.

Dictate whole words to the student frequently during instruction, emphasizing the beginning letters of the words. Select words for dictation that involve a consistent CVC order. If possible, avoid words that contain blends for the initial sounds.

Phonetic/Linguistic Approaches with Auditory Deficits

Teachers in regular classrooms where the reading materials are limited to a basal reading series that follows a phonetic or linguistic approach often experience difficulty in teaching reading to students with mild to moderate auditory channel deficits. These teachers should begin by reinforcing the regular class use of a phonics-based series. They should adapt instruction as much as possible to emphasize word patterns if the basal series does not work after a reasonable trial period. They may find it necessary to teach the words that appear in the basal series as sight words before they can teach their phonetic equivalents. They should also emphasize the identification of word families and the determination of how the words are alike and different.

Teachers using a linguistically oriented basal series are encouraged to emphasize skill development in the auditory deficit areas as soon as possible. The activities described in Chapter 9 for use with students who have auditory processing problems should be used to reinforce and strengthen the students' understanding of sound-symbol relationships. The words from linguistic word families should be taught initially as sight words.

INSTRUCTIONAL APPROACHES FOR VISUAL AND AUDITORY CHANNEL DEFICITS

Visual-auditory dyslexic students experience impaired perception, memory, and integration in both the visual and the auditory channels. Their learning problems are nearly always severe. Educators should observe these students and experiment with the following types of multisensory and single-sensory approaches before choosing an instructional procedure to use:

multisensory: tactual-kinesthetic, visual, and auditory-vocal
primarily auditory-vocal input
primarily visual input
primarily graphic: tactual-kinesthetic input
equal emphasis on auditory and visual inputs
equal emphasis on visual and vocal inputs

These students usually require extensive readiness experiences in their deficit areas. Activities for establishing visual-auditory association such as labeling the pictures and objects in the room are helpful, as well as visual perceptual activities involving manipulative materials, plastic or cut-out letters and geometric forms, and pencil-and-paper tasks. Language development activities should include grammatic closure and auditory association training and other experiences designed to facilitate development of automatic level responses in the auditory-vocal channel.

Educators should also experiment with the phonetic, sight-word, and global approaches to see which works best. The global approach utilizes context clues, such as associating a sound with its meaningful use in pronouncing actual words. Questions that these procedures should answer include: Can the student learn the letter sounds? Can the student learn whole words? Can the student learn an entire sentence?

Educators should assess the student's need for repetition to determine if one-half hour a day, fifteen minutes twice a day, ten minutes three times a day, or five minutes six times a day would be the most desirable schedule for the student.

One of the following instructional approaches may be effective in reaching these students. Each approach emphasizes simultaneous instruction in reading and writing.

the *language experience approach,* which emphasizes the use of key words drawn from sentences the students dictate

the *Orton-Gillingham method,* which is a highly structured phonetic approach that involves some use of input through the kinesthetic modality

the *Fernald method,* which is a mildly structured whole-word approach that utilizes language experience and the tactual-kinesthetic channel

Slingerland's multisensory approach, which is an adaptation of Orton-Gillingham's phonetic method that includes the use of sight words

INSTRUCTIONAL APPROACHES FOR AUTOMATIC LEVEL RESPONSE DEVELOPMENT

Some students who are able to respond correctly fall behind in their school work because of their need to consciously reason through each response before making it. These students need assistance in learning to make most of their responses at the automatic level. Automatic level responses are made without a conscious effort that requires the student's total attention. The spontaneous correct pronunciation of a word as soon as it is seen and the use of correct verb tenses while speaking are examples of automatic level responses.

Instructional activities designed to facilitate development of automatic level response patterns should always begin and end with material that is easy enough to assure the student of obvious success. The level of difficulty and the complexity of the material should increase rapidly during instruction until the student is being challenged to a point just below the frustration level.

The length of time students will be able to devote to a specific task before taking a break will vary from between two and three minutes to up to fifteen minutes. Students who are being required to work near their frustration level will tend to tire much faster than usual. The number of short breaks—from thirty seconds to two or three minutes—that will be needed during an instructional period will vary among students and from day to day. It is not unusual for students who have learning problems to vary in their ability to perform on a minute-to-minute, hourly, daily, or weekly basis. What determines the need for breaks is the student's ability to perform. Teachers can get an idea about how long a student can continue before taking a break by working with the student and observing his or her performance. A short break should be taken as soon as the student's level of effective efficiency begins to decrease.

Teachers may find it necessary to vary the difficulty level and complexity of the task as the student's performance varies, asking the student to work longer and harder on the good days and demanding less of the student on bad days. Teachers who ask students to perform near their frustration level should be prepared for the possibility that a student may "frustrate out," "blow up," or otherwise lose control. If this occurs the student will probably feel irritated, upset, angry, and guilty about failing. At this point, the teacher should assume full responsibility for pushing the student into the frustration level. He or she should discontinue the task immediately and replace it with simpler material or a game that is not anxiety producing. After devoting a few minutes to this substitute activity, the student can resume activities directed toward developing automatic level responses. Each instructional period should end with the successful production of a series of correct responses.

INSTRUCTIONAL APPROACHES FOR OLDER STUDENTS READING AT THE PRIMARY LEVEL

Older students who read at a second- or third-grade level are almost certain to fail in most of their other academic efforts. These students should be tested with comprehensive individual reading tests. Teachers can then task analyze the errors students make to pinpoint the areas of difficulty and formulate methods of remediation.

For example, a silent reading comprehension score that is higher than the oral reading comprehension score suggests that the student may have a verbal fluency or anomia problem. *Anomia* is the inability to recall words and the names of objects. An oral reading score that is higher than the silent reading score, on the other hand, suggests that the student probably needs to reauditorize words to comprehend them. *Reauditorization* consists of remembering and vocalizing the sounds of letters or words that are seen in print.

Students' auditory comprehension is usually higher than their reading comprehension. Exceptions to this general rule occur when the student is able to adjust reading speed to facilitate his or her own comprehension needs, go back in the passage being read to make a correction in word interpretation, or reauditorize words or passages to gain greater meaning. The student whose reading comprehension is lower than his or her auditory comprehension should be able to improve the reading comprehension with instruction and practice. The student whose auditory and reading comprehension scores are both low should start by working on auditory comprehension and memory.

Comparison of word pronunciation and comprehension errors should indicate if the student is able to pronounce words without comprehending them or comprehend words he or she cannot pronounce. Most students with learning problems tend to be weaker in word pronunciation than in comprehension. Teachers should be particularly careful while testing these students to avoid yielding to their natural tendency to assist the student on words he or she cannot pronounce. Assisting the student tends to result in inflated comprehension scores, and eliminates the chance for the teacher to observe how the student uses or fails to use word attack skills and context clues. The student who guesses or skips words should be permitted to do so without being given assistance during testing. The words that are skipped may be words that the student is able to comprehend without word calling.

Pronunciation errors should be examined to determine if the words mispronounced are multisyllable or one-syllable words, if they are located at the beginning, at the end, or in the middle of a line, and if they relate to regressions and/or omissions of words. Finally, they should be analyzed to determine if they consist of context or structural (such as *the, and, that*) words. Do the errors occur in the beginnings, middles, or endings of the words? In root words, prefixes, or suffixes?

Older students who are not reading at the appropriate level should also be tested with flash word lists to assess the speed with which they recognize words. Finally, their fluency, phrasing, intonation, pauses and hesitations, and general reading speed should also be checked.

INSTRUCTIONAL APPROACHES FOR STUDENTS WITH BETTER SILENT READING SKILLS

Students whose silent reading skills are better than their oral reading skills are probably having difficulty with reauditorization or verbal fluency. Phonetic word callers, who read without comprehending what they read should be changed to a sight-word approach, which should be accompanied by separate activities designed to facilitate development of phonetic skills. These activities should not be included in the students' general reading instruction program. These students should not be expected to pass criterion-referenced phonics tests with fluency.

Teachers should check to see if these students are using context clues as word-attack skills. The cloze method or the *Context Clues* volume from the *Specific Skills Series* by Bonning (1962, 1976) are helpful in developing the ability to use context clues.

Commercially published materials that contain reading lists and phrases for use in drills designed to increase verbal fluency include the *SRA Reading Lab: Word Games* (Parker and Scannell 1962), *Cues and Symbols* (Wehrli, 1971), and the *Flash-X* (1962) and *Word Clues: GHI and JKLM Vocabulary Sets* (Morris, 1979). Fry's instant word lists and the Dolch basic word lists are sometimes helpful when teaching older students. Heckelman's neurological impress method can also be used to encourage the development of oral reading skills (see Chapter 12). Students should be asked to work at their frustration level. Mumbling over unknown words should not be permitted.

Fluency and Speed of Reading

Tachistoscopic presentation of letters, groups of letters, and words often helps students who lack sufficient reading fluency. Timing devices such as stop watches and egg timers can be used to determine the student's rate of response.

The following methods are suggested for use with students whose poor phrasing and intonation are due primarily to word calling and lack of meaningful language:

the sight-word approach (if the phonetic approach has been used unsuccessfully)
the cloze technique
choral reading activities
large amounts of phrase-reading under pressure
the dual-track Language Master

Students who make frequent pauses, hesitations, and regressions can be helped by means of the neurological impress method, weekly speed tests, and techniques such as having the student keep the place in the book with a finger or draw phrase lines under the lines of print while listening to a tape recording of the material.

Comprehension Problems

A large number of commercially published materials are available for use in building comprehension skills. Included among these materials are the *Specific*

Skill Series (Bonning, 1962, 1976), Reader's Digest *Skillbuilders* (Blake, 1977), and SRA's *Reading for Understanding* cards (Thurstone, 1958).

The cloze method, which is discussed in detail in Chapter 12, is frequently used with students who have comprehension problems. It is sometimes helpful to have students who have severe problems read the sentence and then tell what it said in their own words. This approach can be expanded to paragraph-length passages after success with sentence-length passages. Students who are having comprehension problems should also be assisted in developing and applying visual imagery skills to reading.

SUMMARY

1. Students with auditory strengths and visual deficits usually learn best from instruction that emphasizes a phonetic approach.
2. Visual dyslexics often experience difficulty learning and remembering the shapes of letters and words.
3. The alphabetic or phonetic approach emphasizes the teaching of letter and letter group sounds and the blending of these sounds into words.
4. The consistent linguistic patterns found in linguistic material are well suited for use with students who have auditory strengths.
5. Auditory dyslexics experience difficulty learning and retaining the sounds of letters and words.
6. A sight-word approach should be used initially in providing reading instruction to auditory dyslexics.
7. Repetition and overlearning under pressure are helpful in developing the ability to produce sounds and read phrases automatically.
8. Visual-auditory dyslexics experience impairment of perception, memory, and integration in both the visual and auditory channels.
9. Senior high school students who are reading at the second- and third-grade level are almost certain to fail in most of their academic efforts.
10. The cloze procedure is frequently used with students who have comprehension problems.

REFERENCES

Blake, S. 1977. *Reading Skillbuilders.* Silver ed. Pleasantville, N. Y.: Reader's Digest.

Bloomfield, L., and C. L. Barnhart. 1961. *Let's Read: A Linguistic Approach.* Detroit: Wayne State University Press.

Bonning, R. A. 1962, 1976. *Specific Skill Series.* Baldwin, N. Y.: Barnell Loft.

Buchanan, C. D. 1973. *Programmed Reading.* 3rd ed. New York: McGraw-Hill.

Cureton, G. 1974. *Action Reading: A Participatory Approach.* Boston: Allyn and Bacon.

Durr, W. K. et al. 1976. *Houghton Mifflin Reading Series: Getting Ready to Read.* Boston: Houghton Mifflin.

Englemann, S., and E. Bruner. 1969. *DISTAR Reading I and II.* Chicago: Science Research Associates.

Fernald, G. M. 1943. *Remedial Techniques in Basic School Subjects.* New York: McGraw-Hill.

Flash-X. 1962. New York: EDL–McGraw-Hill.

Fries, C. C. et al. 1973. *Merrill Linguistic Reading Program.* Columbus, Ohio: Charles E. Merrill.

Geake, R. R. 1967. *Primary Alphabet Tracking.* Worthington, Ohio: Ann Arbor Publishers.

Gillingham, A., and B. W. Stillman. 1975. *Remedial Training for Children with Specific Learning Disability in Reading, Spelling and Penmanship.* Cambridge, Mass.: Educators Publishing Service.

Gunn, M. A. 1967. *Ginn Basic Reading Program.* Lexington, Mass.: Ginn and Company.

Harris, A.J. et al.1970. *Macmillan Reading Program.* Riverside, N.J.: Macmillan.

Harris, T. L., and M. Creekmore. 1972. *Phonetic Keys to Reading.* Oklahoma City: Economy Company.

Hegge, T. G., S. A. Kirk, and W. D. Kirk. 1936. *Remedial Reading Drills.* Ann Arbor, Mich.: George Wahr Publisher.

Johnson, D. J., and H. R. Myklebust. 1967. *Learning Disabilities: Educational Principles and Practices.* New York: Grune and Stratton.

McCracken, G., and C. C. Walcutt. 1970. *Lippincott's Basic Reading.* Philadelphia: J. B. Lippincott Company.

Morris, H. 1979. *Word Clues: GHI and JKLM Vocabulary Sets.* New York: EDL–McGraw-Hill.

Parker, D., and G. Scannell. 1962. *Reading Lab: Word Games.* Chicago: Science Research Associates.

Rasmussen, D., and J. Goldberg. 1965. *Basic Reading Series: Levels A through F.* Chicago: Science Research Associates.

Reiss, E., and R. Friedman. 1969. *Alpha I.* Norwalk, Conn.: New Dimensions in Education.

Reiss, E., and R. Friedman. 1972. *Alpha Time.* Norwalk, Conn.: New Dimensions in Education.

Schoolfield, L. D., and J. B. Timberlake. 1965. *Phonovisual Charts.* Washington, D. C.: Phonovisual Products, Inc.

Slingerland, B. H. 1964, 1970, 1974. *Slingerland Screening Tests.* Cambridge, Mass.: Educators Publishing Service.

Slingerland, B. H. 1971. *A Multi-Sensory Approach to Language Arts for Specific Language Disability Children.* Cambridge, Mass.: Educators Publishing Service.

Smith, D. E. P. 1970. *Word Tracking.* Worthington, Ohio: Ann Arbor Publishers.

Sullivan, M. W. 1966. *Sullivan Reading Series.* Palo Alto, Calif.: Behavior Research Laboratories.

Thurstone, T. G. 1969. *Reading for Understanding.* Chicago: Science Research Associates.

Wehrli, K. 1971. *Cues and Symbols.* Worthington, Ohio: Ann Arbor Publishers.

Weinberg, J. S. et al. 1966. *Macmillan Spectrum Reading: Vocabulary Development.* New York: Macmillan Company.

TWELVE

Visual/Sight-Word Methods for
Teaching Problem Readers

Students who learn best when visual and/or tactual kinesthetic inputs are emphasized usually benefit from one of the approaches discussed in this chapter. The visualization and writing activities involved in these approaches serve as a meaningful foundation to which the corresponding auditory attributes of words can be linked.

THE FERNALD APPROACH (VAKT)

The Fernald approach was developed at the University of Southern California Clinic School by Grace Fernald (1943) for use with disabled readers. It uses the tactual-kinesthetic sensations involved in tracing to help students learn and remember the visual and auditory attributes of words. The Fernald approach can be used successfully with students who have trouble processing both visual and auditory stimuli, but is most effective with students who have difficulty with visual perception and imagery.

Fernald (1943) devotes considerable discussion to the emotional effect reading failure has on students, observing that "The greatest handicap of the non-reader . . . is the complex which accompanies it" (p. 10). She points out that the remedial process must help restore students' self-confidence at the same time as it teaches them to read.

Fernald suggests that teachers should begin remedial procedures by telling students that there is a new way of learning words that they want them to try, and

Dr. Douglas E. Wiseman, associate professor of special education at Arizona State University, Tempe, Arizona, coauthored this chapter.

163

that many bright people with reading problems have learned to read by this method. She outlines a four-stage method for use in helping these students progress from zero reading performance to normal reading.

In the first stage, the student is permitted to select any word he or she wants to learn, regardless of its length. The teacher writes this word in blackboard-size letters on a large piece of paper while the student watches. Either manuscript or cursive writing can be used. Fernald prefers manuscript writing because it resembles the printing found in books.

The first and second fingers are used to trace the words written by the teacher. Fernald reports that chalk, crayon, or a stylus do not produce the desired results. The student should pronounce the word each time it is traced.

The student writes the word once on a piece of scrap paper and then as part of a sentence or story written in the student's own vocabulary. The student's sentences and stories are used during reading instruction in place of a basal reading series. He or she then files the word alphabetically in a card box. This helps the student learn to identify the first letter of each word and the sequence of letters in the alphabet. Next the student writes the entire word without looking back and forth to the example written by the teacher. Looking back and forth while the word is being written breaks it up into small meaningless units and interrupts the flow of movements involved in writing. If a mistake is made, the entire word is covered or erased and rewritten. This insures that words are always written as whole units.

It is permissible to teach words during the first few instructional sessions that may not be used in a story. The main purpose of instruction at this point is to convince the student that he or she can learn and remember words. After the first few sessions, however, each word should be one that the student wishes to use in the sentence or story that is being written. Using a word in context, in a sentence that he or she has written, greatly increases the likelihood that the student will remember that word.

To summarize, the steps contained in stage 1 are as follows: (1) student chooses a word, (2) student sees teacher write word, (3) student traces the word, (4) student writes the word, (5) student sees the word in typed form, (6) student feels and sees the word as he or she pronounces and traces it, (7) student feels the arm movements used to write the word, (8) student feels the movement of his or her lips, tongue, jaw, and vocal cords when pronouncing the word, and (9) the student hears the word pronounced.

The number of tracings required gradually decreases until tracing is no longer necessary. The length of time required for a student to complete stage 1 depends on the degree of disability involved.

The student is ready to begin stage 2 when he or she is able to learn new words without tracing them. The teacher writes the words the student cannot read in small script on a card and pronounces it. The student then writes the word as a whole without looking back and forth to the example written by the teacher. The student says each part of the word silently or aloud as he or she writes the word. This effort to establish the connection between the sound of a word and its form is a necessary step in learning to recognize words from visual stimuli alone. The sounds of individual letters or syllables should not be distorted or given undue emphasis. The longer words are pronounced syllable by syllable as these parts of the word are written.

When the student makes an error, the entire word is rewritten. Some students may be able to rewrite the word correctly after reexamining it visually and saying it several times. Others will find it necessary to trace the word several times before attempting to write it a second time.

The teacher should type the student's composition immediately so that the student can read it. Silent reading is used to prepare the student for fluent oral rereading. No attempt is made to simplify the vocabulary, sentence structure, or concepts contained in the student's composition. The learning and retention of larger words is reported to be better than for shorter words. As in stage 1, the large cards containing the words selected by the student are filed in a small box. These cards are used for checking the student's immediate and delayed recall of words. The only mode of learning eliminated during stage 2 is tracing.

In stage 3, students learn from the printed word by looking at it and saying it before writing it. Students are ready to begin stage 3 when they can write a word after looking at its printed form. The teacher pronounces the word for the student but does not need to write it. The student looks at the printed word, says it silently, and then writes it from memory without looking back to the printed copy. When difficulty is encountered, it is sometimes necessary to return to stage 2 activities for a while before resuming stage 3 activities.

The stage 3 student is ready to begin reading from books. The teacher initiates this activity by having the student read the passage silently before attempting to read it orally. Each new word is placed on a card for use in assessing the student's immediate and delayed recall.

In stage 4, students no longer need to write a word to remember it. They are able to look at a new word and recognize its resemblance to words or parts of words they have already learned. Fernald (1943) indicates that, "As he looks at the word, the simultaneous association by similarity with words he already knows, together with the meanings inferred from the context, gives him an instant perception of the word" (p. 52).

The student may want to skim over difficult or scientific material before trying to read it to clear up the meaning of any words he or she does not know. The use of silent reading to locate and clear up the meaning of new words helps improve the student's phrasing during oral study.

Users of the Fernald approach should remember the following points:

The approach is most effective when used with disabled readers who are having difficulty with visual perception and imagery.
Words are never spelled orally.
Words are always written as a whole, never as separate letters.

The student never copies a word. It is always written from memory.

The correct form of the word is emphasized. The entire word is always erased or covered up when an error is made.

Instruction should continue beyond stage 4 to the point where the student is able to immediately recognize groups of words arranged in all the combinations in which they occur in printed matter.

THE LANGUAGE EXPERIENCE APPROACH

The language experience approach brings reading, listening, speaking, and writing skills together into a single instructional program. The skills are taught as they are needed to write stories based on students' oral descriptions of their own experiences. For example, students are taught to capitalize the first letter of the first word in a sentence as sentences describing the student's personal experiences are being written.

The language experience approach is suitable for students who learn best from a visually oriented whole-word approach. It can be used remedially with older students who have basic decoding skills but who need an alternative to the standard primary-level materials that are available for use in developing comprehension skills.

Instruction begins with a discussion designed to prepare students for the activities involved in developing language experience charts. This discussion identifies the reasons for preparing an experience chart and describes how the topic to be covered on the first chart should be selected. This topic can be varied to correspond with other parts of the school curriculum. It may contain a narrative description of the student's experiences, a report of a science experiment, classroom or school news, or a story made up by the student.

The preparation of a language experience chart begins with the student's oral description of a personal experience. The teacher writes what the student says on the chalkboard. A preliminary draft of the student's story is completed, followed by an editing and revision phase. Specific skills such as capitalization, punctuation, spelling, grammar, correct sentence structure, and left-to-right progression are taught while editing and revision are taking place.

The student writes the edited form of the story or passage on a permanent or semipermanent chart. Instruction in handwriting is provided at this time if needed. The completed experience chart becomes the basic instructional material used in teaching the student to read.

Rebus figures* may be substituted for some of the words. For example, a drawing or picture of an apple may be substituted for the word *apple*. Some students enjoy adding illustrations to their charts.

---

*Rebus figures can be obtained from American Guidance Services, Circle Pines, Minnesota 55014.

The language experience approach can also be used to develop readiness for formal reading instruction in kindergarten and first grade, introduce new units of instruction, summarize and unify a unit of instruction, teach the correct use of letter forms, handwriting, and spelling, and help students develop creative writing skills. It places high value and emphasis on the following goals:

freedom of oral and written self-expression
individual authorship
the development of self-confidence in all language usage including grammar, punctuation, capitalization, spelling, and word recognition
communication between the student and teacher
the development of a basic sight-word vocabulary that corresponds to students' own oral language
the teaching of phonetic concepts as they are needed to write and spell words occurring in students' oral language
the motivation to read fostered by showing students that their own oral language can be written and then read orally

Allen (1976) suggests that the following language experiences and abilities can be emphasized during reading instruction:

Sharing experiences. The ability to tell or illustrate something on a purely personal basis.
Discussion experiences. The ability to interact with what other people say and write.
Listening to stories. The ability to hear what others have to say and relate what is heard to their own experiences.
Telling stories. The ability to organize one's thinking so that it can be used to share clearly dictated oral accounts of others' experiences.
Dictating. The ability to choose, from all that might be said, the most important part for someone else to write and read.
Developing speaking, writing, and reading relationships. The ability to conceptualize reading as speech that has been written.
Making and reading books. The ability to organize one's ideas into a form that others can use and to use the ideas that others have shared through books.
Developing awareness of common vocabulary. The ability to recognize that our language contains many common words and patterns of expression.
Expanding vocabulary. The ability to expand one's vocabulary through listening and speaking, followed by writing and reading.
Writing independently. The ability to record one's own ideas in a form that will make them available for others to read.
Reading whole books. The ability to read books for information, recreation, and improvement of reading skills.

Improving style and form. The ability to profit from reading and listening to well-written materials.

Using a variety of resources. The ability to recognize and use many resources in expanding vocabulary, improving oral and written expression, and sharing.

Reading a variety of symbols. The ability to read symbols found in one's environment—the clock, calendar, radio dial, thermometer.

Studying words. The ability to find the correct pronunciation and meaning of words and to spell the words in writing activities.

Improving comprehension. The ability, through oral and written activities, to gain skill in following directions, understanding words in the context of sentences and paragraphs, reproducing the thought in a passage, and reading for general significance.

Outlining. The ability to use various methods of briefly restating ideas in the order in which they were written or spoken.

Summarizing. The ability to get the main impression, outstanding ideas, or details of what has been read or spoken.

Integrating and assimilating ideas. The ability to use reading and listening for specific purposes of a personal nature.

Reading critically. The ability to determine the validity and reliability of statements.

These language experiences become the major framework within which children learn to read. The activities at the beginning of the list require less background and maturity than those at the end of the list.

The advantages of the language experience approach include the following:

Each lesson is based on the experiences of the student who is being instructed.

The students' experiences are first expressed in their own wording and then edited and revised until they read correctly.

Students' level of interest tends to be higher than usual because they are reading about something that actually happened.

Students tend to learn to read material based on their personal word patterns much faster than language patterns contrived by someone else.

Disadvantages of the language experience approach include:

There is a good likelihood that this approach will already have been used with the student.

Students with a limited vocabulary may not receive enough encouragement to learn new words.

Students with faulty language patterns will tend to practice rather than correct the errors they have been making.

The amount of teacher time required to write life experience stories for each student places a heavy burden on the teacher.

Allen (1976) contains an in-depth discussion of the use of the language experience approach in teaching reading.

THE CLOZE PROCEDURE

The *cloze procedure* can be used to determine the level of students' understanding of printed materials that are read silently. It can also be used to determine if students are capable of comprehending a particular text and to assess students' ability to use context clues (Bloomer, 1962; Bormuth, 1968; Jongsma, 1971). It is based upon the psychological theory of closure, which suggests that people want to complete any pattern that is nearly complete. It can be used at the various reading levels found in the elementary, intermediate, and secondary schools.

Cloze exercises are constructed by selecting 250- to 300-word passages from the middle of basal readers or elementary-, intermediate-, and secondary-level textbooks. Every seventh to tenth word should be omitted in lower-grade-level material, and every fifth word can be omitted from upper-grade-level material. Proper nouns, scientific terms, and mathematical terms should not be omitted, nor should words from the first and last sentences of a passage. The blanks for the deleted words should all be the same length. From thirty-five to fifty deletions should appear in each passage used diagnostically. Shorter passages and fewer deletions are often used during instruction.

The following cloze exercise was developed from a fourth-grade-level story:

Equal Pay for Equal Work *

Two men went to a cadi, or judge, for help in settling

a disagreement. "I (1) _____ a woodchopper,"   am

said the first man. "(2) _____ chopped down   I

twenty-eight loads of (3) _____ for this bag   wood

of gold coins. (4) _____ man did not do any   this

of (5) _____ work, but he wants half the (6)   the

_____."   coins

   "I was your partner," said the (7) _____ man.   second

"Partner!" the woodchopper exclaimed. (8) _____   who

struck the trees? Who chopped the (9) _____   fallen

trees, tied the wood in bundles, (10) _____   loaded

*Adapted from D. Murdoch, "Equal Pay for Equal Work: An Old Fable." Copyright © 1966 Highlights for Children, Inc., Columbus, Ohio. Reprinted with permission.

the donkey, and drove it to the customer's

(11) _____, unloaded it, and drove it back

(12) _____ the mountain? You did none of it."

"(13) _____ what this man says true?" asked

the cadi.

"(14) _____," said the partner, "I did my

share too. I (15) _____ all the groaning and

grunting when the work was (16) _____. I did

the complaining when the day (17) _____ hot

and the donkey became lazy. I also (18) _____

up the woodchopper whenever he became tired."

"Do you (19) _____ that work?" the woodchopper

asked angrily.

"If you had (20) _____ to do all those things

yourself it (21) _____ have taken twice as

long to finish the job," (22) _____ his partner.

I should receive half the pay, (23) _____ I

did half the work."

"Yes," agreed the (24) _____ thoughtfully.

"You certainly should receive your fair share

(25) _____ the money."

The woodchopper cried out (26) _____. But the

cadi roared, "Be silent! Guard, (27) _____

me a metal tray. Woodchopper, hand me the (28) _____

of coins."

The cadi took a coin (29) _____ the bag and

dropped it on the (30) _____. The coin rang

loud and clear. The woodchopper gritted (31) _____

teeth at the sound, but (32) _____ partner grinned.

One by one he let coins drop (33) _____ the tray with

clangs. The cadi listened to the (34) _____ of

the coins, one hand to his ear, looking (35) _____

house
up
is
well
did
heavy
grew
cheered
call
had
might
replied
for
cadi
of
angrily
bring
bag
from
tray
his
his
on
ring
questioningly
nodded
half
but
out
not
partner
been

at the partner. As each coin fell, the partner   all

(36) _____ happily at the sound.   tossed

When the bag was (37) _____ empty, the   fair

woodchopper reached for it. (38) _____ the cadi   your

stopped him and continued to take (39) _____   you

coins, dropping them loudly onto the tray. "Do   share

(40) _____ interrupt these pleasant sounds,"   received

shouted the cadi.   while

    The (41) _____ nodded greedily. When the

last coin had (42) _____ dropped onto the

pile, the cadi shoveled (43) _____ the

coins back into the bag, and (44) _____

it to the woodchopper.

    "You have each received your (45) _____

share," announced the cadi.

    The partner gasped. "But, (46) _____

Honor, I don't have any of it. (47) _____

said—"

    "I said you should receive your fair (48) _____ ,"

replied the cadi, "and you have just (49) _____

it. You made the sounds of work (50) _____

the woodchopper did the work. Now, you have heard

the sounds of the coins, but the woodchopper shall

have the money."

Three different approaches can be used in designing cloze passages, each involving a different level of difficulty. On the two easiest levels, a column containing the words that have been omitted is typed to the right of the cloze passage. At the easiest level these words are listed in the same order as they appear in the passage, as in the example shown. At the second level of difficulty the omitted words are listed in a scrambled order. Finally, at the most difficult level, the omitted words are not listed on the page containing the passage at all. Teachers using the cloze procedure as an instructional technique find it helpful to start with the easiest form. They can shift to the more difficult forms as the students' comprehension and ability to use context clues improves.

The student reads the passage silently and then writes the missing word in the blanks or on a separate sheet of paper. The student should supply the exact word that has been omitted; this helps determine the student's independent, instructional, and frustration levels. Spelling errors are disregarded during the scoring process as long as the correct word is supplied. The student should be permitted to use as much time as needed to complete each cloze exercise.

Responses are scored by dividing the number of correct responses by the number of blanks to determine the percentage of correct responses, for example, 25 of 50 words correct = 50 percent, 30 of 50 words correct = 60 percent.

If fewer than 40 percent of the blanks are filled in correctly, the difficulty of the material is at the student's frustration level. Miller (1974) suggests that success in supplying 60 percent or more of the words corresponds to the independent reading level, whereas from 40 to 59 percent success corresponds to the instructional level. Acceptance of synonyms for omitted words increases the level of success required for the independent level to 80 percent and to 60 to 79 percent success for the instructional level. Success in supplying fewer than 60 percent of the words suggests that the materials are at the student's frustration level.

Miller (1974) indicates that the student's average level of comprehension can be determined by multiplying the percentage of blanks successfully completed by 1.67. She uses the following two examples to explain this process:

Example 1

22 exact replacements
50 blank spaces
$22 \div 50 = 44\%$ correct replacements
$44 \times 1.67 = 73.48\%$ comprehension

Example 2

29 exact replacements
50 blank spaces
$29 \div 50 = 58\%$ correct replacements
$58 \times 1.67 = 96.86\%$ comprehension

Betts (1957) indicates that 95 percent or better comprehension is needed at the independent level and 75 percent or better at the instructional level. He reports that students who are comprehending less than 50 percent of what they read are at their frustration level. Cloze exercises can be used to evaluate the readability level of books or instructional materials that are being considered for adoption.

Cloze exercises can be used to assess and instruct students who are unable to use a specific part of speech. In each case, the words omitted can be representative of the troublesome part of speech. For example, a student who has trouble reauditorizing nouns can be given cloze exercises that provide an opportunity to practice this specific task; students who have trouble distinguishing among verb tenses can be given cloze passages that have blanks in place of the verbs; and students who have trouble distinguishing among the prepositions used to describe spatial relationships, such as up-down, over-under, above-below, and in front of–behind, can be given cloze exercises that require them to practice making these types of choices.

THE NEUROLOGICAL IMPRESS METHOD (NIM)

The neurological impress method (NIM) is a remedial reading technique developed by Heckelman (1969) and first used by him in the Merced and Sonoma County (California) schools. It is an instructional procedure that utilizes a whole-word approach to the development of reading fluency, phrasing, and visual-auditory channel integration. It is not recommended for use with students who need assistance in developing comprehension skills.

The NIM is well suited for students 10 years old and older who devote excessive amounts of time to sounding out words. These students should have at least second-grade-level word-attack skills and comprehension skills to benefit from the NIM. It helps these students synthesize their labored letter-by-letter and syllable-by-syllable reading into fluently read whole words, sentences, and passages. It also helps them learn how to read material in phrases rather than as isolated words. It is particularly helpful to students who tend to ignore commas and periods while they are reading.

The NIM is most effective when used on a one-to-one basis. It can be used with groups when the teacher speaks into a microphone that is connected to individual headsets worn by the students. Groups of students who are not equipped with headsets do not usually benefit from the NIM because they cannot hear the instructor's voice clearly and also because they become disorganized after hearing one another's mistakes.

The final goal of the NIM is fluent reading at an automatic response level. Heckelman (1969) reports that when NIM is used, the student's word recognition skills will improve but at a slower rate than reading speed. He indicates that word recognition skills will continue to increase gradually after the NIM training period is over. The most rapid growth tends to occur when the student gains sufficient confidence in reading to begin reading newspapers and magazines on a voluntary basis.

Unison Reading Procedure

The student receiving assistance by the NIM should be seated slightly in front of the teacher so that the teacher's voice is close to the student's ear. Older students and tactually defensive students usually prefer to sit beside the teacher. The student and teacher begin by reading the same passage together orally. They continue with the teacher smoothly moving his or her finger along the line of words so that it points to the word that is to be read next.

During the early sessions, the teacher should read a little faster and louder than the student. The student who complains that the teacher is going too fast should be encouraged to continue trying and to not worry about mistakes. It may be necessary at times to slow down slightly to a speed that is more comfortable for the student. The nearer the teacher's reading speed is to the student's reading frustration rate, the sooner the student's fluency will increase to a level near his or her comprehension level.

The teacher and student should reread the initial lines and paragraphs several times before going on to new material. This repetition permits the student to experience early success in reading fluently. The student who is able to read a passage fluently after a try or two should not be asked to read it over and over. Two or three minutes of repetitious patterning is usually sufficient.

Starting Level, Rate of Growth, Failure to Respond

Teachers should start remedial instruction at a level slightly below the level where the student can read successfully. They should not start so low that time will be wasted before the student begins expanding his or her skills. Heckelman (1969) indicates that students who are started at the first- or second-grade reading level should advance to the third-grade level by the end of the second hour of remedial instruction, to the fifth- or sixth grade-level by the sixth hour, and to the seventh- or eighth-grade level by the end of the twelfth hour. The student should not be pushed beyond the grade level at which a person of his or her age and intelligence should normally be reading.

Students who fail to respond rapidly and easily within four hours of the initiation of the NIM should be considered for assignment to a program that uses a kinesthetic approach.

Heckelman (1969) indicates that most students may be exposed to as many as two thousand words during an ordinary fifteen-minute NIM session. In some cases, it is necessary to start with much shorter instructional sessions and work up to fifteen-minute periods. This emphasis on overexposure to difficult words is a major factor in the rapid progress made with this method.

Voice-Finger Synchronization

Heckelman (1969) advises teachers to make sure during their early attempts to use NIM that their voices are synchronized with their fingers. He points out that many teachers have difficulty doing this and that they are not always aware of this problem. This lack of natural voice-finger synchronization is attributed to the tendency for a good reader to look ahead of the word being vocalized. Heckelman emphasizes voice-finger synchronization because he believes that many children do not read well because of malfunctioning eye movements.

When the reader's finger reaches the end of the line, it should move rapidly back to the point where the next line begins. The speed of this movement should resemble that of a typewriter carriage returning to the beginning of the next line.

Teacher-Student Alternation

The teacher and student may trade off leading the reading of the passage. The student should move his or her finger along the line of words as they are read. It may be necessary for the teacher to guide the student's finger so that it continues to move in a smooth fashion at exactly the same speed the words are being read. The student's pronunciation of the words will be a letter or syllable behind the teacher's when the teacher is leading the reading; the teacher's pronunciations are slightly behind the student's when the student is leading. Often the student must be pushed to maintain the desired speed when he or she is leading the reading.

Correcting Mispronunciations

Heckelman (1969) advises teachers not to stop students to go back to correct a mispronounced word or words. This type of interruption of the flow of the student's reading for the sake of accuracy or a comprehension check tends to defeat the main objective of the NIM, which centers on the need to increase the student's reading fluency. Other instructional techniques should be selected when the primary instructional concern is developing word-attack skills.

Rate Acceleration

Teachers should speed up the reading rate for a few minutes during each instructional session after two or more hours of instruction have been completed; they should literally drag the student to higher rates of reading speed (Heckelman, 1969). The reading speed should be the fastest rate at which the teacher can read clearly without discomfort.

In reading phrases, students should not revert back to word calling. They should develop the skills needed to appropriately vary their rhythmic patterns while reading. Also, they should not mumble while reading multiple-syllable words. The only time a student is asked to repeat a passage for the purpose of correcting an error is when he or she is mumbling. The reading model provided by the teacher should demonstrate the rhythmic and phrasing patterns and the reading rate the student is expected to use.

Echo Reading

Echo reading, a supplemental procedure described by Heckelman, may be introduced at any point during the NIM. It is most frequently used with students who have auditory discrimination and verbal expression problems. First the teacher reads a phrase or sentence while the student listens. Then the student repeats, or "echoes," the phrase or sentence. Sentences may need to be broken down into sections that are practiced individually before being recombined and again repeated in a conversational tone. As soon as the student is able to successfully echo read the sentence, the student and teacher reread it using regular NIM unison reading.

NONVISUAL AKT

Nonvisual AKT (auditory, kinesthetic, tactual) is a modality-blocking procedure for teaching reading. Developed by Harold and Harriet Blau (1969) it is designed for use with students whose reading problems are caused by interference of visual stimuli with the reception of stimuli through the auditory and tactual-kinesthetic modalities. It is possible to avoid this interference by blocking off or preventing the reception of visual stimuli.

Students who require nonvisual AKT procedures generally have well-developed speech patterns, which suggests that they are receiving auditory stimuli properly. They tend to be more successful in writing when their movements are based on their tactual-kinesthetic memory than when they attempt to copy a word they can see. These factors, combined with their failure to develop a sight-word vocabulary, suggest that they may benefit from instruction following the nonvisual AKT procedure.

Nonvisual AKT follows the general instructional sequence described by Fernald for the VAKT method, except that the visual modality is not used when new material is introduced. The student's eyes may be covered with a blindfold or sleep shade, or closed to prevent the reception of visual stimuli. All new material is introduced and learned auditorily, kinesthetically, and tactually before its visual form is introduced. Three modifications of standard VAKT procedures are made to fill in the gap created by blocking out the visual stimuli. The first modification calls for the teacher to print the word lightly on the student's back. In the second modification, the student responds by voicing each letter of the word as the teacher traces it. The third modification consists of a combination of the first two adjustments.

These modifications are designed to help the student develop a strong mental image of the word to be read. As soon as this happens, modality blocking is discontinued and VAKT procedures are resumed. The student's strong auditory imagery and the repertoire of tactual-kinesthetic responses associated with the word serve as a foundation on which the word's visual image can be based.

KINETIC PATTERNING

Kinetic patterning is an instructional sequence developed by Scottsdale, Arizona reading specialist Gerry Lee and learning disability specialist Virginia Young. It is designed for use with students who are unable to gain meaning from isolated sounds or to blend these isolated sounds into a meaningful whole.

In kinetic patterning, the sounds and letter symbols are introduced in linguistic clusters (such as *nat, rat, fat, that, at, sat, cat*). These clusters are introduced one at a time. Each set of words is repeated over and over until the student's tongue automatically falls into the correct position when a visual symbol is introduced. The sounds and symbols are introduced in clusters in order to prevent the perseveration of individual sounds, which often happens when sounds are taught in isolation. Each cluster of sounds is introduced and repeated until all the consonants and vowels are mastered. The vocabulary and language are carefully controlled so that the student can deal with the material without becoming frustrated.

The eight levels covered on the 506 drill cards found in the *Kinetic Patterning Kit* (Lee and Young, 1974) extend from beginning reading to high school material. Levels I through VI emphasize teaching the sound patterns found in the English language so that they are produced as fully integrated automatic responses. Level VII teaches a vocabulary that is designed to allow the student to function successfully in any low-track, primary basal reading program. Level VIII concentrates on specific word concepts related to paragraph meaning in the content material the student will be asked to read while in school. *Kinetic Patterning Kits* can be obtained from Learning Systems, P.O. Box 1674, Scottsdale, Arizona 85252.

THE SECONDARY CORRECTIVE READING SEQUENCE

The secondary corrective reading sequence (SCRS) is a simple, inexpensive, flexible, comprehensive sequence for teaching reading to adolescents with learning problems. Developed by Douglas Wiseman and first used in the model demonstration project for learning disabled students at Mountain View High School in Mesa, Arizona, the SCRS does not usually require commercial materials and equipment except those commonly found in classrooms and resource centers. All materials are made either by teachers or students. The procedures are flexible enough to be used with individuals, small groups, or large groups, and by teachers, teacher aides, or peer tutors. The SCRS is comprehensive, covering any area of instruction related to reading, including handwriting, spelling, written or oral composition, phonics, sight-vocabulary, silent reading, choral reading, oral reading, language stimulation, syllabication, thinking skills, and dictionary skills. Designed to help adolescents develop the reading and language skills needed to successfully participate in secondary school classrooms, SCRS procedures make it possible for them to escape much of the humiliation and embarrassment they experience when confronted with materials whose ideational content is at the level of their reading vocabulary rather than their intellectual level. The general components in the SCRS include (1) listening comprehension, (2) choral reading, (3) oral reading, and (4) review. This suggested sequence should be used on each passage selected by the student and teacher.

Listening Comprehension

The teacher should identify the student's listening comprehension level and areas of special interest before selecting the passages to be read. The materials selected should be based on the student's level of listening comprehension, not reading level. They can be content materials from class work in areas such as social science, career education, or literature; they can be from special interest areas such as auto mechanics or flying; or they can be job-related materials. A passage is acceptable if the student can comprehend the material when it is read aloud by the teacher.

There are five steps in the listening comprehension component:

1. The teacher reads the passage aloud to the student at least once.
2. The teacher determines the student's comprehension level by asking questions directly related to the passage. The student may be asked to retell the content in his or her own words. The teacher should discuss all the word meanings about which the student is uncertain.
3. The teacher then asks standard comprehension questions of the type adolescents are expected to answer. These questions might ask the student to identify the main idea, discover the answers by reading between and beyond the lines, and complete a set of directions.
4. The teacher encourages the student to participate in an active learning situation by stimulating higher-level intellectual participation through mind-expanding questions such as the following: "What would happen if another character or problem had been added to the passage?" "How is this character or idea similar to another character or idea?" "In what other way could the passage have ended?"

5. The teacher encourages the student's oral expression by urging him or her to retell the story or make up a fantasy story or passage related to the original passage. The student can also discuss a personal experience that is related to the story.

Choral Reading

The choral reading component is much like the neurological impress method suggested by Heckelman (1974). The teacher and student read together in unison, with the teacher assuming the dominant role. The teacher sits behind or beside the student so that the teacher's voice will be directed toward the student's ear. The teacher or student should follow the line being read with a smooth finger motion. Reading should not stop when the student falters or makes an error, but should continue on as if nothing had occurred. The passage should be read and reread chorally until the student reads smoothly with the teacher.

Echo or staggered reading can be used with students who are having difficulty with choral reading. The teacher reads a sentence or part of a passage and then the student rereads it aloud. This procedure is followed until the entire passage has been read. It may be necessary to repeat this echo reading procedure several times before successful choral reading is possible.

Oral Reading

The inclusion of oral reading in the SCRS makes it possible to identify any problems the student has not overcome during step A (listening comprehension) and step B (choral reading). The student reads the passage aloud while the teacher records errors on a second copy of the passage. The student and teacher then compile an error list, which the teacher can use as the basis for prescribing skill-building activities such as sight-word drills, phonics instruction, and so on.

The multidimensional nature of reading forces the reader to apply mechanical skills smoothly and systematically while simultaneously comprehending what is being read. Poor readers with inconsistent mechanical skills tend to divide their attention between the multiple tasks of word attack and those of comprehension. If the student attends to word attack, his or her comprehension tends to suffer, and vice versa. The SCRS attempts to eliminate this inhibiting distraction by emphasizing comprehension before mechanical skill development is attempted. It encourages the student to use comprehension or context clues to assist in the systematic application of word-attack skills much as the experienced adult reader does.

Adult readers rely heavily on their vast store of experience as they read. This prior experience permits and encourages idea reading rather than word reading. When the adult reader is confronted with a completely unfamiliar vocabulary and/or subject matter, his or her reading rate decreases, often to the point of reading word by word. Subvocal utterances, repetition of words and phrases, and sentence regressions also tend to occur more often. This behavior closely resembles the reading style of adolescents who have trouble reading. The SCRS provides this prior experience in steps A and B. Step B also serves as a transition stage between listening comprehension and the systematic application of mechanical skills, or independent reading. The program uses successive approximations to move the student toward independent reading.

The suggested steps for the oral reading component are as follows:

1. The student orally reads the passage.
2. The teacher records errors.
3. The teacher and student analyze the errors together, compiling a word error list and planning an instructional and self-instructional program that could include
   a. dictionary drills to correct errors in
      (1) vocabulary
      (2) spelling
      (3) phonics, including syllabication
      (4) handwriting
   b. sentence writing using problem words, emphasizing
      (1) composition
      (2) grammar
      (3) punctuation and capital letters
      (4) spelling and handwriting
   c. development of a sight-word list, using
      (1) tracing
      (2) flashcards
      (3) tachistoscopic drills
4. Evaluation:
   a. the student rereads the passage orally and
      (1) the teacher records the errors and compares the new error list
      (2) the teacher and student jointly agree to go on to the next passage or to return for additional work on the original error list
   b. the student is given a spelling quiz of words selected for spelling mastery
   c. the student defines words from the original error list

Review

Review is an essential step in the SCRS and must receive considerable emphasis to insure overlearning and long-term retention. Procedurally, the student and teacher develop a file of completed passages and error lists to be utilized in the review and practice process. The review process should be an independent activity planned by the student with only occasional teacher involvement. A weekly review of each completed passage and error list should be required. Periodic spelling and vocabulary tests could be scheduled to assist in the process of overlearning. As the student becomes more adept, a variety of dictation activities can be initiated to eliminate the need for separate spelling and vocabulary quizzes. Scheduled review activities are an integral part of the successful application of the SCRS.

Other Considerations

The SCRS was designed for students in grades 7 through 12 who have at least an advanced grade 2 reading level or higher. Students with little or no reading skills and possible severe processing disabilities may not profit from this approach. Remedial approaches like those developed by Gillingham and Stillman (1966) and Fernald (1943), which were designed for use with students who have severe reading disabilities, are recommended in these cases.

The passages to be read in the SCRS must be selected with care. They should usually be at the student's comprehension level. The teacher should read the prospective paragraphs to the student, and then question the student to determine the student's level of listening comprehension. If the student shows interest in the content and can respond appropriately to the questions, the material is acceptable. The teacher should also determine the readability of the passages. Three of the most frequently used readability formulas are found in Fry (1968), Flesch (1951), and McLaughlin (1969).

Finally, the SCRS was designed for ease of grouping. It can be effectively used in individual tutoring situations controlled by the teacher, student, a teaching aide, an adult volunteer, or a carefully selected peer who has already mastered the assigned passage. Tape-recordings and overhead transparencies can be used when working with groups.

The suggested activities listed in the SCRS are guidelines to be used at the discretion of the teacher. The needs of the student must be a primary ingredient in the teacher's decision-making process.

SUMMARY

1. Visual sight-word methods are recommended for use with students who learn best when visual and tactual-kinesthetic inputs are stressed.
2. The Fernald VAKT approach emphasizes the use of tactual-kinesthetic sensations involved in tracing to aid students in learning to read.
3. According to Fernald, the greatest handicap of the nonreader is the emotional complex that accompanies reading failure.

4. The language experience approach uses students' oral descriptions of their own experiences as a basis for teaching speaking, listening, reading, and writing skills.

5. The cloze procedure involves having the reader fill in words that have been left out of a passage.

6. The teacher and student who are using the neurological impress method read together orally while developing reading fluency, phrasing, and visual-auditory channel integration.

7. Nonvisual AKT is a modality-blocking procedure for teaching reading to students whose reception of visual stimuli is interfering with the reception of stimuli through the auditory and tactual-kinesthetic modalities.

8. Kinetic patterning introduces sounds and letter symbols as linguistic clusters (such as fat, cat, rat, hat).

9. The secondary corrective reading sequence is a simple, flexible, comprehensive sequence for teaching reading to adolescents with reading problems.

REFERENCES

Allen, R. V. 1976. *Language Experiences in Communication.* Boston: Houghton Mifflin Company.

Betts, E. A. 1957. *Foundations of Reading Instruction.* New York: American Book Company.

Blau, H., and H. Blau. 1969. "A Theory of 'Modality Blocking'." In *Successful Programming: Many Points of View.* J. I. Arena, Ed. Pittsburg: Association for Children with Learning Disabilities.

Bloomer, R. H. 1962. "The Cloze Procedure as a Remedial Reading Exercise." *Journal of Developmental Reading,* 5 (Spring), 173–181.

Bormuth, J. 1968. "The Cloze Readability Procedure." *Elementary English,* 45 (April) 429–436.

Fernald, G. 1943. *Remedial Techniques in Basic School Subjects.* New York: McGraw-Hill.

Flesch, R. 1951. *How to Test Readability.* New York: Harper & Row.

Fry, E. 1968. "A Readability Formula that Saves Time." *Journal of Reading,* 11, 513–516.

Gillingham, A., and B. Stillman. 1966. *Remedial Training for Children with Specific Disability in Reading, Spelling, and Penmanship.* 7th ed. Cambridge, Mass.: Educators Publishing Service.

Heckelman, R. G. 1969. "The Neurological Impress Method of Remedial Reading Instruction." *Academic Therapy,* 4 (Summer), 277–282.

Heckelman, R. G. 1974. *Solutions to Reading Problems.* San Rafael, Calif.: Academic Therapy Publications.

Jongsma, E. 1971. *The Cloze Procedure as a Reading Technique.* Newark, Del.: International Reading Association.

Lee, G., and V. Young. 1974. *Kinetic Patterning to Cognition in Reading.* Scottsdale, Ariz.: Learning Specialists.

McLaughlin, H. G. 1969. "SMOG Grading—A New Readability Formula." *Journal of Reading,* 12, 639–646.

Miller, W. H. 1974. *Reading Diagnosis Kit.* New York: Center for Applied Research in Education, Inc.

THIRTEEN

Auditory Phonetic Methods
of Teaching Reading

Auditory phonetic methods of teaching reading emphasize word recognition as a sound-blending process. Their primary goal is to develop proficiency in decoding the words contained in written language. Two general approaches are followed in teaching phonics. The *synthetic phonics approach* emphasizes learning the sounds of letters in isolation and blending these sounds into words (Kaluger and Kolson, 1978). The *analytic approach* emphasizes breaking down or analyzing the phonetic content of words the student has learned as sight words.

Kaluger and Kolson (1978) report that the advantages of phonics instruction, "are that phonics produces efficiency and independence in unlocking new words and that the child learns of the association between printed letters and the sounds they represent" (p. 195). They list the disadvantages as (1) a tendency of some teachers to teach phonics as isolated sounds without associating the sounds to unlocking words, (2) the emphasis on the pronunciation of words without stressing comprehension, and (3) a confusion that arises with words that are exceptions to the rules.

The three phonetically oriented approaches to teaching reading discussed in this chapter emphasize the use of students' auditory strengths to learn phonetic skills. Mastery of these skills provides a foundation on which to base the corresponding visual and tactual-kinesthetic attributes of the words.

THE ORTON-GILLINGHAM METHOD

The Orton-Gillingham approach to teaching reading is a synthetic phonetic or alphabetic approach. It begins with the names and sounds of the letters in the alphabet, and follows by combining or blending these sounds together to make words. The kinesthetic sensations involved in vocalizing these sounds, feeling the shapes of the letters in the alphabet, and writing words are sometimes used to reinforce the association between the sound and corresponding visual form of each letter.

The Orton-Gillingham approach is well suited for students whose diagnostic profiles reveal what Johnson and Myklebust (1967) call *visual dyslexia* — strong auditory skills and visual processing problems. It is a multisensory procedure that permits students to use their auditory strengths to learn the names, sounds, and kinesthetic sensations associated with vocalizing the letters of the alphabet. They can then use this information as they learn to perceive and remember the visual equivalents of these sounds and kinesthetic sensations.

The Orton-Gillingham instructional approach is based on the symptoms described by neurologist Samuel T. Orton in 1929 and 1937 as a result of his studies of reading disabled students. Orton described these students as having adequate visual acuity and normal or above average intelligence, but poor auditory and visual memory. The symptoms he found most frequently included confusion of lower-case letters, uncertainty in reading short palindromical words such as *saw* and *was*, a tendency to reverse parts of words or whole syllables, and greater facility than usual in reading from the mirror and a frequent facility for producing mirror writing.

Orton (1937) suggests that children with specific developmental language disabilities in areas such as reading may have these problems because they fail to establish dominance of one hemisphere of their brain over the other. According to Orton, the associations involved in reading and gaining meaning from written words are stored in the dominant hemisphere of the brain; a mirror image of this information is stored in the nondominant hemisphere. The absence of a clearly dominant hemisphere results in incomplete or mixed dominance and an increased tendency for these mirror images to be expressed as reversals.

Orton's theories were developed into special procedures for teaching reading by Anna Gillingham and her associate, Bessie Stillman. These procedures have been carried on and extended by a number of others, including Beth Slingerland, Sally Childs, and Aylett Cox.

The Orton-Gillingham method is intended for use with reading disabled students who are in grades 3 through 6 (practitioners report that it is also effective when used with younger and older students, including adults), have normal visual and auditory acuity, tend to reverse letters or words and write mirror images of words, have trouble pronouncing words, and have failed to learn reading and spelling skills when taught with a combination of sight-word reading and phonics. Gillingham advised those who use this method to make sure that the students receiving special instruction are removed from their classrooms whenever the other students are receiving reading or spelling instruction, that instruction always starts at the beginning of the logical sequence of structured steps that she outlined, and that steps or parts of the procedure are not omitted. She also outlined the following six combinations of the auditory, visual, and kinesthetic modalities:

V-A—translation of visual symbols into sounds (vocalized or in thought)

A-V—translation of auditory symbols into visual images

A-K—translation of auditory symbols into the muscle responses involved in speaking and writing

K-A—movement of a passive hand by another hand to produce a letter to prompt naming or production of the sound of a letter

V-K—translation of a visual symbol into the muscular action required to speak or write it

K-V—use of the muscular "feel" associated with vocalizing a sound or writing a letter to prompt the visualization of that letter

Teaching Letter Names and Sounds

The instructional sequence used in the Orton-Gillingham approach starts with the introduction of the letters in the alphabet. Words and sentences are introduced following mastery of the names and sounds of the letters. A *key word* is used to introduce each new sound. Cox (1975) describes a key word as a word that illustrates the sound and serves as a key to "unlocking" the student's memory of that sound, its connection with the letter, and its position in the word. The following series of steps is used to assist the student with the formation of linkages or associations between the auditory, visual, and kinesthetic characteristics of each letter.

Linkage 1—Association of letter's name, shape, and sound with its kinesthetic "feel" in the muscles of the student's mouth.

a. Therapist shows student new "reading" letter (printed form) on letter card and names letter.

b. Student repeats letter name.

c. Therapist gives key word and isolates speech sound which letter represents.

d. Student repeats key word and sound while therapist describes its "feel" in mouth and throat.

e. Therapist and student look into mirror while both make speech sound and match their mouth shapes.

f. Student discovers letter's category (vowel or consonant) by noting his mouth's position. He designates a voiced or unvoiced consonant and the role of his tongue, lips, and teeth in its production.

Linkage 2—Association of student's kinesthetic memory of letter's cursive shape (in his hand and arm) with its name.

a. Therapist prints "reading" letter on board and writes cursive letter over it, showing the relationship of "writing" letter to "reading" letter.
b. Therapist places small arrow at starting point and writes large cursive letter carefully on board (or unlined paper) while describing strokes and rhythm. Student observes closely.
c. Student traces letter several times, first in air and then on chalkboard, naming letter just before writing it every time. He always starts on the arrow and names letter before he writes.
d. Student copies letter several times on board or paper until he has the "feel" in his muscles. He always names letter before he begins to write it.
e. Therapist erases letter from chalkboard or provides clean paper when letter shape seems to be clearly established in student's arm muscles.
f. Student writes large letter several times from memory, always naming letter first.
g. Student writes large letter several times with eyes closed or averted, each time "telling his hand" the letter's name.

Linkage 3 — Association of graphic symbol with letter's name — alphabet and reading.
a. Student sees "reading" letter on card and names it. This part of linkage may be continued as alphabet drill until student is assured that his eyes convey the correct messages.
b. Therapist moves student's passive hand to form large letter in air while student's arm is straight.
   or
   Class of students move own arms in writing large letter shape in air, while imitating teacher's motions (teacher's back to class). Therapist walks behind class and assists each student by guiding arm movement.
c. Student names letter his hand is forming without watching his hand.

Linkage 4 — Association of written cursive shape with letter's name-writing.
a. Therapist names letter.
b. Student writes large cursive letter on chalkboard or large unlined paper, naming letter just before writing it. This linkage becomes a part of daily writing practice.

Linkage 5 — Association of printed symbol with speech sound — reading.
a. Student sees printed letter on card.
b. Student gives key word and speech sound which letter represents. This part of linkage becomes the daily reading deck drill.

   c. Therapist moves student's hand in the air to form large cursive letter (student's arm straight) while student looks away.
   or
   Class follows teacher's motion in making the shape of a letter, without watching their own hands.
   d. Student again gives key word and speech sound for which letter stands.

Linkage 6 — Association of speech sound with letter's name.
a. Therapist names letter.
b. Student gives key word and speech sound.

Linkage 7 — Association of letter's name with speech sound — oral spelling.
a. Therapist makes sound which letter symbolizes.
b. Student gives key word and names letter which stands for sound. This linkage is used as oral spelling drill. It is especially valuable in advanced training for the study of multiple spellings.

Linkage 8 — Association of letter's name and cursive shape with speech sound — written spelling.
a. Therapist makes speech sound.
b. Student repeats sound and names letter which stands for sound.
c. Student writes letter, sometimes with eyes averted or closed. This linkage becomes the daily written spelling deck drill. (Cox, 1975, pp. 102–104).

Each letter that is introduced is printed on a card that is included in the student's personal deck of drill cards. The distinction between vowel and consonant sounds is shown by printing the consonants on white cards and vowels on salmon-colored cards. The student repeats the linkages described above for the sounds represented by each of these cards during daily review sessions. These review sessions continue until the student acquires the ability to recognize the alphabet automatically and use it reliably.

The following ten letters and the key words that introduce them are taught first. Each is taught as if it had only one sound. Other sounds for these letters are taught later.

a	apple	/a/		*j*	jam	/j/
b	boy	/b/		*k*	kite	/k/
f	fun	/f/		*m*	man	/m/
h	hat	/h/		*p*	pan	/p/
i	it	/i/		*t*	top	/t/

(Gillingham and Stillman, 1975, p. 44)

Students must master one sound for each of these first ten letters and the associated linkages before they move on to blending them into words. Additional letters may be introduced while instruction in blending these first ten letters into words is taking place. These new letters and their corresponding sounds may be introduced in the following sequence at a rate of one or two words a day.

g	go	*s*	sat
o	olive	*sh*	ship
r	rat	*d*	dog
l	lamp	*w*	wind
n	nut	*wh*	whittle
th	this	*y*	yes
ch	chin	*v*	van
e	elephant	*z*	zebra

(Gillingham and Stillman, 1975, pp. 55–57)

Reading Words

Simple words made from combinations of the first ten letters are printed on yellow cards and placed in a box of drill words for use by the student. Among these words might be the following:

bat	map	him
tap	at	mat
hip	if	fat
hit	Jim	bib
pat	pit	bit
hat	fib	knit
jab	it	

(Gillingham and Stillman, 1975, p. 49)

Instruction in the reading of words starts with placement of the drill cards for one word—say, *b-a-t*—in a row on a table in front of the student. The student is asked to produce the sound for each of the letters—for example, /b/ /a/ /t/—and to repeat these sounds again and again. Each repetition should be faster and smoother until the first two letters, /ba/, are blended together with the last letter /t/ following. Finally, the entire series of sounds should become smoothly blended together into a correctly pronounced word. The yellow drill card containing the word is then exposed so that the student can read it. This procedure continues until the student can read all of the words on the yellow cards in the original deck. Additional words are added to the deck each time a new letter and sound is mastered and combined with previously learned letters. The student's progress can be plotted on a graph showing the number of drill word cards read correctly and incorrectly during each day of instruction. The cards read incorrectly are placed in a separate pile for further study during later instructional periods.

Spelling Words

Gillingham and Stillman (1975) believe that *oral spelling* is the translation of sounds into letter names and that *written spelling* is the translation of sounds into letter forms. They suggest that instruction in spelling should start a few days after the initiation of the blending of sounds into words.

They begin spelling instruction by analyzing or breaking down a word into its component sounds. This is the reverse of the blending procedure used to teach the students to read the word. Called *simultaneous oral spelling (SOS)*, this procedure emphasizes the simultaneous naming of letters. The following five steps in Childs's adaptation of the Orton-Gillingham SOS procedures are described by Cox (1975).

1. The student *listens* to the word as it is pronounced by the teacher (auditory) and looks at the teacher's mouth as it is pronounced.
2. The student *echoes* or repeats the word aloud (kinesthetic and auditory).
3. The student *spells* the word aloud, naming each letter (kinesthetic and auditory).
4. The student *writes* the word, naming each letter immediately before writing it (visual, auditory, kinesthetic).
5. The student *reads* (proofreads) the word aloud to be certain that his or her hand wrote it correctly.

The teacher will sometimes find it necessary to assist students by slowly pronouncing the words while they listen for the first, middle, or final sounds. It is also helpful at times to use drill cards to reconstruct a word.

Spelling rule 1 is taught after the student has learned the sounds for each of the letters. This rule states that, "Words of one syllable ending in *f, l,* or *s* after one vowel usually end in double *f,* double *l,* or double *s*" (Gillingham and Stillman, 1975, p. 59). The following words are written on yellow cards and added to the student's deck of drill cards when this rule is introduced.

doll	muff	puff
doff	whiff	hell
buff	bell	sell
huff	fell	tell
well	ill	dill
fill	hill	kill

mill	pill	rill
sill	till	will
gull	hull	mull
bass	mass	chess
less	mess	muss
hiss	kiss	

(Gillingham and Stillman, 1975, p. 58)

Spelling instruction is discussed further in Chapter 14.

Handwriting

Cursive handwriting is introduced in linkage 2. This linkage emphasizes the student's association of the kinesthetic sensations experienced while writing the letter with its name. Written spelling is usually not introduced until the student can automatically name and write the letters.

Cursive handwriting is used because it provides the writer with a natural left-to-right progression. Cursive handwriting also eliminates the question of where to start each letter and reduces the tendency to reverse letters by eliminating the need to raise the pencil. Finally, if they use cursive handwriting at this stage, young children will not have to learn two different writing skills.

The teacher's manual for *Alphabetic Phonics Workbook I* (Green, 1971) includes the following verbal directions for use in telling students how to form the lower-case cursive letters of the alphabet. The formation of each letter begins with placement of the pencil point on the line.

a 1. Curve up and over, stop
   2. Swing left, down, around and close
   3. Pull down
   4. Turn out

b 1. Swing way up
   2. Loop left
   3. Pull straight down
   4. Curve around and up
   5. Turn out

c 1. Curve up and over, stop
   2. Swing left, down, around
   3. And out

d 1. Curve up and over, stop
   2. Swing left, down, around and close
   3. Push straight up

    4. Pull straight down
    5. Turn out

e 1. Swing up
    2. Loop left
    3. Pull straight down
    4. Turn out

f 1. Swing way up
    2. Loop left
    3. Pull way down straight
    4. Loop right, curve up to join
    5. Turn out

g 1. Curve up and over, stop
    2. Swing left, down, around and close
    3. Pull way down straight
    4. Loop left, curve up and out

h 1. Swing way up
    2. Loop left
    3. Pull straight down
    4. Curve over, pull down
    5. Turn out

i 1. Swing up
    2. Pull down
    3. Turn out
    4. Then dot

j 1. Swing up
    2. Pull way down straight
    3. Loop left, curve up and out
    4. Then dot

k 1. Swing way up
    2. Loop left
    3. Pull straight down
    4. Curve over and in
    5. Pull down and out

l 1. Swing way up
    2. Loop left
    3. Pull straight down
    4. Turn out

m 1. Curve up and over
    2. Pull straight down

    3. Up and over
    4. Pull straight down
    5. Up and over
    6. Pull straight down
    7. Turn out

n 1. Curve up and over
    2. Pull straight down
    3. Up and over
    4. Pull straight down
    5. Turn out

o 1. Curve up and over, stop
    2. Swing left, down around and close
    3. And out

p 1. Swing up
    2. Pull way down straight
    3. Loop left
    4. Curve up, around, close
    5. Turn out

q 1. Curve up and over, stop
    2. Swing left, down, around and close
    3. Pull way down straight
    4. Loop right, curve up to join
    5. Turn out

r 1. Swing up, stop
    2. Down a little
    3. Swing up and over
    4. Pull down and out

s 1. Swing up, stop
    2. Curve down, around, close
    3. Turn out

t 1. Swing way up
    2. Pull straight down
    3. Turn out
    4. Then cross

u 1. Swing up
    2. Straight down, around
    3. Swing up
    4. Straight down
    5. Turn out

v 1. Curve up and over
   2. Down, around, swing up
   3. Turn out

w 1. Swing up
   2. Straight down, around
   3. Swing up
   4. Straight down, around
   5. Swing up
   6. Turn out

x 1. Curve up and over
   2. Slant down
   3. Turn out
   4. Slant down left

y 1. Curve up and over
   2. Down, around, swing up
   3. Pull way down straight
   4. Loop left, curve up and out

z 1. Curve up and over
   2. Down, around, stop
   3. Curve around and way down
   4. Curve up and out

Additional material regarding handwriting instruction appears in Chapter 16.

Reading and Writing Dictated Stories

After students have become proficient at reading and writing three-letter phonetic words, they can combine these words into sentences and stories. First the students read the sentences silently, asking for assistance with troublesome words. Then they read the sentences out loud. Finally, they group them into short stories. The teacher dictates these short stories to the students, who write them on paper. The teacher writes the nonphonetic words in these stories on paper so they are available for the students to copy when they reach the points in the story where they appear.

Teaching Consonant Blends

Consonant blends are taught after students have become proficient at reading, writing from dictation, and spelling the words contained in the short stories introduced earlier. First the teacher prepares a deck of cards containing consonant blends. These cards are shuffled and read by the student each day. Emphasis is placed on the development of linkages among the auditory, visual, and kinesthetic attributes of the consonant letters being blended together. The following words are representative of those included by Gillingham and Stillman (1975) in blending instruction.

risk	spot	staff
slit	lend	dress
skin	trot	press
slab	flash	smell
plot	hand	swell

(Gillingham and Stillman, 1975, p. 62)

Other Activities

A number of other activities are included in the Orton-Gillingham approach. For example, the use of affixes to build words is introduced after the ability to blend consonants has been integrated with previously learned material. *Affixes* are meaningful syllables that are placed before or after a basic word for the purpose of modifying the idea expressed by the base word. *Prefixes* are affixes attached to the beginning of a base word to add the concept of "before" to the basic meaning. The addition of the prefix *pre-* to the base word *date* means that the item was dated *before* the time that is stated. *Suffixes* are affixes placed after the base word. The addition of the suffix *-er* means "one who performs" some action. The *reporter* is one who performs the act of making a report.

Additional spelling rules are introduced as the student moves through the carefully sequenced instructional activities outlined by Gillingham and Stillman. The five-step program for teaching spelling is repeated in each case. Throughout the instructional sequence, newly introduced material and rules are reviewed and linked with previously learned material.

Separated syllables are connected in instruction to further assist students with building, reading, and spelling more complex words. The five-step program is again utilized in teaching students to spell the words created by combining syllables. Students are also taught to place the appropriate accent on each syllable as they read multiple-syllable words. Understanding of the effect of accent on various syllables is related to later instruction in dictionary usage.

As new ways of pronouncing previously learned letters are taught, the various symbols, or diacritical marks, used in the dictionary to indicate pronunciation are systematically introduced. This new marking system should be integrated with previously learned sounds and key words. Drill cards, graphing of words read, spelling by the five-point program and story reading are used when each new sound is introduced.

Gillingham and Stillman make frequent use of the dictionary during the advanced stages of reading and spelling instruction. They place particular emphasis on alphabetical sequence, the use of the guide words at the tops of the pages, multiple spellings of words, syllabication, definitions, the use of diacritical marks, and pronunciation of words.

THE HEGGE, KIRK, AND KIRK REMEDIAL READING DRILLS

The Hegge, Kirk, and Kirk (1936) *Remedial Reading Drills* were developed for use in teaching phonetic reading to students who require remedial assistance. The drills emphasize learning the sounds of letters and blending letters together. These features make the drills well suited for use with students who have strong auditory processing skills. Their primary focus is on development of the word-attack skills needed to pronounce independently new words that are encountered in sentence and story reading. They are most effective when used with students who are reading below the fourth-grade level, have a severe special reading disability, are able to learn to blend sounds, do not have extreme visual or auditory deficits that have not been corrected, are motivated, and need drill in phonics.

Teachers using the remedial reading drills should always begin instruction at a level where the material can be mastered easily. Success is one of the greatest incentives for a student whose previous attempts to learn have ended in failure.

Psychological Basis for the Drills

The *Remedial Reading Drills* are based on the following psychological principles:

The presentation of two possible sounds for one letter may confuse the student, who may be unable to reproduce either sound the next time he or she sees that letter. The drills are constructed so that only one sound is presented for a letter; for example, the letter *a* is always a short *ă* when it appears alone. Additional sounds for a letter are taught by presenting the letter in combination with another letter; for example, the long form of *ā* is presented as *āy* as in say or *āi* as in said.

Frequent repetition of letter-sound combinations helps the student learn to associate them with each other. The drills are sequenced so that many more repetitions are involved than are usually found in instructional materials.

Motivation facilitates learning. The drills are carefully structured so that the easiest material is presented first. Success in these tasks motivates the student for the more difficult material appearing later in the drills.

Articulation aids retention. The student's oral production of the words also gives the teacher a chance to correct errors as soon as they appear and helps prevent the development of habitual errors that might arise from mistakes made during silent reading.

Pre-Drill Exercises

The first few days of instruction should focus on securing the student's cooperation, showing the student that he or she can perform successfully, and introducing the synthetic phonic method used in the drills. The length of time needed for this pre-drill phase will depend on the student's proficiency in producing the sounds of letters, writing letters, and blending letters into words.

The student is shown the letters *s, a, c, t,* and *p.* The following procedures are used to instruct the student who does not know the sounds of these letters. The teacher introduces each letter by writing it on the chalkboard and saying the sound of the letter at the same time. For example, the *a-a-a* sound made by a crying baby is voiced by the teacher as the letter *a* is written on the board. The student is asked to write the letter *a* from memory and to simultaneously make the *a* sound as soon as the teacher erases it. Mastery of these sounds is followed by a review of most of the other consonant sounds. Those that are not known are taught. Only one sound per letter is introduced in the beginning. The sounds of the other vowels, remaining consonants, and multiple sounds for letters are systematically introduced as the student moves through the drills.

Mastery of letter-sound correspondence is followed by instruction in sound blending. The teacher begins by writing the word *cat* on the board and asks the student to call out the sounds one at a time. The student is then shown how these individual sounds can be blended together into a word. Success with this word is followed by the introduction of the words *pat, tap, cap, at, sap,* and *sat.* Emphasis during the pre-drill period is on producing the sounds contained in the words rather than on naming the letters that spell the word.

The teacher then dictates these words and asks the student to write them. The student who is unable to perform this task successfully is asked to say the word slowly so that it can be analyzed into its parts. This enables the student to identify the first sound of the word and write it before moving on to the next letter.

Practice in writing dictated words is followed by additional practice in blending sounds together to make words. The instructor says the sounds that occur in a word slowly, leaving an interval between each sound. The student is then asked to blend these sounds into words. Hegge, Kirk, and Kirk (1965) state that, "When the child knows the sounds of most consonants and the sound of the vowel *a,* and is able to blend three sounds into a word (even inadequately or slowly) he is ready to begin practicing the Remedial Reading Drills."

The Remedial Reading Drills

There are fifty-five remedial reading drills. They are divided into three parts: introductory sounds, combinations of sounds, and advanced sounds. A fourth part consists of thirty-seven supplementary exercises which cover exceptions to previously taught configurations. Each drill provides the student with an opportunity to practice reading a list of words containing a specific sound or combination of sounds. Drills that review previously taught sounds or combinations of sounds are located throughout. Each of the first three parts ends with a general review and a test.

The authors give the following specific directions for using the drills and supplementary exercises:

1. *Always begin with drill 1.* This drill should be very easy for the student who has successfully completed the pre-drill exercises. Success on this drill will help build the student's confidence.
2. *Teach the child to respond to individual symbols.* The combination of the vowel with the final consonant may confuse the student. Do not teach this form of blending until after the student learns to produce the sounds for the individual letters.
3. *Read all drills orally.* The articulation of the sounds serves as an aid to learning and retention. Oral responses also provide the teacher with an opportunity to initiate instruction designed to correct incorrect responses that the student may be making.
4. *Stress accuracy and disregard speed.* The drills should be read at a slow enough rate to permit accuracy.
5. *Do not rush the child or allow skipping of drills.* Failure to devote sufficient time to each drill, skipping drills, or completing too many drills in one lesson may cause the student to forget some of the sounds that should have been learned.
6. *Present the drills in the order given.* The drills are sequenced so that each drill depends on what has been taught in earlier drills.
7. *Use the grapho-vocal method.* The grapho-vocal method consists of writing letters from memory while saying the sound of the letter. This method is used to introduce new sounds before they are inserted in the drills.
8. *Use concrete associative aids.* Practical examples such as a mother saying "sh" to quiet her noisy children can be used as an associative aid when teaching the student to make the *sh* sound.
9. *Introduce sentence reading.* Introduce sentence reading after the student has successfully completed a number of the drills. Words that appear in the sen-

tences that have not been covered in the drills already completed are taught as whole words.

DISTAR READING

DISTAR Reading (Engelmann and Bruner, 1973, 1974, 1975) is a highly structured, auditory phonetic instructional program. The name DISTAR stands for Direct Instructional System for Teaching Arithmetic and Reading. Its design is based on the belief that an intense, systematic, structured, direct oral teaching approach can prevent failure in the primary grades and help low achievers in the upper grades catch up. DISTAR was originally developed for use with preschool, culturally different, and economically disadvantaged children. Engelmann (1967) reports that the use of the first level of the program can begin as soon as the student's mental age reaches 4.

Each DISTAR group consists of from four to six students. The students sit on chairs in a quarter-circle within reach of the teacher. The thirty-minute lessons are presented on a daily basis. The sequence of presentation, teacher verbalization, and hand movements to be used to elicit group responses are specified in the manual for each DISTAR kit. The teacher models the procedures to be followed by the students and reinforces correct responses and appropriate behavior. Praise, points, or both are used to reinforce the desired responses.

The first two levels emphasize "learning to read" or basic decoding skills. The third level emphasizes "reading to learn." It includes material dealing with science, social studies, and social relations. The reading program is carefully cross-referenced to the lessons in the language kits.

DISTAR Reading follows well-sequenced scripts based on behavioral objectives. The use of highly repetitive scripts allows slow students to grasp the material's content. Specific correction procedures for use with various types of student errors are built into the program, as is repetition, which facilitates overlearning. The criterion for mastery of each instructional task is close to 100 percent.

Some teachers reject the DISTAR program as too rigid (Kirk, Kliebhan, and Lerner, 1978); others find the system to be a well-written, well-organized procedure that is highly effective in teaching reading to children (Boyd, 1975). The *SRA Corrective Reading* program (Engelmann, Becker, Hanner, and Johnson, 1978) is an advanced remedial program that follows DISTAR instructional concepts.

SUMMARY

1. Auditory phonetic methods of teaching reading emphasize word recognition as a sound-blending process.
2. The synthetic phonics approach emphasizes learning the sounds of letters in isolation and blending these sounds into words.

3. The analytic approach to teaching phonics emphasizes breaking down or analyzing the phonetic content of words the student has learned as sight words.
4. The phonetic approach gives students who have auditory strengths a foundation on which to base the corresponding visual and tactual-kinesthetic attributes of the words.
5. The Orton-Gillingham method is a synthetic phonetic approach that begins with teaching the names and sounds of the alphabet and advances to include blending of sounds into words.
6. Orton believed that developmental language problems are caused by the failure to establish dominance of one hemisphere in the brain over the other hemisphere.
7. The teaching method developed by Gillingham emphasizes six combinations of the visual auditory and kinesthetic modalities: V-A, A-V, A-K, K-A, V-K, and K-V.
8. The Hegge, Kirk, and Kirk *Remedial Reading Drills* emphasize learning the sounds of letters and blending these letters together.
9. *DISTAR reading* is a highly structured, phonetic instructional approach to teaching reading that is based upon carefully sequenced behavioral objectives.

REFERENCES

Boyd, J. E. 1975. "Teaching Children with Reading Problems." In *Teaching Children with Learning and Behavior Problems.* D. Hammill and N. Bartel, Eds. pp. 15–60. Boston: Allyn and Bacon.

Childs, S. 1968. *Sound Spelling.* Cambridge, Mass.: Educators Publishing Service.

Cox, A. R. 1975. *Structures and Techniques—Remedial Language Training: Multisensory Teaching for Alphabetic Phonics.* Cambridge, Mass.: Educators Publishing Service.

Engelmann, S. 1967. "Classroom Techniques: Teaching Reading to Children with Low Mental Age." *Educational Training of the Mentally Retarded,* 2 (January), 77–127.

Engelmann, S., W. C. Becker, S. Hanner, and G. Johnson. 1978. *New Corrective Reading.* Chicago: Science Research Associates.

Engelmann, S., and E. Bruner. 1974. *DISTAR Reading Level I.* Chicago: Science Research Associates.

Engelmann, S., and E. Bruner. 1975. *DISTAR Reading Level II.* Chicago: Science Research Associates.

Engelmann, S., and E. Bruner. 1973. *DISTAR Reading Level III.* Chicago: Science Research Associates.

Gillingham, A., and B. W. Stillman. 1975. *Remedial Training for Children with Specific Disabilities in Reading, Spelling and Penmanship.* Cambridge, Mass.: Educators Publishing Service.

Green, G. F. 1971. *Teachers' Manual for Alphabetic Phonics Workbook I.* Cambridge, Mass.: Educators Publishing Service.

Heckelman, R. G. 1969. "The Neurological Impress Method of Remedial Reading Instruction." *Academic Therapy,* 4 (Summer), 277–282.

Hegge, T. G., S. A. Kirk, and W. D. Kirk. 1936. *Remedial Reading Drills.* Ann Arbor, Mich.: George Wahr Publisher.

Johnson, D. J., and H. R. Myklebust. 1967. *Learning Disabilities: Educational Principles and Practices.* New York: Grune and Stratton.

Kaluger, G., and C. J. Kolson. 1978. *Reading and Learning Disabilities.* Columbus, Ohio: Charles E. Merrill.

Kirk, S. A., J. M. Kliebhan, and J. W. Lerner. 1978. *Teaching Reading to Slow and Disabled Learners.* Boston: Houghton Mifflin Company.

Orton, S. 1937. *Reading, Writing and Speech Problems in Children.* New York: Norton.

Orton, S. 1929. "The Sight Reading Method of Teaching Reading, as a Source of Reading Disability." *Journal of Educational Psychology,* 20, 135–143.

Slingerland, B. 1975. *A Multi-Sensory Approach for Specific Language Disability Children: A Guide for Primary Teachers.* Cambridge, Mass.: Educators Publishing Service.

PART FOUR

Diagnosis and Remediation of Spelling and Handwriting Problems

FOURTEEN

Diagnosis and Remediation of
Spelling Problems

Learning problems in spelling rarely appear as a student's only problem. They are usually combined with problems in one or more other areas, including reading, auditory discrimination, auditory sequential memory, reauditorization, visual sequential memory, revisualization, auditory blending, handwriting, writing from recall, impulse control, proofreading and self-monitoring, sensory integration, visual discrimination, eye-hand coordination, form constancy, position in space, spatial relations, kinesthetic recall, and associating sounds with symbols. Some students are able to spell words orally but unable to write them from dictation. Others are able to recognize the correct spelling of a word when they see it in print but are unable to spell it orally or write it correctly. Still others may be able to write the word from dictation but be unable to write it when they must initiate the response.

The relationship between spelling and reading has been examined by many educators. Johnson and Myklebust (1967) observe, "As reading improves, spelling also improves; as revisualization improves, spelling improves" (p. 239). Wallace and McLoughlin (1975) indicate that, "Children who lack basic phonics ability usually do not have any dependable method to spell words and often rely upon guessing. The students who have visual memory problems tend to experience difficulty storing and retrieving the visual image of the word" (p. 182). Fernald (1943) indicates that some spelling problems are due to bad habits forced on the student by the school during attempts to teach him or her to spell. She reports that these bad habits develop because of methods that make it impossible for certain students to learn and then insistence that the words be written over and over, limitations on the length of time devoted to spelling to the extent that the responses do not become habitual, disregard for well-established laws of learning, and arousal of negative emotions, which tend to block the voluntary production

205

of the desired responses. And Aho (1968) states that, "Written spelling requires the automatic recall of the correct letter formation, letter connections, and exact letter sequence in association with its correct sound and feel. The response must be so secure that this sequential movement pattern does not take all the attention" (p. 8).

INFORMAL SPELLING ASSESSMENT

Many spelling problems can be identified informally by observing the student's performance and then answering the following questions (Linn, 1967):

Can the student recall the letter and sound symbols quickly and accurately?
Can the student produce them correctly on paper?
Can the student fuse (blend) the sound parts together into whole words?
Does the student reverse letters in sound parts?
Can the student remember what the teacher has written on the board a few minutes after it is erased?
Does the student learn words from hearing the letter sequence rather than from seeing it?
Does the student appear to block out or not hear sounds?
Can the student write the correct symbol for single sounds when they are dictated orally?
Can the student identify sounds?

An informal diagnostic spelling test was suggested for classroom use by Watson (1935). The essentials of Watson's diagnostic method are summarized by Lerner (1976) as follows:

1. Select thirty to fifty words based on a graded list at the grade level of the student or class.
2. Administer the spelling test.
3. Score the test and tabulate the results.
4. Have the student define words he or she misspelled. Omit words that are misspelled because they are not in the student's vocabulary.
5. Have students spell any remaining words orally. Keep a record of the spelling errors, noting syllabication, phonetic use, and speech or hearing difficulties.
6. Compare the oral spelling with the written spelling to note differences.
7. Ask the students to study words missed (for about ten minutes) and observe their method of study.
8. Analyze errors and incorporate information from the data obtained from other sources.
9. Draw conclusions as to the nature of the spelling problem. Plan educational strategies to overcome the difficulties.

10. Discuss the analysis and teaching plan with the student. Make provision for the student to see his or her own progress.

Edgington (1968) recommended a careful analysis of the student's errors, suggesting that they be tabulated to determine if an identifiable pattern exists in material written spontaneously and material written from dictation. The error patterns described by Edgington included the following:

addition of unneeded letters (for example, *dressess*)
omission of needed letters (*hom* for *home*)
reflections of student's mispronunciations (*pin* for *pen*)
reflections of dialectical speech patterns (*Cuber* for *Cuba*)
reversals of whole words (*eno* for *one*)
reversals of vowels (*braed* for *bread*)
reversals of consonant order (*lback* for *black*)
reversals of consonant or vowel directionality (*brithday* for *birthday*)
reversals of syllables (*telho* for *hotel*)
phonetic spelling of nonphonetic words or parts thereof (*cawt* for *caught*)
wrong associations of a sound with a given set of letters, such as *u* having been
    learned as *ou* in *you*
"neographisms," such as an extra letter that bears no discernible relationship
    to the word dictated
varying degrees and combinations of these or other possible combinations

These error analyses and tabulation procedures can also be applied to the students' oral reading errors.

FORMAL SPELLING ASSESSMENT

The number of standardized spelling tests that are available is limited. The following four instruments are representative:

Gates-Russell Spelling Diagnostic Test (Gates and Russell, 1940). Grade-level scores are provided for each of the following nine subtests: (1) spelling words orally, (2) word pronunciation, (3) giving letters for sounds, (4) spelling one syllable, (5) spelling two syllables, (6) word reversals, (7) spelling attack, (8) auditory discrimination, and (9) effectiveness of visual, auditory, kinesthetic, and combined methods of study.

Peabody Individual Achievement Test (Dunn and Markwardt, 1970). The spelling subtest of the PIAT is made up of multiple-choice items. Each test item consists of four possible spellings of each word, including the correct spelling. The student points to the correct spelling of the word without needing to revisualize the image of the word.

Test of Written Spelling (Larsen and Hammill, 1976). This test involves the administration of predictable and unpredictable words. Test scores are in terms of spelling age, spelling quotient, and spelling grade equivalent.

Wide Range Achievement Test (Jastak, Bijou, and Jastak, 1978). The spelling subtest consists of copying marks that resemble letters, writing one's own name, and writing single dictated words.

The error analyses and tabulation procedures described in the informal assessment section of this chapter may also be applied to the students' responses on these tests.

REMEDIATING SPELLING PROBLEMS

Hanna, Hodges, and Hanna (1971) list the following eight basic objectives for beginning spelling. They also suggest that these basic purposes and activities should be kept in mind while the student is being taught to analyze the spoken word.

1. Teaching students that a word is composed of sounds (phonemes). The students should listen to the sounds in a word and note their position and sequence. They should also understand what is meant by the first or beginning sound in a word, the second or middle sound, and the last or final sound.
2. Teach students to pronounce the sounds in a word. The students should realize that the sounds in a word are arranged in order and that knowledge of this order is an essential condition for spelling. The teacher should clearly enunciate the sounds to provide students with a model that can be heard and imitated.
3. Teach awareness of the alphabetic nature of written English. The students should be able to say and recognize the letters of the alphabet.
4. Teach students how to form (write) the letters of the alphabet neatly and legibly. A carefully devised system of letter strokes for use in forming the letters of the alphabet should be followed. The steps involved in developing handwriting proficiency are described in Chapter 16.
5. Teach the students to coordinate listening, speaking, spelling, handwriting, and reading.
6. Develop automatic, highly predictable phoneme-grapheme correspondence. Include most consonant and short-vowel phonemes that occur in the monosyllabic words most frequently used by students.
7. Start the students toward general spelling power by helping them use the sound-to-letter responses they have learned to spell words that they now use only in their spoken form.
8. Teach students to use as many learning modalities (ear, voice, eyes, and hand) as possible while acquiring spelling mastery.

Fernald's Approach to Spelling

Fernald (1943) outlines the following series of steps. It can be used in either the formal or informal teaching of spelling.

1. The teacher writes the word to be learned on the chalkboard or on paper. The word may have been requested by the student or it may be selected from a spelling lesson.
2. The student pronounces the word after hearing the teacher pronounce it correctly. The student should always look at the word as he or she pronounces it.
3. The student studies the word in order to develop an image of the word that will help the student think of it after the copy is removed. Emphasis during this step is on tracing the word. The student should use a finger to trace the word rather than a pencil or stylus.
4. The word is erased or covered. The student should write the word from memory as soon as he or she is sure of it, but should not be forced to do this until he or she wishes. Students who attempt to write words before the image of the word is clear frequently make errors, which can easily lead to the formation of bad habits.
5. The student turns the paper over and writes it a second time without copying it.
6. The teacher provides the student with frequent opportunities to use the word he or she has learned in written expression.
7. The teacher encourages the student to use books and dictionaries to find the correct form of a word any time he or she is doubtful about its spelling.
8. The teacher organizes spelling matches that require written instead of oral responses.

The Fernald approach is well suited for use with students who require strong tactual-kinesthetic inputs to learn, remember, and write the words they want to spell.

Simultaneous Oral Spelling

Slingerland (1975), Cox (1975), Childs (1968), and others who follow Orton-Gillingham related procedures, teach reading, spelling, and handwriting simultaneously as an integrated set of skills. They call the spelling component of their procedures simultaneous oral spelling, or SOS. The statement of purpose that accompanies the Cox (1975) adaptation of SOS emphasizes the following goals:

1. coordination of the student's auditory, visual, and kinesthetic senses in the written spelling of words, using the student's strongest modality to develop and reinforce the weaker ones

2. structuring of the student's spelling by the development of precise, habitual responses that involve instant translation of speech sounds into probable symbols

3. fortification of the student's confidence in his or her own written expression

4. prevention of careless errors and development of the student's confidence that his or her hand can be depended on to write the words he or she wants to write

Cox (1975) suggests remedial procedures consisting of five steps. The first three steps emphasize the oral aspects of spelling. The written aspects (steps 4 and 5) are taught as soon as the oral responses are firmly established.

1. The student *listens* and watches the mouth of the therapist as he or she carefully pronounces one word. The more obscure sounds are exaggerated slightly.

2. The student *echoes* or repeats the word, feeling it in his or her mouth and hearing it again.

3. The student *spells* the word orally, naming the letters in succession. The longer words are spelled in syllables with a pause between each syllable. The student's response is considered to be wrong if the correct letters are not grouped in syllables.

4. The student *writes* the word, naming each letter just before writing it.

5. The student *reads* the word to insure that it is written the way he or she planned to write it. This proofreading should follow step 4 immediately.

The Orton-Gillingham approach to teaching reading was discussed in detail in Chapter 13.

Other Procedures and Activities for Teaching Spelling

A large number of workbooks, several kits, and many informal instructional activities are available for use in teaching spelling. Some of the more useful ones are summarized here:

Glue letters. Write a letter on yellow paper with a magic marker and then have the student put a bead of white glue over the line. The next day the student has a beaded glue letter, which can be traced with a finger to get the feel of writing the letter.

Screen letters. Mount a piece of window screen on cardboard and cover the rough edges with masking tape. Place a piece of paper on top of the screen and have the student write on it with the side of a piece of crayon between ⅝ inch and 1 inch long. The bumpy sensation created as the crayon passes over the rough surface will provide the student with kinesthetic feedback.

Spelling Concentration. Place spelling words on three-by-five cards and cut the cards in half. Place the halves for several words face down and have the student practice finding the matching halves for each word. Have the student read and then spell the word. Return those cards not read or not spelled correctly to the table top (face down).

Hershey Syrup letters.   Pour a bead of syrup, whipping cream, frosting, or cheese spread on a clean surface in the shape of a letter or word. Have the student pick it up by tracing the letter or word with a finger and then licking it off the finger. The contact with the surface while picking up the syrup provides kinesthetic feedback.

Filling in missing letters.   Develop visual memory and closure with activities that require the student to fill in letters that have been omitted from a word. For example:

  r a g   r _ g   r _ _   _ _ g   _ a _   _ _ _

The blank in a word should be filled in before attempting to complete the next word. This activity is helpful in developing visual memory before age 8 and visual imagery after age 8.

Using the typewriter.   Have the student use a typewriter to copy his or her spelling list.

Matching spelling word cards.   Place library card pockets on a large piece of poster board. Write a different spelling word on each pocket. Have the student sort a deck of three-by-five cards containing the same words by placing each card in the correct pocket.

Color-coded letters.   Use colored letters to emphasize certain letter attributes such as consonants, vowels, and short or long letters.

SUMMARY

1. Spelling problems are usually found in combination with difficulties in one or more areas of visual or auditory perception.
2. Johnson and Myklebust state that, "As reading improves, spelling also improves; as revisualization improves, spelling improves."
3. Aho states that, "Written spelling requires the automatic recall of the correct letter formation, letter connections, and exact letter sequence in association with its correct sound and feel."
4. The limited number of formal diagnostic spelling instruments makes it necessary to rely heavily on informal diagnostic procedures.
5. Error analysis and tabulation procedures play an important role in both formal and informal spelling diagnoses.
6. The Fernald approach to teaching reading and spelling is well suited for students who require strong tactual-kinesthetic inputs to learn, remember, and write words.
7. The Orton-Gillingham procedures teach reading, spelling, and handwriting as an integrated set of skills.

REFERENCES

Aho, M. S. 1968. "Teaching Spelling to Children with Specific Language Disability." In *Building Spelling Skills in Dyslexic Children.* Ed. J. I. Arena. San Rafael, Calif.: Academic Therapy Publications.

Childs, S. 1968. *Sound Spelling.* Cambridge, Mass.: Educators Publishing Service.

Cox, A. R. 1975. *Structures and Techniques—Remedial Language Training: Multi-Sensory Teaching for Alphabetic Phonics.* Cambridge, Mass.: Educators Publishing Service.

Dunn, L. M., and F. C. Markwardt. 1970. *The Peabody Individual Achievement Tests.* Circle Pines, Minn.: American Guidance Service.

Edgington, R. 1968. "But He Spelled Them Right this Morning." In *Building Spelling Skills in Dyslexic Children.* Ed. J. I. Arena. San Rafael, Calif.: Academic Therapy Publications.

Fernald, G. 1943. *Remedial Techniques in Basic School Subjects.* New York: McGraw-Hill.

Gates, A. I., and D. H. Russell. 1940. *Gates-Russell Spelling Diagnostic Test.* New York: Bureau of Publications, Teachers College, Columbia University.

Gillingham, A., and B. Stillman. 1967. *Remedial Training for Children with Specific Disability in Reading, Spelling and Penmanship.* 7th ed. Cambridge, Mass.: Educators Publishing Service.

Hanna, P. R., R. E. Hodges, and J. S. Hanna. 1971. *Spelling: Structure and Strategies.* Boston: Houghton Mifflin Company.

Jastak, J. F., S. Bijou, and S. R. Jastak. 1978. *The Wide Range Achievement Test.* Wilmington, Del.: Guidance Associates.

Johnson, D. J., and H. R. Myklebust. 1967. *Learning Disabilities: Educational Principles and Practices.* New York: Grune and Stratton.

Larsen, S. C., and D. D. Hammill. 1976. *The Test of Written Spelling.* Austin, Tex.: Empiric Press.

Lerner, J. W. 1976. *Children with Learning Disabilities.* 2nd ed. Boston: Houghton Mifflin Company.

Linn, S. H. 1967. "Spelling Problems: Diagnosis and Remediation." *Academic Therapy Quarterly,* 3, 62–63.

Slingerland, B. 1975. *A Multi-Sensory Approach for Specific Language Disability Children: A Guide for Primary Teachers.* Cambridge, Mass.: Educators Publishing Service.

Wallace, G., and J. A. McLoughlin. 1975. *Learning Disabilities: Concepts and Characteristics.* Columbus, Ohio: Charles E. Merrill.

Watson, A. E. 1935. *Experimental Studies in the Psychology and Teaching of Spelling.* Contributions to Education, no. 638. New York: Teachers College, Columbia University.

FIFTEEN

Diagnosis of Handwriting Problems

Johnson and Myklebust (1967) describe *handwriting* as "one of the highest forms of language, hence, the last to be learned" (p. 193). They describe *writing* as "a form of expressive language, a visual symbol system for conveying thoughts, feelings, and ideas" (p. 193). The writer records his or her thoughts in the form of graphic symbols, which the reader decodes to gain the message they contain.

Chalfant and Scheffelin (1969) describe four tasks involved in the production of graphic language symbols:

Task I. Intention The student must feel the need to communicate and decide to send a message in graphic form before he or she can write.

Task II. Formulation of a Message The need and decision to write are followed by formulation of the sequence in which the general content of the message will appear.

Task III. Retrieval of Graphic-Language Symbols The formulation of the message that is to be communicated is followed by the retrieval of the graphic-language symbols that correspond to the selected auditory-language signals.

Task IV. Organizing the Graphic-Language Sequence Selection of the graphic-language symbols that represent the message the person wants to communicate is followed by organization of the graphic-language symbols into a sequence and then producing them.

Chalfant and Scheffelin (1969) describe a developmental handwriting hierarchy containing six steps:

1. *Scribbling* This step involves grasping the pencil and manipulating the fingers to perform random pencil movements. It is often necessary to teach dysgraphics how to hold and manipulate a pencil and position the paper on their desks.

2. *Tracing*   Development of the ability to control pencil movements makes it possible to introduce tracing activities. Tracing of connected letters and figures is followed by practice in tracing disconnected letters or figures.
3. *Copying*   Proficiency in tracing prepares the student for copying. Copying should start with reproduction of a visible model. Success on this task leads to reproduction of the model from memory. Copying of symbolic and non-symbolic figures (for example, scribbles) should follow.
4. *Completion of Tasks*   Mastery of the pencil control and manipulation skills required to copy figures prepares the student for completion of these same figures when portions of them are missing. Transfer from the tracing to the completion task can be accomplished by gradually removing portions of the lines. Connecting dashes can be followed by connecting dots and then the insertion of missing sides of the figures.
5. *Writing from Dictation*   Four types of tasks are involved in this step: writing letters as they are spoken, writing words and sentences, supplying missing words, and supplying missing sentences.
6. *Propositional Writing*   In this step, handwriting is used to record and convey thoughts, ideas, and questions to others.

Breakdowns in the student's written communication may occur on any one of the above steps or tasks.

TYPES OF HANDWRITING DISORDERS

Johnson and Myklebust (1967) describe three types of writing disorders: dysgraphia, defective revisualization, and formulation and syntax deficits. *Dysgraphia* is a partial inability to write caused by a visual motor integration disorder that interferes with memory and execution of the motor patterns needed to form letters, words, or numbers. The term *agraphia* describes the total inability to write. The agraphic's inability to copy differentiates his or her problem from other writing disorders. Revisualization problems are discussed in Chapter 8, and formulation and syntax problems in Chapter 9.

Jordan (1972) divides common handwriting errors into three areas: difficulty with symbols, confusion of directionality, and difficulty in copying simple shapes.

1. Difficulty with alphabet symbols:
   a. Does not remember how to write certain letters or numerals.
   b. Distorts shapes of certain letters or numerals.
   c. Overall writing effort is awkward and uneven.
   d. Has difficulty transferring from manuscript to cursive style.
   e. Continues to print manuscript style long after introduction to cursive style.
   f. Fragments certain letter or numeral forms.
   g. Writing resembles "bird scratching"; is virtually illegible.

    h. Has difficulty distinguishing between capital and lower case letter forms.

    i. Mixes capital and lower case forms.

2. Confusion with directionality:

    a. Writes certain letters, numerals, or words in mirror image.

    b. Tends to write on mirror side (left side) of vertical midline when moving to next column.

    c. Marks from bottom to top when moving to next column.

    d. Uses backward (clockwise) motions when forming loops in certain letters or numerals.

    e. Erases or overprints habitually to change directions of certain letters or numerals.

    f. Writing tends to slant up, down, or to wobble up and down.

3. Difficulty copying simple shapes:

    a. Distorts simple shapes.

    b. Fails to close corners.

    c. Tends to draw "ears" where lines meet or change direction.

    d. Has difficulty producing simple designs from memory.

    e. Work deteriorates toward end of writing exercise.

    f. Has difficulty staying on lines when tracing. (p. 63)

Newland's (1932) analysis of the errors in the handwriting of 2,381 people revealed that their ten most common errors were as follows:

1. Failure to close letters (e.g. *a, b, f*, etc.) accounted for 24 per cent of all errors.

2. Closed top loops (*l* like *t, e* like *i*) accounted for 13 per cent of all errors.

3. Looping nonlooped strokes (*i* like *e*) accounted for 12 per cent.

4. Using straight up-strokes rather than rounded strokes (*n* like *U, c* like *i*) accounted for 11 per cent.

5. End-stroke difficulty (not brought up, not brought down, not left horizontal) accounted for 11 per cent.

6. Top short (*b, d, h, k*): 6 per cent.

7. Difficulty crossing *t*: 5 per cent.

8. Letters too small: 4 per cent.

9. Closing *c, h, u, w*: 4 per cent.

10. Part of letter omitted: 4 per cent. (p. 252)

EVALUATING HANDWRITING PROFICIENCY

The Zaner-Bloser manuscript and cursive writing scales (Zaner-Bloser Staff, 1974) are the most frequently used commercially published measures of handwriting proficiency. The teacher writes the sentence the student is to write on the chalkboard. After practicing it several times, the student writes the sentence carefully on a piece of paper. The teacher then evaluates it by comparing it to examples of writing shown on the scale. The scale for each grade level contains five examples of handwriting, which represent different levels of proficiency for students at that grade level.

A series of "peek thru" templates are also available from Zaner-Bloser. Each clear plastic template contains guidelines that correspond to those on writing paper distributed by Zaner-Bloser for use in the primary grades. The templates contain upper- and lower-case manuscript and cursive letters and the numerals 1 through 9. They are placed over the page containing the student's work when it is being evaluated, making it easy for both the student and teacher to identify discrepancies existing between the student's graphic production and the examples shown on the template.

The *Handwriting Skill Analysis and Check List* on pages 218–222 was developed for use in the informal assessment of handwriting proficiency. Specific suggestions for use in helping students with the development of these skills are found in Chapter 16.

THE HANDWRITING SKILL ANALYSIS AND CHECK LIST

Handwriting deficiencies that suggest this scale should be used include the inability to hold and manipulate the writing instrument correctly; poorly formed geometric figures, numerals, or letters; inconsistent size of writing; writing above, below, and sometimes on the lines; reversal of letters, numbers, or words; incorrect sequence or direction of strokes; inconsistent slant or pencil pressure; improper or inconsistent spacing between letters or words; and pausing in the middle of words or between words.

This check list is designed for use as a sequence of steps that can be followed in assessing handwriting proficiency and as a check list that can be used to record the specific handwriting skills a student has mastered. It can also be used to record the results of an analysis of a student's handwriting errors and changes that occur in a student's mastery of specific handwriting skills during the remediation process.

Following is a list of procedures for using the *Handwriting Skill Analysis and Check List:*

1. Collect a sample of the student's handwriting. Have younger children and those with severe handwriting problems draw the basic geometric figures and write the letters of the alphabet and the numbers 1 to 10. Older students can be asked to copy groups of numbers, groups of words, and short sentences and to write them as they are dictated.

2. Check off (✔) those skills the student has mastered. Record the date of the evaluation on the last three or four tasks that have been mastered. These dates can be used later when assessing the effectiveness of the remediation program.

3. Analyze the errors for the next five tasks on the scale and circle the initials F (formation), SZ (size), SL (slant), SP (spacing), and H (hesitation or pause) in the "Analysis" column adjacent to these tasks to indicate the types of errors made. Formation, size, and slant errors can be assessed by using a yellow felt-tip pencil (⅛-inch wide) to superimpose the correct letter, number, or line over the student's work. The points where the student's lines extend beyond the superimposed line can then be noted and analyzed.

4. Begin remediation with the task on the scale following the last one *checked off* during the evaluation. Continue moving through the tasks listed on the scale until the desired level of proficiency has been attained.

5. Refer to Chapter 16 for specific remedial suggestions related to each task.

Name_____Grade_____	**HANDWRITING SKILL ANALYSIS AND CHECK LIST**
Birthdate_____CA_____	
School_____Teacher_____	Experimental Edition
Date of Initial Evaluation_____	© 1979 by: Larry A. Faas
Right-handed ( ) Left-handed ( )	

Task #	Task (Skill) Descriptions	Example	Check-Off or Date	Error Analysis
	PRE-WRITING SKILLS (1-19)			
1	Works the thumb in opposition to the first and second finger to correctly grasp, hold, manipulate and release the writing instrument.			
2	Produces random (freeform) scribbles.			
3	Produces vertical scribbles and lines			
4	Produces horizontal scribbles and lines			
5	Draws loops and circles			F SZ
6	Positions the paper in the proper relationship to the body and the hand which is being used to write.			
7	Draws a single line cross.	+		F SZ SL SP H
8	Draws a square			F SZ SL SP H
9	Draws a rectangle			F SZ SL SP H
10	Draws lines which slant to the left of the vertical axis.			F SZ SL SP H
11	Draws lines which slant to the right of the vertical axis.			F SZ SL SP H
12	Draws an "X".	X		F SZ SL SP H
13	Joins rows of dots with slanting lines.			F SZ SL SP H
14	Draws an equilateral triangle.	△		F SZ SL SP H
15	Draws vertical and horizontal lines using guidelines.			F SZ SL SP H
16	Draws large and small circles between guidelines.			F SZ SL SP H
17	Draws full, three-quarter and half circles.			F SZ SL SP H
18	Draws lines between guidelines which slant to the right and left of the vertical axis. (Up and down the mountain)			F SZ SL SP H
19	Draws squares, rectangles and triangles between guidelines.			F SZ SL SP H

Task #	Task (Skill) Description	Example	Check-Off or Date	Error Analysis
	MANUSCRIPT AND NUMBER WRITING SKILLS (20-48)			
20	Prints the upper case forms of the letters L, F and E between guidelines.	L FEL		F SZ SL SP H
21	Prints the upper case forms of the letters H, I and T between guidelines.	HIT		F SZ SL SP H
22	Prints the letters C and O in their upper and lower case forms.	OoCoc		F SZ SL SP H
23	Prints the upper and lower case forms of L, F, E, H, I and T between guidelines.	LiTtfe		F SZ SL SP H
24	Combines lower case letters to make two and three letter words.	it the		F SZ SL SP H
25	Prints letters which are combinations of slanting lines (V, v, W, w, and X, x and) slanting horizontal lines (Z, z).	Vv Wwz		F SZ SL SP H
26	Prints the upper and lower case letters B, b, M, m, N, n, R, r, U and u.	BbmRu		F SZ SL SP H
27	Prints the upper and lower case letters A, a, D and d.	Aa Dd		F SZ SL SP H
28	Prints the upper and lower case letters of S and s.	Ss Ss		F SZ SL SP H
29	Prints the upper or lower case form of letters which have tails. (G, g, J, j, P, p, Q, q, Y, y)	JjPpy		F SZ SL SP H
30	Prints the upper and lower case forms of the letters K and k.	KkKk		F SZ SL SP H
31	Writes numbers that start on the left side and move to the right. (2, 3, 4, 7)	2347		F SZ SL SP H
32	Writes numbers that start on the right side and move to the left. (0, 5, 6, 8, 9)	0689		F SZ SL SP H
33	Copies groups of multiple digit numbers on lined paper.	23		F SZ SL SP H
34	Copies columns of multiple digit numbers on lined paper.			F SZ SL SP H
35	Copies phone numbers in columns.			F SZ SL SP H
36	Writes dictated lists of multiple digit numbers on lined paper.			F SZ SL SP H
37	Writes dictated lists of multiple digit numbers on paper which does not contain lines.			F SZ SL SP H
38	Copies lists of three and four letter words which do not contain tails and are all the same height.			F SZ SL SP H
39	Leaves an appropriate amount of space between letters and words.			F SZ SL SP H
40	Copies lists of two and three letter words which have letters of varying height and tails on lined paper.			F SZ SL SP H

Task #	Task (Skill) Description	Example	Check-Off or Date	Error Analysis
41	Copies pairs of two, three and four letter words with letters of varying height and tails on lined paper.	hop egg		F SZ SL SP H
42	Copies two word sentences which contain a capitalized first word and a period at the end.	He ran		F SZ SL SP H
43	Copies three, four and five word sentences.			F SZ SL SP H
44	Writes numbers which are one space high.	12345678		F SZ SL SP H
45	Writes individual numbers and groups of numbers as they are dictated.			F SZ SL SP H
46	Prints individual letters and groups of letters as they are dictated.			F SZ SL SP H
47	Uses numerals spontaneously to record and convey numerical information.			F SZ SL SP H
48	Uses printing spontaneously to record and convey numerical information.			F SZ SL SP H
TRANSITION FROM MANUSCRIPT TO CURSIVE WRITING (49-50)				
49	Connects cursive letters correctly.	it it		F SZ SL SP H
50	Slants cursive letters correctly.	it it		F SZ SL SP H
CURSIVE WRITING SKILLS-LOWER CASE (51-74)				
51	Makes tall, middle-size and short swing strokes.			F SZ SL SP H
52	Makes tall, middle-size and short pull strokes.			F SZ SL SP H
53	Combines swing and pull strokes without lifting pencil.			F SZ SL SP H
54	Connects a series of swing and pull strokes without lifting pencil.			F SZ SL SP H
55	Uses loops to connect middle-size swings and pulls with short swings and pulls without lifting pencil.			F SZ SL SP H
56	Connects the letters l, e, i, t and u to make words.	little		F SZ SL SP H
57	Writes the letters w and b.	w b		F SZ SL SP H
58	Combines the letters b and w with l, e, i, u and t.	bill		F SZ SL SP H
59	Writes the letters f and j.	f f j j		F SZ SL SP H

Task #	Task (Skill) Description	Example	Check-Off or Date	Error Analysis
60	Makes the over-stroke correctly.			F SZ SL SP H
61	Combines over and pull-strokes to write the letters m and n.			F SZ SL SP H
62	Writes the letter h correctly.			F SZ SL SP H
63	Writes the letters v and x.			F SZ SL SP H
64	Writes the letters y and z.			F SZ SL SP H
65	Writes the letter c correctly.			F SZ SL SP H
66	Writes the letter a correctly.			F SZ SL SP H
67	Writes the letter d correctly.			F SZ SL SP H
68	Writes the letter g correctly.			F SZ SL SP H
69	Writes the letter q correctly.			F SZ SL SP H
70	Writes the letter o correctly.			F SZ SL SP H
71	Writes the letter r correctly.			F SZ SL SP H
72	Writes the letter s correctly.			F SZ SL SP H
73	Writes the letter p correctly.			F SZ SL SP H
74	Writes the letter k correctly.			F SZ SL SP H
	CURSIVE WRITING SKILLS-UPPER CASE (75-93)			
75	Makes the cane stroke correctly.			F SZ SL SP H
76	Writes the letter H correctly.			F SZ SL SP H
77	Writes the letters M and N.			F SZ SL SP H
78	Writes the letter Q correctly.			F SZ SL SP H
79	Writes the letters U and V.			F SZ SL SP H
80	Writes the letter W correctly.			F SZ SL SP H
81	Writes the letter X correctly.			F SZ SL SP H
82	Writes the letters Y and Z.			F SZ SL SP H
83	Makes tall ovals and the letter A.			F SZ SL SP H

Task #	Task (Skill) Description	Example	Check-Off or Date	Error Analysis
84	Writes the letters C and O.			F SZ SL SP H
85	Writes the letter D correctly.			F SZ SL SP H
86	Writes the letter E correctly.			F SZ SL SP H
87	Writes the letters S and G.			F SZ SL SP H
88	Writes the letters T and F.			F SZ SL SP H
89	Writes the letters P, R and B.			F SZ SL SP H
90	Writes the letter K correctly.			F SZ SL SP H
91	Writes the letter L correctly.			F SZ SL SP H
92	Writes the letter I correctly.			F SZ SL SP H
93	Writes the letter J correctly.			F SZ SL SP H
	USE OF CURSIVE HANDWRITING SKILLS (94-97)			
94	Copies short sentences which contain capitalized first letters and proper nouns and a period at the end.			F SZ SL SP H
95	Writes words in cursive form from a model which is being viewed in print.			F SZ SL SP H
96	Writes dictated letters, words and sentences in cursive.			F SZ SL SP H
97	(TARGET BEHAVIOR) Uses cursive writing spontaneously to record and/or convey information.			F SZ SL SP H

Remarks and Observations:

SUMMARY

1. Johnson and Myklebust describe handwriting as a visual symbol system for conveying thoughts, feelings, and ideas.
2. The development of handwriting skills follows an orderly sequence of steps.
3. The three types of handwriting disorders described by Johnson and Myklebust are dysgraphia, defective revisualization, and formulation and syntax deficits.
4. The term *agraphia* refers to a total inability to write; *dysgraphia* refers to a partial inability to write.
5. The Zaner-Bloser manuscript and cursuve writing scales are the most frequently used commercially published measures of handwriting proficiency.
6. The *Handwriting Skill Analysis and Check List* was developed for use in the informal assessment of handwriting.

REFERENCES

Chalfant, J. C., and M. A. Scheffelin. 1969. *Central Processing Dysfunctions in Children: A Review of Research.* Washington, D.C.: U.S. Government Printing Office.

Johnson, D. J., and H. R. Myklebust. 1967. *Learning Disabilities: Educational Principles and Practices.* New York: Grune and Stratton.

Jordan, D. R. 1972. *Dyslexia in the Classroom.* Columbus, Ohio: Charles E. Merrill.

Newland, T. E. 1932. "An Analytical Study of the Development of Illegibilities of Handwriting from the Lower Grades to Adulthood." *Journal of Educational Research*, 26, 249–258.

Zaner-Bloser Staff. 1974. *Creative Growth Alphabet: Peek Thru Templates.* Columbus, Ohio: Zaner-Bloser Inc.

Zaner-Bloser Staff. 1974. *Cursive Writing Evaluation Scale.* Columbus, Ohio: Zaner-Bloser Inc.

Zaner-Bloser Staff. 1974. *Manuscript Writing Evaluation Scale.* Columbus, Ohio: Zaner-Bloser Inc.

SIXTEEN

Developing Proficiency in Handwriting

Children who have trouble with the development of handwriting skills are likely to be having difficulty with one or more of the ninety-seven tasks or steps that lead to proficiency in handwriting. These tasks which are among those most frequently used in instructing children who are experiencing difficulty in developing handwriting skills, fall into six skill groups: pre-writing skills (tasks 1–19), manuscript and number writing skills (tasks 20–48), transition from manuscript to cursive writing (tasks 49–50), cursive writing skills—lower case (tasks 51–74), cursive writing skills—upper case (tasks 75–93), and use of cursive handwriting skills (tasks 94–97).

PRE-WRITING SKILLS

Task 1. *Holding and Manipulating the Writing Instrument*

Suggested activities

1. squeezing a sponge between the thumb and first and second fingers
2. squeezing a soft rubber ball, then a harder rubber ball
3. picking up objects (for example, grasping the pegs on the inserts of geometric form boards)
4. pouring from a pitcher containing rice, beans, or water
5. lacing shoes and cards
6. stacking blocks
7. assembling simple puzzles
8. assembling parquetry blocks
9. clipping pinch-type clothespins on the edge of a can or bucket
10. cutting with a scissors
11. picking a pencil up, holding it correctly, and releasing it

Note   The following drawing shows the recommended procedure for holding the writing instrument.

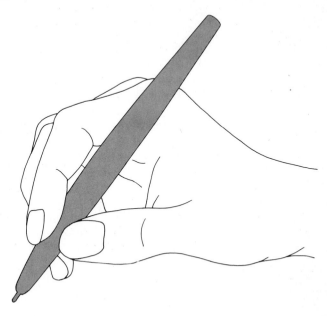

SOURCE: From *The Whys and Hows of Teaching Handwriting* by E. H. Myers. Zaner-Bloser Company, Columbus, Ohio, 1963, p. 56.

Caution   Children who experience difficulty with this step tend to substitute pressure of the third, fourth, and fifth fingers on the palm of the hand for the desired proficiency in thumb to first- and second-finger opposition.

Task 2. *Production of Random (Freeform) Scribbles*

Procedure   1.   Demonstrate production of large freeform scribble marks on the chalkboard, being sure that your marks frequently cross in front of the vertical midline of your body.

2. Ask the student to make large freeform scribbles on the chalkboard like the ones you have just made.
3. Grasp the hand of the student who is not able to scribble spontaneously and guide it through the movements involved in the production of random scribble marks. Alternate guiding the student's hand with having the student attempt the task without assistance until proficiency can be demonstrated without assistance.
4. Repeat steps 2 and 3, confining the scribbling to a 2-foot square box that you have drawn on the chalkboard.
5. Repeat step 4, confining the scribbling to a 1-foot square box that you have drawn on the chalkboard.
6. Repeat steps 2 through 5, using a crayon or marking pencil to scribble on a piece of unlined paper.

Suggestions   Finger-painting activities that involve repetition of these movement patterns can be used to transfer this pattern of random scribble marks from the vertical surface to a table or desk top where handwriting activities usually occur.

Task 3. *Production of Vertical Scribbles and Lines*

Procedure   1. Demonstrate production of *vertical* scribble marks on the chalkboard.

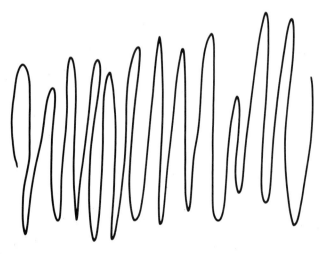

2. Ask the student to make scribble marks on the chalkboard that go up and down.
3. Guide the hand of the student who is unable to produce spontaneously the hand movements involved in the production of *vertical* lines. Alternate guiding the student's hand with having the student attempt the task without assistance until proficiency can be demonstrated without assistance.

4. Repeat steps 1 through 3, using a crayon or marking pencil to make *vertical* lines on a piece of unlined paper.

Note   If proficiency is not observed during step 4, proceed with step 5 and as many additional steps as are required to develop proficiency.

5. Have the student practice making *vertical* lines on the chalkboard. Use a template containing 3-inch, then 2-inch, and finally 1-inch wide *vertical* slots, which can serve as boundaries while the student practices making these lines. Be sure that the student starts at the top of the slot in the template and moves toward the bottom of the chalkboard each time a line is drawn.

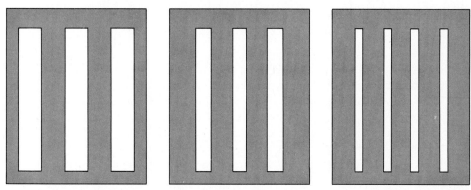

6. Have the student use colored chalk to superimpose *vertical* lines over (but within the boundaries of) 3-inch, then 2-inch, then 1-inch, and finally ½-inch wide *vertical* guidelines that have been drawn on the chalkboard by placing lengths of white chalk flat against the writing surface.
7. Have the student repeat step 6, superimposing *vertical* lines over narrow vertical lines that you have drawn on the chalkboard.
8. Have the student practice drawing solid lines over *vertical* lines of dashes on the chalkboard. Be sure that the student starts at the top of the line each time.
9. Have the student practice drawing solid lines over a *vertical* line of dots on the chalkboard.

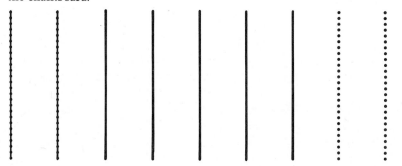

10. Remove every other dot and repeat step 9.
11. Repeat steps 9 and 10, removing more and more of the dots after mastery of each difficulty level until the student can draw *vertical* lines by connecting two dots.

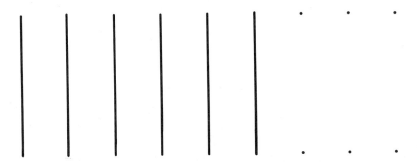

12. Have the student practice making long *vertical* lines on the chalkboard until the task can be performed in an easy, relaxed manner.
13. Have the student practice making *vertical* lines between guidelines on a piece of paper. Gradually decrease the distance between these lines until the student is superimposing the line that is being produced over a single narrow vertical guideline.
14. Repeat steps 7 through 11, using a crayon or marking pencil on a piece of paper.
15. Have the student practice making long *vertical* lines on unlined paper until the task can be performed in an easy, relaxed manner.

Suggestion Inexpensive templates of this type can be easily cut from ⅛-inch tempered hard board.

Task 4. *Production of Horizontal Scribbles and Lines*

Procedure 1. Demonstrate production of *horizontal* scribble marks on the chalkboard. Be sure to mark from your left to right, crossing your midline.

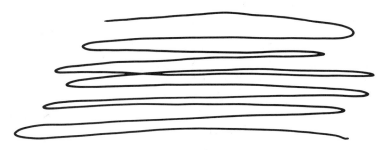

2. Ask the student to make scribble marks that go across the chalkboard.
3. Guide the hand of the student who is unable to produce spontaneously the hand movements involved in the production of *horizontal* lines.
4. Repeat steps 1 through 3 using a crayon or marking pencil on a piece of unlined paper.

Note   If proficiency is not observed during step 4, proceed with step 5 and as many of the following steps required to develop proficiency.

5. Have the student practice making *horizontal* lines on the chalkboard. Use a template containing 3-inch, then 2-inch, and finally 1-inch wide *horizontal* slots that can serve as boundaries when the student practices making these lines.

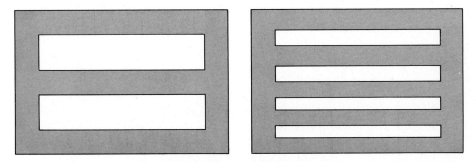

6. Have the student use colored chalk to superimpose *horizontal* lines over (but within the boundaries of) 3-inch, then 2-inch, 1-inch, and finally ½-inch wide *horizontal* guidelines that have been drawn on the chalkboard by placing lengths of chalk flat against the writing surface.
7. Have the student repeat step 6, superimposing *horizontal* lines that you have drawn on the chalkboard.
8. Have the student practice drawing solid lines over *horizontal* lines of dashes on the chalkboard. Be sure that the student starts at the left end of the line each time and that each line crosses in front of the midline of the body.
9. Have the student practice drawing solid lines from left to right over a *horizontal* line of dots on the chalkboard.

10. Remove every other dot and repeat step 9.

11. Repeat steps 9 and 10, removing more and more of the dots after mastery of each difficulty level until the student can draw *horizontal* lines by connecting two dots.

12. Have the student practice making long *horizontal* lines on the chalkboard until the task can be performed in an easy, relaxed manner.
13. Have the student practice making *horizontal* lines between guidelines on a piece of paper. Gradually decrease the distance between these lines until the student is superimposing the line that is being produced over a single, narrow *horizontal* line.
14. Repeat steps 7 through 11, using a crayon or marking pencil on a piece of paper.
15. Have the student practice making long *horizontal* lines on unlined paper until the task can be performed in an easy, relaxed manner.

Task 5. *Drawing a Circle*

Procedure 1. Repeat as many of the steps listed under tasks 3 and 4 as are needed to develop proficiency in drawing circles. (In other words, substitute drawing a circle for drawing a vertical or horizontal line.)
2. Be sure that the large circle you draw as a model crosses in front of the vertical midline of your body.
3. Right-handed students should move their writing hands in a counterclockwise direction when drawing a circle.

4. Left-handed students should move their writing hands in a clockwise direction.

Suggestion   Students whose freehand circles turn out to be egg-shaped can be helped to correct the shape by going around the circle several times after the first revolution has been completed. This procedure provides the child with continuous feedback about the improvement made in the shape of the circle with each successive revolution.

Materials   1. Chalkboard templates of a circle are found in McGraw-Hill's *Developing Learning Readiness Program* (Getman et al., 1968).
2. Chalkboard and desk templates containing circles are found in the Winterhaven materials, which are available from the Winterhaven, Florida, Lions Club.

Task 6. *Positioning the Paper in the Proper Relationship to the Body and Writing Hand*

Procedure   1. Position the paper so that the lower left corner points to the navel of the right-handed writer, or so that the lower right corner points to the navel of the left-handed writer.
2. The nonwriting hand should be resting on the paper with the elbow of that arm off the desk.
3. The writing hand and that arm's forearm and elbow must be on the desk.
4. The body of the right-handed writer should be turned slightly to the left while the body of the left-handed writer should be turned slightly to the right.
5. The writer's eyes should be approximately 16 inches from the paper.

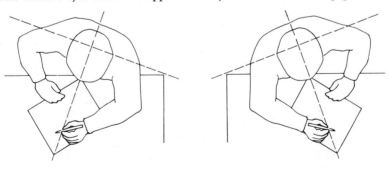

Left-handed   Right-handed

SOURCE: From B. Crontch "Handwriting & Correct Posture" in John I. Arena's *Building Handwriting Skills in Dyslexic Children.* Reprinted by permission of Academic Therapy Publications, San Rafael, California, 1970.

Caution   The left-handed student's tendency to write hook-handed is an unnatural position that causes discomfort, fatigue, and poor posture. It should be revised according to the procedure just outlined.

Suggestions
1. Do not attempt to force the child who is definitely left-handed to switch to the right hand for writing.
2. Moving the paper up as each line of writing is completed eliminates the need to constantly reposition the arm after each line.
3. The chair and desk should be of a height that permits the seated student to sit with feet flat on the floor.
4. A desk top that slopes at a 20-degree angle is regarded as best for writing.

Task 7. *Drawing a Single-Line Cross*

Procedure
1. Repeat as many of the steps listed under tasks 3 and 4 as are needed to develop proficiency in drawing straight lines.
2. The horizontal line you draw as part of the model should cross in front of the midline of your body.
3. Right-handed students who are drawing large crosses on the chalkboard should learn to comfortably reach across in front of the vertical midlines of their bodies so that they can pull the writing instrument from left to right when they are drawing the horizontal line.
4. Left-handed students should learn to start at the left end of the horizontal line and to move their writing hand comfortably across in front of their bodies without leaning or stepping to the right.
5. The vertical line should start at the top and extend downward to dissect the horizontal line into two equal parts.

Task 8. *Drawing a Square*

Procedure
1. Repeat as many of the steps listed under tasks 3 and 4 as are needed to develop proficiency in drawing a square.
2. It is sometimes helpful to verbalize the direction of each stroke involved in drawing a square (for example, *across, down, back across,* and *up*). This procedure may be used in producing freehand squares, tracing squares, or using a template to make a square.
3. Occasionally a student can draw a perfect square as long as the eyes are kept closed. Have this student first draw a square with the eyes closed, then open, then closed, then open, until proficiency is demonstrated with the eyes open.

Materials   1. A chalkboard template of a square is included in McGraw-Hill's *Developing Learning Readiness Program* (Getman et al., 1968).
2. Chalkboard and desk templates containing squares are included in the Winterhaven materials.

Task 9. *Drawing a Rectangle*

Procedure   The difference in the length of time required to draw the short and long sides of a rectangle is the main difference between production of a square and a rectangle. The temporal-spatial differences between a square and a rectangle are best taught at the chalkboard, where these differences can be exaggerated. This exaggeration makes it easier for the student to note differences in the time and kinesthetic effort involved in producing a square and a rectangle.

Materials   1. Chalkboard templates containing a rectangle are included in McGraw-Hill's *Developing Learning Readiness Program* (Getman et al., 1968).
2. Chalkboard and desk templates are found in the Winterhaven materials.
3. Chalkboard templates of the various geometric figures can be easily cut out of ⅛-inch tempered hard board.

Task 10. *Drawing Lines that Slant to the Left of the Vertical Axis*

Procedure   1. Start with a vertical line and then practice drawing rows of lines that each slant more and more to the left until proficiency is demonstrated at a 45-degree angle.

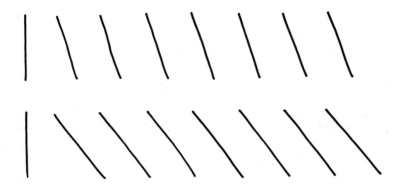

2. If difficulty is experienced with this task, refer to tasks 3 and 4 and break the tasks into smaller steps, using templates; tracing over lines, dashes and dotted lines; joining two dots; and finally achieving freehand production on the chalkboard followed by transfer of the task to unlined paper.

Task 11. *Drawing Lines that Slant to the Right of the Vertical Axis*

Procedure   1. Start with a vertical line and then practice drawing rows of lines that each slant more to the right until proficiency is demonstrated at a 45-degree angle.

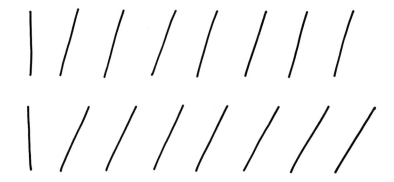

2. Repeat as much of the procedure used in task 10 as is needed to develop proficiency in drawing lines that slant up to 45 degrees to the right of the vertical axis.

Task 12. *Drawing an X*

Procedure   1. Combine the line that slants 45 degrees to the left of the vertical axis (task 10) with the line that slants 45 degrees to the right (task 11) to produce an *X*.
2. Break the task down into smaller steps involving tracing and connecting dot-to-dot patterns if necessary.
3. Development of proficiency in making an *X* should include skill in drawing two lines that dissect each other into two equal parts.
4. Drawing of lines that dissect each other equally can be taught by first drawing one of the slanting lines and then placing a dot in the center of it. The points in space that should serve as the start and stop points for the other slant line can be added to assist the student.

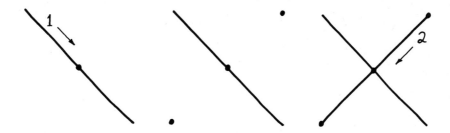

Task 13. *Joining Lines that Slant to the Left and Right*
(Up and Down the Mountain)

Procedure 1. Place two rows of large dots across the page. Be sure that the dots in each row are close together.

2. Demonstrate joining rows of dots with slanting lines.

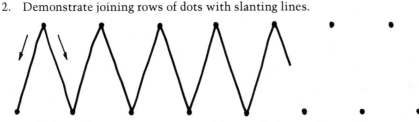

3. Ask the student to join two rows of dots with slanting lines.
4. Break the task down into smaller steps involving the use of stencils, tracing and marking over dotted lines if proficiency is not demonstrated in step 3.
5. Practice the preceding steps until the student is able to make and join slanting lines spontaneously without the use of dots.
6. Gradually widen the distance between the dots as the student's proficiency increases until the lines are being drawn at a 45-degree angle from the vertical axis.

Suggestions 1. Gradually reduce the size of the dots as proficiency increases.
2. Use of a chalkboard eraser initially while working on the chalkboard will give the student more to grasp and therefore tactual feedback.
3. Follow the use of the chalkboard eraser with the use of a wet finger and then chalk as a writing instrument.

Task 14. *Drawing an Equilateral Triangle*

Procedure   Repeat as many of the steps listed under tasks 3 and 4 as are needed to develop proficiency in drawing an equilateral triangle.

Materials   1. A chalkboard template of a triangle is included in McGraw-Hill's *Developing Learning Readiness Program.*
2. Chalkboard and desk templates containing triangles are included in the Winterhaven materials.

Task 15. *Drawing Vertical and Horizontal Lines Using Guidelines*

Procedure   1. Draw wide guidelines on the chalkboard using a colored or broken line for the center line.

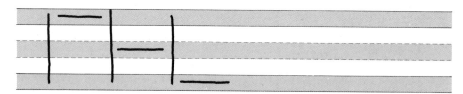

2. Draw vertical and horizontal lines between the guidelines. Alternate or mix figures of various height so that some of the marks are tall ones extending from the top guideline to the bottom guideline while others extend from the center line to the top or bottom guideline.

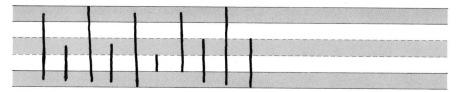

3. Regard as successful any attempt in which the end of the line being drawn does not extend beyond the outer edge of the wide guidelines.

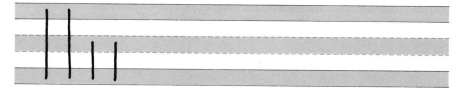

4. Gradually reduce the width of the guidelines until the student must touch but not go beyond thin guidelines.

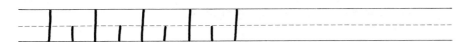

5. Gradually reduce the width between the guidelines until this activity can be performed on commercial writing paper.

Suggestion The wide guidelines that are needed when students have trouble marking between the lines can be made on the chalkboard by placing a short length of chalk flat against the chalkboard.

Note If the student has reached the age where his or her classmates are learning cursive writing, you should move directly to task 31. It is advisable to move immediately into cursive writing when instructing students who are over 8 years old. This procedure is recommended because students of this age seldom use manuscript writing in their written communication. It is also important to note that manuscript writing consists in large part of putting parts (segments) of letters together to make a whole whereas cursive writing stresses total movement patterns.

Task 16. *Drawing Large and Small Circles Between Guidelines*

Procedure 1. Repeat as many of the steps outlined in task 15 as are needed to develop proficiency.

2. Break the production of large and small circles into smaller steps involving tracing, marking over broken lines, and completing partially drawn figures if difficulty is encountered in step 1.

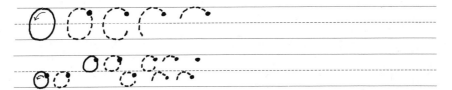

Task 17. *Drawing Full, Three-Quarter, and Half Circles*

Procedure 1. Break the production of a circle into parts and practice drawing each part until proficiency is demonstrated while moving in both the counter-clockwise and clockwise directions.

2. Practice those strokes on which difficulty is encountered by going back to tracing, marking over broken lines, and connecting dots if proficiency is not demonstrated in step 1.

Task 18. *Drawing Lines that Slant to the Right and Left of the Vertical Axis Between Guidelines*

Procedure   1. Repeat as many of the steps outlined in task 15 as are needed to develop proficiency.

2. Break the production of tall and short slanting lines between guidelines into smaller steps involving tracing, marking over broken lines, and connecting dots.

Task 19. *Drawing Squares, Rectangles, and Triangles Between Guidelines*

Procedure   Repeat as many of the steps outlined in task 15 as are needed, substituting squares, rectangles, and triangles for the vertical, horizontal, and slanting lines drawn in that task.

MANUSCRIPT AND NUMERAL WRITING SKILLS

Task 20. *Printing the Upper-Case Forms of the Letters L, F, and E Between Guidelines*

Procedure   1. Have the students combine vertical and horizontal strokes to print the letters *L, F,* and *E* on a chalkboard that does not contain guidelines.

2. Repeat step 1 on paper without guidelines.
3. Print the letters *L, F,* and *E* on the chalkboard using guidelines.

4. Repeat step 3 between guidelines on paper.

Suggestions   1. Students should pronounce each letter as they begin to print it.
               2. Be sure to tell the student that this is one way to print these letters and that you will teach them another way later. This will help eliminate problems that may occur later when the lower-case equivalents of these letters are taught.

Task 21. *Printing the Upper-Case Forms of the Letters* H, I, *and* T *Between Guidelines*

Procedure   Repeat as much of the procedure outlined in tasks 15 and 20 as is needed to develop proficiency.

Assumption   It is assumed that teachers who have followed the step-by-step procedure to this point are familiar with how to break individual tasks down into smaller steps. If not, refer back to tasks 3, 4, 15, and 20 for detailed procedures.

Task 22. *Printing the Letters* C *and* O *in Upper- and Lower-Case Forms Between Guidelines*

Procedure

Task 23. *Printing the Upper- and Lower-Case Forms of the Letters* L, F, E, H, I, *and* T *Between Guidelines*

Procedure

Suggestions   1. The teacher should pronounce the word first, then say each letter as it is being printed, and then use the word in a sentence.
2. The student should pronounce the word first and then say each letter as he or she begins to print it.

Note   Tasks 23 and 24 appear out of order in the logical sequence of skill development. They are introduced at this early point to provide the student with a sample of the payoff that lies at the end of this sequence of developmental tasks.

Task 24. Combining Lower-Case Letters to Make Two- and Three-Letter Words

Procedure

it

if

the

Suggestion   Writing these words in a vertical column eliminates the need for the student to cope with leaving proper spaces between words.

Task 25. Printing Letters that Are Combinations of Slanting Lines (V, v, W, w, and X, x) and Slanting and Horizontal Lines (Z, z)

Procedure

Task 26. Printing the Upper- and Lower-Case Letters B, b, M, m, N, n, R, r, U, and u

Procedure

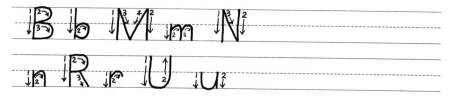

Task 27. *Printing the Upper- and Lower-Case Letters*
A, a, D, *and* d

Procedure

Task 28. *Printing the Upper- and Lower-Case Forms*
of the Letter S *and* s

Procedure

Task 29. *Printing Letters that Have Upper- or Lower-Case*
Forms with Tails (G, g, J, j, P, p, Q, q, Y, *and* y)

Procedure

Task 30. *Printing the Upper- and Lower-Case Forms*
of the Letter K *and* k

Procedure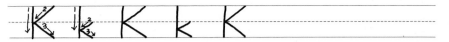

Note   The letter *K* is not introduced earlier because it is one of the hardest for children to learn to make.

Task 31. *Writing Numbers that Start on the Left Side*
and Move to the Right (2, 3, 4, *and* 7)

Procedure

Task 32. *Writing Numbers that Start on the Right and Move
to the Left (0, 6, 8, and 9) and the Number 5*

Procedure

0 5 6 8

9

Task 33. *Copying Groups of Multiple-Digit Numbers
on Lined Paper*

Procedure

23 157

Suggestion Emphasize the importance of leaving the proper amount of space between the
numbers in each group and between each group of numbers. Refer to task 39 if
difficulty is encountered regarding proper spacing between letters or words.

Task 34. *Copying Columns of Multiple-Digit Numbers
on Lined Paper*

Procedure

23 568
67 992
41 705

Suggestion One-inch graph paper provides both the horizontal and vertical lines needed for
performance of this task.

Task 35. *Copying Phone Numbers in Columns*

Procedure

902-1168
421-6171
872-3315

Suggestions
1. The student's own phone number should be among the first ones taught.
2. Paper can be used more efficiently if you divide the page with two vertical lines. This allows the student to proceed without worrying about leaving the appropriate amount of space between sets of numbers.

Task 36. *Writing Dictated Lists of Multiple-Digit Numbers on Lined Paper*

Procedure

Suggestion
Emphasize the importance of maintaining proper horizontal and vertical spacing between the groups of numbers.

Task 37. *Writing Dictated Lists of Multiple-Digit Numbers on Paper that Does Not Contain Lines*

Task 38. *Copying Lists of Three- and Four-Letter Words that Do Not Contain Tails and Are All the Same Height*

Procedure
1. Prepare a list of words on five-by-eight cards that fall within the student's range of skills.
2. Reduce the number of words on each card for the student who tends to be easily distracted or who is unable to handle the amount of stimuli that is involved when several words appear on a single card.

Task 39. *Learning to Leave an Appropriate Amount of Space Between Letters and Words*

Procedure

Suggestion
Instruct the right-handed student to print the first word and then to place the thumb of the left hand over the line immediately to the left of the word. If the second word is then printed immediately to the right of the thumb, an appropriate space will exist between the words when the thumb is removed. Reverse this procedure if the student is left-handed.

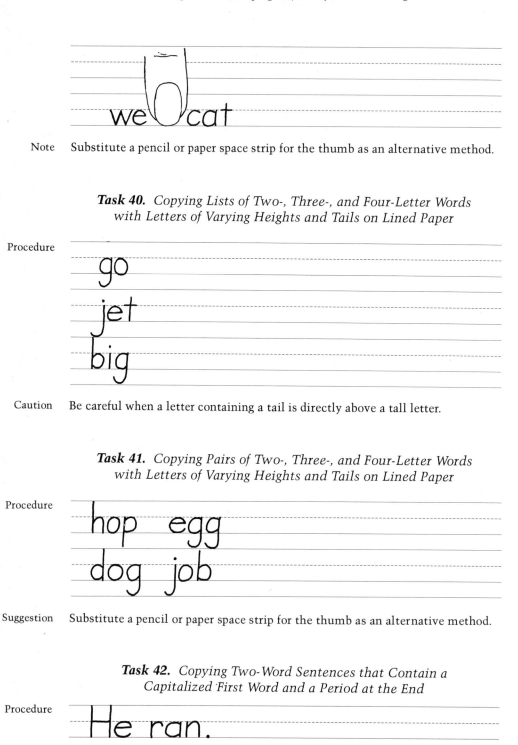

Note   Substitute a pencil or paper space strip for the thumb as an alternative method.

Task 40. *Copying Lists of Two-, Three-, and Four-Letter Words with Letters of Varying Heights and Tails on Lined Paper*

Procedure

> go
>
> jet
>
> big

Caution   Be careful when a letter containing a tail is directly above a tall letter.

Task 41. *Copying Pairs of Two-, Three-, and Four-Letter Words with Letters of Varying Heights and Tails on Lined Paper*

Procedure

> hop egg
>
> dog job

Suggestion   Substitute a pencil or paper space strip for the thumb as an alternative method.

Task 42. *Copying Two-Word Sentences that Contain a Capitalized First Word and a Period at the End*

Procedure

> He ran.

Task 43. *Copying Three-, Four-, and Five-Word Sentences*

Procedure   Repeat the procedure outlined in task 42, gradually lengthening the number of words in the sentences.

Task 44. *Writing Numbers that Are One Space High*

Procedure

0123456789

Task 45. *Writing Individual Numbers and Groups of Numbers as They Are Dictated*

Procedure   Have the student write single- and then multiple-digit numbers as they are dictated.

Task 46. *Printing Individual Letters and Groups of Letters as They Are Dictated*

Procedure   Have the student print single letters, groups of letters, single words, and short sentences as they are dictated.

Task 47. *Spontaneous Use of Numerals to Record and/or Convey Numerical Information*

Note   Observation of a student's successful performance of the activities described in this task would suggest that he or she has mastered the skills involved in the graphic production of numbers.

Task 48. *Spontaneous Use of Printing to Record and Convey Information*

Note   Observation of a student's successful performance of the activities described in this task would suggest that he or she has mastered the skills involved in printing.

TRANSITION FROM MANUSCRIPT TO CURSIVE WRITING

Tasks 49 and 50 are suggested for use in assisting students who are involved in making the transition from manuscript to cursive writing.

Task 49. *Learning to Connect Cursive Letters*

Procedure
1. Print a two-letter word such as *it* on the chalkboard.
2. Use dotted lines to show the student how to change manuscript letters into cursive letters.
3. Have the student practice joining manuscript letters.

Task 50. *Learning to Slant Cursive Letters*

Procedure
1. Write the letters in a word in both the vertical manuscript and vertical cursive forms while the student watches.
2. Write the cursive form of the word with the letters slanting at the desired angle.
3. Have the student practice tracing and then copying these connected letters in their slanting form.

CURSIVE WRITING SKILLS: LOWER CASE

Cursive writing may be introduced following mastery of the tasks involved in manuscript writing or as an alternative form of initial instruction. It is often advisable to move directly to instruction in cursive writing when teaching handwriting to students who have perceptual problems.

Students with visual perceptual problems often experience difficulty with the degree of segmentation and the number of starts and stops involved in the production of manuscript letters. They are, however, sometimes able to master the flowing strokes involved in cursive writing.

Young children have traditionally been taught to print first because of the belief that simultaneous instruction in manuscript writing and learning to read print reinforce each other. If a child reaches age 8 or 9 without mastering manuscript writing, it is suggested that the instructional effort be redirected to developing proficiency in cursive writing. Instruction in cursive writing at age 8 and older provides the student with skill in the form of writing they will see their peers and teachers use in the years following.

Task 51. *Making Tall, Middle-sized, and Short Swing Strokes*

Procedure

Task 52. *Making Tall, Middle-sized, and Short Pull Strokes*

Procedure

Suggestion   The degree of slant in a student's pulls and swings should be consistent.

Task 53. *Combining Swing and Pull Strokes Without Lifting Pencil*

Procedure

Task 54. *Connecting a Series of Swing and Pull Strokes Without Lifting Pencil*

Procedure

Task 55. *Use of Loops to Connect Middle-sized Swings and Pulls and Short Swings and Pulls Without Lifting Pencil*

Procedure

l l l   elelele

Suggestion Change the color of the line when changing the direction of the strokes for those students who have difficulty in recognizing changes in direction.

Task 56. *Connecting the Letters* l, e, i, t, *and* u *to Make Words*

Procedure

let lite

tut little

Suggestion If the suggestion in task 55 regarding the use of different-colored lines does not work, use heavy rug yarn to make tactile cursive letters so that the student may move his or her finger and eyes over the route followed while correctly making each letter. Each letter should consist of one continuous strand of yarn that is glued to oak tag or cardboard.

Task 57. *Writing the Letters* w *and* b

Procedure

w w w

b b b

aution Be sure that the student begins the letter *w* on the base line so that this and all other lower-case cursive letters start with a lead-in line. This eliminates any confusion that may exist regarding where to start various letters and which direction to move.

Task 58. *Combining the Letters* b *and* w *with* l, e, i, u, *and* t

Procedure

be we bet

web will

bill but

Task 59. *Writing the Letters* f *and* j

Procedure

f f f f f f

j j j j j j

fill jet

Task 60. *Making the Over Stroke*

Procedure

Task 61. *Combining the Over and Short Pull Strokes to Write the Letters* m *and* n

Procedure

n n n n n mm

n n n n net

m m met

men men

Suggestion   Numbering the humps is sometimes helpful to the student who has difficulty transferring from the manuscript to the cursive forms of *m* and *n*.

Task 62. *Writing the Letter* h

Procedure

h n h h h h

hen him

Task 63. *Writing the Letters* v *and* x

Procedure

v v v vet

v x x next

Task 64. *Writing the Letters* y *and* z

Procedure

y y y y yet

z z z z buzz

Task 65. *Writing the Letter* c

Procedure

c c c c

Task 66. *Writing the Letter* a

Procedure

a a a at

an tan

Task 67. Writing the Letter d

Procedure

a l d dad

dim had

Task 68. Writing the Letter g

Procedure

o g g get

Task 69. Writing the Letter q

Procedure

o q q quit

Task 70. Writing the Letter o

Procedure

x c o o

out good

Task 71. Writing the Letter r

Procedure

r r r rrr

run car

Task 72. *Writing the Letter* s

Procedure

sam set

Task 73. *Writing the Letter* p

Procedure

pit puppy

Task 74. *Writing the Letter* k

Procedure

k k k kite

CURSIVE WRITING SKILLS: UPPER CASE

Task 75. *Making the Cane Stroke*

Procedure

Suggestions
1. The handles of all of the canes should slope to the right to the same degree.
2. The loop at the top of the cane should close well to the left of the handle.

Task 76. *Writing the Letter* H

Procedure

Hal

Task 77. *Writing the Letters* M *and* N

Procedure

M May

N N Nate

Task 78. *Writing the Letter* Q

Procedure

Q Q Quit

Task 79. *Writing the Letters* U *and* V

Procedure

U U Up

V V Vern

Task 80. *Writing the Letter* W

Procedure

W W W When

Task 81. *Writing the Letter* X

Procedure

X X X

Task 82. *Writing the Letters Y and Z*

Procedure

Y Y You

Z Z Zoo

Task 83. *Making Tall Ovals and the Letter A*

Procedure

O A A

Ann Amy

Task 84. *Writing the Letters C and O*

Procedure

C C C Carl

O O O On

Task 85. *Writing the Letter D*

Procedure

I I D D D Del

Task 86. *Writing the Letter E*

Procedure

E E E Eric

Task 87. *Writing the Letters* S *and* G

Procedure

/ / S S Sam

/ / / G Go

Task 88. *Writing the Letters* T *and* F

Procedure

/ / T Tim

/ / F Fred

Task 89. *Writing the Letters* P, R, *and* B

Procedure

P P P Pat

/ R R Rae

B B B Bob

Task 90. *Writing the Letter* K

Procedure

K K Kay

Task 91. *Writing the Letter* L

Procedure

L L L Lot

Task 92. *Writing the Letter* I

Procedure

ℐ ℐ ℐke

Caution   Students learning to write the upper-case letter *I* often need extra emphasis and assistance because of the initial direction of movement and the letter's unconventional starting point.

Task 93. *Writing the Letter* J

Procedure

(𝒥 𝒥 𝒥 𝒥im

USING CURSIVE HANDWRITING SKILLS

Task 94. *Copying Short Sentences that Contain a Capitalized First Letter, Proper Nouns, and a Period at the End*

Procedure

ℐ see the cat.

Caution   Remember to emphasize the importance of leaving the correct amount of space between words.

Task 95. *Writing the Cursive Forms of Words from a Model that Is Being Viewed in Print*

Task 96. *Writing Dictated Letters, Words, and Sentences in Cursive*

Procedure   Have the student write single letters, groups of letters, single words, and short sentences in cursive as they are dictated, using both upper- and lower-case forms.

Task 97. *Spontaneous Use of Cursive Writing to Record and/or Convey Information*

Note Observation of a student's successful, spontaneous production of cursive writing suggests that he or she has mastered cursive writing.

SOURCES OF MATERIAL FOR TEACHING HANDWRITING

Materials for use in teaching handwriting are available from most of the major publishers. Catalogs containing materials for use in teaching specific types of handwriting skills can be obtained from the following sources: Educators Publishing Service, Inc., 75 Moulton Street, Cambridge, Massachusetts 02138; The A. N. Palmer Company, 1720 West Irving Park Road, Schaumburg, Illinois 60172; and Zaner-Bloser Company, 612 North Park Street, Columbus, Ohio 43215.

SUMMARY

1. The development of proficiency in handwriting evolves through a series of steps that begin with learning to grasp the writing instrument and extend through spontaneous use of cursive writing to convey information.
2. The right-handed student's hand should move in a counterclockwise direction when a circle is being drawn; the left-handed student's hand should move in a clockwise direction.
3. The writing paper should be positioned for the right-handed student so that a line drawn from the upper right-hand corner to the lower left-hand corner would extend straight to the writer's navel.
4. The left-handed student should not be forced to switch to his or her right hand for writing.

REFERENCES

Crontch, B. 1970. "Handwriting and Correct Posture." In *Building Handwriting Skills in Dyslexic Children.* Ed. J. I. Arena. San Rafael, Calif.: Academic Therapy Publications.

Getman, G. N., E. R. Kane, M. R. Halgren, and G. K. McKee. 1968. *Developing Learning Readiness.* New York: McGraw-Hill.

PART FIVE

Diagnosis and Remediation of Arithmetic and Mathematics Problems

SEVENTEEN

Diagnosis of Arithmetic
and Mathematics Problems

Children who have learning problems frequently experience difficulty with arithmetic and mathematics. Johnson and Myklebust (1967) suggest that problems in this area may be due to disturbances of quantitative thinking; difficulties with language or reading; or an inability to revisualize numbers, to form written numbers graphically, or to remember instructions. Chalfant and Scheffelin (1969) refer to these problems as *quantitative language disorders.* Herman (1959) indicates that students who are unable to read numerals should be classified as dyslexic. He suggests that the term *acalculia* should be used to describe children who are unable to perform calculations. *Dyscalculia,* a form of acalculia, involves a partial inability to perform calculations.

In their discussion of central processing dysfunctions, Chalfant and Scheffelin (1969) make the following distinction between arithmetic and mathematics: "Mathematics is the abstract science of space and number which deals with space configuration and the interrelations and abstractions of numbers. Arithmetic is a branch of mathematics that deals with real numbers and their computation (p. 119)." They indicate that the student with a mathematics disability might have trouble "handling the operations, interrelations and abstractions of numbers, or the structure, measurement and transformation of space configurations" (p. 119). Furthermore, the student may have difficulty "reading or writing isolated numerals or a series of numerals, reading and writing numbers whose names are not written the way they are spoken (twenty-one = 21, not 201), recognizing the categorical structure of numbers (units, tens, hundreds, thousands), and doing computational operations" (p. 119).

TYPES OF ARITHMETIC AND MATHEMATICS PROBLEMS

Students who are having trouble in arithmetic may be unable to do the following:

1. determine if the *size* of objects is the same or different
2. determine if the *shape* of objects is the same or different
3. determine if the *quantity* of objects in one group is greater, the same as, or less than in another group
4. effectively use basic quantitative language
5. understand one-to-one correspondence (for example, between the number of books and the number of students in a classroom)
6. count meaningfully, in other words, recognize the numeral and the quantity it represents
7. associate the names of numerals with their corresponding visual symbols
8. learn the cardinal system of counting (1, 2, 3, 4, 5, and so on)
9. learn the ordinal system of counting (1st, 2nd, 3rd, 4th, and so on)
10. visualize clusters or groups of objects that appear as sets within a larger group without counting each individual object
11. grasp the meaning of Piaget's principle of conservation of quantity (for example, that ten cents is the same when it consists of one dime, two nickels, or ten pennies)
12. organize the numbers on a page so that they clearly appear in columns that each represent a specific place value
13. perform the operations involved in addition, subtraction, multiplication, and division
14. understand the meaning of the process signs (for example, $+$, $-$, $\div$, $\times$)
15. remember and follow the sequence of steps involved in various mathematical operations
16. understand fractions
17. tell time
18. understand the principles of measurement
19. understand the values of money
20. read maps and graphs
21. solve problems that require reading

Buswell and Johns (1926) report finding the following errors and faulty habits in the addition, subtraction, multiplication, and division of elementary school students.*

---

*From G. T. Buswell and L. Johns, *Diagnostic Studies in Arithmetic.* Chicago: University of Chicago Press, 1926. Reprinted by permission of University of Chicago Press.

Addition

Errors in combinations
Counting
Added carried number last
Forgot to add carried number
Repeated work after partly done
Wrote number to be carried
Irregular procedure in column
Carried wrong number
Grouped two or more numbers
Split numbers into parts
Used wrong fundamental operation
Lost place in column
Depended on visualization
Disregarded column position
Omitted one or more digits

Errors in reading numbers
Dropped back one or more tens
Derived unknown combination from familiar one
Disregarded one column
Error in writing answer
Skipped one or more decades
Carried when there was nothing to carry
Used scratch paper
Added in pairs, giving last sum as answer
Added same digit in two columns
Wrote carried number in answer
Added same number twice

Subtraction

Errors in combinations
Did not allow for having borrowed
Counting
Errors due to zero in minuend
Said example backwards
Subtracted minuend from subtrahend
Failed to borrow; gave zero as answer
Added instead of subtracted
Error in reading
Used same digit in two columns
Derived unknown from known combination
Omitted a column
Used trial-and-error addition
Split numbers

Deducted from minuend when borrowing was not necessary
Ignored a digit
Deducted 2 from minuend after borrowing
Error due to minuend and subtrahend digits being same
Used minuend or subtrahend as remainder
Reversed digits in remainder
Confused process with division or multiplication
Skipped one or more decades
Increased minuend digit after borrowing
Based subtraction on multiplication combination

Multiplication

Errors in combinations
Error in adding the carried number
Wrote rows of zeros

Carried a wrong number
Errors in addition
Forgot to carry

Used multiplicand as multiplier

Error in single zero combinations, zero as multiplier

Errors due to zero in multiplier

Used wrong process—added

Error in single zero combinations, zero as multiplicand

Confused products when multiplier had two or more digits

Repeated part of table

Multiplied by adding

Did not multiply a digit in multiplicand

Based unknown combination on another

Errors in reading

Omitted digit in product

Errors in writing product

Errors in carrying into zero

Counted to carry

Errors due to zero in multiplicand

Error in position of partial products

Counted to get multiplication combinations

Illegible figures

Forgot to add partial products

Split multiplier

Wrote wrong digit of product

Multiplied by same digit twice

Reversed digits in product

Wrote tables

Omitted digit in multiplier

Division

Errors in division combinations

Errors in subtraction

Errors in multiplication

Used remainder larger than divisor

Found quotient by trial multiplication

Neglected to use remainder within problem

Omitted zero resulting from another digit

Counted to get quotient

Repeated part of multiplication table

Used short division form for long division

Wrote remainders within problem

Omitted zero resulting from zero in dividend

Omitted final remainder

Used long division form for short division

Said example backwards

Used remainder without new dividend figure

Derived unknown combinations from known one

Had right answer, used wrong one

Grouped too many digits in dividend

Error in reading

Used dividend or divisor as quotient

Found quotient by adding

Reversed dividend and divisor

Used digits of divisor separately

Wrote all remainders at end of problem

Misinterpreted table

Used digit in dividend twice

Used second digit of divisor to find quotient

Began dividing at units digit of dividend

Split dividend

Counted in subtracting

Used too large a product

Used endings to find quotient

INFORMAL DIAGNOSIS

Experienced teachers frequently find it helpful to use informal diagnostic questions and activities to determine what assistance is needed by students who are having trouble learning arithmetic and mathematics concepts. These same informal questions can be used by the inexperienced teacher who is trying to decide if the student should be referred to an arithmetic or learning disabilities specialist for diagnostic services. The following are examples of such questions:

1. Can the student match objects or figures that are the same shape or size?
2. Can the student identify circles, squares, triangles, and other geometric shapes?
3. Can the student identify the object in a group of objects that is different from the others?
4. Can the student identify the largest or smallest member of a group of objects?
5. Can the student identify the tallest or shortest member of a group of objects?
6. Can the student identify the longest or shortest member of a group of objects?
7. Can the student identify those sets in a group of sets that contain the same number of members?
8. Can the student identify the set in a group of sets that contains the most or fewest members?
9. Does the student understand the one-to-one correspondence that exists between a number and a specific quantity of objects?
10. Can the student count meaningfully using cardinal numbers (1, 2, 3, 4, and so on) and ordinal numbers (1st, 2nd, 3rd, and so on)?
11. Does the student associate number names with their corresponding visual symbols (sets or numerals)?
12. Can the student write the numerals?
13. Does the student organize the numerals that are written so that they appear in clearly identifiable rows and columns?
14. Can the student perform the operations involved in addition?
15. Can the student perform the operations involved in subtraction?
16. Can the student solve problems involving carrying and regrouping?
17. Can the student perform the operations involved in multiplication?
18. Can the student perform the operations involved in division?
19. Does the student understand and correctly use place value?
20. Does the student understand the meaning of process signs $(+, -, \times, \div)$?
21. Can the student remember and follow the sequence of steps involved in various mathematical operations?
22. Does the student understand and use fractions and decimals correctly?
23. Can the student tell time?

24. Does the student understand and use measurements of length, volume, and weight correctly?
25. Does the student understand the value of money and count change correctly?
26. Can the student read maps and graphs?
27. Can the student read well enough to successfully answer story problems?

Bartel (1975) suggests the following series of questions for use in determining why a student is having trouble with story problems:

1. Can the student orally read the problem?
2. Can the student restate what it is that is to be computed?
3. Can the student determine if all of the necessary information is given?
4. Can the student determine if irrelevant information is given?
5. Can the student decide whether to add, subtract, etc.?
6. Can the student decide whether some conversions are required before solving the problem (e.g., changing feet to inches)?
7. Can the student organize a procedure?
8. Can the student estimate an answer, or decide if his obtained answer is reasonable?
9. Does the student know how to check his answer? (pp. 71 and 74)

STANDARDIZED ARITHMETIC TESTS

The *KeyMath Diagnostic Arithmetic Test* (Connolly, Natchman, and Pritchett, 1971) and the *Stanford Diagnostic Arithmetic Test* (Beatty, Madden, and Gardner, 1966) are two of the most frequently used standardized arithmetic tests. KeyMath is a diagnostic instrument for assessing students' arithmetic strengths and weaknesses, and provides information on which to base an appropriate instructional program. It contains fourteen subtests divided into three areas. Area 1 (content) includes the Numeration, Fractions, and Geometry and Symbols subtests. Addition, Subtraction, Multiplication, Division, Mental Computation, and Numeric Reasoning subtests are in Area 2 (operations), and Area 3 (applications) contains Word Problem, Missing Elements, Money, Measurement, and Time subtests. A metric supplement to Key Math is also available.

The *Stanford Diagnostic Arithmetic Test* is used to identify areas in which instruction is needed. The three tests in Level I are used for students with arithmetic skills between grade levels 2.5 and 4.5. The Level I tests and their subparts include the following:

Test 1: Concepts of Numbers and Numerals
    Part A: Number system and counting
    Part B: Operations
    Part C: Decimal place value
Test 2: Computation
    Part A: Addition
    Part B: Subtraction
    Part C: Multiplication
    Part D: Division
Test 3: Number Facts
    Part A: Addition
    Part B: Subtraction
    Part C: Multiplication
    Part D: Division

The five subtests in Level II are used with students who are performing between grade levels 4.5 and 8.5. The Level II tests and their subparts include the following:

Test 1: Concepts of Numbers and Numerals
    Part A: Number system and operations
    Part B: Decimal place value
Test 2: Computation with Whole Numbers
    Part A: Addition and subtraction
    Part B: Multiplication
    Part C: Division
Test 3: Common Fractions
    Part A: Understanding
    Part B: Computation
Test 4: Decimal Fractions and Percent
Test 5: Number Facts
    Part A: Addition
    Part B: Subtraction
    Part C: Multiplication
    Part D: Division
    Part E: Carrying

Specific objectives are available for each item in KeyMath and the *Stanford Diagnostic Arithmetic Test*. This feature makes it possible to use them as criterion-referenced tests.

The arithmetic subtest from the *Wide Range Achievement Test* (Jastak, Bijou, and Jastak, 1978) and the *Peabody Individual Achievement Test* (Dunn and

Markwardt, 1970) are useful when a quick indication of the student's approximate grade placement in arithmetic is needed. These subtests lack the detail needed for diagnostic use, however. Finally, the *Kraner Preschool Math Inventory* (Kraner, 1976) is used to determine which quantitative concepts have been acquired by children between ages 3 and 6. The seventy-seven concepts assessed by the inventory are divided into counting, sequence, positional, directional, and geometry/measurement areas. Receptive and mastery age norms are provided for each concept. Kraner describes the *receptive age* as that age level where 50 percent of the children answer the question correctly. The *mastery age* is the age level where 80 percent of the children respond correctly on an item. The inventory can be used as a norm- or criterion-referenced test.

CRITERION-REFERENCED ARITHMETIC TESTS

Criterion-referenced arithmetic tests are useful for determining which arithmetic skills have been mastered and which skills should be taught next. They produce the type of information about student performance that is needed to plan instruction on a day-to-day basis.

The lack of general agreement as to the sequence of skills each student must master in order to become proficient in arithmetic greatly complicates the development of criterion-referenced arithmetic tests. However, the linear nature of arithmetic skill development does make test development much easier than in areas such as reading. Although many publishers are now offering lists of objectives for the items contained in standardized tests for those who wish to use these instruments as criterion-referenced tests, many teachers are still finding it necessary to design their own. The following criterion-referenced arithmetic test is provided in an effort to relieve teachers of some of the burden involved in this time-consuming task.

THE CRD ARITHMETIC TEST

The *CRD Arithmetic Test* (pp. 274–290) is a criterion-referenced diagnostic arithmetic test. It is designed for use in assessing those skills that fall between $1 + 1 = 2$ and mastery of basic arithmetic computation. It does not contain items suitable for assessing precomputational or higher mathematical concepts.

In each of the eight subtest areas, I have arranged the items in a sequence of developmental tasks on the basis of my professional judgment. Those who wish to rearrange the order in which these objectives and test items appear may simply renumber the items on the *CRD Arithmetic* Skill Analysis and Check List form (pp. 270–273) with no adverse effect on the usefulness of the subtest involved.

Each subtest appears on the front and back of one page. When a teacher wishes to assess a student's mastery of certain skills, the student receives only one page of problems on those skills. The test should be presented as untimed, and the student should answer as many of the problems as possible. The length of time required to complete the test should be recorded for use in determining the student's rate of response to problems. The teacher can read the instructions aloud to students who have reading problems for those items with printed directions.

The teacher will not usually administer all eight subtests to a student. Those who wish to have a student complete all the subtests are advised to spread the administration of the tests over several days.

The tasks for the items passed should be checked off on the student's individual copy of the *CRD Arithmetic* Skill Analysis and Check List form. An examination of this form will give an approximate indication of the point in the sequence of tasks where instruction should begin. Instruction should generally start on a task level that corresponds with the next to last item passed. This will help insure that the student experiences success before encountering difficult material, and will ascertain that the last one or two items weren't lucky guesses suggesting mastery that doesn't actually exist.

Each task is coded for easy use in writing individualized education programs (IEPs). For example, a student's IEP might call for instruction designed to achieve mastery of the skills involved in arithmetic objectives A5 through A9 and $2 through $5. The preparation of IEPs is discussed thoroughly in Chapter 4.

Name _____ Grade _____ Birthdate _____

Teacher _____ School _____

© 1979 by: Larry A. Faas

CRD* ARITHMETIC SKILL ANALYSIS AND CHECK LIST

ADDITION

Task #	Task (Skill) Description	Check off date/form			Error Analysis Circle type of Error
A1	Addition of two 1-digit numbers with sums of 2 to 5				CE SA F
A2	Addition of two 1-digit numbers with sums of 5 to 9				CE SA F
A3	Addition of 0 to 1-digit numbers from 1-9				CE SA F
A4	Addition of two 1-digit numbers with sums of 10 to 18				CE SA F
A5	Addition of a 1-digit number to a 2-digit number which ends in 0 (20 + 3 = 23)				CE SA F
A6	Addition of two 2-digit numbers which end in 0 (20 + 30 = 50)				CE SA F
A7	Addition of three 1-digit numbers with sums under 10				CE SA F
A8	Addition of three 1-digit numbers with sums under 20				CE SA F
A9	Addition of a 1-digit number to a 2-digit number without regrouping				CE SA F
A10	Addition of a 2-digit number to a 1-digit number without regrouping				CE SA F
A11	Addition of two 2-digit numbers without regrouping				CE SA F
A12	Addition of two 3-digit numbers without regrouping				CE SA F
A13	Addition of a 1-digit number to a 2-digit number with regrouping to 10's				CE SA F R
A14	Addition of two 2-digit numbers with regrouping to 10's				CE SA F R
A15	Addition of two 3-digit numbers with regrouping to 10's				CE SA F R
A16	Addition of two 3-digit numbers with regrouping to 100's				CE SA F R
A17	Addition of two 2-digit numbers with regrouping to 10's and 100's				CE SA F R
A18	Addition of two 3-digit numbers with regrouping to 100's and 1000's				CE SA F R
A19	Addition of two 4-digit numbers with regrouping to 100's and 1000's				CE SA F R
A20	Addition of three 2-digit numbers without regrouping				CE SA F R
A21	Addition of three 2-digit numbers with regrouping to 10's				CE SA F R
A22	Addition of three 2-digit numbers with regrouping to 10's and 100's				CE SA F R
A23	Addition of three 4-digit numbers with regrouping to 10's, 100's and 1000's				CE SA F R
A24	Addition of several numbers of varying length, regrouping when necessary				CE SA F R

*Criterion-Referenced Diagnostic

Error Analysis
CE = Computational Error
SA = Spacing or Alignment Problem
F = Number or Symbol Formation Problem
R = Regrouping or Remainder Problem

SUBTRACTION

Task #	Task (Skill) Description	Check off date/form			Error Analysis Circle type of Error
S1	Subtraction of a 1-digit number from another 1-digit number with differences of 1 to 4				CE SA F
S2	Subtraction of a 1-digit number from another 1-digit number with differences of 5 to 9				CE SA F
S3	Subtraction of 0 from a 1-digit number				CE SA F
S4	Completion of a number sentence by filling in the missing number				CE SA F
S5	Subtraction of a 1-digit number from another 1-digit number with a difference of 0				CE SA F
S6	Subtraction of a 2-digit number which ends in 0 from another 2-digit number which ends in 0 (30 - 10 = 20)				CE SA F
S7	Subtraction of a 1-digit number from 10				CE SA F
S8	Subtraction of a 1-digit number from a 2-digit number with differences of 1 to 18				CE SA F
S9	Subtraction of a 1-digit number from a 2-digit number with differences larger than 20 without regrouping				CE SA F
S10	Subtraction of one 2-digit number from another 2-digit number without regrouping				CE SA F
S11	Subtraction of a 2-digit number which ends in 0 from a 2-digit number without regrouping				CE SA F
S12	Subtraction of a 2-digit number from a 3-digit number with regrouping and a zero in the ans.				CE SA F
S13	Subtraction of a 3-digit number from another 3-digit number without regrouping				CE SA F
S14	Subtraction of a 1-digit number from a 2-digit number with regrouping from 10's				CE SA F R
S15	Subtraction of a 1-digit number from a 2-digit number which ends in 0 with regrouping from 10's				CE SA F R
S16	Subtraction of a 2-digit number from another 2-digit number with regrouping from 10's				CE SA F R
S17	Subtraction of a 2-digit number from a 2-digit number which ends in 0 with regrouping from 10's				CE SA F R
S18	Subtraction of a 1-digit number with regrouping from 10's				CE SA F R
S19	Subtraction of a 3-digit number from another 3-digit number with regrouping from 100's and 10's				CE SA F R
S20	Subtraction of a 3-digit number from another 3-digit number with regrouping from 100's and 10's				CE SA F R
S21	Subtraction of a 3-digit number containing a 0 from another 3-digit number with regrouping from 10's				CE SA F R
S22	Subtraction of a 3-digit number from another 3-digit number which ends in two zeros, with regrouping from 100's and 10's				CE SA F R
S23	Subtraction of a 4-digit number from another 4-digit number with regrouping from 100's				CE SA F R
S24	Subtraction of a 4-digit number from another 4-digit number with regrouping from 1000's, 100's and 10's				CE SA F R

Sondra Frankland, learning resource specialist at the Hohokam School in the Scottsdale, Arizona, public schools, served as my graduate assistant during the development of the *CRD Arithmetic Test.*

MULTIPLICATION

Task #	Task (Skill) Description	Check off date/form			Error Analysis Circle type of Error
M1	Multiplication of 1-digit numbers by 1				CE SA F
M2	Multiplication of 1-digit numbers by 2				CE SA F
M3	Multiplication of 1-digit numbers by 3				CE SA F
M4	Multiplication of 1-digit numbers by 0				CE SA F
M5	Multiplication of 1-digit numbers by 4				CE SA F
M6	Multiplication of 1-digit numbers by 5				CE SA F
M7	Multiplication of 1-digit numbers by 6				CE SA F
M8	Demonstrates understanding of commutative property $(32 \div \square = 9)$				CE SA F
M9	Multiplication of 1-digit numbers by 7				CE SA F
M10	Multiplication of 1-digit numbers by 8				CE SA F
M11	Multiplication of 1-digit numbers by 9				CE SA F
M12	Multiplication of 2-digit numbers by 1-digit number w/o regrouping				CE SA F
M13	Multiplication of 3-digit numbers by 1-digit numbers without regrouping and a zero in the ans.				CE SA F
M14	Multiplication of 3-digit numbers, which contain a zero, by 1-digit numbers without regrouping				CE SA F
M15	Multiplication of 2-digit numbers by 1-digit numbers with regrouping to 10's				CE SA F R
M16	Multiplication of 2-digit numbers by 1-digit numbers with regrouping and products of 100 or more				CE SA F R
M17	Multiplication of 3-digit numbers by 1-digit numbers with regrouping to 10's and 100's				CE SA F R
M18	Multiplication of 2-digit numbers by 2-digit numbers with emphasis upon alignment of partial products				CE SA F
M19	Multiplication of 2-digit numbers by 2-digit numbers with regrouping to 10's and 100's				CE SA F R
M20	Multiplication of 2-digit numbers by 2-digit numbers ending in zero with regrouping				CE SA F R
M21	Multiplication of 3-digit numbers by 2-digit numbers with regrouping				CE SA F R
M22	Multiplication of 3-digit numbers by 2-digit numbers ending in zero with regrouping (342 X 20 = 6840)				CE SA F R
M23	Multiplication of 3-digit numbers by 3-digit numbers with regrouping				CE SA F R
M24	Multiplication of 2 through 5-digit numbers requiring rewriting of the problem and regrouping				CE SA F R

DIVISION

Task #	Task (Skill) Description	Check off date/form			Error Analysis Circle type of Error
D1	Division of 1-digit numbers by 1-digit numbers with no remainders				CE SA F
D2	Division of 1-digit numbers by 1-digit numbers resulting in quotients of one				CE SA F
D3	Division of 1-digit numbers by 1-digit numbers with remainders				CE SA F R
D4	Division of 1-digit numbers by 1				CE SA F
D5	Demonstrates understanding of commutative property $\square$ x 8 = 48				CE SA F
D6	Division of 2-digit numbers by 1-digit numbers with 1-digit quotients, no remainders				CE SA F
D7	Division of 2-digit numbers by 1-digit numbers with 1-digit quotients and remainders				CE SA F R
D8	Division of 2-digit numbers by 1-digit numbers with 2-digit quotients, no remainders				CE SA F
D9	Division of 2-digit numbers by 1-digit numbers with 2-digit quotients and remainders				CE SA F R
D10	Division of 3-digit numbers by 1-digit numbers, no remainders				CE SA F R
D11	Division of 3-digit numbers by 1-digit numbers with remainders				CE SA F R
D12	Division of 4-digit numbers by 1-digit numbers with remainders				CE SA F R
D13	Division of zero by 1-digit numbers				CE SA F
D14	Division of 2-digit numbers ending in zero by 2-digit numbers ending in zero, no remainders				CE SA F
D15	Division of 2-digit numbers by 2-digit numbers with 1-digit quotients, no remainders				CE SA F
D16	Division of 2-digit numbers by 2-digit numbers with 1-digit quotients and remainders				CE SA F R
D17	Division of 3-digit numbers by 2-digit numbers with 2-digit quotients, no remainders				CE SA F
D18	Division of 3-digit numbers by 2-digit numbers with 2-digit quotients and remainders				CE SA F R
D19	Division of 3-digit numbers by 2-digit numbers with 1-digit quotients and remainders				CE SA F R
D20	Division involving zero in the dividend with remainders				CE SA F R
D21	Division involving zero in the divisor with remainders				CE SA F R
D22	Division involving zero in the quotient with remainders				CE SA F R
D23	Division involving zeros in the divisor, dividend and quotient				CE SA F
D24	Division of 4 or 5-digit numbers by 3-digit numbers with remainders				CE SA F R
D25	Division of multiple-digit numbers requiring rewriting of the problem and remainders				CE SA F R

Name_____ Birthdate_____ Grade_____ School_____ Teacher_____

FRACTIONS

Task #	Task (Skill) Description	Check Off Date	Error Analysis Circle type of Error
F1	Shading one-half of a geometric figure		
F2	Identification of one-half of an existing set		
F3	Shading one-fourth of a geometric figure		
F4	Identification of one-fourth of an existing set		
F5	Division of an existing set into two equal sets		
F6	Shading one-third of a geometric figure		
F7	Identification of one-third of an existing set		
F8	Writing the fraction which describes the shaded part of a geometric figure		
F9	Shading one-third of a box that is divided into sixths		
F10	Writing the fraction which describes circled part of a set		SA F
F11	Finding a fractional part of a number (e.g. 3/4 of 16 = 12)		SA F
F12	Finding the missing numerator		SA F
F13	Reduction of a fraction to the lowest terms		SA F
F14	Conversion of improper fractions to a mixed number (e.g. 7/5 = 1 2/5)		SA F
F15	Conversion of mixed numbers to improper fractions (e.g. 1 2/5 = 7/5)		SA F
F16	Completion of a number sentence by inserting ∟, 7 or =		F
F17	Ordering of fractions from smallest to largest		SA F
F18	Identification of smallest common multiples		SA F
F19	Addition of fractions with common denominators and sums less than one		CE SA F
F20	Subtraction of fractions with common denominators		CE SA F
F21	Addition of fractions which have different denominators and sums less than one		CE SA F R
F22	Subtraction of fractions which have different denominators		CE SA F R

MONEY & DECIMALS

Task #	Task (Skill) Description	Check Off Date	Error Analysis Circle type of Error
$1	Identification of a penny		
$2	Identifcation of a nickel		
$3	Identification of a dime		
$4	Identification of a cent sign		
$5	Identification of a coin as 1¢		SA F
$6	Identification of a coin as 5¢		SA F
$7	Identification of a coin as 10¢		SA F
$8	Identification of a coin as a quarter		
$9	Identification of a coin as 25¢		
$10	Indication of the value of a set of coins (Value under 50¢)		SA F
$11	Identification of a dollar sign		SA F
$12	Indication of the value of a specified number of pennies or nickels		SA F
$13	Addition of pennies, nickels and/or dimes		CE SA F
$14	Addition of money without regrouping		CE SA F
$15	Indication of the value of a set of coins (Value between 40¢ and $1.00)		CE SA F
$16	Computation of the amount of change which should be received when making a purchase with a quarter		CE SA F R
$17	Indication of the number of pennies, nickels, dimes and quarters in a dollar		SA F
$18	Multiplication of dollars and/or cents by a one-digit number		CE SA F R
$19	Computation of wage earned for a specified number of hours at a specified hourly rate		SA F
$20	Conversion of money written in words to numerals using a dollar sign and decimal point		SA F
$21	Addition of dollars and cents with regrouping		CE SA F R
$22	Indication of the value of a dollar bill and a mixture of coins		CE SA F
$23	Addition of dollars and cents when the problem is written in linear form		CE SA F R
$24	Computation of a story problem requiring summing of money earned		CE SA F R

CE=Computational Error
SA=Spacing or Alignment Problem
F =Number or Symbol Formation Problem
R =Regrouping Problem

Name_____ Birthdate_____ Grade_____ School_____ Teacher_____

MEASUREMENT (time, linear, volume, weight)

Task #	Task (Skill) Description	Check Off Date	Error Analysis Circle type of Error
TM1	Identification of tallest and shortest		
TM2	Identification of longest and shortest		
TM3	Telling time to the hour		SA F
TM4	Sequencing the days of the week		
TM5	Measurement to the nearest inch		SA F
TM6	Sequencing the months of the year		
TM7	Measurement to the nearest centimeter		SA F
TM8	Telling time to the half-hour		
TM9	Indication of the day of the week on which a given date in a month falls		SA F
TM10	Identification of words that are units of weight		
TM11	Telling time to the quarter hour		SA F
TM12	Indication of the number of seconds in a minute, months in a year, minutes in an hour, hours in a day, days in a week		SA F
TM13	Identification of the seasons of the year		
TM14	Indication of the number of degrees shown on a thermometer		SA F
TM15	Indication of the number of inches in a foot, feet in a yard, and centimeters in a meter		SA F
TM16	Measurement of lines to the nearest ¼ inch or nearest mm		SA F
TM17	Telling time to five minutes		SA F
TM18	Conversion of pints to cups, cups to quarts and pints to quarts		SA F
TM19	Addition of feet and inches with regrouping		CE SA F R
TM20	Conversion of gallons to quarts, half-gallons to pints and quarts to half-gallons		SA F
TM21	Conversion of inches to feet and inches (18 inches = 1 foot, 6 inches)		SA F
TM22	Indication of the fractional part of cup which is filled		SA F
TM23	Conversion of yards to inches, feet to yards and pounds to ounces		SA F
TM24	Conversion of meters to dm or cm, liters to ml, and kilograms to grams		SA F

CE=Computational Error
SA=Spacing or Alingment Problem
F =Number or Symbol Formation Problem
R =Regrouping Problem

PLACE VALUE

Task #	Task (Skill) Description	Check Off Date	Error Analysis Circle type of Error
PV1	Addition of one or more single sticks to a bundle of 10 sticks		CE SA F
PV2	Indication of the number of tens and ones in an existing set		CE SA F
PV3	Addition of one or more single sticks to 2 or 3 bundles of 10 sticks		CE SA F
PV4	Addition of one or more single sticks to more than 3 bundles of 10 sticks		CE SA F
PV5	Indication of the number of tens and ones in a set containing over 20 dots		CE SA F
PV6	Addition of bundles of ten sticks and single sticks, values to 50		CE SA F
PV7	Indication of the number shown on an abacus (values under 100)		CE SA F
PV8	Indication of the number of tens in 100, 200		SA F
PV9	Indication of the number shown on an abacus, values from 100 to 500		CE SA F
PV10	Addition, using an abacus with no regrouping		SA
PV11	Indication of the number of ones, tens and/or hundreds in specified numbers		SA F
PV12	Addition of bundles of ten sticks and single sticks, values from 51 to 99		CE SA F
PV13	Indication of the number represented by a specified number of ones, tens, and hundreds		SA F
PV14	Indication of the number shown on an abacus, values from 100 to 5000		CE SA F
PV15	Indication of the digit in multiple digit numbers which is of GREATEST value		SA
PV16	Makes marks on an abacus to represent a number that is given		CE SA
PV17	Transcribing number words to numerals, values from 500 to 9000		SA F
PV18	Transcribing number words to numerals, values from 10,000 to 900,000		SA F
PV19	Indication of the number represented by a specified number of ones, tens, hundreds and thousands - in no special order		SA F
PV20	Indication of the number of thousand(s) in (10) hundreds		SA F
PV21	Rounding numbers to the nearest thousand, hundred and ten		SA F

CRD ARITHMETIC TEST (ADDITION)

Experimental Edition

ⓒ 1979 by: Larry A. Faas

Directions: Write the answers.

Name_____Date_____

Grade____CA_____Time_____

CAP_____ Number Correct_____

A1

$$\begin{array}{r} 1 \\ +\ 1 \\ \hline \end{array}$$

A2

$$\begin{array}{r} 4 \\ +\ 3 \\ \hline \end{array}$$

A3

$$\begin{array}{r} 3 \\ +\ 0 \\ \hline \end{array}$$

A4

$$\begin{array}{r} 7 \\ +\ 6 \\ \hline \end{array}$$

A5

$$\begin{array}{r} 20 \\ +\ 3 \\ \hline \end{array}$$

A6

$$\begin{array}{r} 30 \\ +\ 20 \\ \hline \end{array}$$

A7

$$\begin{array}{r} 3 \\ 2 \\ +\ 4 \\ \hline \end{array}$$

A8

$$\begin{array}{r} 6 \\ 4 \\ +\ 5 \\ \hline \end{array}$$

A9

$$\begin{array}{r} 42 \\ +\ 7 \\ \hline \end{array}$$

A10

$$\begin{array}{r} 6 \\ +\ 33 \\ \hline \end{array}$$

A11

$$\begin{array}{r} 61 \\ +\ 24 \\ \hline \end{array}$$

A12

$$\begin{array}{r} 361 \\ +\ 234 \\ \hline \end{array}$$

A13

$$\begin{array}{r} 76 \\ +\ 7 \\ \hline \end{array}$$

CRD ARITHMETIC TEST (ADDITION)   PAGE 2

A14

```
    47
  + 38
  ────
```

A15

```
   437
 + 328
 ─────
```

A16

```
   564
 + 253
 ─────
```

A17

```
    87
  + 55
  ────
```

A18

```
   684
 + 565
 ─────
```

A19

```
  2685
 +1534
 ─────
```

A20

```
    32
    25
  + 11
  ────
```

A21

```
    34
    29
  + 15
  ────
```

A22

```
    65
    34
  + 53
  ────
```

A23

```
  2341
  6374
 + 3857
 ──────
```

A24

627 + 43 + 1536 + 314 =

CRD ARITHMETIC TEST (SUBTRACTION)

Experimental Edition

© by Larry A. Faas

Directions: Write the answers.

Name_____Date_____

Grade_____CA_____Time_____

CAP_____Number Correct_____

S1
```
    6
  - 3
  ___
```

S2
```
    9
  - 4
  ___
```

S3
```
    8
  - 0
  ___
```

S4

6 + [   ] = 8

S5
```
    2
  - 2
  ___
```

S6
```
    50
  - 30
  ____
```

S7
```
    10
  - 3
  ____
```

S8
```
    15
  - 8
  ____
```

S9
```
    49
  - 6
  ____
```

S10
```
    36
  - 24
  ____
```

S11
```
    95
  - 60
  ____
```

CRD ARITHMETIC TEST (SUBTRACTION)   PAGE 2

S12	S13	S14	S15
316 - 12	589 - 264	64 - 5	60 - 3

S16	S17	S18
65 - 37	50 - 13	436 - 8

S19	S20	S21
542 - 44	623 - 457	542 - 106

S22	S23	S24
500 - 296	6289 - 4195	4826 - 2869

CRD ARITHMETIC (MULTIPLICATION)

Experimental Edition

© 1979 by: Larry A. Faas

Directions: Write the answers.

Name_____Date_____

Grade_____CA_____Time_____

CAP_____Number Correct_____

M1]
$$\begin{array}{r} 4 \\ \times\, 1 \\ \hline \end{array}$$

M2]
$$\begin{array}{r} 7 \\ \times\, 2 \\ \hline \end{array}$$

M3]
$$\begin{array}{r} 8 \\ \times\, 3 \\ \hline \end{array}$$

M4]
$$\begin{array}{r} 2 \\ \times\, 0 \\ \hline \end{array}$$

M5]
$$\begin{array}{r} 7 \\ \times\, 4 \\ \hline \end{array}$$

M6]
$$\begin{array}{r} 7 \\ \times\, 5 \\ \hline \end{array}$$

M7]
$$\begin{array}{r} 9 \\ \times\, 6 \\ \hline \end{array}$$

M8]
$$32 \div \boxed{} = 9$$

M9]
$$\begin{array}{r} 8 \\ \times\, 7 \\ \hline \end{array}$$

M10]
$$\begin{array}{r} 9 \\ \times\, 8 \\ \hline \end{array}$$

M11]
$$\begin{array}{r} 7 \\ \times\, 9 \\ \hline \end{array}$$

M12]
$$\begin{array}{r} 21 \\ \times\, 3 \\ \hline \end{array}$$

CRD ARITHMETIC TEST (MULTIPLICATION)   PAGE 2

M13	M14	M15	M16
312 x 3	402 x 2	48 x 2	96 x 6

M17	M18	M19	M20
132 x 7	32 x 21	36 x 12	67 x 40

M21	M22	M23	M24
573 x 65	765 x 40	835 x 263	28,765 x 436 =

CRD ARITHMETIC TEST (DIVISION)
Experimental Edition
 © 1979 by: Larry A. Faas

Directions: Write the answers

Name_____Date _____

Grade____CA____Time_____

CAP_____Number Correct_____

D1
$$3\overline{)6}$$

D2
$$8\overline{)8}$$

D3
$$5\overline{)9}$$

D4
$$1\overline{)9}$$

D5
$$\boxed{}\ X\ 8\ =\ 48$$

D6
$$9\overline{)63}$$

D7
$$4\overline{)33}$$

D8
$$3\overline{)72}$$

D9
$$3\overline{)82}$$

D10
$$6\overline{)186}$$

D11
$$3\overline{)472}$$

D12
$$3\overline{)2876}$$

D13
$$7\overline{)0}$$

D14
$$20\overline{)60}$$

CRD ARITHMETIC TEST (DIVISION)   PAGE 2

D15	D16	D17
$22\overline{)44}$	$33\overline{)67}$	$23\overline{)943}$

D18	D19	D20
$56\overline{)749}$	$25\overline{)135}$	$65\overline{)790}$

D21	D22	D23
$30\overline{)493}$	$83\overline{)8675}$	$50\overline{)4500}$

D24	D25
$543\overline{)7689}$	$3976 \div 365 =$

CRD ARITHMETIC TEST (MONEY/DECIMALS)

Experimental Edition
© 1979 by: Larry A. Faas
Directions: Write the answers

Name_____ Date_____

Grade_____ CA_____ Time_____

CAP_____ Number Correct_____

$1 Make an X on the penny.

$2 Make an X on the nickel.

$3 Make an X on the dime.

$4 Circle the cent sign.

÷   ¢ $

$5

= _____ ¢

$6

= _____ ¢

$7

= _____ ¢

$8 Make an X on the quarter.

$9

= _____ ¢

$10 Add.

= _____ ¢

$11 Circle the dollar sign.

÷   ¢ $

$12

5 pennies = _____ ¢

2 nickels = _____ ¢

5 nickels = _____ ¢

10 pennies = _____ ¢

CRD ARITHMETIC TEST (MONEY/DECIMALS)

$13

3 dimes + 5 pennies = _____ ¢

2 nickels + 2 dimes = _____ ¢

$14

$1.05 $ .07
+ .10   + .42

$15

= _____ ¢

$16

How much change would you get back if you gave the storekeeper a quarter for a 15¢ candy bar?

_____

$17

_____quarters = $1.00

_____dimes   = $1.00

_____nickels = $1.00

_____pennies = $1.00

$18

$ .25 $1.40
X 3   X 5

$19

How much would you earn if you were paid $2.00 an hour for three hours?

_____

$20

Write one dollar and ten cents using numerals, a dollar sign and decimal point.

_____

$21

$6.67 $8.39
+ 1.75   + 3.83

$22

= $_____

$23

$5.02 + $10.37 + $ .53 + 25¢ =

_____

$24

If you earned 75¢ on Saturday, 50¢ on Monday and $1.00 on Wednesday, how much money would you have?

_____

CRD ARITHMETIC TEST (MEASUREMENT - TIME, LINEAR, VOLUME AND WEIGHT)

Experimental Edition

© 1979 by: Larry A. Faas

Directions: Write the answers.

Name_____Date_____

Grade_____CA_____Time_____

CAP_____Number Correct_____

TM1	Circle the TALLEST tree. Make an X on the SHORTEST tree.

TM2	Circle the LONGEST rope. Make an X on the SHORTEST rope.

TM3

____o'clock   ____o'clock   ____o'clock

TM4 Circle the day of the week that comes after Wednesday.

Monday	Thursday
Sunday	Tuesday

TM5 Measure the line to the nearest inch.

____inches

TM6 Fill in the months of the year in order.

January, February, _____,
April, _____, _____,
July, August, September, October,
_____, December

TM7 Measure the line to the nearest centimeter (cm).

____cm

TM8 Draw hands to show:

10:30   half past 4   6:30

TM9 What day of the week is May 8th?

May						
S	M	T	W	Th	F	S
		1	2	3	4	5
6	7	8	9	10	11	12
13	14	15	16	17	18	19
20	21	22	23	24	25	26
27	28	29	30	31		

_____

TM10 Circle the words which are units of weight.

quart	ounce	milligram
pound	liter	centimeter

TM11 Write the time that is shown on each clock.

____:____   ____:____   ____:____

TM12

____seconds = 1 minute
____months = 1 year
____minutes = 1 hour
____hours   = 1 day
____days   = 1 week

CRD ARITHMETIC TEST (TIME AND MEASUREMENT)   PAGE 2

TM13	Circle the seasons of the year.

SATURDAY   WINTER   SPRING

FALL   FRIDAY   SUMMER

TM14 What temperature is shown:

_____degrees

TM15

_____inches = 1 foot

_____feet = 1 yard

_____cm = 1 meter

TM16 Measure the lines to the nearest ½ in. or nearest mm.

_____ inches

_____ mm

TM17 Write the time that is shown on each clock.

___:___   ___:___   ___:___

TM18

1 pint = _____ cup/s

4 cups = _____ quart/s

4 pints = _____ quart/s

TM19 Add.

3 feet 7 inches   9 feet 8 inches
+5 feet 6 inches   +5 feet 7 inches

TM20

1 gallon = _____ quart/s

½ gallon = _____ pint/s

2 quarts = _____ half-gallon/s

TM21

36 inches = _____feet_____inches

30 inches = _____feet_____inches

49 inches = _____feet_____inches

TM22 How full is each cup?

_____   _____   _____

TM23

1 yard = _____ inches

6 feet = _____ yards

3 yards = _____ inches

2 pounds = _____ ounces

TM24

1 meter = _____ dm

3 meter = _____ cm

2 liter = _____ ml

1 kilogram = _____ g

CRD ARITHMETIC TEST (FRACTIONS)

Experimental Edition

© 1979 by: Larry A. Faas

Directions: Write the answers.

Name_____Date_____

Grade_____CA_____Time_____

CAP_____Number Correct_____

F1 | Shade one-half of this figure:

F2 | Draw a circle around one-half of the dots

F3 | Shade one-fourth of this figure:

F4 | Draw a circle around one-fourth of the dots

F5 | Draw a line which divides these dots into two equil sets

F6 | Shade one-third of this figure:

F7 | Draw a circle around one-third of the dots

F8 |

$\rightarrow \frac{1}{4}$ shaded

$\rightarrow$ — shaded

F9 | Shade 1/3 of this figure

$\leftarrow \frac{1}{3}$

F10 | What fraction of the objects is circled?

—

CRD ARITHMETIC TEST (FRACTIONS)   PAGE 2

F11	F12 Find the missing numerator
$\dfrac{3}{4}$ OF 16 = _____	$\dfrac{4}{5} = \dfrac{}{10}$

F13 Reduce to lowest terms	F14 Change to a mixed number (eg. $\dfrac{7}{6} = 1\dfrac{1}{6}$)
$\dfrac{4}{10} =$ _____	$\dfrac{5}{3} =$ _____

F15 Change to an improper fraction (eg. $2\dfrac{1}{4} = \dfrac{9}{4}$)	F16 Complete these number sentences with $>$, $<$, or $=$
$1\dfrac{3}{8} =$ _____	$\dfrac{5}{4} \square 1 \qquad \dfrac{3}{8} \square \dfrac{1}{16}$ $\dfrac{2}{4} \square \dfrac{6}{8} \qquad \dfrac{2}{3} \square \dfrac{4}{6}$

F17 Write these fractions in order beginning with the smallest	F18 Find the smallest common multiple
$\dfrac{1}{2}$, $\dfrac{1}{8}$, $\dfrac{1}{3}$, $\dfrac{1}{6}$, $\dfrac{1}{5}$	3 — 3, 6, 9, 12, (15) 15 — (15), 30, 45 $> \dfrac{6}{8} < \square$

F19	F20
$\dfrac{1}{4}$ $\dfrac{2}{4}$ $+\dfrac{4}{}$	$\dfrac{2}{3}$ $\dfrac{1}{3}$ $+\dfrac{3}{}$

F21 Add	F22 Subtract
$\dfrac{1}{3}$ $\dfrac{1}{2}$ $+\dfrac{2}{}$	$\dfrac{3}{4}$ $\dfrac{1}{3}$ $-\dfrac{3}{}$

CRD ARITHMETIC TEST (PLACE VALUE)

Experimental Edition

© 1979 by: Larry A. Faas

Directions: Write the sums.

Name_____Date_____

Grade_____CA_____Time_____

CAP_____Number Correct_____

PV1 Write the number.	PV2 Write the number of 10's and 1's in this set.

PV1 Write the number.

＋ = _____

PV2 Write the number of 10's and 1's in this set.

= _____tens_____ones

PV3 Write the number.

= _____

PV4 Write the number.

= _____

PV5 Write the number of 10's and 1's in this set.

= _____tens_____ones

PV6 Add

＋

= _____

PV7 Write the number shown.

= _____

PV8

_____tens = 100

_____tens = 200

PV9 Write the number shown.

= _____

PV10 Show 54 on the abacus.

PV11	hundreds	tens	ones
32 =			
17 =			
503 =			

PV12 Add.

＋

= _____

CRD ARITHMETIC TEST (PLACE VALUE

PV13	Write the number that contains 2 ones, 7 tens, and 3 hundreds. _____	PV14	Write the number shown. = _____
PV15	Circle the digit of greatest value in this number. 6666	PV16	Show 507 on the abacus.
PV17	Write the numeral. Seven hundred thirty nine	PV18	Write the numeral. Sixty-six thousand seven hundred one
PV19	Write the number that contains 8 tens, 4 hundreds, 3 ones and 5 thousands _____	PV20	 10 hundreds = _____ thousand(s)

| PV21 | Round 18674 to the nearest ten _____

Round 18674 to the nearest hundred_____

Round 18674 to the nearest thousand_____ |

Answer Key---CRD Arithmetic Test   © 1979 by: Larry A. Faas

Addition	Subtraction	Multiplication	Division	Money and Decimals	Time/Measurement	Fractions
A1-------2	S1------3	M1------------4	D1---------2	$1 ---___ ___ X	TM1-Score visually	F1 through F7-Score visually
A2-------7	S2------5	M2-----------14	D2----------1	$2--- X ___ ___	TM2-Score visually	F8---1/3
A3-------3	S3------8	M3----------24	D3------ 1 r4	$3---___ X ___	TM3------4---12---6	F9 Score visually
A4------13	S4------2	M4------------0	D4---------9	$4------------¢	TM4----Thursday	F10---2/5
A5------23	S5------0	M5----------28	D5---------6	$5------------1¢	TM5-------------2"	F11-------12
A6------50	S6-----20	M6----------35	D6---------7	$6------------5¢	TM6-Score visually	F12----8
A7-------9	S7------7	M7----------54	D7------8 r1	$7-----------10¢	TM7----------4cm	F13------2/5
A8------15	S8------7	M8------------4	D8-------24	$8---___ X ___	TM8-Score visually	F14--1 2/3
A9------49	S9-----43	M9----------56	D9-----27r 1	$9----------25¢	TM9----Tuesday	F15--------11/8
A10-----39	S10----12	M10---------72	D10------31	$10---------36¢	TM10-Pd,Oz, Millgm	F16-Score visually
A11-----85	S11----35	M11----------63	D11---í57 r1	$11-----------$	TM11-9:45-5:15-5 45	F17-Score visually
A12----595	S12---304	M12----------63	D12---958 r2	$12---5-10-25-10	TM12--60-12-50-24-7	F18----24
A13-----83	S13---325	M13--------936	D13--------0	$13-----35¢--30¢	TM13-Score visually	F19----3/4
A14-----85	S14----59	M14--------804	D14--------3	$14--$1.15--$.49	TM14----------40°	F20--1/3
A15----765	S15----57	M15----- -----96	D15-------2	$15---------43¢	TM15---12--3--100	F21-------5/6
A16----817	S16 ---28	M16--------576	D16-----2 r1	$16---------10¢	TM16--2 1/2"-55mm	F22--5/12
A17----142	S17----37	M17--------924	D17-------41	$17---4_10_20_100	TM17-9:55-1:10-4:35	
A18---1249	S18---428	M18--------672	D18---13 r21	$18--$.75--$7.00	TM18---2---1---3	
A19---4219	S19---498	M19--------432	D19----5 r10	$19-------$6.00	TM19-9'1"- 15"3"	
A20-----68	S20---166	M20 ------2,814	D20---12 r10	$20-------$1.10	TM20---4---4---1	
A21-----78	S21---436	M21 -----37,245	D21---16 r13	$21--$8.42-$12.22	TM21-3'-2'6"-4'1"	
A22----152	S22---204	M22 -----30,600	D22--104 r43	$22-------$1.42	TM22--1/2-1/3-3/4	
A23--12572	S23--2094	M23 ----219,605	D23------90	$23------$16.17	TM23-36-2-108-32	
A24---2520	S24--1957	M24---12,541,540	D24---14 r87	$24-------$2.25	TM24-10-300-2000-1000	
			D25---10 r326			

Note: All parts of multiple answer items should be correct before credit is given.

Place Value

PV1---------12
PV2--1 ten 2 ones
PV3-----33
PV4-----55
PV5-2 tens 4 ones
PV6-----38
PV7------43
PV8---10--20
PV9-----132
PV10-Score visually
PV11-Score visually
PV12----61
PV13----372
PV14--------2025
PV15---⑥666
PV16-Score visually
PV17---739
PV18---66,701
PV19----5483
PV20--- ----1
PV21-Score visually

SUMMARY

1. Arithmetic and mathematics problems may be due to an inability to revisualize numbers, an inability to form written numbers graphically, or an inability to remember instructions.

2. Chalfant and Scheffelin use the term *quantitative language disorders* to refer to learning problems in arithmetic and mathematics.

3. The *acalculic* student is unable to perform calculations while the *dyscalculic* student has a partial inability to perform calculations.

4. Mathematics is the abstract science of space and number that deals with space configuration and the interrelations and abstractions of number.

5. Arithmetic is a branch of mathematics that deals with real numbers and their computation.

6. Informal arithmetic diagnosis consists of having students perform computational activities related to specific arithmetic tasks that the student may not have mastered.

7. The *KeyMath Diagnostic Arithmetic Test* and the *Stanford Diagnostic Arithmetic Test* are two of the most frequently used standardized arithmetic tests.

8. The *CRD Arithmetic Test* is a criterion-referenced diagnostic arithmetic test based on a task analysis of eight areas of arithmetic.

REFERENCES

Bartel, N. R. 1975. In *Teaching Children with Learning and Behavior Problems.* Ed. D. D. Hammill and N. R. Bartel. Boston: Allyn and Bacon, pp. 61–88.

Beatty, L. S., R. Madden, and E. F. Gardner. 1966. *Stanford Diagnostic Arithmetic Test.* New York: Harcourt Brace Jovanovich.

Buswell, G. T., and L. Johns. 1926. *Diagnostic Studies in Arithmetic.* Chicago: University of Chicago Press.

Chalfant, J. C., and M. A. Scheffelin. 1969. *Central Processing Dysfunctions in Children: A Review of Research.* Washington, D.C.: U.S. Government Printing Office.

Connolly, A. J., W. Natchman, and E. M. Pritchett. 1971. *KeyMath Diagnostic Arithmetic Test.* Circle Pines, Minn.: American Guidance Service.

Dunn, L. M., and F. C. Markwardt. 1970. *Peabody Individual Achievement Test.* Circle Pines, Minn.: American Guidance Service.

Herman, K. 1959. *Reading Disability.* Springfield, Ill.: Charles C Thomas.

Jastak, J. F., S. W. Bijou, and S. R. Jastak. 1978. *Wide Range Achievement Test.* Wilmington, Del.: Jastak Associates.

Johnson, D. J., and H. R. Myklebust. 1967. *Learning Disabilities: Educational Principles and Practices.* New York: Grune and Stratton.

Kraner, R. E. 1976. *Kraner Preschool Math Inventory.* Austin, Tex.: Learning Concepts.

EIGHTEEN

Remediation of Arithmetic and Mathematics Problems

Mathematics is a symbolic language whose practical function is to express quantitative and spatial relationships (Brown, 1953). Students who have visual perceptual problems tend to have problems in arithmetic and mathematics because of their inability to visualize and group objects in space. Johnson and Myklebust (1967) suggest that there are inner, receptive, and expressive aspects of mathematical language just as there are in other forms of symbolic behavior. They indicate that children first assimilate and integrate nonverbal experiences, then learn to associate numerical symbols with the experience, and finally express ideas of quantity, space, and order by using the language of mathematics.

Instructional activities should be designed so that numbers and arithmetic facts are integrated with meaningful experiences. Without meaning, numbers and arithmetic facts do not make sense. Also, the student's conceptual development and readiness should be considered whenever a new concept is presented. Many adults disregard these factors, trying to impose mathematical concepts on a student before he or she is ready to learn them. As a result, these concepts tend to be learned as auditory patterns that the student does not associate with the related spatial symbols and concepts.

Johnson and Myklebust relate the concept of inner language to arithmetic by referring to it as *number sense*. An internalized quantitative sense that gradually evolves out of young children's meaningful experiences, number sense is a prerequisite for quantitative thinking about relationships of quantity, space, form, distance, order, and time.

REMEDIATION OF SPECIFIC PROBLEMS

Matching, Sorting, and Classifying

The first step in the development of number concepts is to learn to focus on and recognize a single object or shape (Lerner, 1976). Activities designed to develop those concepts are also helpful in building a basic quantitative vocabulary. Words such as *big* and *little, round* and *square, thick* and *thin, tall* and *short, long* and *short,* and so forth, can be taught while the student learns to match objects.

Many students who experience difficulty in learning to match, sort, and classify objects are having trouble visualizing the differences between the objects. It may be necessary to use many of the procedures that were originally designed for teaching blind students. By having students close their eyes or by placing the objects in a bag where they can be felt but not seen, teachers can help students develop their ability to feel the differences in the objects and to describe them verbally. Encourage students to think about how the objects would look if they could be seen. The ability to discriminate tactually between objects can then be linked to visualization of those same objects.

Each student-teacher interaction should be accompanied by carefully chosen descriptive verbalization and questioning. For example:

> *Teacher:* "Give me the ball."
> *Student:* (Hands the ball to the teacher.)
> *Teacher:* "What did you give me?"
> *Student:* "I gave you the ball."

Structure the initial matching activities so that only one attribute of the objects being matched varies at any one time. For example, objects being matched on the basis of *shape* should differ only on the basis of shape. Presenting objects that also differ in color and size tends to confuse the student. Practice in matching objects on the basis of size, shape, length, and so on can be followed by matching configurations of dots or numerals. Next, matching on the basis of single attributes can be followed by matching based on multiple attributes. For example, "Give me the red blocks." Or ask the student to arrange a series of objects according to increasing or decreasing size. When the student has mastered this activity, have the student match pictures or drawings of these objects. Finally, ask the student to select or sort out those objects from a group of objects that are not the same. Matching, sorting, and classifying objects also helps teach the student to notice and discriminate among visual stimuli.

Attribute blocks that vary in size, shape, color, and thickness are commonly found in catalogs containing materials for use in mathematics instruction, language development, and early childhood education. The geometric figures and form boards included in the Montessori materials can be used in teaching the visual-spatial skills needed to match geometric figures to specific positions in space. The use of the first two fingers in opposition to the thumb to grasp the handles on the Montessori materials also helps develop the finger muscles needed to hold a writing instrument.

Students who are unable to manipulate the objects to match, sort, or classify them can verbally direct the teacher to move each object to its correct location. In this way, students who are cerebral palsied or poorly coordinated can concentrate on learning concepts rather than on movement of the objects involved.

These activities all contribute to the development of the students' *number sense.* Emphasis on developing the ability to visualize relationships among the objects being matched, sorted, or classified helps prepare the students for the more complex visualization activities involved in associating numerical concepts with their corresponding numerals and for the activities involved in computation.

One-to-One Correspondence

One-to-one correspondence is an important prerequisite to meaningful counting and the development of addition and subtraction skills. Practice in pairing objects gives both student and teacher an opportunity to create combinations involving one-to-one correspondence. This practice should be accompanied by a verbal description of what is being done, for example, "One boy goes with one chair," or "One knife goes with one fork." Some of the activities that help develop one-to-one correspondence include the following:

Set the correct number of table settings for a given number of people (Bartel, 1975).

Give each student in the class one cookie (Lerner, 1976).

Arrange a row of pegs in a pegboard to match a prearranged row on a pegboard (Lerner, 1976).

Pass out one pencil, one piece of paper, or one book to each student in the class (Wallace and McLoughlin, 1975).

Make one tally mark for each time a bell is rung, a note is played on the piano, hands are clapped, or a beat is heard on a drum (Wallace and Kauffman, 1978).

Give examples of one-to-one correspondence, such as one person—one shirt; one dog—one bone; one teacher—one desk; one button—one buttonhole.

Visualizing Groups and Sets

Students who have visual-spatial problems often find it difficult to visualize clusters of objects or figures as groups or objects. This is particularly so when the student has *form constancy* and *spatial relations* problems. For example, the student with a form constancy problem usually fails to see any relationship between the four-dot pattern $\vdots\ \vdots$ and the $\cdot\!\cdot\!\cdot$ pattern created by rotating the original 90 degrees. The configuration of dots or objects being used to represent each quantity should be kept stable until the concepts involved are fully mastered.

The use of various configurations of dots to represent different activities should precede instruction in learning to count. Activities involving matching of cards containing various configurations can be used in teaching one-to-one correspondence. Other standard configurations can be used to teach the concepts of more and less. As soon as these concepts are understood, the student can be asked to practice organizing the cards into a series in which each card contains more dots than the one to its left.

Later on the student can be asked to point to the dots on the various cards while he or she learns to count. Cards containing dot patterns that correspond to the basic numbers are available commercially from a number of different distributors of educational materials.

The following activities and suggestions are helpful in teaching students to visualize clusters of objects as groups or sets:

Have the student match groups or sets of objects containing the same number of objects.
Use colored discs, domino games, playing cards, concrete objects, felt boards, magnetic boards, and workbooks containing sets that can be viewed and counted (Lerner, 1976).
Have the student arrange sets of different size into a sequence according to increasing or decreasing size.
Have the student draw a set containing more or less than the one shown on a card or drawn by the teacher.
Use the Cuisenaire (Davidson, 1969), Montessori, or Stern instructional programs.
Have the student sort cards containing various groupings of symbols into piles according to number.

Counting

Wallace and McLoughlin (1975) describe counting as a fundamental skill by which the child determines the number of elements in a set. Students who have trouble with counting fail in three concepts: one-to-one correspondence, associating the number with the spatial quantity of the set or group of objects it represents, and remembering the auditory series of numbers. One of the objectives of instruction in counting should be the integration of these three concepts into one process. For example, the student who hears the word *four* should be able to visualize a set or group of four objects. When a set or group of four objects is seen, the student should automatically think of the number four and if necessary state that there are four objects present. Students who have not fully integrated these concepts may not be able to look at objects and count aloud at the same time. Others may be unable to remember the auditory sequences of numbers that describe different visual sequences.

Activities that are helpful in teaching students to count include the following:

Use concrete objects such as pegs in a pegboard, beads on a string, bottle caps, poker chips, and attribute blocks that can be arranged in a series and touched as the corresponding numbers are said.

Organize animal crackers in a row and have the student count them. Give the student a cracker to eat for each correct response in the beginning and for each five or ten correct responses as proficiency increases.

Have students count drum beats while their eyes are closed (Johnson and Myklebust, 1967). Have them make a mark on paper for each sound they hear.

Use number lines. Start with large intervals marked off on the floor, playground, or balance beam. Gradually reduce the size of the intervals until the line can be placed on top of the chalkboard and on top of the student's desk.

Use motor activities such as clapping the hands together three times, jumping four times, or tapping on the table two times (Lerner, 1976).

Use counting boxes that require a motor response such as placing a peg in a hole as each number is said (Strauss and Lehtinen, 1947).

Have the student practice counting anything countable, for example, desks in the classroom, doorknobs, windows, sections in the chalkboard, doors in the corridor, light fixtures in the classroom, and so forth.

Assign dot-to-dot puzzles that require the student to connect numbered dots to complete a picture (Wallace and Kauffman, 1978).

Also effective are the instructional materials outlined by Davidson (1969). Montessori (1964, 1965a, 1965b), and Stern and Stern (1971).

The student should master the use of cardinal numbers (1, 2, 3, 4, and so on) before being introduced to ordinal numbers (first, second, third, and so on). Many of the above activities can be repeated during instruction in the use of ordinal numbers.

Quantitative Language Vocabulary

Students often experience difficulty in arithmetic and mathematics because they lack an adequate quantitative language vocabulary. This tends to occur because the student's teacher incorrectly assumes that he or she has already mastered the basic vocabulary. Many of these concepts are found in Boehm (1970) and Kraner (1976). The quantitative concepts covered by Boehm include:

1. some, not many	6. second	11. not first	16. left
2. few	7. several	12. not last	17. pair
3. widest	8. almost	13. medium-sized	18. equal
4. most	9. half	14. zero	19. third
5. whole	10. as many	15. every	20. least

The quantitative concepts covered by Kraner include:

1. all	18. after	36. nearest	54. short
2. empty	19. next to	37. farthest	55. largest
3. each	20. ahead of	38. right	56. tallest
4. same object	21. before	39. left	57. same size
5. same number	22. beginning	40. forward	58. triangle
of objects	23. in	41. backward	59. circle
6. more than	24. out	42. up	60. smallest
7. less than	25. top	43. down	61. same shape
8. one more	26. together	44. toward	62. square
9. smallest	27. apart	45. around	63. rectangle
10. largest	28. bottom	46. away from	64. shortest
11. first	29. under	47. to the right	65. different shape
12. behind	30. over	48. to the left	66. different size
13. in front of	31. between	49. big	67. straight line
14. in back of	32. inside	50. little	68. one-half
15. middle	33. outside	51. longest	69. closed curve
16. end	34. highest	52. all	
17. last	35. lowest	53. tall	

These concepts should be taught as part of meaningful instructional activities. Cawley et al. (1976) suggest that a "do, say, and see" procedure should be used during arithmetic instruction. The student manipulates objects, describes what he or she is doing, and then visualizes the process after the objects have been removed.

Visual Recognition of Numbers and Number Words

Students who experience difficulty in learning to recognize written numbers and number words can be assisted by the following activities and procedures:

matching the written number with a corresponding set of objects
tracing numbers or number words that have been written on felt or cardboard, formed in clay, or cut out of sandpaper
using numbers in a concentration game to help the student develop the ability to remember the visual image of the written number or number word
reassembling cut-up numbers or number words

Writing Numbers and Number Words

Additional suggestions for use in teaching students to write numbers are found in Chapter 16 as part of the discussion of instruction in handwriting.

Associating Number Names with Written Numerals and Number Words

Some students are able to say the correct number name in response to a group or set of objects they see but are unable to identify the written numeral or number word that describes this same quantity. This problem is essentially a reading problem, which suggests that the student did not learn to associate the written numbers or number words with their corresponding number names and spatial values in the final stages of learning to count.

Activities that can help students learn these relationships include practice in selecting cards containing written numbers or number words that correspond to dictated number words, matching cards containing written numbers with their corresponding number words, and writing numbers and number words as they are dictated.

Addition, Subtraction, Multiplication, and Division

Computational skills grow out of the student's mastery of one-to-one correspondence, counting, and perception of groups or sets of objects. Many students' errors can be traced to difficulties with one of these foundation skills. The types of computational errors observed most frequently are the following (Otto and Smith, 1980):

Addition	*Subtraction*
errors in combinations	combinations
counting	counting
carrying	regrouping
faulty procedures	faulty procedures

Division	*Multiplication*
combinations	combinations
counting	counting
remainder difficulties	carrying
faulty procedures	faulty procedures

Manipulative, structural materials such as those developed by Cuisenaire (Davidson, 1969), Stern and Stern, (1971), and Montessori (1964, 1965a, 1965b) should be used to introduce and teach these fundamental operations. The use of these materials enables the student to observe the manipulation of rods, blocks, and groups of beads to solve problems. Only after a student has mastered an operation using these concrete manipulative materials should the abstract representation of the spatial values involved in the use of numerals be introduced. Many who are having difficulty with computation do not fully understand the manipulation of objects in space that basic computations represent.

Once an operation is fully understood, the teacher can use drill to bring the student's mastery of it to the automatic response level. If drill is used before this stage, memorized responses tend to be substituted for understanding. As soon as the student memorizes a response to a number combination, it is very hard to convince him or her of the need to go back and work out the answer using exploratory procedures with manipulative materials.

Teachers should find the following suggestions and activities helpful with students who are having trouble with the fundamental operations involved in computation:

Make slash marks representing the value of the numbers before attempting to add or subtract.

Use concrete objects such as paper clips, poker chips, or attribute blocks that can be grouped to represent the numbers being added or subtracted.

Make drill sheets for each of the *CRD Arithmetic* objectives for use after the student understands the operations required to solve the problems.

Permit the student to count on his or her fingers.

Use auditory clues, such as clapping out addition and subtraction combinations (Wallace and Kauffman, 1978).

Use consistent language to refer to an operation. Be sure the student understands the words that are used.

Use tape recorders, number lines, and other auxiliary aids to reinforce the student's understanding of concepts and skills.

Use problems that require the student to fill in the process signs needed to complete the number sentence (for example, $4 \boxed{} 2 = 6$; or $9 \boxed{} 3 = 3$).

Spatial Organization of Numbers/Place Value

Failure to organize numbers into clearly identifiable columns on a page makes it difficult to determine the place value of each digit. Students with this difficulty may have spatial relationship problems, or they may have handwriting problems that command their attention at the expense of everything else. One of the easiest ways to deal with this problem is to rotate the student's paper 90 degrees so that the lines run vertically and can be used as guides for organizing the numbers into columns as they are written. This adjustment makes it possible to clearly identify the columns while providing instruction in the techniques of regrouping and borrowing.

The structural instructional approaches developed by Cuisenaire (Davidson, 1969), Montessori (1964, 1965a, 1965b), and Stern and Stern (1971) are particularly well suited for teaching place value. Each approach uses manipulative materials that give the student an observable, concrete accumulation of items. For example, the student has ten blocks or beads to use during the addition of the one's column; these ten tangible items can then be exchanged (or regrouped) for one block or set of beads that has a value of ten when it is necessary to regroup from the one's column to the ten's column. These manipulative materials can also be used to teach the students to borrow. Again, mastery of these concepts while using concrete manipulative materials should be followed, not preceded, by the use of columns of numerals to represent place values during computational activities.

Fractions

Students who are having problems with fractions usually do not understand how the parts of an object contribute to making up the whole object. Geometric shapes have traditionally been used to introduce fractional numbers. Manipulative materials for use in teaching fractions are found in most catalogs containing materials for use in mathematics education, early childhood education, and special education. The Cuisenaire (Davidson, 1969), Montessori (1964, 1965a, 1965b), and Stern and Stern (1971) approaches are helpful in this area, as well as the following activities, suggestions, and procedures:

Have students cut shapes out of flannel, tag board, or paper plates. Start with halves, follow with quarters, and then eighths (Wallace and Kauffman, 1978).

Have students put fractional parts together to make whole figures while verbally describing each step.

Cut strips of paper into fractional parts and have students reassemble the parts on equivalent strips that haven't been cut.

Cut familiar pictures into halves, quarters, and eighths and have students put them back together (Wallace and Kauffman, 1978).

Use measuring cups to experiment and prove fractional values (for example, have student count the number of ¼-cup measures needed to fill one cup).

Help the students read fractions by telling them that the top number tells the number of parts present while the bottom number indicates the total number of parts that exist (Lerner, 1976).

Conservation of Properties

Students who have problems grasping the principle of conservation of properties frequently experience difficulty learning to count, add, and subtract. Piaget (1953) described the principle of conservation of properties as the ability to change the shape, color, or organization of the items in a group without changing the number of items involved. In other words, the student can rotate, invert, reverse, or scramble the organization of a group of objects without having any effect on the number of objects. Bartel (1975) indicates that understanding the principle of conservation of properties gives the student the flexibility and reversibility needed to grasp the relationship between addition and subtraction, for example, $5 + 4 = 9$ and $9 - 4 = 5$. It tells the student that the same total number of items is involved in both problems. This principle can be readily demonstrated with the Cuisenaire (Davidson, 1969) and Stern and Stern (1971) materials. The experience in manipulating observable objects enables the student to prove the relationship between addition and subtraction.

Telling Time

Students who experience difficulty telling time may not understand the relationship between the time sequence and the clock's number system (Peterson, 1973); they may be reversing the face of the clock; or they may be unable to read the numbers, to differentiate the big hand from the little hand, or to count the time from one hour to the next.

Teachers should use consistent terminology when referring to time (for example, a quarter after five or five-fifteen but not both). Instruction usually starts with telling time to the nearest hour. It then moves on to telling time to the nearest half-hour, quarter hour, five minutes before and after the hour, minutes, and seconds. Calendar time usually starts with years and moves on to months, weeks, days, hours, and so on. The inability to remember the sequence of the months in a year or days in a week can sometimes be remedied by taping the calendars into a long series of pages that can be folded and opened accordian style. This arrangement helps the student gain perspective of the linear nature of passage through time and facilitates memory of the correct sequence.

When teaching students how to tell time, teachers should emphasize the practical uses of these skills. Ask the student questions about when it will be time to have lunch, recess, or go home from school. Time every conceivable event in the classroom—the time needed to read a story, finish one's arithmetic problems, erase the chalkboard, straighten the chairs, and so on.

Mastery of the use of a clock to tell time can be followed by practice in writing the numerals that express the various times. The conversion of minutes to hours or hours to minutes can be taught after the more basic concepts have been mastered.

Money

Students who have difficulty counting money may be confusing the names of coins, misnaming the coins, or failing to discriminate visually and tactually between coins of different sizes. They may be unable to make change, not recognizing that ten pennies, two nickels, and one dime all represent the same monetary value.

Activities and procedures that are often helpful in teaching students to effectively handle money include the following:

Use real money when it is available.

Use rubber stamps of the various coins when preparing special problems for the student.

Give the student an imaginary $100 and the Christmas Catalog to use in preparing a Christmas wish list.

Set up a classroom store where the student can practice using money to make purchases.

Have the student make out a grocery list showing the price of each item and the total cost.

Have the student sell lunch tickets to his or her classmates.

It is sometimes necessary to give a dollar bill to the student who has serious visual and tactual discrimination problems. This enables the student to ride the bus or buy a school lunch without counting out change. Each day the change the student returns home with can be exchanged for another bill. This survival technique should be reserved for use by parents in cases of extreme disability.

Measurement (Length, Volume, and Weight)

Difficulties with linear measurement and the measurement of volume usually involve problems with spatial perception. Instruction in these areas should start with the actual measurement of gross differences such as long and short, full and empty, and move on to more precise units of measurement such as yards, feet and inches, and half-full, one-fourth full, gallons, quarts, and so forth. Each measurement should be accompanied by a verbal description of the units involved. Use of consistent terminology is a must.

Teach the measurement of weight by actually weighing different objects in the classroom. You might begin these activities by having the student hold objects of the same size that differ widely in weight. Materials of this type are included in the Montessori (1964, 1965a, 1965b) materials. Inexpensive scales that have the capacity to weigh ounces and a few pounds are usually sufficient for teaching the basic concepts of weight. Bathroom scales can be used to make larger comparisons, such as those involved in weighing the student.

You can combine instruction in fractions and volume by using measuring cups, spoons, and containers used for cooking and canning. Encourage the student to perform the actual measurements, verbally describe them, and then record them in writing. The final goal of instruction should be the full integration and use of these three aspects of measurement. Avoid introducing metric measurements and traditional American measurements at the same time, as this is apt to confuse the student. It is usually best to teach one system to the point of mastery before introducing the other one.

Map and Graph Reading

Those who have spatial relationship, left-right discrimination, and directionality problems frequently experience difficulty reading maps. They forget that north is usually represented by the top of a map, do not understand the distances between the various points on a map, fail to associate the map with personal experience or needs, do not understand the quantitative relationships represented by the axes on a graph, and cannot project the quantitative values listed along the axes of a graph to the point plotted.

Activities and procedures that students may find helpful in learning map reading include the following:

drawing a map of the street where they live, using squares for each neighbor's house
drawing a map showing the route from their home to school
designating the directions on each map
drawing a map of the school building
locating the street where they live and the location of the school on a map of the city
locating the city where they live on a county or state map
locating neighboring cities near their hometown on a county or state map
finding the city or state where their grandparents or other relatives live on a state or national map
reading the legend on the map that indicates distances, capital cities, parks, churches, schools, and so forth

Graph reading is usually easiest to understand when instruction begins with the actual construction of a bar graph. A column of blocks can be placed on a paper so that it rests on the base line of the graph. The student then draws around the blocks, creating the bar. Numbers are written along the vertical line to the left of the column of blocks. Lines can be drawn around additional columns of blocks as they are placed on the paper. The student can be taught to project the value along the left axis to each new column, and the blocks can be counted to verify the accuracy of this projection. This procedure can be repeated to construct other graphs and prove the quantities represented. The construction of each graph should be accompanied by a verbal description of the activities and concepts involved.

MATHEMATICS AND ARITHMETIC PROGRAMS AND MATERIALS

A large variety of commercially published programs and materials are available for use in teaching mathematical reasoning and arithmetic computation. Many fine materials and programs have also been developed by local school personnel and individual teachers. The following programs and materials are representative of those that are available commercially.

The Montessori Materials

The manipulative materials developed by Italian physician Maria Montessori were among the first available for use in teaching mathematical concepts and arithmetic computational skills. Sets of solid inserts, sets of solids in graduated sizes, cubes, prisms, rods, tablets of different weights, sticks for counting, and strings of beads on wires that represent the different numbers are all used at various points during instruction. The Montessori materials are designed so that they are self-correcting, so the students know immediately if their responses are correct or incorrect. They are divided into three parts: motor education, sensory education, and language (Montessori, 1964, 1965a, and 1965b.).

Structural Arithmetic

Structural Arithmetic is an approach to teaching mathematics developed by Catherine Stern that employs manipulative devices to give students an opportunity to discover arithmetic facts and to learn how to record their findings by writing equations. Stern and Stern (1971) indicate that *Structural Arithmetic* achieves its objectives through the following approaches: (1) It uses concrete materials that allow the student to discover number facts for himself; (2) It follows a carefully arranged sequence of experiments whereby the student advances step by step from simple number concepts to the mastery of arithmetic computation and problem solving; and (3) It presents functional illustrations in workbooks that help the student reconstruct any forgotten number fact. The materials consist of four kits, appropriate for use in kindergarten and grades 1, 2, and 3. Each kit contains a teacher's manual, student workbooks, and manipulative materials. The instructional activities for each level include carefully sequenced demonstrations, experiments, and games designed to help students develop insights that will make it possible for them to use manipulative materials to represent these quantitative concepts. The eventual goal of *Structural Arithmetic* is for students to visualize the quantities represented by these groups of blocks in their minds.

Cuisenaire Rods

The Cuisenaire rods are instructional aids for use in teaching mathematical concepts. The rods consist of 291 wood blocks that vary in length and color. Each block is one centimeter square and from one to ten centimeters long. The quantitative value of the white cube is 1. Red rods represent 2, 4, and 8. The blue-green rods represent 3, 6, and 9, the black rod represents 7, and the yellow rod 5 and 10.

The use of the rods closely resembles Stern's use of blocks of varying length and Montessori's use of varying numbers of beads strung on a wire. Teachers are instructed to ask questions that encourage the student to observe and discover the relationships involved in the basic structure of mathematics; the manipulative skills needed to handle the rods operate as a vehicle leading to discovery of these relationships. Davidson (1969) indicates that, "The rods are useful in the teaching of arithmetic at all grade levels, in conjunction with any textbook and within the framework of any mathematics curriculum" (p. 7).

DISTAR Arithmetic

The *DISTAR* arithmetic kits I, II, and III (Engelmann and Carnine, 1970, 1975, 1976) are designed to provide direct instruction to small groups of students. Each kit contains a carefully sequenced series of structured instructional activities that are presented by the teacher to the student in a highly prescriptive fashion. The objectives of and criteria for each lesson are stated explicitly. The program indicates specifically what the teacher should say and do, and what the student is required to say and do.

Project MATH

Project MATH (Cawley et al., 1976) is a mathematics program for students who have special education needs for instruction on content ranging from preschool through grade 6. According to the authors, this approach to mathematics instruction gives a balanced emphasis to the development of skills, concepts, and social growth. They state that *Project MATH* is designed to:

1. provide the teacher with a number of instructional options, so that handicaps to learning might be circumvented;
2. enhance the learner's chances of success in a mathematics program;

3. provide the learner with a substantial mathematics curriculum designed to facilitate his use of mathematics in daily life;
4. maximize the instructor's opportunity for individualizing instruction;
5. provide a framework in which mathematics content can be used as a tool for enhancing the development of the total child—socially and emotionally, as well as academically;
6. provide a supplement to the regular mathematics program for those not-so-handicapped learners for whom such a supplement may be desirable. (p. 1)

Each of the four levels in the program covers an approximate grade and age range. Level I covers content for prekindergarten through grade 1 (ages 4 to 6). Level II presents mathematical content usually covered in first and second grades by students with mental ages of about 6 to 8. Level III is for the 8- to 10-year olds who are functioning between the middle of second grade and fourth grade. Level IV concentrates on content usually covered in grades 4–6. The guides are coded to indicate the type of inputs (constructing, presenting, stating, and graphically symbolizing) and outputs (constructing, identifying, stating, and graphically symbolizing) involved in each activity (Cawley et al., 1976).

SUMMARY

1. Mathematics is a symbolic language that expresses quantitative and spatial relationships.
2. Johnson and Myklebust report that there are receptive, inner, and expressive aspects of mathematical language just as there are in other forms of symbolic behavior.
3. The sequence of mathematical concept development includes (1) assimilation and integration of nonverbal experience, (2) learning to associate numerical symbols with experience, and (3) expression of ideas of quantity, space, and order.
4. Number sense is a prerequisite for quantitative thinking about relationships of quantity, space, form, distance, order, and time.
5. One-to-one correspondence is an important prerequisite to meaningful counting and development of addition and subtraction skills.
6. Mastery of the basic quantitative language vocabulary (for example, many, few, all) is an important early step in the development of proficiency in arithmetic and mathematics.
7. Piaget's principle of conservation of properties is described as the ability to change the shape, color, or organization of items in a group without changing the number of items involved.

8. The Montessori materials, Stern's *Structural Arithmetic,* and the Cuisenaire rods all contain manipulative materials for use in teaching arithmetic and mathematics concepts.
9. *DISTAR Arithmetic* and *Project MATH* are commercially published instructional kits used in teaching arithmetic and mathematics.

REFERENCES

Bartel, N. R. 1975."Problems in Arithmetic Achievement." In *Teaching Children with Learning and Behavior Problems.* Ed. D. D. Hammill and N. R. Bartel. Boston: Allyn and Bacon, pp. 61–88.

Boehm, A. E. 1970. *Boehm Test of Basic Concepts.* New York: The Psychological Corporation.

Brown, C. 1953. *The Teaching of Secondary Mathematics.* New York: Harper and Brothers.

Cawley, J. F. et al. 1976. *Project MATH, Level I.* Tulsa, Okla.: Educational Progress, a division of the Educational Development Corporation.

Davidson, J. 1969. *Using the Cuisenaire Rods.* New Rochelle, N. J.: Cuisenaire of America.

Engelmann, S., and D. Carnine. 1970, 1975, 1976. *DISTAR:* Arithmetic I, II, and III. Chicago: Science Research Associates.

Johnson, D. J., and H. R. Myklebust. 1967. *Learning Disabilities: Educational Principles and Practices.* New York: Grune and Stratton.

Kraner, R. E. 1976. *Kraner Preschool Math Inventory.* Austin, Tex.: Learning Concepts, Inc.

Lerner, J. W. 1976. *Children with Learning Disabilities.* 2nd ed. Boston: Houghton Mifflin Company.

Montessori, M. 1964. *The Montessori Method.* New York: Schocken.

Montessori, M. 1965a. *Dr. Montessori's Own Handbook.* New York: Schocken.

Montessori, M. 1965b. *The Montessori Elementary Material.* Cambridge, Mass.: Robert Bentley, Inc.

Otto, W., and R. Smith. 1980. *Corrective and Remedial Teaching.* 3rd ed. Boston: Houghton Mifflin Company.

Peterson, D. L. 1973. *Functional Mathematics for the Mentally Retarded.* Columbus, Ohio: Charles E. Merrill.

Piaget, J. 1953. "How Children Learn Mathematical Concepts." *Scientific American* 189 (November), 74–79.

Stern, C., and M. B. Stern. 1971. *Children Discover Arithmetic: An Introduction to Structural Arithmetic.* Revised and Enlarged Edition. New York: Harper & Row.

Strauss, A. A., and L. Lehtinen. 1947. *Psychopathology and Education of the Brain-Injured Child.* Vol. 1. New York: Grune and Stratton.

Wallace, G., and J. M. Kauffman. 1978. *Teaching Children with Learning Problems.* 2nd ed. Columbus, Ohio: Charles E. Merrill.

Wallace, G., and J. A. McLoughlin. 1975. *Learning Disabilities: Concepts and Characteristics.* Columbus, Ohio: Charles E. Merrill.

PART SIX

Other Considerations

NINETEEN

Working with Parents of Children with Learning Problems

Effective communication with parents of children who have learning and behavioral problems is a vital component in helping these children. Teachers and other professionals who are able to involve their students' parents in the planning and delivery of remedial services are usually more effective than those who ignore parents. Each major section of this chapter deals with one aspect of working with parents of children who have learning problems.

CONDUCTING PARENT-TEACHER CONFERENCES *

Parent-teacher conferences are an important part of working with students who have learning and behavioral problems. The following suggestions are offered for review by teachers who are preparing to conduct a parent-teacher conference.

Preparing for Parent-Teacher Conferences

Before each parent-teacher conference teachers should do the following:

1. Plan carefully.
2. Become familiar with all available information on the parents and their child.

*Adapted from L. Kay Hartwell. *The Art of Conducting Parent-Teacher Conferences.* Unpublished class material, Department of Special Education, Arizona State University, Tempe, Arizona.

3. Arrange the items in the student's conference folder in chronological order by date.

4. Make notes regarding things to discuss with the parents. These might be organized into positive areas in the student's performance, areas showing improvement, areas that need improvement, specific questions, and possible ways of helping the student.

5. Schedule conferences so that there will be a ten-minute break after each conference for making notes about the conference just completed and reviewing materials related to the next conference.

6. Schedule a conference that will be an easy, pleasant experience to start and end each day.

7. Leave a complete schedule of your conferences with the school secretary the day before they are scheduled so that they can be canceled if you are absent.

8. Prepare or secure a neat sign for your door reading CONFERENCE IN SESSION. PLEASE DO NOT DISTURB. Interruptions are often disturbing to parents and break the flow of thought.

9. If parents have more than one child in school, schedule their conferences in succession so the parents do not have to make repeated trips to school.

During the Conference

During parent-teacher conferences, teachers should do the following:

1. Greet the parents and help them feel at ease. Relax and be a good host.

2. Encourage the student's parents to do most of the talking early in the conference and listen carefully to what they say.

3. Attempt to learn how the parents feel about their child before bringing up the child's problem.

4. Express sincere interest in receiving the parents' assistance and suggestions.

5. Accept what the parents say without showing surprise or disapproval.

6. Begin and end the conference with a positive comment about the child.

7. Arrange for a few minutes of casual conversation or devote a few minutes to showing the parents the student's classroom and the materials being used. Express your appreciation of their willingness to come to visit with you. This often helps you develop a rapport with the parents before directly approaching the reason for the conference.

8. Avoid letting your desk serve as a barrier between you and the parents. A grouping of three or four chairs in a circle or around a small table creates a more comfortable environment.

9. Restrict note taking to a minimum, using key words or phrases that will

enable you to reconstruct the conference later. Make specific notes of information that will appear in the student's IEP.

10. Accept criticism of yourself and your colleagues gracefully. Ask for suggestions while avoiding arguments.

11. Try to picture how you would react if you were the parent before making comments and suggestions. Be tactful while pursuing the course you feel is desirable for the student.

12. Avoid being critical of the student while you are evaluating his or her progress.

13. Present several possible alternative solutions to the student's problems. Such a choice is usually easier for parents to accept than a single "sure cure" that may be interpreted as something you are trying to impose upon them. Make sure parents feel they have a role in planning and carrying out their child's remedial program.

14. Accept plans of action suggested by parents and use them whenever possible. There should be no doubt as to the proper roles of the teacher and parents in conducting the business of the classroom.

15. Concentrate on a few things on which you and the parent can work together to help the child.

16. Move on to another topic when the parent appears reluctant to talk about the topic being discussed.

17. Refrain from agreeing with parents if they are critical of their child's previous teachers or schools.

18. Avoid commenting about other students and comparing the student who is having difficulty with his or her brothers and sisters.

19. Do not suggest activities that are clearly the school's responsibility as home activities.

20. Refer students who have serious psychological problems to a counselor or psychologist. Parent-teacher conferences should not be expected to handle these problems.

21. Show parents samples of the student's work, including samples of the poorest and best work. Emphasize how the student's performance has improved or changed.

22. Use professional jargon and terminology only when other terms are not available.

23. Avoid continuing a conference beyond the point where something is being accomplished. You can indicate that the conference is over by tactfully standing up and escorting the parent to the door. End each conference with an indication of your willingness to confer with the parents again either in person or on the telephone.

24. End each conference with a positive feeling. Summarize the major information discussed. Agree on the course of action and the next steps to be taken.

After the Conference

Immediately following each parent-teacher conference, teachers should do the following:

1. Review the main points mentioned by the child's parents.
2. Write down notes summarizing the conference.
3. Evaluate the conference to determine if the objectives for the conference were met and to determine how future conferences might be handled more effectively.
4. Request whatever help or special services may be needed.
5. Begin making whatever changes in the student's program were agreed on during the conference.

Other Guidelines

Other factors to remember while conducting parent-teacher conferences are as follows:

1. The people you are visiting with often tend to act as you act. If you talk loudly they will probably speak loudly. If you speak softly they are much more likely to respond in a soft voice. An enthusiastic approach is much more likely to generate an enthusiastic response than an apathetic approach.
2. First impressions are important. If your greeting to the parents is receptive and friendly they will probably view you as that type of person. If you want the conversation to be informal and friendly be sure it starts out that way.
3. Think and talk positively. Don't ask questions that call for "no" responses if you want "yes" answers.
4. Listen in a sympathetic, understanding way. Look at the parent who is doing the talking. Act interested in what is being said by leaning slightly toward the speaker, asking questions, asking the speaker to tell you more, and repeating some of what the speaker has said.
5. No one ever wins an argument. Let the parents state their case fully before you start to present yours. Be sure that you have considered their point of view fully before responding to their questions. Respond confidently and in objective, impersonal terms.
6. Be free with sincere praise. Think of several nice things that can be truthfully said about the student before going into the conference.
7. Be consistent. What you tell parents in a conference should agree with what you write on the student's report card.

Parent-teacher conferences with parents who are overly timid, worried, or critical require special techniques and understanding. The following adjustments are often helpful in these situations.

Timid parents usually have a very high regard for teachers. As a result, they tend to sit quietly before the teacher waiting to be told what to do. They require a friendly, supportive approach. Sincere compliments often help reassure them that they are adequate parents. Ask them questions that can't be answered with a "yes" or "no."

Worried parents are often concerned about more than just their child. They tend to assume, regardless of what you say, that their child must be in some kind of trouble. Recognize and respect their expression of concern, and assure them that few problems in child adjustment are insolvable. Describe the degree of their child's difficulty clearly, and develop a joint plan of attack on the child's problems. This clarity and support usually relieves the parents' minds.

Critical parents often come to parent-teacher conferences armed with "expert" opinions on how to teach their child. They sincerely believe that phonics, a return to the basics, or some other specific approach is the only way to solve their child's problem. Try to inform these parents without arguing, using both facts and an appeal to the emotions. Talk about only those areas in which you are well equipped. At times you may have to admit you don't have all the answers.

PARENTAL ADJUSTMENT TO LEARNING PROBLEMS

Kronick (1973) saw the adjustment of parents who have children with learning problems as a process involving a series of stages. Each stage is characterized by its own level of understanding, acceptance, hope, and type of response. An understanding of these stages, which are also observed in parents of the handicapped, is helpful to those who are involved in parent counseling and who work with parent groups. The stages are as follows:

Stage 1.   shock
Stage 2.   denial
Stage 3.   isolation and alienation
Stage 4.   "Why did it have to happen to me?"
Stage 5.   anger, envy, and resentment
Stage 6.   guilt
Stage 7.   searching for a magic cure
Stage 8.   depression and mourning
Stage 9.   acceptance
Stage 10. realistic anticipation and planning for the future

As Kronick points out, these stages are essentially the same as those described by Kübler-Ross (1969) in her book on death and dying. Indeed, many parents seem to view the discovery that their child is experiencing significant difficulty in learning as an indication that this child's chances for success and recognition are dead or dying. Awareness and sensitivity regarding the parents' level of adjustment and acceptance of their child's learning problems is a valuable aide in working effectively with parents and in understanding their attempts to provide assistance.

Stage 1. Shock

It is natural for parents to dream and project regarding what they would like their children to become, and these dreams almost always involve the academic success needed to prepare for a trade or profession. Realization that these hopes and dreams for one's child are not going to be fulfilled, therefore, is almost always accompanied by *shock*. The dreams of success are quickly replaced by thoughts of failure, loss of status, and a need to depend on society. These new projections usually place the child's eventual outcome at a much lower level than they had been expecting.

Stage 2. Denial

Denial is described as one of the ways we cope with profound shock. Kübler-Ross (1969) suggests that "Denial functions as a buffer after unexpected shocking news, allows the patient to collect himself and, with time, mobilize other, less radical defenses" (p. 39). Kronick (1973) indicates that it is important for professionals to appreciate that parents must spend some time in the denial stage and the stages that follow before they are ready to accept and realistically deal with their child's problems.

At first this denial may take the form of an outright rejection of the possibility that the child is having a problem. This may be followed by attempts to "explain the problem away" with statements that suggest "it's just a stage" the child is going through. The denial may also take the form of insistence that the child is not as severely disabled as he or she is reported to be. For example, parents may insist that their mentally retarded child is actually learning disabled or that their severely retarded child is actually mildly retarded. This form of denial is frequently accompanied by travel from professional to professional or clinic to clinic in search of someone who will support their belief. Sometimes parental denial of their children's problems is encouraged by professionals who themselves find it necessary to deny the existence of all but the most severe learning problems.

The child's parents do not usually move through the denial stage and the stages that follow at the same rate. Mothers tend to verbalize their concerns, which enables them to talk their child's problem through much more quickly than the fathers, who are much less likely to talk about it to others. This seems to be particularly so when a son is involved. In extreme cases the father may not even be able to talk about his feelings with his wife. This difference in the way a child's parents approach his or her problems can easily develop into an intense conflict between them. The mother's more rapid movement through this stage places her in a position to view her husband as "not caring" about their child or not supporting her efforts to secure help. At the same time, the father's continuing denial makes it appear to him that his wife is overprotecting or spending excessive amounts of time and money searching for services for a child whose only need is discipline or time to mature.

The well-meaning third party who offers assistance at this point is likely to see his or her services rejected. The parents may even become aggressive, claiming any problems their child has are due to his or her teacher's incompetence or the general low quality of the school's offerings. Every effort should be made to avoid polarizing the relationship at this time so that communication can occur later, when the parents have begun to accept the problem.

Stage 3. Isolation and Alienation

Parental realization and acceptance of their child's learning problem is often accompanied by feelings of isolation and alienation. The parents suddenly find themselves in a situation where they don't know what to expect or how to help their child. They can no longer ask parents, brothers, sisters, neighbors, or friends about how they handled similar problems because their children probably didn't have such problems or needs for special assistance. The many child-related factors they have always held in common with others are no longer sufficient to meet their child's unique needs. Also, new questions arise for the parents regarding how others will feel about letting their children play with their child and how he or she will be accepted in the neighborhood school. Kronick (1973) indicates that these fears are often intensified by the refusal of educators to make the curricular and instructional adjustments needed to provide for children who have special needs. Ironically, in the past it has been much easier to secure special consideration for children whose problems were severe and obvious to all than it was to adjust the requirements for those with less severe problems.

Parental feelings of alienation often arise out of fears about how others view them. These fears are often caused by the belief that others feel they caused their child's problems. Unfortunately, these misconceptions have been fostered by the insensitive comments of poorly informed friends, relatives, and some professionals.

Membership in parent organizations, such as the Association for Children with Learning Disabilities, has proven to be very helpful to parents who are experiencing these feelings of isolation and alienation. Not only does it give them an opportunity to become acquainted and to exchange ideas and experiences with other parents of children who have problems similar to their child's, but it also provides them with a source of information regarding the types of services available and those who are providing these services.

Finally, quality services themselves do much to alleviate feelings of isolation and alienation from society.

Stage 4. "Why Did It Have to Happen to Me?"

Parents of children who have special needs eventually ask, "Why did it happen to me?" or "Why did it happen to my child?" There is no easy answer to either question. As a result, many parents must pass through a period of serious reflection and re-examination of their lives.

Stage 5. Anger, Envy, and Resentment

Kronick (1973) indicates that, "As the child's difficulties increase, rationalizations for denial cease to suffice. As more is demanded of him, and as outsiders become less tolerant and more impatient with the denial game, all but the most persistent families progress to the next stage, which includes anger, envy, and resentment" (p. 51). Kübler-Ross (1969) suggests that this anger tends to be randomly projected on to their environment. Kronick indicates that it is often projected on rejecting neighbors, an insensitive teacher, a nonsharing psychologist, their spouse, or the child. Sometimes it is directed toward a doctor who the parents feel was negligent or a teacher who they feel did not do an effective job in teaching their child. At times, however, the risk involved in projecting one's anger on to those outside the family is so great that the only ones left to blame are each other or their child.

Feelings of envy and resentment tend to develop when parents find that their child is not doing as well as their friends' children. As Kronick (1973) states, "North Americans cherish the myth that everyone is owed the right to a perfect life, to be fulfilled and to enjoy oneself much of the time. To find oneself with less is to feel cheated, thereby to resent everyone who is better endowed" (p. 57).

Stage 6. Guilt

Parents who are unable to identify the cause of their child's problems are prime candidates for feelings of guilt. This is in part perpetuated by society's tendency to imply that parents are the cause of their children's problems. This implication leads parents to search for errors in their behavior that might explain the cause of their child's problem. Parental behaviors characteristic of this stage are actually a continuation of stage 4.

Guilt feelings may also develop in response to an endless number of experiences that may be regarded in one's thoughts as bad or sinful acts. Parents may view their child's problems as "punishment" they are receiving for committing these acts or thinking these thoughts. Or the guilt feelings may develop because of feelings of anger toward the child or toward people who have been trying to provide assistance. Those with severe guilt feelings that have persisted for a long time may require professional help in handling their feelings.

Stage 7. Searching for a Magic Cure

Parents who feel the most guilty are often the most vulnerable to the promises of each new therapeutic fad (Kronick, 1973). Their search for a magic cure may consist of frequent changes in the approaches they use with their child. The result may be overindulgence, inconsistency in maintaining limits, and a vacillation between overprotection and underprotection.

Parental bargaining may take the form of negotiating for the child's transfer to another teacher or to an educational setting where a particular new "in" therapy is being used. It may also include statements such as, "We'll hire a tutor this summer, if you will promote my child to the next grade." Kronick reports that many of these attempts to bring about quick cures may be based on the parents' need to "make it up" to the child for having caused the disability.

Stage 8. Depression and Mourning

The realization that bargaining attempts and quick cures are not producing the desired results frequently strips parents of their last delaying devices. A period of depression and mourning often follows. During this stage the parents come face to face with the fact that they will probably need to readjust their goals and expectations to a more realistic level. Kronick (1973) indicates that, "transient mourning has important psychological value," whereas "prolonged mourning requires intervention" (p. 63). Professionals should be sensitive to the importance of transient mourning to parents who are involved in the process of learning to accept and cope with their child's problem or disability.

Stage 9. Acceptance of the Child and His or Her Problems

Kronick (1973) states that, "Acceptance implies coming to terms with that which a person *will* be able to do as well as that which he is unlikely to accomplish" (p. 95). Parental acceptance of the child's problems makes it much easier for the child to accept these problems. Their acceptance of the child's strengths and weaknesses permits them to move on to the development of realistic goals for the child's future.

Buscaglia (1975) emphasizes the importance of one's family in learning to accept and live with problems:

> True acceptance comes when we stop generalizing the effect of a disability and realize that the disability is not *all* of the person, that all aspects of his life will not be influenced by it and that he is more than the sum total of any of his parts. Acceptance comes with a realistic evaluation of the disability and the values which seem lost due to it. Acceptance also arises with the knowledge that there are vast areas of the self which are still very much intact, accessible and waiting to be utilized. These truths are always better experienced in action than formally taught. The family, then, is the person's major day-to-day counselor." (p. 129)

Stage 10. Realistic Anticipation and Planning for the Future

The acceptance of one's strengths and weaknesses and the setting of realistic goals makes renewed hope possible for the child and his or her parents. Kronick (1973) suggests that parents and their child should adopt goals for themselves that lead to integrated adult functioning. Following is a suggested list of possible goals for the child and his or her parents:

1. Expects to be able to exert control over his own behavior and assumes an increasing responsibility for controlling himself. Does not blame behavior on the disability.
2. Strives toward adaptive methods of handling his difficulties, rather than maladaptive. For example, frustration can be overcome by kicking a soccer ball rather than screaming; overstimulation can be handled by removing oneself rather than by displaying a tantrum.
3. Accepts consequences of his behavior.
4. Does not allow himself to be caught up in a situation in which he cannot cope but explains his difficulties so that demands can be modified. By this means he gains some mastery over his environment.
5. Is confident in his strengths and feels that he has something to offer other people and society. Neither distorts his strengths or weaknesses.
6. Has a number of interests where the disability retreats to a minor place in his life. However, he does not pretend that the disability does not exist or feel that he has to compensate. Rather, he is content to do those things that he does adequately.

7. Does not overreact or underreact to stimuli.
8. Expects others to accept him. Is not defensive and does not magnify rejections out of proportion. Takes a reasonable amount of initiative in interactions.
9. Is interested in other people and the well-being of society and the world.
10. Expects to be able to cope with independent adult life. (Kronick, 1973, pp. 95–96)

Kronick (1973) suggests that people who are aware of their strengths and weaknesses can be helped to choose a lifestyle that will enable them to maximize their coping skills. At the same time they can avoid situations that require performance in their weaker areas.

ACCESS TO RECORDS*

Parents and students who are age 18 and over were given the right to see, correct, and control access to the students' records by the Educational Rights and Privacy Act, which became law on November 19, 1974. Known as the "Buckley amendment," this law applies to all schools and universities that receive federal funds from the U.S. Office of Education.

This law applies to *all* records, files, documents, or other materials containing information directly related to a student, including disciplinary folders, health files, grade reports, and other records found in a cumulative record. Records that a school can refuse to show to parents or students include a teacher's or counselor's "personal notes," which are made for his or her own use and are not to be shown to anyone else except a substitute; records of school security police, if they are kept separate from the rest of the school's files, if the security agents do not have access to any other school files, and if they are used for law-enforcement purposes only within the local area; and personnel records of school employees.

Schools are required to establish written procedures insuring that the provisions of this law are carried out. They must supply on request a list of all the records being maintained on a student. Records sent to the school by agencies or individuals who are not a part of the school system must also be made available for examination by parents and older students.

Students who are 18 years old and older are granted the same right as parents to examine their own records. Furthermore, they may examine their records themselves, and may demand an explanation of any item in the records they don't understand. Hearing the records read by a school official does not satisfy the

*Based on *Your School Records: Questions and Answers About a New Set of Rights for Parents and Students.* Children's Defense Fund, 1520 New Hampshire Ave., N.W., Washington, D.C. 20036.

requirements of the law. Students under age 18 who attend elementary or secondary schools must rely on their parents or on state and local laws in order to see, correct, or control their own records.

Parents and students who are 18 and older are entitled to obtain copies of the student's records whenever records are transferred to another school or information is released to third parties. The school has forty-five days to respond to a request to examine student records. It is not permitted to remove or destroy portions of a student's file after receiving a request, but may do so prior to receiving a request. Those receiving copies may be required to pay for the cost of their reproduction.

Parents and students 18 and older have the right to request the removal of information they feel is misleading or false from the records. If their request is not approved, they have the right to a formal hearing. This hearing must be held within a "reasonable" period of time. Questions about hearing procedures should be directed to the Children's Defense Fund, 1520 New Hampshire Ave. N.W., Washington, D.C. 20036.

Access to a student's records without parental consent and the consent of students who are age 18 or older is limited to the following people:

school officials in the same district with a "legitimate educational interest"
school officials in the school district to which the student intends to transfer
   (providing the parent or student has had a chance to request a copy of the
   records and to challenge their contents)
various state and national *education* agencies, when enforcing federal laws
anyone to whom the school must report information as required by a state statute
   in effect prior to November 19, 1974
accreditation and research organizations helping the school
student financial aid officials
those with court orders

The school must maintain a list of every nonschool employee who requests and receives information about a student. Parents and students 18 and older have a right to see this list. Blanket releases of information signed at the beginning of the school year are not permitted; the child's parent must be asked to approve the release of the student's records each time a new request for records is received, and must be told what records are being requested, why the request is being made, and who will receive the records.

PROVIDING NECESSARY INFORMATION

Parents of children with special needs require clear, accurate, easy-to-understand information that they can use while participating in the planning and monitoring of their children's educational programs. Parents need to know the following:

how to obtain services for their children

when they can expect certain services to be available and the types and locations of these services

that written parental permission is required for both assessment and placement of their children in special education programs

the procedures used by local schools

that they have the right to see the school's records and files related to their child

their children's rights

that an individualized education program (IEP) must be developed and written for their child if he or she is identified as having exceptional needs

that they must be invited to participate in the meeting where their child's IEP is developed

what progress their child is making and how the school measures progress

that the educational progress of students with special needs must be reviewed at least once each year

that they have a right to request a review when they disagree with the findings or recommendations of the school

that their child has the right to receive services in the setting that is most suitable to his or her needs and that does not involve any more separation from normal children than is absolutely necessary

what other programs in the community provide services that their child needs

TRAINING PARENTS

There are several recently developed programs designed to prepare parents to work with their children. Each of these programs emphasizes assisting parents with the development of parenting skills and of strategies designed to help them become more effective. Kroth (1975) lists the following four advantages of parent training groups:

1. It is beneficial for parents to realize that they are not the only ones with a particular problem. Often a parent who has a child who has been classified as mentally retarded feels that he is the only one who has to face this problem.

2. Parents can share their strong emotions with others who understand. Feelings of guilt or anger regarding a handicapped child are often alleviated when they are expressed in a group meeting. The realization that other members of the group have similar feelings seems to have a therapeutic effect.

3. Parents can share solutions. Parents will often listen to solutions to problems from other members of the group more readily than they will from an outside authority. Knowing that other parents have been confronted with a situation similar to their own and have resolved it

with a particular action seems to make the proposed solution more
palatable.

4. More parents can be reached in a group than individually. Sometimes
the group procedure results in a commitment to change in a number
of people in an hour session that might take five or six hours of the
leader's time if done individually. The group procedure, therefore, is
an efficient use of the leader's time. (p. 151)

Kroth indicates that parent groups are not a solution to all parent problems.
Some require one-to-one contact with their child's teacher or a counselor. He also
reminds us of the complications that often develop when teachers attempt to
conduct training sessions for the parents of students who are enrolled in their
classes.

Systematic Training for Effective Parenting (STEP)

Systematic Training for Effective Parenting (STEP) was developed by Dinkmeyer
and McKay (1976) for use in parent training groups. The nine parent study sessions in the program focus on a thoughtful, realistic approach to raising children.
The program teaches principles of parent-child relationships that promote responsibility, self-reliance, cooperation, mutual respect, and self-esteem. STEP program
participants learn the following:

an approach to discipline, called "natural and logical consequences," that devel-
ops responsibility and self-discipline in children by permitting them (within
limits) to learn from the consequences of their own actions
how to identify the goals of their children's behavior, and how their own
responses to their children's misbehavior may invite it to continue
how to be encouraging to children
how to identify "who owns the problem" and not assume responsibility for problems that belong to their children
how to use the communication skills of reflective listening, exploring alternatives, and expressing thoughts and feelings to children in a way that encourages mutual respect
how to conduct family meetings in which parents and children share the planning
for family fun, provide encouragement for each other, and solve problems in a
constructive fashion
how to recognize faulty beliefs that underlie ineffective methods of child training,
for example, the mistaken idea that "there really isn't much we can do about
our problems. When it comes right down to it, we are really victims of our
circumstances"

Groups of from ten to twelve parents and a leader meet together for nine 1½-
to 2-hour study sessions. Each STEP study session focuses on a main topic. The

activities center on a prerecorded cassette presentation regarding a typical family situation. This presentation is followed by discussion of the topic and the sharing of experiences. The narrator's analysis of the challenges involved in the topic are also covered in the session. A parents' handbook contains readings and exercises that help the participants clarify the principles illustrated in the recordings. The following topics are covered in the nine STEP sessions:

1. understanding children's behavior and misbehavior
2. understanding how children use emotions to involve parents
3. encouragement
4. communication: listening
5. communication: exploring alternatives and expressing ideas and feelings to children
6. developing responsibility
7. decision making for parents
8. the family meeting
9. developing confidence and using potential

Parent Effectiveness Training (PET)

Parent Effectiveness Training (PET) is a program designed to instruct parents in the techniques of active listening and problem solving (Gordon, 1970). PET emphasizes teaching parents how to analyze the communication transactions they have with their children. Gordon regards the program as a "no-lose" method of raising children.

It takes eight weekly sessions to complete the PET program. A PET group consists of from ten to twelve parents and a group leader. The participants, who sit in a circle, are encouraged to express their agreement and disagreement with the leader and the other group members. Parents are taught how to express their feelings in an open and honest way to their children. Demonstrations and role playing using these approaches are included in the training sessions.

The need for the child to accept *ownership* of his or her own problems is stressed, and training sessions are devoted to learning to analyze this ownership. Gordon believes that by being active listeners, parents can help their children solve their own problems.

The Art of Parenting

The Art of Parenting is a parent training kit developed by Wagonseller, Burnett, Salzberg, and Burnett (1977). The program's focus is on presenting materials that help parents understand their child's behavior patterns, and helping parents to devise techniques and methods for handling whatever problems arise. The program is divided into five parts:

1. communication
2. assertion training
3. behavior management techniques: methods
4. behavior management techniques: motivation
5. behavior management techniques: discipline

The five program parts are designed so that they can be covered in a series of five separate meetings. Individual parts may also be used as PTA presentations. The authors recommend the use of a workshop format that involves the parents as active participants rather than as passive listeners or observers. Each training session consists of a filmstrip/slide presentation, participant reaction to simulations, completion of exercises outlined in a parents' manual, and a group discussion. The average parent training meeting should last about one and a half hours.

SUMMARY

1. Effective communication with parents of students who have learning and behavioral problems is a vital component in helping students.
2. Careful planning is an important prerequisite to conducting effective parent conferences.
3. Parental acceptance of their child's learning problems can be described as a process involving a sequence of steps leading toward understanding, acceptance, and hope.
4. Denial that one's child has a problem functions as a buffer that helps soften the impact of shocking information.
5. A period of depression and mourning is a natural part of the process through which parents must pass in learning to accept and live with the realization that their child may not fulfill all of their dreams.
6. The final stage in the process of learning to accept that one's child has a problem is realistic anticipation and planning for the future.
7. The *Educational Rights and Privacy Act* gives parents and students who are 18 years and older the right to see, correct, and control access to the student's records.
8. Parents need a clear, accurate, easy-to-understand source of information they can use while participating in the planning and monitoring of their child's educational program.
9. The school must keep a list of the names of all persons who examine a student's records.

10. Parent training programs that emphasize the preparation of parents to work with their own children are an important emerging dimension of services for students with special needs.

REFERENCES

Buscaglia, L. 1975. *The Disabled and Their Parents: A Counseling Challenge.* Thorofare, N.J.: Charles B. Slack, Inc.

Dinkmeyer, D., and G. D. McKay. 1976. *Systematic Training for Effective Parenting.* Circle Pines, Minn.: American Guidance Service.

Gordon, T. 1970. *Parent Effectiveness Training.* New York: Peter H. Wyden.

Kronick, D. 1973. *A Word or Two About Learning Disabilities.* San Rafael, Calif.: Academic Therapy Publications.

Kroth, R. L. 1975. *Communicating with Parents of Exceptional Children.* Denver, Colo.: Love Publishing Company.

Kübler-Ross, E. 1969. *On Death and Dying.* New York: Macmillan Company.

Wagonseller, B., M. Burnett, B. Salzberg, and J. Burnett. 1977. *The Art of Parenting: A Complete Training Kit.* Champaign, Ill.: Research Press Company.

TWENTY

Record Keeping

Developing and maintaining a functional record-keeping system is an important part of providing free and appropriate special educational and related services for students who have learning problems. This system should provide for the documentation of each step taken to implement the services needed by the student and required by PL 94-142. It should also record the progress the student is making toward reaching the short- and long-term objectives outlined in his or her individualized education program (IEP).

The record-keeping system that is used should be well organized, easy to follow, and easily understood by the student's teacher, other teachers, the student's parents, and, when appropriate, the student. It should be easy to keep up to date without an undue expenditure of teacher or student time, and should be structured so that information needed to plan and provide quality instruction is readily available. Needless details and requests for unimportant information should be avoided. The system should also provide for the systematic removal of information that is found to be inaccurate or no longer applicable to the student.

DOCUMENTATION OF SERVICES

A folder should be maintained for each student who is receiving special services. This folder should include a "service delivery log" in which an entry is made each time a specific report, completed form, correspondence, or IEP is added to the folder. The location of these materials should be clearly stated on the log whenever an item is located in a place other than the folder.

The materials contained in the student's folder should be organized in chronological order and attached to the top of the folder with a two-hole fastener. This

Service Delivery Log

Name _____ **Birth date** _____ **School** _____

Date	Description of item or service	Location

greatly reduces the possibility of losing a portion of its contents. The preceding "service delivery log" can be used to keep a record of the services that have been provided.

RECORD FORMS

The record forms contained on pages 330–340 are representative of the variety of forms that are used to document the delivery of the various types of special education and related services required to meet the needs of students with learning problems. They were selected from the following two sources:

1. *An Introduction to Individualized Education Program Plans in Pennsylvania: Guidelines for School Age IEP Development,* Revised Edition, National Resource Center of Pennsylvania and the Bureau of Special Education, Pennsylvania Department of Education, 1978. This monograph was prepared in

part with funds from the Bureau of Education of the Handicapped, U.S. Office of Education.

2. S. Torres. *Special Education Administrative Policies Manual.* Council for Exceptional Children, Reston, Virginia, 1977. This manual was developed with funds from a grant from the Bureau of Education of the Handicapped, U.S. Office of Education.

Forms for use in writing individualized education programs (IEPs) were shown and discussed in Chapter 4.

REFERRAL FOR EVALUATION

ORIGINATOR: School personnel (including a teacher), a parent, a judicial officer, a social worker, a physician, a person having custody of the child, any other person including a school age child who may ask for a referral through any one of those listed above.

PURPOSE: To begin the evaluation process.

SEND TO: Special Education Administrator.

Date: _____

STUDENT
1. NAME: _____
   Last   First   Middle
2. ADDRESS: _____
   Number   Street

   _____
   City   State   ZipCode
3. TELEPHONE: _____
   AreaCode   Number
4. BIRTH DATE: _____ / _____ / _____ 5. CURRENT EDUCATION PLACEMENT_____
   Month Day Year
6. Is this student currently receiving
   Special   Education   ☐ Yes   ☐ No
   Related Services   ☐ Yes   ☐ No

PARENT
1. NAME: _____
   Last   First   Middle
2. ADDRESS: (Fill out only if information is different than above) _____
   Number   Street

   _____
   City   State   ZipCode

3. TELEPHONE: _____
   Area Code   Number

4. PRIMARY LANGUAGE OF THE HOME:
   ☐ English   ☐ Other   Specify _____

SPECIFIC REASONS FOR REFERRAL

Please indicate the specific reasons and/or situations which make you feel that a referral for special education evaluation is needed.
1. _____

_____

(continued)

SOURCE: Reprinted from *Special Education Administrative Policies Manual* by S. Torres by permission of the Council for Exceptional Children.

_____
_____
2._____
_____
_____
_____
3._____
_____
_____
_____
4._____
_____
_____
_____

ATTEMPTS TO RESOLVE

Please indicate all attempts to resolve each of the above listed reasons within the current
education program. This should include what was done, for how long, and by whom.
Attempts to resolve should follow the sequence of reasons listed above.

1. _____
_____
_____
2. _____
_____
_____
3. _____
_____
4. _____
_____
_____

PERSON MAKING REFERRAL: NAME _____

POSITION/TITLE_____

PHONE _____

ANECDOTAL RECORD(S)

Student _____

School Year _____

p. ____ of ____

Date of Entry	Recorded by	Time & Date of Observ.	Circumstances Surrounding Behavior (setting, participants, etc.)	Observable Behavior	Relationship to the Student's IEP

SOURCE: Reprinted from *Special Education Administrative Policies Manual* by S. Torres by permission of the Council for Exceptional Children.

REQUEST FOR PERMISSION TO EVALUATE

Address block giving the name and address of the
student, parent, guardian, or surrogate parent.

Address block identifying the name, title, school
and school address of the school official requesting permission for the evaluation (if the letter is
typed on letterhead paper, this block may not be
necessary).

_____
Date

Dear _____ :
    Complete name of student, parent, guardian or surrogate parent

_____ would like to provide an evaluation for
    School District

_____ to assure that he/she has an appropriate education program.
    Student's complete name

The student has been referred for evaluation for the following reasons: _____

_____

Our plan for evaluation includes:

Type of Test/Procedure	Proposed Date of Evaluation
_____	_____
_____	_____
_____	_____

    You have the right to see and study all the information in the student's school record. Since all of your ques-
tions may not be answered by reviewing these records, you may also wish to meet with the evaluator(s) to discuss
the recommended referral and/or the evaluation procedures. To obtain the student's records or to arrange a conference, you may call _____
    Specify staff member, phone number and hours during the day when he/she can be reached

    If this evaluation shows that the student is eligible for special education programs and services, we will ask for
your assistance in preparing an individualized education program.

    You may already have enough information to reach a decision about the evaluation without reviewing the
student's records or requesting a conference. If this is the case, please indicate your decision by signing in the
appropriate space below.

If you agree to an evaluation as outlined above, please
sign here:

If you do NOT agree to an evaluation, as outlined
above, at this time, please sign here. We will contact you to arrange a personal conference as soon
as possible. You also have the right to request a
hearing concerning this proposed evaluation.

_____
*Signature of student, parent, guardian or surrogate
parent*

_____
*Signature of student, parent, guardian or surrogate
parent*

_____
Date

_____
Date

_____
Signature of parent, guardian or surrogate parent

_____
Signature of parent, guardian or surrogate parent

_____
Date

_____
Date

    Please return this letter in the enclosed envelope within 10 days of receipt. Thank you for your cooperation.

SOURCE: Reprinted with permission of the Bureau of Special Education, Department of Education, Harrisburg, Pennsylvania.

REQUEST FOR PARENT PARTICIPATION IN AN IEP PLANNING MEETING

Address block giving the name and address of the student, parent, guardian or surrogate parent.

Address block identifying the name, title, school and school address of the school official sending this letter (if the letter is typed on letterhead, this block may not be necessary).

_____
Date

Dear _____ :

Student, parent, guardian or surrogate parent

We wish to plan an initial or make major revisions in _____

Student's Complete Name

individualized education program plan and <u>encourage</u> you to join with educational personnel in a meeting for this purpose. Your participation is desired so that you may be fully informed concerning program and/or placement revisions we feel may be necessary.

You, as the student, parent, guardian or surrogate parent, may decide not to participate in revising this plan at this time by signing below. If you do not respond to this letter within 10 days, we will hold an IEP planning meeting in your absence. A copy of the IEP will be sent to you.

_____
Individualized Education Program Planner

☐ I would like to participate in planning or revising the student's individualized education program. I can be reached at the following telephone number:

Phone Number: _____

Time of Day: _____

Phone Number: _____

Time of Day: _____

Or at the following address:

_____

_____

_____

_____

☐ I do not desire to participate in the planning or revising of the student's individualized education program.

_____   _____
Date   *Signature of student, parent, guardian or surrogate parent*

_____   _____
Date   *Signature of student, parent, guardian or surrogate parent*

SOURCE: Reprinted with permission of the Bureau of Special Education, Department of Education, Harrisburg, Pennsylvania.

REQUEST FOR ASSIGNMENT OF A SURROGATE PARENT

ORIGINATOR: Any employee of a school district, state education agency, residential school, institution, or hospital; any judicial officer; or any other person whose work involves education or treatment of children who knows of a child possibly needing special educational services and knows that:

● The child's parents or guardians are not known.
● The child's parents or guardians are not available.
● The child is a ward of the state.

PURPOSE: To request assignment of a surrogate parent to the child. The request shall be filed with the local education agency.

Date:_____

CHILD
1. NAME:_____

2. ADDRESS:_____
               Number   Street

              City   State   Zip Code

3. TELEPHONE:_____
               Area Code   Number

4. WITH WHOM IS THE CHILD RESIDING?
    NAME:_____
    RELATIONSHIP:_____

INQUIRER
1. NAME:_____

2. POSITION TITLE:_____
3. EMPLOYER/AGENCY:_____
4. BUSINESS ADDRESS:_____
               Number   Street

              City   State   Zip Code

5. BUSINESS TELEPHONE:_____
               Area Code   Number

6. WHY HAS THIS REQUEST BEEN MADE?

_____

_____

_____

_____

Signature: _____
                       Person Making Request

SOURCE: Reprinted from *Special Education Administrative Policies Manual* by S. Torres by permission of the Council for Exceptional Children.

REQUEST FOR INTERPRETER/TRANSLATOR

ORIGINATOR: Special Education Administrator.

PURPOSE: All communication with parents of children referred for possible special education and related services or currently receiving special education and related services should be conducted in the mode and primary language of the home. If the special education administrator determines that the language is other than English or that the parents are blind or hearing impaired and an interpreter/translator is needed to facilitate communications between the evaluation team members and the parents and/or the child, then this form should be completed.

1. CHILD's NAME: _____

    PARENT's NAME: _____

    ADDRESS: _____
                    Number   Street

                  _____
                    City   State   Zip Code

2. The mode or primary language of the home is_____

3. An interpreter/translator will be needed for the following:

    _____ Development of the individualized education program
    _____ Review of the written individualized education program
    _____ Review of student records (written)
    _____ Hearing procedure
    _____ Identification of a surrogate parent

4. An interpreter/translator is needed on the following date(s):

    _____
    _____
    _____
    _____

SOURCE: Reprinted from *Special Education Administrative Policies Manual* by S. Torres by permission of the Council for Exceptional Children.

Record Forms

ADMINISTRATION OF MEDICATION

ORIGINATOR: Special Education Administrator

PURPOSE: To secure important information regarding the administration of medication and the effects the medication might have or is having on the school performance of the student.

Student name: _____
Duration of this form: _____ school year (or until medication is changed)

Type of prescription:

Recommended dosage:

Time(s) administered:

Reactions: The physician/pharmacologist is urged to list potential reactions the child might have to medication. The teacher or support personnel should note any behavioral changes.

Anticipated Reactions to Medication (potential impact on education)	Observed Reactions to Medication (actual impact on education)	Date	Obs. by
Ex: Increased drowsiness expected for first 4-5 days of medication change	Ex: Student fell asleep while talking during science class. Was asleep for 5 minutes	9/18	ST

During the school hours of _____ and _____, it is my understanding that (person administering medication) _____, who is ____(child's name)____'s (teacher or (type in position) will administer the prescribed medication according to the specified physician's recommendations.

Signatures: Date of Signatures:

_____   Parent   _____

_____   Physician   _____

_____   Person Admin. Med.   _____

_____   Bldg. Level Admin.   _____

SOURCE: Reprinted from *Special Education Administrative Policies Manual* by S. Torres by permission of the Council for Exceptional Children.

REQUEST FOR PERMISSION TO RELEASE PERMANENT
SCHOOL RECORD TO THIRD PARTY

Dear ☐ Parent,

    ☐ Student,   ———————————————, 19 —————.

We have received a request from ——————————————————————————
                                     (Name of requesting individual, agency, etc.)

for ☐ a copy of ☐ access to ——————————————————————— school record.
                                 (name of Pupil)

School Record

Please indicate in the appropriate space below whether you are willing for us to comply with this request.

                               ☐ Yes   ☐ No

————————————————————————— may have ☐ a copy of ☐ access to the
       (Name of requesting party)

following part of——————————————————————————————— record.
                                 (name of Pupil)

☐ Official student academic record (name, address, birthdate, grade level completed, grades, class standing, attendance record, health data, aptitude and achievement test results)

☐ intelligence test scores

☐ personality and/or interest scores

☐ teacher and/or counselor observations, ratings, and recommendations

☐ Family background data

☐ Psychological or social work reports

☐ individualized education program

—————————————————   ————————————————, 19 ———
     Parent or Student Signature   Date

Please return the completed form to: (print name/address of special education administrator)

SOURCE: Reprinted from *Special Education Administrative Policies Manual* by S. Torres by permission of the Council for Exceptional Children.

CONSENT FORM FOR MUTUAL EXHANGE OF INFORMATION

ORIGINATOR: Special Education Administrator

PURPOSE: To obtain parental permission to secure necessary child records from agency and/or personnel outside the school district.

Date _____

Student's Name _____

Birth Date _____

I hereby authorize the mutual exhange of records regarding the above-named child between the School District and (list of all schools, physicians, psychologists, hospitals, clinics, etc. that have had significant contact with your child):

Name	Address
_____	_____
_____	_____
_____	_____

I certify that I am the parent or legal guardian of the above-named child or that I am the student of majority age and have the authority to sign this release.

_____
Signature

_____
Address

_____
City

Please return this form to: (print name/address of special education administrator.)

SOURCE: Reprinted from *Special Education Administrative Policies Manual* by S. Torres by permission of the Council for Exceptional Children.

RECORD OF INSPECTION OF PUPIL RECORDS

Name of Pupil

Record examined by   Date: Purpose

_____   _/_/_   _____

_____   _/_/_   _____

_____   _/_/_   _____

_____   _/_/_   _____

_____   _/_/_   _____

_____   _/_/_   _____

_____   _/_/_   _____

_____   _/_/_   _____

_____   _/_/_   _____

_____   _/_/_   _____

_____   _/_/_   _____

_____   _/_/_   _____

_____   _/_/_   _____

_____   _/_/_   _____

ATTACH THIS FORM TO INSIDE OF STUDENT RECORD FOLDER

SOURCE: Reprinted from *Special Education Administrative Policies Manual* by S. Torres by permission of the Council for Exceptional Children.

RECORDING STUDENT PROGRESS

A record should be kept of each student's daily progress toward mastery of the skills described in the objectives outlined in his or her individualized education program (IEP). The information recorded should be of a type that will help determine if the instructional procedures being used are producing the desired results. It may be stated as the total number of correct responses made during each untimed daily instructional period, the percentage of attempted responses that are correct during each untimed instructional period, the total number of correct responses made during a specific length of time (such as one minute), or the percentage of correct responses made during a specific length of time.

Systematic Progress Reporting

The *Systematic Progress Report* (p. 343) is designed for use in recording the four types of information previously mentioned. This form is designed so that the number, percentage, or number *and* percentage of correct responses made by the student can be recorded. These data may be plotted by the teacher for timed and untimed periods. Points representing the number or percentage of correct responses that occur over a several-day period can be connected to create a line graph.

The form on p. 344 shows how both the number and percentage of correct responses made during untimed daily instructional periods can be plotted on the same form. The number of correct responses made during a one-minute time period is plotted on the form on p. 345. Short, daily timed tests are well suited for use with students who need to increase their rate of response.

A *criterion of acceptable performance* (CAP) statement describes the level of accuracy or rate that must be demonstrated on a task before the student can be considered to have mastered that task. The CAP statement for a specific task may call for a certain number of correct responses within a specific length of time (see p. 345). Or it may call for correct answers to a specific percentage or number of the items attempted during a series of daily instructional sessions (see p. 344). The student who demonstrates mastery of a task is ready to move on to the next task in the instructional sequence.

A form containing the instructional sequence that is being followed should be placed in the student's folder. The student's mastery of each skill should be noted on this form as soon as the CAP is demonstrated. For example, the student's mastery of CRD *Arithmetic* Objective A-8 has been noted on the instructional sequence shown on page 346. The date objective A-8 was mastered is located in the square to the right of the description of that task.

Psychoeducational Test Data Summary

The *Psychoeducational Test Data Summary* (shown on pp. 347–348) is designed to display norm-referenced test scores. The tests listed on the first page include those most frequently used in the evaluation of psycholinguistic, visual perceptual, and intellectual processes. They are organized so that age scores for each of the tests and subtests can be displayed and compared.

Psychologists usually do not report mental age scores for the subtests on the Wechsler intelligence scales (1974). As a result, it may be necessary to request this additional information before using the form to plot Wechsler subtest scores. Teachers and parents readily grasp the degree of variability represented by differences in psycholinguistic ages (PLAs), perceptual ages (PAs), and mental ages (MAs). It is much more difficult for them to grasp the meaning conveyed by differences in a student's scaled scores.

The second page of the *Psychoeducational Test Data Summary* is designed for use in displaying the scores of norm-referenced tests of academic performance. This page is organized so that grade equivalent (GE) for each of these tests and subtests can be plotted. The row of numbers across the top of the page represents the chronological age (CA) that corresponds to each grade level.

A vertical line can be drawn from the top to the bottom of the page starting at the point that corresponds to the student's CA. A second vertical line can be drawn to represent the grade placement whenever it varies from the usual placement for a student of that age. This procedure makes it easy to determine the student's academic strengths and weaknesses.

The use of the *Psychoeducational Test Data Summary* and check lists of the type shown on page 346 help facilitate efficient determination of the student's present level of performance. Information shown on the first page of the *Psychoeducational Test Data Summary* can be used to determine the student's learning style.

Rarely will all of the tests listed on the *Psychoeducational Test Data Summary* be administered to one student. Only those portions of the form that are needed should be used. The remaining sections should be left blank.

Systematic Progress Report

Name_____Beginning Date_____Ending Date_____

Objective (Skill/Task)_____

_____ CAP _____

Untimed --- Tim**ed** (circle one) Time Interval (circle one) 30 sec.; 1 min.;____**min.**; day

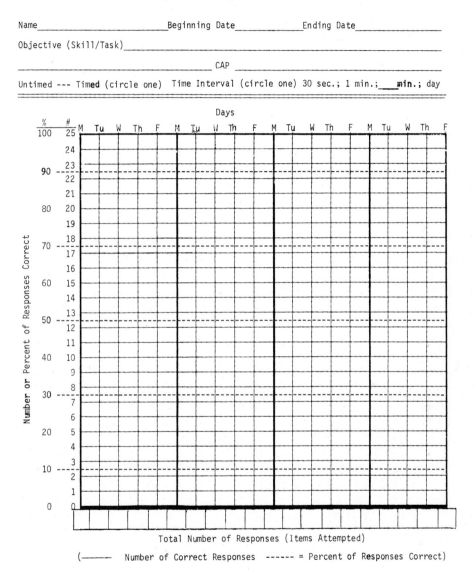

(——— Number of Correct Responses ------ = Percent of Responses Correct)

Systematic Progress Report

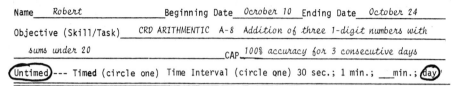

Name *Robert* Beginning Date *October 10* Ending Date *October 24*

Objective (Skill/Task) *CRD ARITHMENTIC A-8 Addition of three 1-digit numbers with*

sums under 20 CAP *100% accuracy for 3 consecutive days*

Untimed --- Timed (circle one) Time Interval (circle one) 30 sec.; 1 min.; ___min.; day

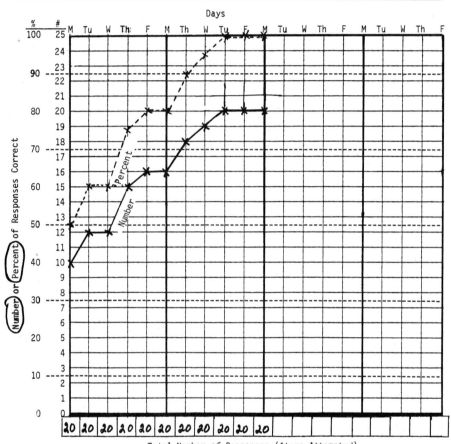

Days

Total Number of Responses (Items Attempted)

(———— = Number of Correct Responses   ------ = Percent of Responses Correct)

Systematic Progress Report

Name___Robert_____ Beginning Date_October 10_ Ending Date___October 24___

Objective (Skill/Task)___CRD ARITHMETIC A-8: Addition of three 1-digit numbers with

___sums under 20._____ CAP___25 correct responses in 1 minute___

Untimed --- (Timed) (circle one) Time Interval (circle one) 30 sec.; (1 min.;) __min.; day

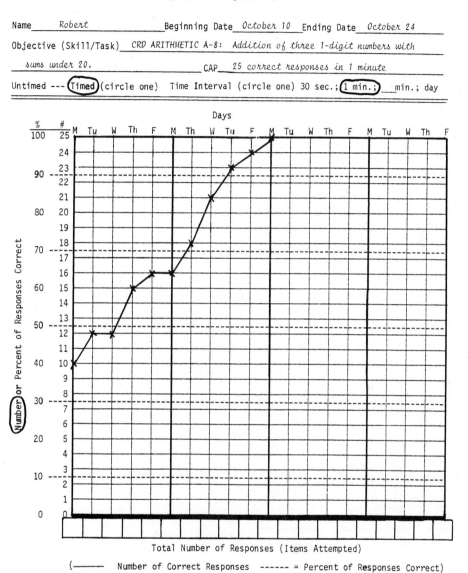

(———— Number of Correct Responses   ------ = Percent of Responses Correct)

ADDITION

Task #	Task (Skill) Description	Check off date/form			Error Analysis Circle type of Error
A1	Addition of two 1-digit numbers with sums of 2 to 5	10/6			CE SA F
A2	Addition of two 1-digit numbers with sums of 5 to 9	10/6			CE SA F
A3	Addition of 0 to 1-digit numbers from 1-9	10/6			CE SA F
A4	Addition of two 1-digit numbers with sums of 10 to 18	10/6			CE SA F
A5	Addition of a 1-digit number to a 2-digit number which ends in 0 (20 + 3 = 23)	10/6			CE SA F
A6	Addition of two 2-digit numbers which end in 0 (20 + 30 = 50)	10/6			CE SA F
A7	Addition of three 1-digit numbers with sums under 10	10/6			CE SA F
A8	Addition of three 1-digit numbers with sums under 20	10/24			(CE) SA F
A9	Addition of a 1-digit number to a 2-digit number without regrouping				(CE) SA F
A10	Addition of a 2-digit number to a 1-digit number without regrouping				(CE) SA F
A11	Addition of two 2-digit numbers without regrouping				(CE) SA F
A12	Addition of two 3-digit numbers without regrouping				(CE) SA F
A13	Addition of a 1-digit number to a 2-digit number with regrouping to 10's				CE SA F R
A14	Addition of two 2-digit numbers with regrouping to 10's				CE SA F R
A15	Addition of two 3-digit numbers with regrouping to 10's				CE SA F R
A16	Addition of two 3-digit numbers with regrouping to 100's				CE SA F R
A17	Addition of two 2-digit numbers with regrouping to 10's and 100's				CE SA F R
A18	Addition of two 3-digit numbers with regrouping to 100's and 1000's				CE SA F R
A19	Addition of two 4-digit numbers with regrouping to 100's and 1000's				CE SA F R
A20	Addition of three 2-digit numbers without regrouping				CE SA F R
A21	Addition of three 2-digit numbers with regrouping to 10's				CE SA F R
A22	Addition of three 2-digit numbers with regrouping to 10's and 100's				CE SA F R
A23	Addition of three 4-digit numbers with regrouping to 10's, 100's and 1000's				CE SA F R
A24	Addition of several numbers of varying length, regrouping when necessary				CE SA F R

Last item passed on pretest

Date objective A-8 was mastered

Type of error made on pretest

Last item given during pretest

PSYCHOEDUCATIONAL TEST DATA SUMMARY

PREPARED BY: LARRY A. FAAS © 1979

NAME_____

GRADE_____ SCHOOL_____

TEACHER_____ EXAMINER_____

DATE OF EXAM: YR.____ MO.____ DAY____

DATE OF BIRTH YR.____ MO.____ DAY____

CHRONOLOGICAL AGE:____ YRS.____ MONTHS

ITPA-REPRESENTATIONAL LVL	SS	PLA	2	3	4	5	6	7	8	9	10
AUDITORY RECEPTION											
VISUAL RECEPTION											
AUDITORY ASSOCIATION											
VISUAL ASSOCIATION											
VERBAL EXPRESSION											
MANUAL EXPRESSION											

ITPA - AUTOMATIC LEVEL	SS	PLA	2	3	4	5	6	7	8	9	10
VISUAL SEQUENTIAL MEMORY											
AUDITORY SEQ. MEMORY											
VISUAL CLOSURE											
GRAMMATIC CLOSURE											

ITPA -SUPPLEMENTARY LEVEL	SS	PLA	2	3	4	5	6	7	8	9	10
AUDITORY CLOSURE											
SOUND BLENDING											

FROSTIG - DTVP PQ ( )	SS	PA	2	3	4	5	6	7	8	9	10
EYE-HAND COORDINATION											
FIGURE-GROUND											
FORM CONSTANCY											
POSITION IN SPACE											
SPATIAL RELATIONS											

WISC-R FULL SCALE IQ( )	SS	MA	STANDARD DEVIATIONS -3 -2 -1 A +1 +2 +3

WISC-R VERBAL IQ ( )	SS	MA	2	3	4	5	6	7	8	9	10	11	12	13	14	15	16	17
INFORMATION																		
SIMILARITIES																		
ARITHMETIC																		
VOCABULARY																		
COMPREHENSION																		
DIGIT SPAN																		

WISC-R PERFORMANCE IQ ( )	SS	MA				5	6	7	8	9	10	11	12	13	14	15	16	17
PICTURE COMPLETION																		
PICTURE ARRANGEMENT																		
BLOCK DESIGN																		
OBJECT ASSEMBLY																		
CODING																		
MAZES																		

DETROIT - VISUAL CHANNEL	MA	3	4	5	6	7	8	9	10	11	12	13	14	15	16	17
( )_____																
( )_____																
( )_____																
( )_____																

DETROIT - AUDITORY CHANNEL	MA	3	4	5	6	7	8	9	10	11	12	13	14	15	16	17
( )_____																
( )_____																
( )_____																
( )_____																

STANFORD-BINET LM IQ ( )	MA	

DRAW A VERTICAL LINE AT THE POINT WHICH REPRESENTS THE STUDENTS CA. PLOT AND CONNECT THE POINTS WHICH REPRESENT THE AGE SCORES EARNED BY THE STUDENT ON EACH SUBTEST THAT IS USED.

NAME_____ CA_____ GRADE_____ SCHOOL_____ TEACHER_____

KEYMATH DIAGNOSTIC ARITHMETIC TEST	CA GE	5	6	7	8	9	10	11	12	13
CONTENT — NUMERATION		K........1........2........3........4........5........6........7........8
CONTENT — FRACTIONS		K........1........2........3........4........5........6........7........8
CONTENT — GEOMETRY/SYMBOLS		K........1........2........3........4........5........6........7........8
OPERATIONS — ADDITION		K........1........2........3........4........5........6........7........8
OPERATIONS — SUBTRACTION		K........1........2........3........4........5........6........7........8
OPERATIONS — MULTIPLICATION		K........1........2........3........4........5........6........7........8
OPERATIONS — DIVISION		K........1........2........3........4........5........6........7........8
OPERATIONS — MENTAL COMPUTATION		K........1........2........3........4........5........6........7........8
OPERATIONS — NUMERICAL REASONING		K........1........2........3........4........5........6........7........8
APPLICATIONS — WORD PROBLEMS		K........1........2........3........4........5........6........7........8
APPLICATIONS — MISSING ELEMENTS		K........1........2........3........4........5........6........7........8
APPLICATIONS — MONEY		K........1........2........3........4........5........6........7........8
APPLICATIONS — MEASUREMENT		K........1........2........3........4........5........6........7........8
APPLICATIONS — TIME		K........1........2........3........4........5........6........7........8

THE WOODCOCK READING MASTERY TEST	CA GE	5	6	7	8	9	10	11	12	13
LETTER IDENTIFICATION		K........1........2........3........4........5........6........7........8
WORD IDENTIFICATION		K........1........2........3........4........5........6........7........8
WORD ATTACK		K........1........2........3........4........5........6........7........8
WORD COMPREHENSION		K........1........2........3........4........5........6........7........8
PASSAGE COMPREHENSION		K........1........2........3........4........5........6........7........8

THE SPACHE DIAGNOSTIC READING SCALES	CA GE	5	6	7	8	9	10	11	12	13
WORD RECOGNITION		K........1........2........3........4........5........6........7........8
INSTRUCTIONAL LEVEL		K........1........2........3........4........5........6........7........8
INDEPENDENT LEVEL		K........1........2........3........4........5........6........7........8
POTENTIAL LEVEL		K........1........2........3........4........5........6........7........8

THE DURRELL ANALYSIS OF READING DIFF	CA GE	5	6	7	8	9	10	11	12	13
ORAL READING		K........1........2........3........4........5........6........7........8
SILENT READING		K........1........2........3........4........5........6........7........8
LISTENING COMPREHENSION		K........1........2........3........4........5........6........7........8
WORD RECOGNITION		K........1........2........3........4........5........6........7........8
VISUAL MEMORY OF WORD FORMS		K........1........2........3........4........5........6........7........8
AUDITORY ANALYSIS OF WORD ELEM.		K........1........2........3........4........5........6........7........8
SPELLING		K........1........2........3........4........5........6........7........8

THE WIDE RANGE ACH'MT TEST (WRAT)	CA GE	5	6	7	8	9	10	11	12	13
SPELLING		K........1........2........3........4........5........6........7........8
ARITHMETIC		K........1........2........3........4........5........6........7........8
READING		K........1........2........3........4........5........6........7........8

THE PEABODY IND. ACH'MT TEST (PIAT)	CA GE	5	6	7	8	9	10	11	12	13
MATHEMATICS		K........1........2........3........4........5........6........7........8
READING RECOGNITION		K........1........2........3........4........5........6........7........8
READING COMPREHENSION		K........1........2........3........4........5........6........7........8
SPELLING		K........1........2........3........4........5........6........7........8
GENERAL INFORMATION		K........1........2........3........4........5........6........7........8

OTHER TESTS GIVEN	CA GE	5	6	7	8	9	10	11	12	13
		K........1........2........3........4........5........6........7........8
		K........1........2........3........4........5........6........7........8
		K........1........2........3........4........5........6........7........8
		K........1........2........3........4........5........6........7........8

Precision Teaching

Precision teaching is a record-keeping system for charting daily improvement and change (Lindsley, 1974). Haring (1978) lists the following five characteristics of precision teaching:

1. *Pinpoint.* Select the specific behavior to be changed.
2. *Aim.* Set a specific rate at which the selected behavior should occur and the date that criterion should be achieved.
3. *Count* the number of times the behavior occurs in one minute.
4. *Chart* on a daily basis the number of times the pinpointed behavior occurs.
5. *Evaluate* the performance of each charted behavior each day. Make changes in instructional techniques if the rate of progress is not satisfactory.

Teachers using precision teaching record the student's performance on standardized six-cycle graph paper. An increase in the frequency of a behavior is viewed as an indication that improvement is occurring.

SUMMARY

1. Development and maintenance of a functional record-keeping system are important in providing free and appropriate special education and related services.
2. The record-keeping system that is used should be well organized and easily understood by teachers, parents, and students.
3. A record should be maintained for each student documenting the dates and types of services that are provided.
4. The location of all reports that document compliance with the requirements of PL 94-142 should be recorded on the student's service delivery log.
5. The items in the student's folder should be organized in chronological order.
6. File materials should be attached to the top of the student's folder so that they will not be lost.
7. A record should be kept of each student's progress toward meeting the objectives outlined in his or her individualized education program.

REFERENCES

Haring, H. G. 1978. *Behavior of Exceptional Children.* 2nd ed. Columbus, Ohio: Charles E. Merrill.

Lindsley, O. R. 1974. "Precision Teaching in Perspective." In *Exceptional Children: Educational Resources and Perspectives.* Eds. S. Kirk and F. Lord, pp. 477–482. Boston: Houghton Mifflin Company.

Wechsler, D. 1974. *Wechsler Intelligence Scale for Children—Revised.* New York: The Psychological Corporation.

TWENTY-ONE

Teaching Study and Location Skills

Special study and location skills should be taught in the elementary and intermediate grades and at the junior and senior high school levels. Proficiency in these areas facilitates learning in content areas, such as social studies, science, geography, literature, and written mathematics, and in industrial-technical courses. Instruction in the use of study and location skills gradually replaces instruction in basic word attack skills as the curricular emphasis shifts from "learning to read" to "reading to learn."

Students need to master some of the basic foundations of study and location skills that are usually taught in primary grades before they can expand and build on these at the higher grade levels. Some of these building blocks for study and location skills are closely related to both the "learning to read" and "reading to learn" processes. Included would be skills such as alphabetization, use of an index, glossary, or table of contents; mastering numerical and chronological order; paying attention; memory; listening; and following directions.

Students with learning problems often require special instruction in study and location skills because of their slower rate of learning and problems with attention, following directions, listening, and sequential memory. These problems often make it difficult for students to learn study and location skills while learning basic academic skills or to learn them as fast as their classmates.

Teachers should begin specific instruction in study and location skills as soon as the student has mastered the prerequisite skills. They may need to individualize instruction because of the slower rate of presentation and the greater number of practice activities required. They may also have to break lessons down into

Dr. T. Patrick Mullen, assistant professor of education at California State College, San Bernardino, wrote this chapter.

basic factors, or subskills, that are carefully sequenced and presented individually, like building blocks.

The reasons students may require special instruction in study and location skills are many and varied, and include problems related to learning rate, adequacy of instruction, and changes in the curriculum. For example, the student who takes longer to learn a skill than expected may have a problem in learning rate. The specialized instruction may consist of a totally slowed down curriculum with no changes in scope and sequence and no additional lessons. On the other hand, it may be necessary to use the same scope and sequence while adding numerous practice exercises to aid the learner in skill mastery. Some students are confused by a speeded-up curriculum in which a number of related skills are presented as a single unit. The curriculum for these students may need to be split into individual skill packages that are taught one at a time, with each skill being mastered before moving on to a next one. The sequence in which skills are presented also makes a major difference to some students who have learning problems. Their teachers often find it necessary to regroup and reteach the skills in a sequence that will be of benefit to the learner. These factors tend to slow students down, making it necessary to devote more time to learning the same skills than is needed by students who are not having trouble.

Some of the greatest problems students with learning problems face in the area of learning rate are those related to instruction that is based on grade placement. These problems arise when teachers proceed with instruction in a specific study or location skill because it is traditionally taught at that grade level even though they know the student(s) lacks the prerequisite skills for success. Intermediate grade or secondary school teachers often place so much emphasis on instruction in the content areas that they fail to take the time to determine if the student is ready to learn new skills. Teachers may also fail to check to see if students have the study and location skills needed to learn the content being presented.

DEVELOPING AN INSTRUCTIONAL PLAN

Providing adequate instruction for problem learners includes assessing the student's strengths and weaknesses and analyzing the tasks to be learned. This information should be taken into consideration when an instructional plan is being developed for students. The plan itself should provide for a continuous process of instruction and diagnosis. Students should not be placed in a situation where an endless stream of tests replaces instruction. Many students who have learning problems need to be taught how to take tests.

Learning takes place through the visual, auditory, kinesthetic, and tactual modalities. Instruction in study and location skills should be organized so that inputs correspond to students' most effective modes of learning.

Instruction in study and location skills should not be limited to the reading and writing areas but should also include skills related to speaking and listening. Attention should be given to sequencing the lessons and providing enough practice to achieve mastery.

Teaching Students to Cope with Curricular Changes

Any major curriculum change can confuse the student who is having trouble learning. The most noticeable changes usually occur in grade 4 and at the beginning of junior or senior high school and college. The fourth grader faces the beginning of the shift in emphasis from basic skills to content material. At the beginning of junior or senior high school, students must adjust to having different instructors for each period of the day. For students entering college, the emphasis placed on *listening to learn* and the need to manage large amounts of unscheduled time may create problems.

The transition from primary grades to the intermediate grades can be made easier by special instruction in applying basic reading skills to learning the content of social studies, science, mathematics, and literature. Throughout the intermediate grades and junior and senior high school, students need instruction in study techniques that are unique to the various content areas. They also need instruction in the use of special reference materials.

Students who are encountering a different teacher and classroom for each content subject for the first time may require help adjusting to the differences between these teachers' rules, expectations, personalities, and teaching styles. Students who are having difficulty with time and space relationships may have difficulty locating their classes. Those with sequential memory problems may have additional problems making use of a combination lock (which may also involve a problem in right-left orientation). Students at this level also need training in organizational skills for writing and speaking.

Some students with excellent high school records encounter difficulty and failure when they enroll in college because they lack the organizational skills needed to complete their homework. Another equally devastating problem facing new college students is the emphasis on listening and taking notes. This becomes particularly critical when a class meeting lasts for more than fifty minutes. Part of this problem may be due to the new vocabulary being encountered, but a much larger portion of these problems is related to poor listening, note-taking, and concentration skills.

Study skills need to be introduced, developed, and practiced throughout the student's school attendance. In the primary grades, the basic reading instruction time provides the most likely situation for the introduction of new study skills. Introduction of new study and location skills in primary and intermediate level reading groups permits students to become acquainted with the skill, its meaning, and its applicability at their own reading level. At the secondary level, where strong emphasis is placed on content instruction, it would be best for teachers in each content area to introduce those study skills that are appropriate to that area. After a skill has been introduced, a period of time follows during which the proficiency needed for individual and independent application is being developed. During this time, it is important that students have a number of opportunities to apply new skills in a meaningful, yet secure, situation. Directed lessons under the guidance of a teacher are advisable. The provision of thorough and timely instruction in skills should be accompanied by an opportunity to strengthen these skills through varied types of experiences. These activities should prepare students to work without the guidance of a teacher.

Each skill should be developed to higher and higher levels of sophistication and applied to more difficult material as students pass from grade to grade. The reading level of materials used should never be above the student's instructional level in reading. This permits students to concentrate on the new study skill involved rather than on the vocabulary of the content. Students who are functioning at the primary level may need instruction in very basic study and location skills.

Teaching Students to Pay Attention

Attention skills are of prime importance. Without development of these skills, efforts to teach other skills may be unproductive. Hewett's (1968) suggestions for helping students pay attention to the instructional task were to remove distracting stimuli; present small, discrete units of work; heighten the vividness and impact of stimuli; and use concrete rather than abstract tasks. The use of behavior modification while teaching may also help students learn to pay attention. Or it may be necessary to set up special lessons to assist students with development of visual attention and auditory attention skills. Highly distractable students may be instructed to point toward the source of the auditory stimuli, or describe the source, rather than turning their whole bodies in that direction. Turning the body may bring forth additional visual and tactile distractions that interfere with paying attention.

Teaching Students to Follow Directions

Learning to pay attention is followed in the instructional sequence by instruction in following oral and written directions. The Language Master is a helpful aide in teaching direction-following skills. Recorded directions may also be useful during the early stages of development of these skills. The greatest benefit comes from activities in which the student actually practices following directions by performing gross motor activities and then moving on to fine motor skills. The game

"Simon Says" provides enjoyable and worthwhile oral direction-following activities. Make sure the vocabulary of the directions is known and understood by the students. A student might be instructed to draw lines on a piece of paper that has been divided into three *columns* and put his or her name and the date in the *upper right-hand corner.*

Teaching Alphabetical Order and Sequence

Two basic academic skills that must be mastered in order to facilitate development of other reading, study, and location skills are the ability to understand and use alphabetical order and the ability to understand and use numerical sequence. Mastery of the alphabet has not been achieved until the learner is able to successfully enter the sequence at any point. With adequate instruction and practice, the learner need not return to *a* in order to place an item beginning with *l* in the correct sequence. Such practice should involve sorting initially into the first and last halves of the alphabet; then into the first, middle, and latter thirds; and finally into specific categories such as *a–e, f–k, l–o, p–t, u–z.* Practice activities like those shown in Figure 21.1, in which the learner indicates the letter that belongs before, after, or between given letters, are also beneficial.

Practice may also be needed in estimating the location of a page with a certain number in a book or a particular point in the alphabet in a dictionary. More advanced skills in alphabetization are necessary in the use of dictionaries and many other reference materials that are organized alphabetically.

Other skills introduced at the primary level are those needed to use and interpret parts of a textbook. Instruction in this area might be on how to use the

FIGURE 21.1 *Practice Sheets for Teaching Alphabetical Order*

g _ h _	_ c _ k	c _ e v _ x
m _ v _	_ g _ p	h _ j p _ r
x _ a _	_ n _ z	o _ q e _ g
d _ r _	_ r _ e	s _ u k _ m
e _ q _	_ v _ x	l _ n g _ i

b _ _ e	_ _ d _ _	_ j _ _ n _
_ o _ q _ _	_ _ j _ _	_ s _ _ e _
g _ _ j _	_ r _ _ _	_ v _ _ k _
s _ _ v _ _	_ _ _ v _	_ d _ _ r _
_ _ c d _	_ _ _ z	_ w _ _ p _

table of contents and glossary, interpret pictures, and understand a book or chapter title. The teacher's guide to most texts at this level contains suggestions for introducing and practicing these skills.

Teaching Students to Listen

Students also need to develop listening skills beyond simple direction following. At the primary level, teachers need to initiate development of basic listening skills, including listening for main ideas, details, and sequences. They should teach students to listen with comprehension for the same kinds of things that will be expected in reading comprehension at the intermediate level. Tape-recorded materials are often used during lessons in listening. Students with learning problems often require more practice than is provided in most commercially published listening programs; for them, supplemental reading materials may be adapted for use as listening lesson scripts. At the primary level, short passages are the most useful.

Teaching Students to Read Maps, Charts, and Graphs

Students should be introduced to simple maps and map making in primary-level social studies. The classroom, the school, the school yard, and the neighborhood provide excellent map-making subjects because they are familiar. This type of activity is particularly valuable to students with spatial orientation problems.

The skills involved in reading charts and graphs may be introduced at the primary level as part of social studies, mathematics, or classroom management. The chart might outline the individual responsibilities of each student in a classroom (for example, who passes out books, waters the plants, feeds the fish, closes the windows, and so on). A daily weather thermometer and weather information chart is a practical way to start in schools located in areas of extreme weather changes.

Teaching Students at the Intermediate Level

Many of the study and location skills taught in the intermediate grades will be closely related to advanced reading skills. Students will need to understand and become skilled in the use of headings, titles, and key words, especially as they are used in indexes of textbooks, encyclopedias, dictionaries, and libraries.

The use of alphabetization skills, first introduced in the primary grades, will take on new dimensions at the intermediate level, especially as students learn to use the library resources. Students will need practical exercises in the use of guide words in reference materials like the telephone book and the dictionary. They should also be introduced to the alphabetical arrangement found in a card catalog and the *Reader's Guide to Periodical Literature.* Numerical sequence again becomes important as students learn to locate nonfiction materials in their school's library. They may also need help in learning to use alphabetically arranged last names of authors to locate fiction and biography materials.

Additional instruction and practice will be required in the skills needed for reading, understanding, and constructing the charts, graphs, and maps that appear in intermediate level science and social studies materials. Skills in the use of almanacs and other indexed materials should also be introduced. These skills are best taught in relation to subjects in which the skills may be needed and used.

Listening skills introduced at the primary level should be expanded and enhanced at the intermediate level with the introduction of note taking. Those students who demonstrate a need for tactile learning should benefit greatly from instruction in note taking. Learning to take notes, at this level, can be taught as both a listening and a reading activity. Students should be taught how to use simple key words, phrases, and summary sentences to record thoughts. Initially they should keep notes on separate pieces of paper that can later be organized into a variety of logical orders. Then they can be taught to establish an outline that organizes these notes into a notebook. Other systems that may be employed, after instruction and practice, include classification, structural analysis, and operational analysis. In classification, the students learn to sort information into appropriate categories. Structural analysis is an organizational system that is useful when studying or writing about things having specific structures, like the parts of a plant in science or the organization of a government in social studies. Operational analysis is an organizational system that is useful when studying or writing about activities such as the steps in a scientific experiment or the rules of a game. When these techniques are introduced at the intermediate level and built on at the secondary level, the possibility that students will master them is greatly increased.

At the intermediate and secondary levels, as students learn to study the various content areas, some modifications need to be made in the approach to reading. The SQ3R technique (survey, question, read, review, recite) is a very popular and useful tool for students in some content areas. Other alternatives, such as outlining, taking summary notes, reading repetitively, and underlining should also be considered. Reading for the main ideas and details is very useful in social studies and literature. When the material being studied consists of technical and scientific reading, this procedure may need to be de-emphasized in favor of skills like reading to locate definitions, examples, contrasts, and classifications. Students who have learning problems may need to be taught to adjust their reading and study techniques as they move from one content area to another. They should be free to try different study techniques until they discover one that works for them without living in constant fear of failure.

Teaching Students at the Secondary School Level

At the secondary level, the skills in alphabetization and numerical order introduced at earlier levels continue to be developed and expanded, especially through use of the library. Dictionaries, encyclopedias, and other reference materials that are organized alphabetically should continue to be used in a practical manner. If not introduced earlier, the thesaurus should become a part of the youngster's repertoire of reference sources. The thesaurus can become a tremendous help to students in preparing compositions for English classes.

Additional counseling and opportunities for practicing listening and note-taking skills should be provided at the secondary school level. Students should be encouraged to record key words and phrases rather than write down every word that is said. They should be allowed to meet in small groups for the purpose of editing their notes. Editing can best be accomplished if initial note-taking instruction at this level employs the use of note paper divided in half vertically. The left half of the page can be used to record the original notes. The edited form of these notes can be written on the right side. The editing of notes includes such elements as spelling key words correctly, filling in items missed, and noting what items seem most important. Also included in the editing process are such skills as outlining or otherwise organizing the notes, writing summary statements, and formulating questions relating to the main points that can be used for review and self-testing. Secondary level students with poor study techniques may need help with organization and concentration. Teachers might assist these students in establishing reachable short-term goals for their study and help them record their success in reaching these goals. Students with poor study techniques may need to be taught to use various memory devices in organizing what they are trying to remember. They should be sure they understand the whole before trying to memorize the parts, breaking long lists into smaller groups using secondary associations (ROYGBIV = red, orange, yellow, green, blue, indigo, violet = colors of the spectrum), writing the material, or repeating it verbally. Some will need additional instruction in how to take tests; others will need assistance in controlling their fear of tests.

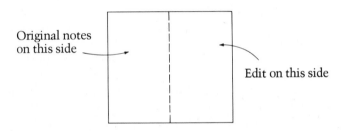

Original notes on this side

Edit on this side

The use of carefully selected study groups can be very helpful. Members of study groups can share techniques that have proven beneficial, assist one another in establishing reasonable study goals, and provide one another with peer approval for effort and achievement. Secondary school students who are having trouble learning will also need help in organizing and selecting a time for their home study. They will require help in determining the amount of time needed to complete various types of assignments. Teachers are usually advised to break longer assignments such as term papers or notebooks into a number of assignments, each with a set due date. They may find it necessary to devote a few minutes of class time to helping students get organized for the studying they should do before the next class meeting.

Teachers introduce, review, repeat, and assess study and locational skills many times throughout the elementary, intermediate, and secondary grades. Systematic repetition plays a major role in students' eventual mastery of these skills. The goal of teachers at all levels should be directed toward helping students develop those skills that are required for functional independent learning.

SUMMARY

1. Study and location skills must be taught in the elementary and intermediate grades and at the junior and senior high school levels.
2. Study skills include tasks such as alphabetization; use of an index, glossary, or table of contents; mastering numerical and chronological order; paying attention; memory; listening; and following directions.
3. Students with learning problems often find it difficult to learn study and location skills while learning basic academic skills.
4. Instruction in study and location skills should be planned so that inputs correspond to students' most effective modes of learning.
5. Study skills need to be introduced, developed, and practiced throughout students' school attendance.
6. Some students require assistance in learning to pay attention to tasks involved in developing study and location skills.
7. It is often necessary to teach study and location skills that are appropriate for use in each content area in junior and senior high schools.
8. Alphabetical order and number order are two basic skills that are necessary for learning to read and for learning more advanced study and location skills such as use of a dictionary.
9. Students with learning problems often require more practice than is provided in most commercially published listening programs.
10. Instruction in how to take notes becomes increasingly important as students enter junior and senior high school and college.

REFERENCES

Hewett, F. M. 1968. *The Emotionally Disturbed Child in the Classroom.* Boston: Allyn and Bacon.

Kaluger, G., and C. J. Kolson. 1978. *Reading and Learning Disabilities.* 2nd ed. Columbus, Ohio: Charles E. Merrill.

Kranyik, R., and F. V. Shankman. 1963. *How to Teach Study Skills.* Englewood Cliffs, N. J.: Teachers Practical Press.

Raygor, A., and D. Wark. 1971. *Systems for Study.* Monterey: McGraw-Hill–California Test Bureau.

TWENTY-TWO

Programs for Secondary School Students
with Learning Problems

Recent years have seen considerable interest and growth in programs for secondary school students who have learning problems. Much of this interest and growth has occurred in programs for learning disabled students (Mann and Goodman, 1976; Marsh, Gearheart, and Gearheart, 1978). In many districts it is a direct result of the implementation of the mandatory service requirements of PL 94-142.

Programming at the secondary level is complicated by serious questions regarding which low-achieving groups should be served in the various programs available. The low-achieving population includes slow learners, the emotionally handicapped, juvenile delinquents, and students who are educable mentally retarded, unmotivated, learning disabled, or having various specific academic problems in areas such as reading. An unusually high percentage of students from bilingual, multicultural, and lower socioeconomic groups tend to end up in the low-achieving population. Many of the solutions appropriate for the learning disabled are also applicable to the learning problems being experienced by the members of the other low-achieving groups.

The issues discussed in this chapter are related to incidence, placement considerations, testing and evaluation, remediation of basic skills, compensatory and other support programs, teacher training, and parent involvement.

PREVALENCE

Efforts to determine the number of students with learning problems in the secondary schools have been complicated by variables and questions relating to the applicability of existing definitions of learning disabilities to secondary level

Dr. Douglas E. Wiseman, associate professor of special education, and Dr. L. Kay Hartwell, assistant professor of special education at Arizona State University, Tempe, Arizona, wrote this chapter.

learning problems, the criteria that should be used when classifying students, the lack of reliable data about the learning problems of adolescents, secondary teachers' lack of preparation to teach students who are having trouble learning, and the lack of systematic procedures for screening and identifying low-achieving students. Tolon (1969) reports that achievement test scores indicated that one-third of the students studied were underachieving in two or more areas while 60 percent underachieved in one or more areas.

Wiseman, Hartwell, and Krus (1978) examined the reading performance of 740 tenth-grade students from a comprehensive high school serving a predominantly middle-class population. They found that 59 percent of these tenth graders performed at a ninth-grade level or below and that 15 percent scored at the fifth-grade level or below. If this figure were applied to the tenth-, eleventh-, and twelfth-grade students in that high school, enough students who were performing 50 percent below grade level would be identified to make twenty learning disability specialists necessary. Including students with less severe deficits would greatly expand the numbers who might require services.

The application of classification criteria as rigorous as a minimum 50 percent deficit in achievement suggests that a large secondary school population is having learning problems. This situation suggests the need for a dramatic change in philosophy and programming in the secondary schools.

TESTING AND EVALUATION

Testing and evaluation services in the secondary schools should include procedures for screening, identifying, classifying, and planning programs for students who are having trouble learning. Relatively few secondary schools have incorporated these systematic procedures into their efforts to identify students who have learning problems, however. Most rely on referrals from junior high schools, teachers, parents, and students. Reliance on referrals has been unsuccessful due to secondary teachers' lack of training in the techniques of identifying learning disabled students, the underemphasis of the need to make referrals, the lack of defined procedures for making referrals, a long-standing lack of interest by secondary school educators in low-achieving students, the cost and time required to perform customary identification procedures, and the lack of programs and personnel needed for educating large numbers of low-achieving students.

Traditional testing and evaluation procedures have relied heavily on teacher referral for screening and a two-phase process of diagnosis and classification. Students who were low achievers were administered a comprehensive battery of psychological and educational tests by a qualified school psychologist or psychoeducational specialist. Past and present records were reviewed by a committee of educators during a staffing and recommendations were made regarding the student's classification and educational needs. Parents have been included in this process since the passage of PL 94-142. Students classified as learning disabled were assigned to learning disability specialists responsible for performing pre-scribed educational intervention programs.

Wiseman and Hartwell (1978) question the use of traditional diagnostic and classification procedures because of the following reasons:

They rely heavily on teacher referral.
Many psychological reports have no value to teachers.
The psychoeducational tests available are often inappropriate for use with adoles-cents.
The test batteries that are administered frequently collect more data than can be utilized effectively.
The diagnostic data collected by the team may not be used by the teacher who will work with the students.
The selection of skills or behaviors to be evaluated may be inappropriate for the low-achieving adolescents. (Many of the skills that are essential for school success—such as listening comprehension, oral language proficiency, facility in handwriting for note-taking, survival reading skills, consumer math skills, and the ability to fill out forms—are ignored.)
Cost and time variables make their use impractical.

The assessment procedures should be tied to intervention systems that will be used in the secondary schools. These procedures should be simple and inex-pensive techniques that make maximum use of available data. They should facili-tate the identification, administrative decision making, program development, and selective placement of low-achieving students who require special assistance.

A Model Testing and Evaluation Procedure

A proposed model for testing and evaluating secondary school students who may have learning problems is described in Figure 22.1 and the following discussion.

Screening High-risk students can be identified by analyzing the scores from achievement tests administered while they are in junior high school. Wiseman, Hartwell, and Krus (1978) found a correlation of .82 between total junior high school achievement test scores and results of a paragraph reading test adminis-tered in the tenth grade. Each school should identify the level of achievement that suggests a person is a possible high-risk student.

Identification High-risk students are administered group tests in areas of sus-pected deficiency to determine if there actually is a deficiency and the extent of the problem. Students falling below the prescribed level of achievement are identified as high-risk students.

FIGURE 22.1 *A Model for Screening, Classifying, and Programming Low-Achieving Adolescents*

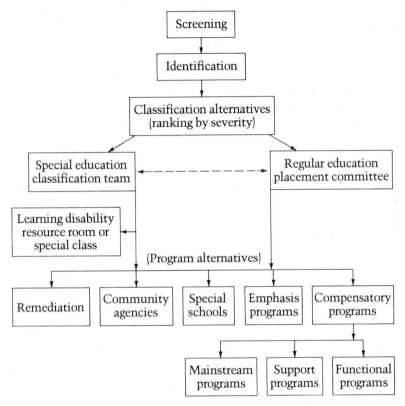

Classification Alternatives High-risk students are rank-ordered by level of deficiency in their respective weak areas. Students with deficiencies severe enough to be considered for special education services are assigned to the Special Education Classification Team. High-risk students with less severe problems are assigned to the Regular Education Placement Committee.

Each school district must decide on the criteria for placement in special education programs. These criteria should be based on local, state, and national guidelines for placing and serving students with special needs.

Each high-risk student who might qualify for special education is staffed by a team consisting of a learning disabilities specialist, regular classroom teacher, school counselor, school administrator or his or her representative, the student, and his or her parents. This team analyzes past and present school performance, past and present school test results, other related considerations such as home and family factors, medical history, and the student's attitude. Following this analysis, the student is either classified as learning disabled or transferred to the Regular Education Placement Committee.

An individualized education program (IEP) is then developed by the Special Education Classification Team for each student identified as learning disabled. The development of this plan includes selection of the program alternative that will best serve the student's needs and the assignment of the student to a learning disability specialist. The learning disability specialist is responsible for providing basic skill instruction and serves as the student's advocate when other services are required.

The Regular Education Placement Committee consists of a school counselor, a teacher from the reading center, a regular education teacher, a special education teacher, and a school administrator or his or her representative. Due to the large number of high-risk students, students and their parents do not participate in the programming procedures unless they specifically request permission.

The committee performs a brief examination of past and present test results and school performance and selects the most appropriate program alternatives for the student. The school counselor is responsible for explaining the program to the student, making modifications when necessary, and contacting parents. The Regular Education Placement Committee may refer students to the Special Education Placement Committee for consideration when special education services appear to be needed.

Program Alternatives   A wide range of program alternatives should be available for both regular and special education students. Possible alternatives, which are listed in Figure 22.1, include remediation, community agencies, special schools, emphasis schools, and compensatory programs. The alternatives will vary from school to school and community to community.

Remediation usually focuses on providing assistance to students who have basic skill deficiencies or language processing problems. Students are usually assigned to special education personnel when the student is learning disabled. Those whose low achievement is primarily in the reading area should be referred to the school's reading center for assistance. Remedial services are discussed later in this chapter. *Community agencies* include out-of-school programs, such as psychiatric clinics and family counseling centers, that can be called on to help students who have special needs. *Special schools* include special-purpose public and private schools such as those that focus on the needs of juvenile offenders. *Emphasis schools* include schools that concentrate on preparing students for specific vocations or trades. Some high-risk students have the ability to profit from required secondary level course work when modifications are made, such as providing a nonreading program or material written at a reduced reading level. The content and expectations in these types of *compensatory programs* remain the same, but the method of acquiring information and testing progress is modified to accommodate the high-risk low achiever. The three types of compensatory programs are discussed further later in this chapter.

This proposed model for screening, classifying, and programming for low-achieving adolescents should provide adequate services for students with learning difficulties whose problems are primarily in academic areas and for other low-achieving groups. Students whose problems are severe or developmental in nature and who do not make adequate progress under the provisions of the above model may require the type of in-depth services provided in traditional diagnostic-remedial approaches.

REMEDIATION

Remediation programs at the secondary level are usually designed to correct or develop basic skills such as reading, spelling, mathematics, and handwriting. Remediation programs at the elementary level generally go beyond teaching basic skills to include process instruction and instruction in language, the perceptual areas, and motor training. The two major assumptions that prevail at both the elementary and secondary levels are that reading is the most important skill learned in schools, and that remediation in reading tends to overcome other problems the student is encountering, such as failure of academic classes and poor self-concept.

Issues at the secondary level that need to be resolved before adequate planning of remedial programs can be initiated include the purpose for remediating the basic skills and how to match the remedial program to the student or teacher. Educators also need to determine if basic skill deficits will be remediated or if tutoring will be provided in academic courses, if training will emphasize basic or survival skills, and if instruction should emphasize isolated or comprehensive skills.

Purpose of Remediating Basic Skills

Students at the secondary level have usually had several years of remedial instruction, particularly when their problem is in reading. The basic decision at the secondary level, then, is whether the instructional emphasis will be on improving the student's academic performance or whether it will be on developing lifemanship skills that will be needed during adulthood. Many secondary level programs have not addressed this question.

A significant number of students in the secondary schools do not progress in basic skills development to the level necessary for success in traditionally taught regular classes, which rely heavily on reading as the principal means for gathering information. Reading is one of the most effective information-gathering tools for those who are proficient in reading; poor readers, however, find it an ineffective or inefficient method of learning. The progress of each secondary level student with learning problems should be reviewed after a period of intense remediation to determine whether future efforts should be directed toward development of academic or survival skills.

Matching the Instruction Program to the Student and Teacher

Educational theory has emphasized the importance of matching instructional procedures to specific needs of learning disabled students. Teacher training programs usually introduce prospective teachers to a variety of instructional methods without devoting enough time to any one approach to insure complete mastery. Special education teachers are expected to develop individualized programs for students that include subskills such as phonics, syllabication, the development of a sight-word vocabulary, and comprehension.

The abilities, needs, desires, and personalities of remedial teachers have frequently been ignored during the development of remedial programs. Some prefer highly structured procedures whereas others prefer more flexible approaches. Some prefer to use commercially published materials and programs, some select teacher-made materials, and others prefer a combination of the two.

Ideally, each teacher will be competent in a wide range of approaches, so he or she can adjust rapidly to the needs of individual students. In actual practice, many teachers tend to use a few favorite techniques without fully adapting instruction to their students' needs. This may be partly a defense mechanism by teachers who find themselves overburdened by too many problems and responsibilities.

Remediation or Tutoring

Educators must determine if the learning disabilities resource room will be used primarily to remediate basic skills or to tutor the students in academic courses. Some advocate remediation of basic skill deficits to prepare students for eventual independent success in course work and later life. Others believe that tutoring students in course work will permit adequate performance in required courses, improve grades, foster the development of a better self-concept, and insure continuance in school until graduation. Still others advocate the inclusion of both remedial and tutorial services in their offerings.

While both options have merit, there is rarely enough time available for learning disability specialists to provide both types of services. This dilemma can be resolved in large part by development of intervention procedures within regular education programs. Designed to assist students who are having difficulty with the content in their regular courses, these intervention procedures permit learning disability specialists to concentrate on remediating basic skill problems. Alternative regular education program offerings might consist of schoolwide peer tutoring programs or courses incorporating a nonreading or learning-by-tape format. These procedures will help insure the integrity of the regular school program while maintaining the intensity of the learning disability program.

Focusing on Basic Skills or Survival Skills

Some students do not progress sufficiently in basic skill development to perform independently and effectively in regular academic programs. At some point in these students' school careers, someone must decide if future instruction will continue to emphasize basic skill development or be shifted to the skills required for survival after school.

Failure in course work can be attributed to causes other than reading problems. An inadequate language foundation, an inability to write well enough to take class notes, faulty listening comprehension, inadequate study skills (see Chapter 21), an inability to organize ideas and materials, limited ability to memorize, an inability to select important facts from lectures and textbooks, and a lack of general strategies for coping with schoolwork are just a few of these possible causes. Remedial reading alone cannot develop all of these prerequisite skills; specific planned intervention is needed.

Schools are responsible for developing and implementing curricular components that deal with survival skills for students who are unable to gain maximum benefit from the regular curriculum. Secondary school programs for learning disabled students can play an important role in encouraging the development of survival programs.

Emphasizing an Isolated Approach or a Comprehensive Program

Remediation programs have traditionally attempted to match specific subskill instruction to each student. Teaching isolated subskills may not be necessary for successful basic skill training in the secondary schools. Another possible approach involves matching a comprehensive basic skills program to a student. Teachers seem to intuitively select decoding activities for severe reading cases, syllabication and comprehension activities for moderate cases, and activities that encourage independent or supplementary reading for mild cases. These teachers could identify and learn to use commercial programs that emphasize each of these priorities, making it possible to eliminate the time-consuming development of teacher-made materials. Commercial programs have the advantage of incorporating entrance and progress tests, a developmental sequence of activities, and instruction on how to use the program materials most effectively.

Teaching skills in isolation from a comprehensive program is also a questionable practice when used with secondary students. Dislike of decoding activities at this level causes students to resist these efforts and prevent attainment of the desired goals. It is important to discuss the instructional program with secondary students to insure program acceptance.

COMPENSATORY PROGRAMS

Compensatory programs are subdivided into three categories: mainstreaming programs, support programs, and functional programs.

Mainstreaming Programs

Many low-achieving students can profit from regular secondary school course offerings. However, modifications and variations in traditional approaches are often necessary to make meaningful education a reality. Four useful classroom modification systems are nonreading curriculums, reading-while-listening options, reduced-reading-level programs, and reduced-difficulty-level options.

Nonreading curriculums vary from conventional approaches by eliminating reading as an information-gathering technique. Audio-cassette tapes, videotapes, talking books, movies, and other systems of information acquisition are used to replace textbooks (Wiseman and Hartwell, 1978). Textbooks and other course-related materials are recorded. Classes are taught at the same difficulty level and with the same general expectations. The students take the same tests as those who can read, with the only exception being that the items are tape-recorded rather than printed. Verbal responses are accepted in place of the usual written responses. Class assignments are modified to suit the skill level of the students. For example, regular students may be assigned term papers requiring high-level reading, organization, and writing skills while low-achieving students may give verbal reports or present hands-on projects or models. Variations in the nonreading curriculum are described by Hartwell, Wiseman, and Van Reusen (1978).

Reading-while-listening options are described by Weinberg and Mosby (1977). They report that giving students the option of reading while listening, listening without reading, or reading without listening was helpful. Their students participated in all general class activities while using any or all of these choices to gain information.

Reduced-reading-level programs utilize reading materials that have been rewritten at a reduced reading level or dictated in a narrative format. Wiseman, Hartwell, and Krus (1978) found that teachers could reduce the readability level of eleventh-grade material to a seventh- or eighth-grade level by translating textbook passages into their own words. This was possible because the conceptual information and facts in these passages were presented at a much higher vocabulary level than necessary. Other techniques used to reduce the readability level involve requesting high-school composition classes and volunteer adults to rewrite the passages. The examination questions for these students also need to be rewritten.

A *reduced-difficulty-option* is needed by students who are unable to read, write, or perform conceptually at the level of the other students in the class. This option is primarily for students who are mentally handicapped.

Support Programs

Support programs are designed to help low-achieving students succeed in regular education classes. They are aimed at students who can make satisfactory progress when they receive tutorial help and assistance in learning the skills necessary for classroom participation. The types of supportive programs most frequently provided are tutoring of regular classroom students, tutoring in the special education resource rooms, and teaching low-achieving students prerequisite skills, such as study skills.

Tutorial efforts often make the difference between success and failure for regular classroom students. Schoolwide peer-tutoring programs are an inexpensive and effective way to assist low-achieving students, and student volunteers can be given course credit for their work. Training peer-tutors in techniques of teaching and organizing instruction requires a small amount of time and can bring about significant returns. Related to peer-tutoring programs is the buddy system, which is an effective classroom approach to helping low-achieving students. The teacher selects a high achiever to assist a low-achieving member of the class. The high achiever shares class notes, discusses the course content, and helps the low achiever study.

Volunteer adult tutors can also provide a strong influence and valuable help for low achievers, and they are able to provide assistance both during and after school hours. Senior citizen groups often provide experienced and reliable volunteers for such a program.

Another technique that can be helpful to low-achieving students are tutorial study halls. These should be reserved for a restricted number of low achievers. A faculty member should be assigned to the study hall to help the students complete assignments for their regular classes.

Academic tutoring in special education resource rooms for learning disabled low achievers is still another effective intervention system. The main drawback to this approach is the cost of the teaching faculty and the need to divert their efforts from providing remediation.

Finally, teaching prerequisite skills to low-achieving students is a cost-efficient way of using instructional time. Many entering students do not possess adequate prerequisite skills such as study skills, note-taking competence, listening comprehension facility, strategies for memorizing, and other techniques for coping with school expectancies. These students can benefit from being assigned during their first year of high school to classes designed to teach prerequisite skills.

Functional Programs

Functional programs are designed to prepare low-achieving students for a life outside the school. Many low-achieving students leave school without the skills needed to cope in an uncaring, competitive society. Functional programs in secondary schools include survival courses, consumer courses, life-skill classes, and programs about the world of work.

Survival classes deal primarily with the reading, writing, math, and spelling skills needed for community living. The course content would emphasize skills needed to read such materials as a telephone book, maps, recipes, medicine labels, and restaurant menus. Writing skills are taught by having students write short notes and fill out job application forms and time cards. *Consumer courses* emphasize the knowledge and skills necessary to participate in a free-enterprise economy. Topics include shopping for groceries, understanding payroll deductions, purchasing a car or large appliance, and buying a home. *Life skill classes* teach low-achieving students health skills, awareness of social responsibilities, food-preparation skills, clothes care, and other skills needed for independent living. Finally, *world of work programs* prepare low-achieving students for entry into the job market. They include career education classes (see Chapter 23) designed to give students an awareness of the work opportunities in the community. Prevocational education classes should teach work attitudes, habits, and skills necessary for entry into vocational education classes. Vocational education classes teach actual job skills, such as auto repair, welding, and maintenance work. Work study programs permit supervised work experience in actual community job situations. Special attention should be directed toward world of work training. Vocational courses typically have artificially high standards for admission, including high reading and math levels. A school committee should be formed to examine standards for vocational classes and to assist the teaching staff in modifying their classes for low-achieving students.

TEACHER TRAINING

Mainstreaming learning disabled students into the regular school programs is an educational fact of life, and its benefits have been tentatively demonstrated by research. Laws have been enacted to assure compliance. Even so, most regular classroom teachers in the secondary schools have been all but ignored in the process of change. Typically, secondary teachers are content specialists who have little experience or training in teaching or modifying programs to meet the instructional needs of the handicapped.

Inservice training of secondary school teachers must be initiated and maintained if mainstreaming efforts are going to be successful. This training should be an ongoing process designed to insure that new faculty are aware of the philosophy and goals of the school, that they have the necessary technical skills to fulfill their goals, and that older faculty are introduced to new techniques and materials.

Initiating an ongoing inservice training program includes four general steps: needs assessment, planning, implementation, and maintenance. Needs assessment involves asking the staff what they need. This can be accomplished in group faculty meetings and through questionnaires. The planning stage should include administrators, curriculum supervisors, teachers, and special educators. Their task is to formulate content needs and format and to select presenters. The content which should reflect both the needs of teachers and the suggestions of experts, may include such topics as techniques of identifying low achievers, alternatives for instruction, methods for monitoring student progress in regular classes, and strategies for counseling and improving communication. Lawrence (1977) states that the active participation of school administrators and supervisors during the planning period helps insure a successful inservice program. The formats generally available include large group workshops, small group instruction, individualized instruction, and self-instructional programs. The large group format is effective for awareness and general knowledge content. Small groups, such as department-sized sessions, can emphasize general curriculum topics. Individualized instruction is most effective for changing classroom performance. Self-instructional programs are inexpensive, once developed, and can teach awareness, knowledge, and techniques. Finally, presenters should be selected from the school faculty whenever possible (Lawrence, 1977).

The implementation step should be planned with great care. After-school and weekend sessions are generally less well accepted than released-time workshops. Active participation workshop formats can be mixed, with large group sessions, small group meetings, and individualized sessions to provide novelty. Lawrence (1977) suggests that emphasizing activities such as making materials or microteaching is preferable to relying on receptive or passive participation.

Maintenance of an ongoing inservice program is particularly important for training new school staff. The delineation of specific program goals and objectives is essential for maintaining an inservice program, and lists of program objectives and a record of each faculty member's progress should be kept throughout. Also, a group of teachers should be selected to serve as a teacher training cadre.

PARENTAL INVOLVEMENT

Little attention has been paid in the secondary schools to programs that involve parents and families of adolescents who have learning problems. This neglect of parental involvement programs may be due to lack of faculty time, the existence of more pressing administrative priorities, and, perhaps, negative attitudes of both teachers and parents toward cooperative involvement. Whatever the reason, both parents and secondary educators are missing an excellent opportunity to provide coordinated services for their handicapped adolescents.

To be effective, parents and educators must see themselves as a working team. In essence, the school is an arm of the home, and the home is an arm of the school. Coordinated efforts usually have a greater chance of helping troubled adolescents than do the efforts of parents and schools who each work alone (Wiseman and Hartwell, 1978). Parents of these adolescents should play a significant role in the total programming of the schools. Similarly, the school faculty must give enthusiastic support. School districts that encourage parental programs generally have more successful programs than those providing only passive support. Parents usually respond when administrators participate and supervise the development of realistic programs.

Parents and educators should select the content for the program jointly. The principal and teaching staff should identify interested parents and faculty to participate in decision making. Or a parental involvement committee can be formed comprised of parents, administrators, and teachers. This committee can develop a needs assessment questionnaire to be distributed to parents and faculty to determine the problems and needs of the school's low achievers. Another source of content for parent involvement programs is professional and lay literature such as journals, books, and newspapers.

The parental involvement committee should be responsible for selecting topics to be presented during the training sessions. The committee should analyze each topic to determine when it should be presented, who should make the presentation, and if a small-group, large-group, individualized, or self-instructional approach will be used. A large-group instructional format is most effective for general overview or awareness topics. Small-group sessions are efficient for in-depth presentations, such as how to help a student in basic skills, how to teach study skills, and how to improve communication techniques. Individual sessions are usually most effective for changing student and parent behavior. They are also the most time consuming and expensive. Special care must be exercised when specific topics are being assigned to parents. Individual training sessions might focus on a particularly difficult home or school problem. The topics covered in these sessions might be identified during communication with the parents, the student, or some outside agency, such as representatives from the court.

A cadre of presenters containing both professionals and parents should be formed. Talented parents, supported by the school faculty, can be trained to perform many of the tasks involved in successful parental involvement programs, including planning, presenting, developing self-instructional materials, forming telephone committees, and selecting sites for meetings. They can also assist schools enormously in the development of communication with other parents of low-achieving adolescents.

Finally, parents and special education teachers should attempt to establish a close working relationship with local and state associations such as the Association for Children with Learning Disabilities (ACLD). These associations can provide valuable assistance and advice for schools and districts interested in expanding and enriching their parental involvement programs.

OTHER PROBLEMS AND ISSUES

Secondary schools have reached a point in their development where new questions need to be asked and fresh alternatives need to be evaluated. The large number of low-achieving students (Wiseman and Hartwell, 1978) and the changing needs of society mean that secondary schools must cope with a number of issues and critical decisions. Five particularly pressing issues that need study are joint planning and decision-making, redefining normalcy, restructuring the curriculum, placement decisions, and the role of the learning disability specialist.

SUMMARY

1. Recent years have seen considerable interest and growth in programs for secondary school students who have learning problems.
2. Programming at the secondary level is complicated by serious questions regarding which low-achieving groups should be served in the various programs available.
3. Testing and evaluation services in the secondary schools should include procedures for screening, identifying, classifying, and planning programs for students who are having trouble learning.
4. Traditional diagnostic and classification procedures are largely irrelevant to the secondary school population with learning problems.
5. Secondary school students whose achievement falls below the prescribed level are referred to as high-risk students by Wiseman and Hartwell.
6. A wide range of program alternatives is required to serve secondary school students who have special needs.
7. Remedial programs at the secondary school level are usually designed to correct or develop basic skills such as reading, spelling, mathematics, and handwriting.
8. Teaching survival skills is an important component of secondary school programs for students with learning problems.
9. Program alternatives, such as a nonreading curriculum, are needed for secondary school students who have serious reading problems.
10. Extensive inservice training for regular secondary school teachers must be initiated and maintained if mainstreaming efforts in the secondary schools are going to be successful.
11. Parents can play a very important role in helping schools develop and maintain quality programs for low-achieving adolescents.

REFERENCES

Hartwell, L. K., D. E. Wiseman, and T. Van Reusen. 1978. *Parallel Alternative Curriculum: A Planning Model for Secondary Level Instructors.* Technical Report Title VI E, Child Demonstration Center, Arizona State University (September).

Lawrence, G. 1977. "Patterns of Effective Inservice Education." *Inservice.* National Council of States on Inservice Education, Syracuse University.

Mann, L., and L. Goodman. 1976. *Learning Disabilities in the Secondary Schools: Issues and Practices.* New York: Grune and Stratton.

Marsh, G. E., II, C. K. Gearheart, and B. R. Gearheart. 1978. *The Learning Disabled Adolescent: Program Alternatives in the Secondary School.* St. Louis: C. V. Mosby Company.

Tolon, A. 1969. "Incidence of Underachievement at the High School Level." *Journal of Education Research,* 63, 63–65.

Weinberg, W. A., and R. J. Mosby. 1977. *Developmental By-Pass Theory and Background Reading.* Vol. 1. Franklin County Education Cooperative Press, Union Missouri Technical Report.

Wiseman, D. E., L. K. Hartwell, and P. Krus. 1978. *Child Service Demonstration Center in Secondary School Age Learning Disabilities.* Title VI E End of Year Report: 1977–1978. Arizona State University (August 25).

Wiseman, D. E., and L. K. Hartwell. 1978. "Alternatives: Programs for Secondary School-Aged Learning Disabled Students." *Learning Disabilities: An Audio Journal for Continuing Education.* Grune and Stratton. (November).

TWENTY-THREE

Career Education for Students
with Learning Problems

Career education is an important but often forgotten aspect of school programs for students who have learning problems. It should begin early in the elementary grades and continue through the secondary schools. In the beginning, career education emphasizes activities that help students become aware of the career options available. As the student grows older, the emphasis switches to development of appropriate attitudes and expectations about the world of work. At the secondary school level, the emphasis shifts to career orientation and preparation for various types of occupations.

Many confuse career education with vocational education and guidance. Vocational education and vocational guidance offerings, which are important aspects of a comprehensive K−12 career education program, are usually confined to secondary school and post-school offerings. Career education is a much broader program designed to help students prepare for career choice and entry into the world of work gradually as they pass through the schools.

DEFINITIONS OF CAREER EDUCATION

The term *career* connotes many settings (such as home, school, occupation, community); many roles (such as student, worker, consumer, citizen, family member); and many events (such as job entry, marriage, and retirement) (Gysbers and Moore, 1973). Career connotes one's role not just as a producer or worker but

Bruno J. D'Alonzo, associate professor of special education at Arizona State University, Tempe, Arizona, wrote this chapter.

as a learner, consumer citizen, family member, and social-political human being (Gordon, 1973).

Professionals in the field of education have defined career education in varying ways. Hoyt, Evans, Mackin, and Mangum (1974) indicate that, "Career education is the total effort of public education and the community to help all individuals become familiar with the values of a work-oriented society, to integrate these values into their personal value systems, and to implement these values in their lives in such a way that work becomes possible, meaningful and satisfying to each individual" (p. 15). Hoyt (1975) revised this statement to read, "the totality of experiences through which one learns about and prepares to engage in work as a part of her or his way of living" (p. 4). In the *Division on Career Development Newsletter,* the board of Governors of the Council for Exceptional Children (1978) states that:

> Career education is a totality of experiences through which one learns to live a meaningful satisfying work life. Within the career education framework, work is conceptualized as a conscious effort aimed at producing benefits for oneself and/or others. Career education provides the opportunity for children to learn, in the least restrictive environment possible, the academic, daily living, personal-social and occupational knowledges and specific vocational skills necessary for attaining their highest levels of economic, personal and social fulfillment. The individual can obtain this fulfillment through work (both paid and unpaid) and in a variety of other social roles and personal life styles including his/her pursuits as a student, citizen, volunteer, family member and participant in meaningful leisure time activities.

Career education applies to handicapped persons in the same manner. However, the special difficulties of the handicapped call for some extra considerations and modifications. A majority of handicapped individuals who receive proper services will be able to pursue careers involving paid employment. For others, paid employment may be a small or nonexistent part of the career. Their careers may consist primarily of avocational, family, and civic pursuits (Brolin and D'Alonzo, 1979).

KEY GOALS AND CONCEPTS OF CAREER EDUCATION

The U.S. Office of Education (1975) developed a list of learner outcome goals for persons leaving the formal education system at the completion of specified levels of education. These goals are commensurate with those traditionally advocated by special educators involved with educating and training students with learning disabilities. According to these goals, students should be:

competent in the basic academic skills required for adaptability in our society

equipped with good work habits

capable of choosing or already equipped with a personally meaningful set of work values that foster a desire to work

equipped with career decision-making skills, job-hunting skills, and job-getting skills

equipped with vocational-personal skills that will allow them to gain entry into and attain a degree of success in the occupational society

equipped with career decisions based on the widest possible set of data concerning themselves and their educational-vocational opportunities

aware of means available to them for continuing and recurrent education once they have left the formal system of schooling

successful in a paid occupation, in further education, or in a vocation consistent with their current career education

successful in incorporating work values into their total personal value structure in such a way that they are able to choose what for them is a desirable lifestyle.

These goals must be individualized to meet the developmental needs and abilities of students who have learning problems.

Brolin (1978) lists several key concepts that must be incorporated into a career education program based on the "life-centered approach." These concepts state that career education

extends from early childhood through the retirement years

focuses on the full development of all individuals

provides the knowledge, skills, and understanding needed by individuals to master their environment

emphasizes daily living, personal-social, and occupational skill development at all levels and ages

encompasses the total curriculum of the school and provides a unified approach to education for life

is a life-centered approach that focuses on the total life roles, settings, events, and relationships that are important in the lives of individuals, including those that pertain to work

encourages all members of the school community to have a shared responsibility and a mutual cooperative relationship among the various disciplines

includes learning in the home, private and public agencies, and the employment community as well as the school

encourages all teachers to relate their subject matter to career implications

includes basic education, citizenship, family responsibility, and other important educational objectives

provides for career awareness, orientation, exploration, and skills development at all levels and ages

provides a balance of content and experiential learning permitting hands-on occupational activities

provides a personal framework to help individuals plan their lives, including career decision making

provides for the acquisition of a saleable occupational entry-level skill upon leaving high school

is a life-long education based on principles related to total individual development

actively involves the parents in all phases of education

actively involves the community in all phases of education

encourages open communication among students, teachers, parents, and the community.

A SCHOOL-BASED CAREER EDUCATION MODEL

Personnel at the Center for Vocational and Technical Education at the Ohio State University developed the original conceptual model for career education. Most models consist of a series of stages through which students must pass, culminating in several possible career options contingent on their developmental level and competence. Other alternative models are described by Bailey and Stadt (1973), Brolin (1974), Brolin and Kokaska (1979), Clark (1979), and Kolstoe (1976). An example of a school-based model is shown in Figure 23.1.

This model represents a sequential career education approach. The students may progress through the activities in these various phases at their own rate. The family, business, industrial, educational, and community agencies should collaborate to offer organized career-oriented activities and experiences for students from preschool through adulthood. The approach used should structure the entire educational plan into one, unified career-based system.

Career education encompasses general and vocational education, job information, skill development, and leadership training, as well as the development of attitudes about the personal, psychological, social, and economic significance of work. Guidance and counseling activities help students to develop self-awareness and to match their interests and abilities with potential careers.

Career education is a comprehensive educational program focusing on careers. It should begin during grade 1 and continue through adulthood. Elementary school students should be made aware of the wide range of careers in our society and the roles and requirements involved. Middle school students may

FIGURE 23.1   *School-Based Career Education Model*

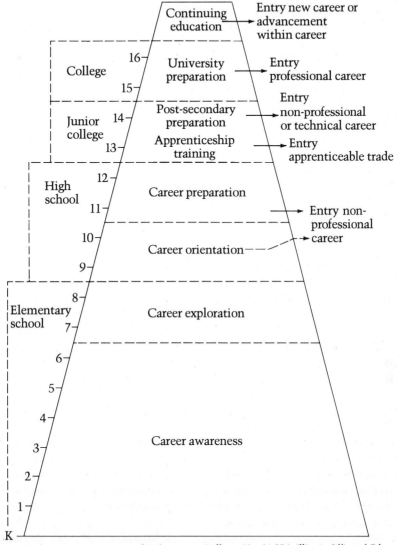

SOURCE: *Elementary Occupational Information Bulletin No. 51-374,* Illinois Office of Education, Department of Adult, Vocational-Technical Education, Springfield, 1973, p. 3.

explore several specific clusters of careers, through hands-on experiences and field observations as well as through classroom instruction. At the senior high school level, students can pursue selected occupational areas and exercise a number of options, including intensive job preparation for entry into the world of work immediately on leaving high school, preparation for post-secondary career education, four-year university career preparation, and preparation or retraining for adult continuing education.

The career education phases described in Figure 23.1 include the following general sequence:

1. *Career awareness*
   a. *Occupational awareness—grades K–3.* The student is informed about occupations through a series of occupational clusters representing the entire world of work.
   b. *Self-awareness—grades 4–6.* The student becomes aware of his or her abilities or aptitudes.
2. *Career exploration—grades 7–8.* The student explores several occupational clusters of his or her choice.
3. *Career orientation—grades 9–10.* The student may select one occupational cluster to explore in depth and starts to develop an entry-level skill. The student has the option of changing the occupational cluster if he or she desires.
4. *Career preparation—grades 11–12.* The student specializes in one occupational area and takes prerequisites for further education and/or intensive skill training for job entry.
5. *Adult and continuing education—post–high school.* The student is employed in the area for which he or she was trained or undertakes further education in an adult education, apprenticeship training, community college, or four-year university program.

OCCUPATIONAL CLUSTERS

An occupational cluster is composed of recognized occupations that are logically related because they include identical or similar teachable skills and knowledge requirements for employability (see Figure 23.2). Vocational or occupational education that centers on the knowledge and skills common to occupations comprising a cluster should prepare students for entry into an "area" or "family" of occupations rather than a specific one.

Occupational clusters, representing the entire world of work and around which a career education system might be designed, include agri-business and natural resource occupations, business and office occupations, community occupations, environmental control occupations, fine arts and humanities occupations, health occupations, hospitality and recreation occupations, manufacturing occupations, marine science occupations, marketing and distributions occupations, personal service occupations, public service occupations, and transportation occupations. Each occupational family has hundreds of occupations within it. General descriptions of each occupation may be found in the fourth edition of

FIGURE 23.2 *Occupational Clusters*

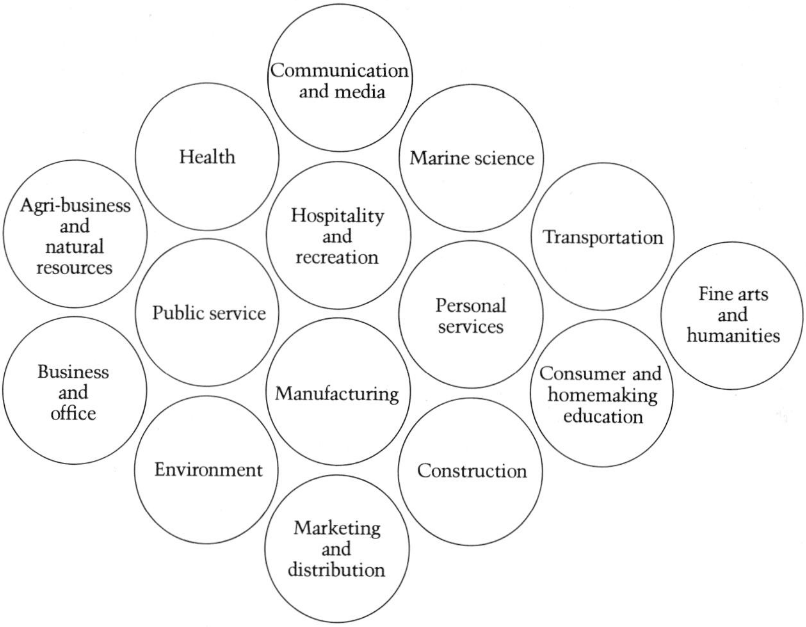

SOURCE: U.S. Office of Education, Office of Career Education. *USOE Career Clusters,* 1971.

the *Dictionary of Occupational Titles* (U.S. Department of Labor, 1977), and the 1978–1979 edition of the *Occupational Outlook Handbook* (U.S. Department of Labor, 1978).

The major difficulty special educators encounter in implementing career education for students who have learning problems is the academic delay these students often exhibit in the basic skill subjects. Because of this delay, many such students are not prepared or ready for the learning experiences and content being presented. Therefore alternative delivery systems must be provided that will present the required content to them, and this information must be presented at a period during the student's development when he or she can master it.

CAREER DEVELOPMENT ENVIRONMENTS

The career development environments described in Figure 23.1 are explained further in Figure 23.3 and the discussion following.

Environment I This environment emphasizes classroom instruction and learning experiences as they relate to career education. As the student progresses through the grade-level hierarchy, the range of experiences increases, career development occurs, career counseling is provided, and the student begins to make

FIGURE 23.3 *Career Development Environments*

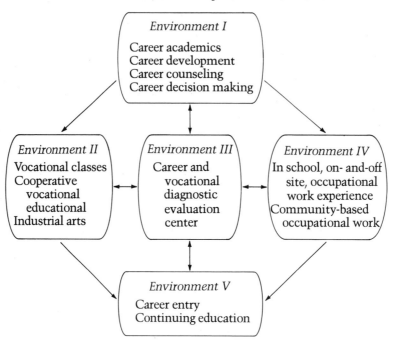

SOURCE: Adapted from B. J. D'Alonzo. "Career Education for Handicapped Youth and Adults in the 70's." *Career Development for Exceptional Individuals,* 1, No. 1 (Spring 1978), p. 9.

appropriate decisions about future career options or goals. A specific occupational cluster is explored.

Environment II   This environment includes specific skill development for a specific occupation within a career cluster. Instruction is given by trained vocational educators, with direct support services provided by special educational personnel. Program modifications such as longer or shorter instructional periods; extended time to complete a course; special texts, instructional materials, and equipment; individualized instruction packages; and minicourses are provided. Additional ancillary services are available through tutorial services, bilingual or bicultural instruction, guidance, job placement, and follow-up. Facilities might require special lighting, acoustical adaptations, and modifications of desks, work benches, and equipment.

Environment III   The Career and Vocational Diagnostic Evaluation Center is designed to assess the career and vocational needs of students who have learning problems. Within the center, diagnostic-evaluative techniques and ameliorative services are provided. Evaluation programs include an assessment of the individual's affective, cognitive, and psychomotor competencies. In this controlled environment, additional competencies are developed through personal adjustment, career and personal counseling, simulated work experience, application of basic academic skills, and development of production competencies essential to meeting the demands of competitive employment. The center and its components add a dimension of precision and ultimate harmony in programming for the career and vocational needs of the student (D'Alonzo, 1974).

Environment IV In this environment, students are engaged in supervised employment on the school campus or in community-based business and industrial settings. Students under 16 are employed in their home school or in a different school within the district. Students 16 and older are usually employed in a business or industry located in their home community.

These work experiences must be considered an extension of classroom learning experiences. Students placed in these work stations must be systematically supervised and their employment coordinated with and related to the school curriculum. Placement is provided in occupations directly related to each student's career training, expressed interests, and level of development.

Environment V Upon graduation the students should be ready for immediate job placement in the community or for entry into continuing career preparation, manpower programs, specific trade unions, sheltered workshops, junior/community colleges, and universities.

TEACHER COMPETENCIES

Special education teachers with elementary level training often employ elementary level approaches and materials with adolescents, whereas teachers with secondary level training usually implement a subject-centered rather than a student-centered instructional approach. Secondary school programs for students with learning problems have traditionally consisted of teacher-directed procedures, using reading, mathematics, and language materials that are "hand-me-down" adaptations or modifications of material borrowed from general elementary education (D'Alonzo and Miller, 1977). The curriculum tends to concentrate on the remediation of the students' perceptual-motor and cognitive deficits with little or no emphasis on career or vocational education.

The actual and desired roles of the high school learning disability resource teacher were investigated by D'Alonzo and Wiseman (1978). They identified five areas in the role of a resource teacher that are related to career education and work experience coordination. Data from the 134 secondary learning disability resource teachers who responded to the study revealed that 37 percent of the teachers seldom or never functioned in the role of planner or implementor of career education programs. Those who performed this duty on a regular basis amounted to only 16 percent; 40 percent felt they should be performing those duties, whereas 17 percent felt this should not be part of their responsibilities. Only 12 percent of the respondents reported that they were always or very often involved in the process of referring students to work-experience programs, and 60 percent indicated that they were very seldom or never involved in work-experience program placements. Approximately 26 percent did not feel work-experience placements should be part of their responsibility, while 23 percent felt that they should be involved to some degree.

Of the resource teachers in the study, 7 percent reported that they regularly participate in securing and supervising job-training sites and serve as liaison between the schools and the state vocational agencies, keeping records and interpreting the programs to the larger community. Approximately 75 percent of the teachers very seldom or never perform in these roles and more than one-third felt that these activities should not be part of their responsibilities. These responses suggest that much more emphasis on career and vocational education training should be provided for teachers at the pre- and in-service levels of preparation. This training should concentrate on the development of the skills and attitudes needed to consider and deliver program options in career and vocational education.

Increased interest in the area of career and vocational education has been appearing in the literature. In 1978, for example, the Division for Children with Learning Disabilities (DCLD) of the Council for Exceptional Children developed a manual entitled *Code of Ethics and Competencies for Teachers of Learning Disabled Children and Youth*. This manual contains a listing of suggested competencies in the area of career and vocational education needed by teachers of the learning disabled.

NEW OPTIONS

The National Panel on High School and Adolescent Education (U.S. Office of Education, 1976) recommends "that the unattained practice and inadequate concept of the comprehensive high school be replaced with the more practical goal of providing a 'comprehensive education' through a variety of means including the schools" (p. 10). Among the many recommendations made by the panel was the creation of a community-based career education center. Each center would serve as a clearinghouse and vehicle for new forms of activities in community-based vocational education, work experience, on-the-job-training, job-finding resources, and career information. To enhance these opportunities for adolescents, the panel urges the removal of those regulations other than minimum wage or safety and health regulations, including tax and insurance penalties, which impede and restrict the employment of adolescents. The panel further recommends that federal and state subsidies for high school vocational classes be made transferable to various on-the-job-training, job-placement, and job-subsidy programs.

This decentralized approach is not intended to replace the formal education structure at the high school level. It does provide diverse learning experiences in the community for students who have learning problems. The panel provides the following recommendations:

> For out-of-school learning opportunities to be most educationally significant for their participants, they have to be designed and operated as independent but integral parts of the total educational environment of adolescents. Thus, effective experience-based learning opportunities and programs must operate neither as a replacement for the existing high school nor as a mere adjunct to it. For community-oriented experiences to be viable components of the adolescent education system, the emphasis in their development should be on opening up alternative educational structures and experiences, not on offering diversity for its own sake or as a substitute for structure in general. Such an approach is necessary if out-of-school learning experiences are to be more than game-playing or officially sanctioned truancy. (U.S. Office of Education, 1976, p. 57)

A matrix of possible structural components and learning situations that can be made available through integrated school and community-based collaborative learning experiences was developed by the panel. Each student would be provided with a personalized series of experiences, customized and tailored to his or her unique needs.

The services of schools and various career and vocational centers must be available to students who have learning problems through an extended school day (evenings) and an extended school year (summers). Collaborative efforts in program options with vocational/technical schools and colleges, community colleges, and university-based instructional programs can be a viable addition to the enhancement of career opportunities for these adolescents. Many of these collaborative efforts can best be delivered in evening or summer programs. They should result in a better student orientation and feel for continuing education opportunities.

METHODS

The most definitive work to date relating specifically to methods of teaching career education to adolescents with learning problems is Brolin (1978). This curriculum approach goes beyond the world of work and encompasses three major domains: daily living skills, occupational guidance and preparation, and personal-social skills. Academic skills are prerequisites to mastery of the twenty-two student competencies and subcompetencies listed under the three domains. For each competency, a unit has been developed that lists the objectives, activities/strategies, and adult/peer roles. Included are lists of instructional materials to assist the teacher in guiding the student toward mastery of the competency. A competency rating scale to be used in assessment and planning and an individualized education program (IEP) form are also provided. This "how-to-do-it" approach to career education should be of immense value to teachers of adolescents with learning problems.

A teacher-made approach to occupational cluster development and career awareness that is personalized for the student and based on the occupations available in the local community was developed by D'Alonzo (1978b). The following six steps are included in the procedures outlined in this personalized occupational cluster development approach:

Step 1. Assessment of the Student's Present Level of Functioning The following types of assessment are included: medical, educational, personal/social, interests, work habits and attitudes, aptitudes, and learning style. Data may be obtained through the use of a medical examination, paper-and-pencil tests, manual dexterity tests, commercially developed assessment systems, self-developed work samples, behavior analysis, and situational assessment (Sitlington and Wimmer, 1978). For additional reading in this area, see Clark (1974).

Step 2. Survey of Local Community Employers The purpose of the survey is to identify agencies, businesses, and industrial sites that are available and appropriate for students.

Step 3. Preparation of a List of Occupations This list should contain every occupation within a specific employing agency and analyze it according to *Common Job Characteristics and Requirements*, a check list developed by the U.S. Department of Labor (1975). This check list follows:

1. high school degree—high school diploma generally required
2. technical school or apprenticeship—some form of nondegree post–high school training required
3. junior college—requires Associate of Arts degree
4. jobs widely scattered—jobs are located in most areas of the United States
5. jobs concentrated in localities—jobs are highly concentrated in one or a few geographical locations
6. works with things—jobs generally require manual skills
7. works with ideas—uses one's intellect to solve problems
8. helps people—assists people in helping relationship
9. works with people—job generally requires pleasing personality and ability to get along well with others
10. able to see physical results of work—work produces a tangible product
11. opportunity for self-expression—freedom to use one's own ideas
12. works as part of a team—interacts with fellow employees in performing work
13. works independently—requires initiative, self-discipline, and the ability to organize
14. work is closely supervised—job performance and work standards controlled by supervisor

15. directs activities of others—work entails supervisory responsibilities
16. generally confined to work area—physically located at one work setting
17. overtime or shift work required—work hours other than normal daytime shifts
18. exposed to weather conditions—works outside or is subjected to temperature extremes
19. high level of responsibility—requires making key decisions involving property, finances, or human safety and welfare
20. requires physical stamina—must be in physical condition for continued lifting, standing, and walking
21. works with details—works with technical data, numbers, or written materials on a continuous basis
22. repetitious work—performs the same task on a continuing basis
23. motivates others—must be able to influence others
24. competitive—competes with other people on the job for recognition and advancement

Step 4. Task Analysis Task analyze each occupation and list every major requirement of that particular occupation. Identify and analyze relevant careers within the local community. Initiate the inclusion of this information into the curriculum. The tasks involved in applying this step to food store occupations might include the following:

Task 1. *Establishing educational goals*
    a. to become aware of the world of work by exploring occupations in food stores that are both familiar and unfamiliar to the exceptional child
    b. to become aware of various occupations in food stores and their roles in society
    c. to introduce the concept that all jobs are important and every food store worker has a contribution to make to society
    d. to introduce the concept that most people work and assume responsibilities
    e. to understand that each food store occupation requires different abilities and knowledge

Task 2. *Occupations introduced*
    bakery clerk
    carry-out person
    chef kitchen clerk
    janitor
    manager
    meat cutter
    produce person
    service corps
    stock person

Task 3. *Vocabulary*
food store
produce
cardboard
supermarket
stocking
wages
produce
customer
fork lift
brands
pallet
cashier

Task 4. *Motivators*
    a. Have you ever been to a food store?
    b. What did you do there?
    c. Are there any food stores in our town? What is another name for a food store?
    d. Do you know anyone who works in a food store? What are some of the jobs they do?

Step 5. Presentation of Occupational Clusters   The food store concept is presented to the student through a variety of learning experiences and audiovisual methods. This is done through:

1. slide-cassette presentations of the specific food store being studied
2. video-taping various individuals as they perform their occupational tasks in the food store
3. printed materials from the food store or teacher-made materials about the food store
4. movies or filmstrips about the food industry
5. art activities focusing on the food store
6. a simulated food store in the classroom with role-playing activities that emphasize the various occupations being studied
7. discussions and guest speakers from the food store
8. field trips to the food store

Step 6. Placement on the Job   The student is placed in the occupation best suited to his or her abilities and interests. Employment is supplemented with job-related experiences in the school. Supervision of the student at work is provided by qualified school and employing agency personnel.

    This approach adds realism to the curriculum by providing opportunities for direct application of student knowledge and skills to community settings. It enables adolescents to become assimilated into the adult environment during these experiences. It also encourages community involvement by giving employers an opportunity to provide input into the school curriculum.

MODEL PROGRAMS

The following model programs serve students who have learning problems. They were selected because they focus totally or in part on the areas of career and vocational education.

Experience-Based Career Education for the Handicapped

The Portland, Connecticut, Public School model program is designed to meet the career education needs of handicapped children of high school age. An adaptation of a validated exemplary program for regular secondary school students known as Experience Based Career Education (EBCE), it combines the documentation features of EBCE with the IEP process. It also includes a revision of the existing site analysis process to accommodate handicapping conditions. Program activities are structured so that they cycle consecutively through design development, pilot operations, demonstration, dissemination, and replication.

Data-Based Cascade Model

This Indianapolis Public School program employs a data-based service-delivery cascade that is designed to facilitate the academic, social, and vocational achievement of mildly handicapped high school students in least restrictive environments. The program provides inservice training to content area specialists that will add methodological skills and strategies, individual pupil programming, and behavior management to their content area expertise. Concurrent activities combine assessment, programming, systematic instruction, data-based management, and computer technology to develop and implement effective IEPs that encompass academic, social, and vocational programming recommendations at the secondary level. The entire process includes continuous evaluation designed to document the efficiency of the program.

Project CLUE (Career Laboratories Utilizing Experiences)

Project CLUE serves Des Moines, Iowa, high school students in grades 7 to 12 who have severe learning disabilities that require more intensive assistance than is provided in the usual special education programs. The students receive assistance in self-contained classrooms called *career laboratories*, which are located in junior and senior high schools. Project CLUE staff members teach students basic math and reading skills and survival skills. Students also attend regular classes that have been carefully selected to achieve the objectives of their individual education programs. A key feature of Project CLUE is its career component. Project CLUE arranges work experiences in the community for each student, ranging from career exploration for younger students to actual job training for seniors. Such experience is intended to integrate the overall educational experience and to develop the knowledge, skills, and behavior patterns necessary for a student to find and hold a job. The small student-teacher ratio in Project CLUE—about 8:1—allows for individual attention to each student's emotional, social, academic, and vocational development.

Handicapped Out-of-School Youth Model Program

The purpose of the St. Paul Public School's special education handicapped student's model program is to initiate the establishment of a vocationally oriented model program to serve handicapped out-of-school youth in the district. An ancillary goal is to help establish new, high-quality programs for handicapped youth and their families in other districts, and to encourage the improvement of existing out-of-school youth programs.

The components in the program include education, consisting of basic skills and life/survival skills; home/school, consisting of social services and home/school communication liaison; vocational, consisting of career exploration and work experience; student advocacy, consisting of cooperation with community agencies and the court system; and outreach, consisting of child-find and assessment activities, consisting of dissemination and replication activities. Handicapped students enrolled in this program can expect to develop the necessary skills to become self-sufficient, income-producing young adults who are able to compete on the job market to the best of their abilities.

SUMMARY

1. The delivery of new and more effective career education services to students with learning problems should be one of our highest priorities.
2. Career education offerings should begin in the elementary grades and continue through the secondary schools.
3. Career education is a K–12 program whereas vocational education and guidance programs are primarily secondary school programs.
4. Hoyt defines career education as "the totality of experiences through which one learns about and prepares to engage in work as part of his or her way of living."

5. The school-based career education model consists of a series of stages through which students pass as they become aware of, explore, and become prepared for entry into several occupations.
6. Clusters of occupations, each containing hundreds of specific job titles, can be included in the options studied in career education programs.
7. A variety of career development environments, ranging from classroom instruction to supervised on-the-job training, should be included in a comprehensive career education program.
8. Preservice and inservice teacher preparation should place a much greater emphasis on career education and vocational education.
9. The services of schools and various career and vocational centers must be made available to students who have learning problems through extended day (evening) and an extended school year (summer) programs.
10. The number of public school career education programs for handicapped students is increasing rapidly.

REFERENCES

An Aid for Planning Programs in Career Education. 1973. Springfield: State of Illinois Division of Vocational and Technical Education.

Bailey, L. J., and R. Stadt. 1973. *Career Education, New Approaches to Human Development.* Bloomington, Ill.: McKnight Publishing Company.

Brolin, D. 1974. *Programming Retarded in Career Education:* Working paper no. 1. Columbia: University of Missouri. (ED 097777)

Brolin, D., Ed. 1978. *Life-Centered Career Education: A Competency-Based Approach.* Reston, Va.: Council for Exceptional Children.

Brolin, D., and C. Kokaska. 1979. *Career Education for Handicapped Individuals.* Columbus, Ohio: Charles E. Merrill.

Brolin, D., and B. J. D'Alonzo. 1979. "Critical Issues in Career Education for Handicapped Students." *Exceptional Children,* 45, No. 4 (January), 246–253.

Clark, G. M. 1979. *Career Education for the Handicapped Child in the Elementary School.* Denver, Colo.: Love Publishing Company.

D'Alonzo, B. J. 1978a. "Career Education for Handicapped Youth and Adults in the 70's." *Career Development for Exceptional Individuals,* 1, No. 1 (Spring), 4–12.

D'Alonzo, B. J. 1978b. *Developing Career Clusters for Exceptional Children.* Unpublished Document. Arizona State University.

D'Alonzo, B. J. 1974. "A Team Approach: Career Education for the Handicapped." *Update,* 2, 14–15.

D'Alonzo, B. J., and S. R. Miller. 1977. "A Management Model for Learning Disabled Adolescents." *Teaching Exceptional Children,* 9, No. 3, 58–60.

D'Alonzo, B. J., and D. Wiseman. 1978. "Actual and Desired Roles of the High School Learning Disabilities Resource Teacher." *Journal of Learning Disabilities*, 11, No. 6, 390–397.

Division for Children with Learning Disabilities. 1978. *Code of Ethics and Competencies for Teachers of Learning Disabled Children and Youth*. Reston, Va.: Council for Exceptional Children.

Division on Career Development Newsletter. 1978. Policy Statement. Reston, Va.: The Council for Exceptional Children (January), 3.

Gordon, E. W. 1973. "Broadening the Concept of Career Education." In *Essays on Career Education*. Ed. L. McClure and C. Buan. Portland, Ore.: Northwest Regional Educational Laboratory.

Gysbers, N., and E. Moore. 1973. "Career Conscious Individual Model." *Life Career Development: A Model*. Columbia: University of Missouri.

Hoyt, K. B. 1975. *An Introduction to Career Education: A Policy Paper of the U.S. Office of Education* (DHEW Publications No. 75-00504). Washington, D.C.: U.S. Government Printing Office.

Hoyt, K. B., R. N. Evans, E. F. Mackin, and G. L. Mangum. 1974. *Career Education: What It Is and How to Do It*. Salt Lake City: Olympus Publishing Company.

Kolstoe, O. P. 1976. "Developing Career Awareness: The Foundation of Career Education Programs." In *Colloquium Series on Career Education for Handicapped Adolescents*. Ed. G. Blackburn. West Lafayette, Ind.: Purdue University.

Sitlington, P. L., and D. Wimmer. 1978. "Vocational Assessment Techniques for the Handicapped Adolescent." *Career Development for Exceptional Individuals*, 1 (Fall), 74–87.

U.S. Department of Labor. 1975. *Common Job Characteristics and Requirements*. Washington, D.C.: U.S. Government Printing Office.

U.S. Office of Education. 1976. *The Education of Adolescents*. HEW Publication No. (OE) 76-00004. Washington, D.C.: U.S. Government Printing Office.

U.S. Office of Education, Office of Career Education. 1975. *An Introduction to Career Education*. Washington, D.C.: U.S. Government Printing Office.

U.S. Office of Education, Office of Career Education. 1971. *USOE Career Clusters*. Washington, D.C.: U.S. Government Printing Office.

U.S. Department of Labor. 1977. *Dictionary of Occupational Titles*. 4th ed. Washington, D.C.: U.S. Government Printing Office.

U.S. Department of Labor. 1978. *Occupational Outlook Handbook*. 1978–1979 ed. Washington, D.C.: U.S. Government Printing Office.

APPENDIX A

Publishers

The following names and addresses include many of the primary sources of textbooks, reference books, and instructional materials used by professionals who work with children with learning problems. The many changes in names and addresses that occur as businesses move and reorganize will most likely cause this list to become out of date during the life of this handbook.

Academic Therapy Publications, 1539 Fourth St., Novato, CA 94947

Adapt Press, Inc., 808 West Avenue North, Sioux Falls, SD 57104

Addison-Wesley Publishing Company, 2725 Sand Hill Rd., Menlo Park, CA 94025

Allied Education Council, P.O. Box 78, Galien, MI 49113

Allyn and Bacon, 470 Atlantic Ave., Boston, MA 02210

American Guidance Service, Inc. (AGS), Publishers' Building, Circle Pines, MN 55014

Ann Arbor Publishers, P.O. Box 338, Worthington, OH 43085

Barnell-Loft, 958 Church St., Baldwin, NY 11510

Behavioral Research Laboratories, P.O. Box 577, Palo Alto, CA 94302

Bell and Howell, 7100 McCormick Rd., Chicago, IL 60645

Benefic Press, 10300 W. Roosevelt Rd., Westchester, IL 60153

The Bobbs-Merrill Company, 4300 W. 62 St., Indianapolis, IN 46206

Borg-Warner Educational Systems, 7450 N. Natchez Ave., Niles, IL 60648

Bowmar, Box 3623, Glendale, CA 91201

William C. Brown Co., 2460 Kerper Blvd., Dubuque, IA 52001

California Test Bureau, A Division of McGraw-Hill, Del Monte Research Park, Monterey, CA 93940

Communication Research Associates, P.O. Box 110012, Salt Lake City, UT

Consulting Psychologists Press, 577 College Ave., Palo Alto, CA 94306

Continental Press, Inc., Elizabethtown, PA 17022

Council for Exceptional Children, 1920 Association Dr., Reston, VA 22091

Creative Playthings, Inc., Edinburg Rd., Cranbury, NJ 08540

Cuisenaire Company of America, Inc., 12 Church St., New Rochelle, NY 10885

Developmental Learning Materials, 7440 N. Natchez Ave., Niles, IL 60648

Devereau Foundation, Devon, PA 19333

Dexter & Westbrook, Ltd., 958 Church St., Rockville Centre, NY 11510

DIAL, Inc., Box 911, Highland Park, IL 60035

The Economy Company, 1901 N. Walnut Ave., Oklahoma City, OK 74103

Edmark Associates, 655 S. Orcas St., Seattle, WA 98108

Educational Activities, Inc., 1937 Grand Ave., Baldwin, NY 11520

Educational Development Laboratories, A Division of McGraw-Hill, 1121 Avenue of the Americas, New York, NY 10020

Educational Performance Associates, 563 Westview Ave., Ridgefield, NJ 07657

Educational Teaching Aids Division, A. Daigger & Co., 159 W. Kinzie St., Chicago, IL 60610

Educational Testing Service, Princeton, NJ 08540

Educator's Publishing Service, 75 Moulton St., Cambridge, MA 02138

Electronic Future, Inc. 57 Dodge Ave., North Haven, CT 06473

Encyclopedia Britannica Educational Corporation, 425 N. Michigan Ave., Chicago, IL 60611

Fearon Publishers, 6 Davis Dr., Belmont, CA 94002

Field Educational Publications, Inc., 2400 Hanover St., Palo Alto, CA 94002

Follett Educational Corporation, 1010 W. Washington Blvd., Chicago IL 60607

Garrard Publishing Company, 1607 N. Market St., Champaign, IL 61820

General Learning Corporation, 250 James St., Morristown, NJ 07960

Ginn and Company, 191 Spring St., Lexington, MA 02173

Globe Book Company, 175 Fifth Ave., New York, NY 10010

Grune and Stratton, 111 Fifth Ave., New York, NY 10003

Harcourt Brace Jovanovich, Inc. 757 Third Ave., New York, NY 10017

Harper & Row Publishers, Inc., 10 East 53 St., New York, NY 10022

D. C. Heath & Company, 125 Spring St., Lexington, MA 02173

Marshall S. Hiskey, 5640 Baldwin, Lincoln, NB 68507

Hoffman Information Systems, Inc. 5632 Peck Rd., Arcadia, CA 91006

Holt, Rinehart and Winston, Inc., 383 Madison Ave., New York, NY 10017

Houghton Mifflin Company, One Beacon St., Boston, MA 02107

Ideal School Supply Company, 11000 South Lavergne, Oak Lawn, IL 60453

Instructional Industries, Inc., Executive Park, Ballston Lake, NY 12019

Instructo Corporation, 200 Cedar Hollow Rd., Paoli, PA 19301

The Instructor Publications, 7 Bank St., Dansville, NY 14437

International Reading Association, 800 Barksdale Rd., Newark, DE 19711

The Judy Company, 310 N. Second St., Minneapolis, MN 55401

Laidlaw Bros., Thatcher and Madison Sts., River Forest, IL 60305

Learning Concepts, 2501 N. Lamar, Austin, TX 78705

J. P. Lippincott Company, E. Washington Square, Philadelphia, PA 19105

Love Publishing Company, 6635 E. Villanova Pl., Denver, CO 80222

Lyons and Carnahan Educational Publishers, 407 E. 25 St., Chicago, IL 60616

The Macmillan Company, 866 Third Ave., New York, NY 10022

Mafex Associates, Inc., 111 Barron Ave., Johnstown, PA 16906

McCormick-Mathers Publishing Co., 450 W. 33rd St., New York, NY 10001

McGraw-Hill Book Company, 1221 Avenue of the Americas, New York, NY 10020

McGraw-Hill/Early Learning, Paoli, PA 19301

David McKay Company, 750 Third Ave., New York, NY 10017

Charles E. Merrill, 1300 Alum Creek Dr., Columbus, OH 43216

Milton Bradley Company, 74 Park St., Springfield, MA 01101

The C. V. Mosby Company, 11830 Westline Industrial Dr., St. Louis, MO 63141

National Council of Teachers of English, 1111 Kenyon Rd., Urbana, IL 61801

National Education Association Publications, 1201 16 St., N.W. DC 20036

Northwestern University Press, 1735 Benson Ave., Evanston, IL 60201

Open Court Publishing Co., Box 599, 1039 Eighth St., LaSalle, IL 61301

Orton Society, 8415 Bellona Lane, Towson, MD 21204

Phonovisual Products, 12216 Parklawn Dr., Rockville, MD 20852

Prentice-Hall, Inc., Englewood Cliffs, NJ 07632

The Psychological Corporation, 304 E. 45 St., New York, NY 10017

Rand McNally & Company, P.O. Box 7600, Chicago, IL 60680

Random House, 201 E. 50 St., New York, NY 10022

Reader's Digest Services, Educational Division, Pleasantville, NY 10570

Scholastic Magazine and Book Services, 50 W. 44 St., New York, NY 10036

Science Research Associates, 259 E. Erie St., Chicago, IL 60611

Scott, Foresman and Company, 1900 East Lake Ave., Glenview, IL 60025

Silver Burdett Company, A Division of General Learning Corporation, 250 James St., Morristown, NJ 07960

Slosson Educational Publications, 140 Pine St., East Aurora, NY 14052

Special Child Publications, 4635 Union Bay Place N.E., Seattle, WA 98105

Steck-Vaughn Company, Box 2028, Austin, TX 78767

Teachers College Press, Teachers College, Columbia University, 1234 Amsterdam Ave., New York, NY 10027

Teaching Resources Corporation, 100 Boylston St., Boston, MA 02116

Charles C Thomas Publisher, 301-27 E. Lawrence Ave., Springfield, IL 62717

3 M Visual Products, 3 M Center, St. Paul, MN 55101

University of Illinois Press, Urbana, IL 61801

University of Iowa Press Bureau of Educational Research, Iowa City, IA 52242

George Wahr Publishing Company, 316 State St., Ann Arbor, MI 41808
Webster Division, McGraw-Hill, Manchester Rd., Manchester, MO 63011
Western Psychological Services, 12031 Wilshire Blvd., Los Angeles, CA 90025
John Wiley & Sons, 605 Third Ave., New York, NY 10016
Winter Haven Lions Research Foundation, Box 1112, Winter Haven, FL 33880
Zaner-Bloser Company, 612 North Park St., Columbus, OH 43215

APPENDIX B

Journals and Periodicals

The following journals and periodicals frequently contain articles; program descriptions; discussions of instructional techniques; reviews of books, tests, and instructional materials; and research reports that are helpful to those working with students who have learning problems.

Academic Therapy, 1539 Fourth St., Novato, CA 94947

Arithmetic Teacher, National Council of Teachers of Mathematics, 1906 Association Dr., Reston, VA 22091

ASHA, A Journal of the American Speech and Hearing Association, 9030 Old Georgetown Rd., Washington, DC 20014

Association for Children with Learning Disabilities Newsletter, P.O. Box 3303, Glenstone Sta., Springfield, MO 65804

Bulletin of the Orton Society, 8415 Bellona La., Towson, MD 21204

Elementary English, 111 Kenyon Rd., Urbana, IL 61801

Exceptional Children, 1920 Association Dr., Reston, VA 22091

The Exceptional Parent, P.O. Box 101, Boston, MA 02117

Focus on Exceptional Children, 6635 East Villanova Pl., Denver, CO 80222

Journal for Special Educators, 179 Sierra Vista La., Valley Cottage, NY 10989

The Journal of Applied Behavior Analysis, Department of Human Development, University of Kansas, Lawrence, KS 66044

Journal of Learning Disabilities, 101 E. Ontario St., Chicago, IL 60611

Journal of Rehabilitation, 1522 K Street N.W., Washington, DC 20005

Journal of Special Education, 3515 Woodhaven Road, Philadelphia, PA 19154

Journal of Speech and Hearing Disorders, 10801 Rockville Pike, Rockville, MD 20852

The Learning Disabilities Quarterly, 1920 Association Dr., Reston, VA 22091
Psychology in the Schools, Business Office, 4 Conant Sq., Brandon, VT 05733
Reading Research Quarterly, 800 Barksdale Rd., Newark, DE 19711
The Reading Teacher, 800 Barksdale Rd., Newark, DE 19711
School Psychology Digest, P.O. Box 184, Kent, OH 44240
Teaching Exceptional Children, 1920 Association Dr., Reston, VA 22091

APPENDIX C

Glossary

Acalculia A loss of the ability to manipulate arithmetic symbols and perform simple mathematical calculations.

Acuity Level of functioning capability of a sensory mode, for example, visual acuity.

Adaptive behavior Behavior that meets the standards of personal-occupational independence consistent with one's age and culture.

Adaptive physical education Physical education programs designed to meet the specific needs of handicapped children and youth.

Agitographia A writing disability characterized by very rapid writing movements and the omission or distortion of letters, words, or parts of words.

Agnosia Loss of or impairment of the ability to recognize objects or events presented through the various modalities when the sense organ is not significantly defective.

    Astereagnosis Disorder of body orientations, characterized by an inability to recognize objects or conceive of their forms by touching or feeling them.

    Auditory An inability to attach meaning to speech and other environmental sounds.

    Autotopagnosia Disorder of body orientation, characterized by an inability to identify body parts.

Agraphia An inability to recall the kinesthetic patterns required to write words or express oneself in writing.

Alexia Loss of the ability to read written or printed language.

Amnesia Lack or loss of memory.

Amusia Loss of the ability to produce or comprehend musical sounds.

Annual goals Activities or achievements to be completed or attained within a year. Annual goals must be stated for handicapped children when writing individualized education programs (IEPs), as directed in PL 94-142.

Anomia Difficulty in recalling words or the names of objects.

Anoxia The lack of an oxygen supply to the brain.

Aphasia Loss of the ability to comprehend, manipulate, or express words in speech, writing, or signs. Usually associated with injury or disease in brain centers controlling such processes.

  Auditory aphasia Inability to comprehend spoken words; the same as word deafness and receptive aphasia.

  Formulation aphasia Inability to formulate sentences properly. Confusion occurs in relationships and tenses rather than in words themselves (for example, Betty give I flowers).

Apraxia Loss of the ability to produce expressive motor movements; medical term reflecting an abnormality of the central nervous system.

Asymbolia Loss of the ability to use or understand symbols, such as those used in mathematics, chemistry, music, and so on.

Ataxia A condition in which deficits of the central nervous system lead to incoordination in motor activity—jerky movements, balance problems, and sometimes speech and writing problems.

Auding Listening, hearing, recognizing, interpreting, and responding to spoken language.

Audiometer A hearing screening device, either a pure-tone audiometer or a speech threshold audiometer.

Auditory association The ability to relate concepts presented orally.

Auditory blending The ability to synthesize the phonemes of a word, when they are pronounced with separations between phonemes, so that the word can be recognized as a whole.

Auditory closure Ability to recognize the whole from the presentation of a partial auditory stimulus.

Auditory discrimination Ability to distinguish auditorily among slight differences in sounds.

Auditory memory Ability to recall words, digits, and so on in a meaningful manner; includes memory of meaning.

Auditory perception Ability to receive sounds accurately and to understand what they mean.

Auditory reception Ability to derive meaning from orally presented material.

Auditory sequential memory Ability to reproduce a sequence of auditory stimuli.

Aura, epileptic A subjective sensation that precedes and marks the onset of an epileptic attack.

Basal-reader approach A method of teaching reading in which instruction is given through the use of a series of basal readers. Sequence of skills, content, vocabulary, and activities is determined by the authors of the series. Teacher's manuals and children's activity books accompany the basal reading series.

Behavior modification A technique for changing human behavior based on the theory of operant behavior and conditioning. Requires careful observation of events preceding and following the behavior in question. The environment is manipulated to reinforce the desired responses, thereby bringing about the desired change in behavior.

Bibliotherapy The use of reading, particularly the use of characters in books with whom the child identifies, for therapeutic purposes.

Binocular difficulties A visual impairment due to the inability of the two eyes to function together.

Blend Combining of two letters into a sound in which each retains its distinctive sound.

Body image Awareness of one's own body and its orientation, position, and movement in space and time.

Brain damage Any structural injury or insult to the brain, whether by surgery, accident, or disease, that is substantiated by hard neurological signs.

Bureau of Education for the Handicapped (BEH) The major unit within the federal government responsible for administration and educational policies affecting handicapped children and youth.

Catastrophic reaction Response to a shock or a threatening situation with which the individual is unprepared to cope. Behavior is inadequate, vacillating, inconsistent, and generally retarded.

Central nervous system (CNS) The part of the nervous system to which the sensory impulses are transmitted and from which motor impulses pass out; in vertebrates, the brain and spinal cord.

Cerebral dominance The assumption that one cerebral hemisphere generally leads the other in control of bodily movements. In most individuals, the left side of the brain controls language and is considered the dominant hemisphere.

Channels of communication The sensory-motor pathways through which language is transmitted, for example, auditory-vocal, visual-motor, among other possible combinations.

Choreiform movements Spasmodic or jerky movements that occur quite irregularly and arrhythmically in different muscles. Characteristically, these movements are sudden and of short duration, distinguishing them clearly from slow tonic athetoid movements.

Chronological age Refers to the number of years a person has lived.

Clinical teaching An approach to teaching that attempts to tailor learning experiences to the unique needs of a particular child. Consideration is given to the child's individualistic ways of learning and processing information.

Closure The ability to recognize a whole or gestalt, especially when one or more parts of the whole are missing or when the continuity is interrupted by gaps.

Cloze procedure A technique used in testing, teaching reading comprehension, and determining readability that involves deleting words from the text and leaving blank spaces. Measurement is made by rating the number of blanks that are filled in correctly.

Cognition The act or process of knowing. The various thinking skills and processes are considered cognitive skills.

Comprehension Understanding the meaning of printed or spoken language.

Conceptual disorders A disturbance in the thinking process, in cognitive activities, or in the ability to formulate concepts.

Conceptualization The ability to infer from what is observable.

Congenital Present at birth; usually a defect of either familial or exogenous origin that exists at the time of birth.

Conservation In Piaget's theory, the ability to retain a concept of area, mass, length, and so on when superficial changes are made in the appearance of an object or scene.

Convulsive disorder A clinical syndrome, the central feature of which is recurrent seizures or convulsions; recurrent disturbances of consciousness, with or without muscular components, and accompanied by changes in the electrical potentials of the brain.

Criterion-referenced tests Mastery tests in which achievement is determined by assessing the student's performance on an orderly sequence of skills.

Cross-modality perception The neurological process of converting information received through one input modality to another system within the brain; also referred to as "intersensory transfer," "intermodal transfer," and "transducing."

Cutaneous Pertaining to the skin.

Decoding The receptive habits in the language process, for example, sensory acuity, awareness, discrimination, and vocabulary comprehension.

Delivery systems The various ways of offering educational services to children, for example, self-contained classes, resource rooms, regular classrooms, and so on.

Developmental imbalance A disparity in the developmental patterns of intellectual skills.

Developmental reading The pattern and sequence of normal reading growth and development in a child who is learning to read.

Developmental disabilities Conditions originating in childhood that result in a significant handicap for the individual. These include mental retardation, cerebral palsy, epilepsy, and conditions associated with neurological damage.

Digraph Two letters representing a single sound, for example, *sh, th,* and *wh.*

Diphthong A blend of two vowels that seem to flow together without losing the identity of each vowel, for example, *oy* in *boy* and *oi* in *oil.*

Directionality Awareness of laterality (the two sides of the body) and verticality (vertical axis awareness), as well as the ability to translate this discrimination within the organism to similar discrimination among objects in space.

Discrimination The process of detecting differences among stimuli.

Auditory Identification of likenesses and differences among sounds.

Visual Ability to recognize differences among similar but slightly different forms or shapes, as in alphabetic letters.

Disinhibition The inability to refrain from responding to what is perceived, often resulting in hyperactivity and distractability.

Distractability The tendency to be easily drawn away from any task at hand and to focus on extraneous stimuli of the moment.

Due process In an educational context, the procedures and policies established to insure equal educational opportunities for all children. PL 94-142 contains due process procedures specifically for handicapped children.

Dysarthria Difficulty in the articulation of words due to involvement of the central nervous system.

Dyscalculia Partial loss of the ability to calculate and to manipulate number symbols.

Dysdiadochokinesis The inability to perform repetitive movements such as tapping with a finger.

Dysgraphia Partial inability to express ideas by means of writing or written symbols; usually associated with brain dysfunction.

Dyskinesia Partial impairment of voluntary movement abilities, resulting in incomplete movements, poor coordination, and apparently clumsy behavior.

Dyslexia Partial inability to read, or to understand what one reads, silently or aloud; usually, but not always, associated with brain impairment. (Some authors refer to genetic dyslexia, affective dyslexia, experiential dyslexia, congenital dyslexia, and so on).

Dysnomia A condition in which an individual knows the word he or she is trying to recall, recognizes it when said, but cannot recall it at will.

Dysphasia Partial inability to comprehend the spoken word (receptive dysphasia) and to speak (expressive dysphasia), believed to be the result of injury, disease, or maldevelopment of the brain.

Dyspraxia Partial loss of the ability to perform purposeful movements in a coordinated manner in the absence of paralysis, cerebral palsy, or sensory loss.

Dysrhythmia Abnormal speech fluency, characterized by defective stress, breath control, and intonation.

Echolalia Meaningless "echoing" or repetition of words or sometimes of sounds.

Educational therapist A teacher who teaches or treats a child who has difficulty in learning. Specialized materials and methods are used.

Electroencephalograph (EEG) An instrument for graphically recording electrical currents developed in the cerebral cortex during brain functioning.

Emotional blocking The inability to think or make satisfactory responses due to excessive emotion, usually related to fear.

Emotional liability Tendency toward cyclic emotional behavior, characterized by sudden, unexplainable shifts from one emotion to another.

Encoding The expressive habits in the language process; response formation, including word selection, syntax, grammar, and the actual motor production of the response.

Endogenous Describing a condition or defect based on hereditary or genetic factors.

Etiology The cause or origin of a condition.

Exogenous Describing a condition or defect resulting from other than hereditary or genetic factors (such as environment or trauma).

Expressive language skills Skills required to produce language for communication with other individuals, for example, speaking and writing.

Feedback The sensory or perceptual report of the result of a somatic, social, or cognitive behavior.

Figure-ground The tendency of one part of a perceptual configuration to stand out clearly while the remainder forms a background.

Figure-ground disturbance Inability to discriminate a figure from its background.

Finger agnosia Inability to recognize the name of or identify the individual fingers of one's own hand.

Flow-through funds Federal funds that are distributed by the state educational agency directly to local districts. Also called pass-through funds.

Formulation The organization of relevant elements of a specific project into a clear and concise pattern.

Free appropriate public education A term used in PL 94-142 to mean special education and related services that are provided at public expense, that meet requirements of the state educational agency, and that conform to the individualized education program (IEP) requirement of PL 94-142.

Gerstmann syndrome A constellation of symptoms indicating lack of laterality and a disturbance of body image. The symptoms are agraphia, acalculia, right-left disorientation, and finger agnosia.

Gestalt A term used to express any unified whole whose properties cannot be derived by adding the parts and their relationships; an entity that is more than the sum of its parts.

Global Perceived as a whole without attempt to distinguish separate parts or functions.

Gnosia The faculty of perceiving and knowing.

Grammatic closure The ability to make use of the redundancies of oral language in acquiring automatic habits for handling syntax and grammatic inflections.

Grapheme A written language symbol representing an oral language code.

Gustatory Pertaining to taste.

Handedness Referring to hand preference of an individual.

Hand-eye coordination Ability of the hand and eye to perform easily together.

Hard neurological signs Physical symptoms of brain injury that can be identified medically.

Hemiopia The condition where one has only one-half of the field of vision in one or both eyes.

Hemispherical dominance Referring to the fact that one cerebral hemisphere generally leads the other in control of body movement, resulting in the preferred use of left or right (laterality).

Hyperactivity Constant and excessive movement and motor activity.

Hypoactivity Insufficient motor activity, characterized by lethargy.

Imagery Representation of images.

Impulsivity Initiation of sudden action without sufficient forethought or prudence.

Individualized education program (IEP) Required by PL 94-142, a written educational plan that must be developed and maintained for each handicapped child. The IEP must state the child's current level of educational performance, annual goals, short-term instructional objectives, specific services to be provided, dates services are to be provided, and criteria for evaluation.

Individualized reading The method of teaching reading that utilizes the child's interest; learning is structured through the child's own reading selections, using a variety of books. The teacher acts as a consultant, aid, and counselor.

Inner language The process of internalizing and organizing experiences without the use of linguistic symbols.

Interindividual Pertaining to a comparison of one person with another person or with a group of individuals.

Intraindividual Pertaining to a comparison of different characteristics within an individual.

Itinerant teacher A teacher who moves about a school district to several schools and schedules children for teaching periods; children leave their regular classrooms to work with such a teacher.

Kinesthesis The sense by which muscular motion, position, and weight are perceived, resulting from stimulation of sensory nerve endings in the muscles, joints, and tendons caused by bodily movements and tensions.

Language arts School curricular activities that utilize language, namely, listening, speaking, reading, writing, handwriting, and spelling.

Language-experience approach to reading A method of teaching reading and other language skills, based on the experiences of children. Frequently involves the generation of experience-based materials that are dictated by the child, written down by the teacher, then used in class as the material for teaching reading.

Laterality The internal awareness of the two sides of one's body. A sense of sidedness that includes the tendency to use one hand for specific tasks.

Least restrictive environment When applied to the education of exceptional children, a term referring to the principle that handicapped children should be educated with nonhandicapped peers in regular educational settings whenever possible. Allowances are made for placement in special classes or other settings when they are the least restrictive based on needs of the individual involved.

Local education agency (LEA) A term often used in referring to public school districts.

Locomotion Movement from one location to another (walking, crawling, rolling, and so on).

Mainstreaming The practice of educating handicapped children in regular educational settings. Generally involves placing handicapped children in regular classrooms and providing support services when necessary. The practice is gaining wide popularity in meeting educational needs of the mildly handicapped.

Memory The ability to store and retrieve on demand previously experienced sensations and perceptions, even when the stimulus that orginally evoked them is no longer present. Also referred to as "imagery" and "recall."

Memory span The number of related or unrelated items that can be recalled immediately after presentation.

Mental age The level of mental ability.

Minimal brain dysfunction A mild or minimal neurological abnormality that causes learning difficulties in the child with near-average intelligence.

Mirror writing A term applied to writing that is completely reversed in letters and form, for example, *emoc* for *come.* May be upside down and/or backwards.

Mixed laterality or lateral confusion The tendency to perform some acts with a right-side preference and others with a left, or the shifting from right to left for certain activities.

Modality The pathways through which an individual receives information and thereby learns. The "modality concept" postulates that some individuals learn better through one modality than through another. For example, a child may receive data better through the visual modality than through the auditory modality.

Movigenics The motor-based curriculum developed by Barsch for children with specific learning disorders.

Native language The language normally used by an individual.

Neurological examination An examination of sensory or motor responses, especially of the reflexes, to determine whether there are localized impairments of the nervous system.

Noncategorical Referring to a system of grouping handicapped children together without reference to a particular label or category of exceptionality.

Nondiscriminatory testing Instruments for assessing performance of individuals that allow for the individual being tested to perform maximally on those skills or behaviors being assessed. Tests discriminate against individuals when the norms are inappropriate, the content of the items does not relate to the individual's cultural background, the examinee does not understand the language of the items or of the person administering the test, or sensory problems interfere with performance on the test.

Occupational therapy Engaging individuals or groups in activities designed to enhance their physical, social, psychological, and cognitive development. A major service provided by most rehabilitation centers.

Ocular pursuit Eye movement caused by visually following a moving target.

Olfactory Pertaining to the sensation of smell.

Ophthalmologist A vision specialist with an M.D. degree, licensed to prescribe refractions, treat eye diseases, and perform ocular surgery.

Optometrist A vision specialist with an O.D. degree, licensed to prescribe refractions and to treat the functional aspects of vision but not permitted to treat eye diseases.

Organicity Referring to impairment of the central nervous system.

Paraprofessional A person trained as an assistant to a professionally qualified teacher. Some states have certification requirements for paraprofessionals.

Perception The process of organizing or interpreting the raw data obtained through the senses.

Perceptual constancy The ability to perceive accurately the invariant properties of objects—such as shape, position, size, and so on—in spite of the variability of the impression these objects make on the senses of the observer.

Perceptual disorder A disturbance in the awareness of objects, relations, or qualities involving the interpretation of sensory stimulation.

Perceptually handicapped A term applied to a person who has difficulty in learning because of disturbance in his or her perception of sensory stimuli.

Perceptual motor Describing the interaction of the various channels of perception with motor activity. These channels include visual, auditory, tactual, and kinesthetic.

Perceptual-motor match The process of comparing and collating the input data received through the motor system and through perception.

Perseveration The tendency for a specific act of behavior to continue after it is no longer appropriate; related to difficulty in shifting from one task to another.

Phoneme The smallest unit of sound in a particular language.

Phonics The application of portions of phonetics to the teaching of reading, particularly the teaching of reading in English. The establishment of the sound (or phoneme) of the language with the equivalent written symbol (or grapheme).

Phonology The linguistic system of speech sounds in a particular language.

Physical therapy Services provided by trained physical therapists in the general area of motor performance. Provided upon prescription by a physician. Services focus on correction, development, and prevention.

Process analyses Psychoeducational evaluation data analysis for the purpose of identifying strengths and weaknesses in students' visual, auditory, and tactual-kinesthetic processing skills.

Programmed reading A method of teaching reading that uses programmed self-instructional and self-corrective materials.

Protective safeguards Procedures established to insure that the rights of the individual are protected.

Psychoeducational diagnostician A specialist who diagnoses and evaluates a child who is having difficulty learning. A variety of psychological and educational testing instruments are used.

Psycholinguistics The field of study that blends aspects of two disciplines—

psychology and linguistics—to examine the total picture of the language process.

Psychomotor Pertaining to the motor effects of psychological processes. Psychomotor tests are tests of motor skill that depend on sensory or perceptual motor coordination.

Public Law 94-142 The Education for All Handicapped Children Act. (See *Federal Register,* August 23, 1977, Vol. 42, No. 163, for details on the rules governing this act.)

Reauditorization The ability to recall the name or sounds of visual symbols (letters). Some individuals remember what letters look like but not which sound they make.

Rebus A method of expressing words or phrases with pictures of objects whose names resemble these words, for example, a picture of a bird substitutes for the written word *bird* in a sentence.

Receptive language Language that is spoken or written by others and received by the individual. The receptive language skills are listening and reading.

Resource teacher A specialist who works with children with learning disabilities and acts as a consultant to other teachers, providing materials and methods to help children who are having difficulty within the regular classroom. The resource teacher may work from a centralized resource room within a school where appropriate materials are housed.

Reversal A transposition of letters.

Revisualization Ability to retrieve a visual image of a letter or word that is heard from one's memory so that it can be written.

Right-left disorientation Inability to distinguish right from left; having no awareness of directionality.

Rigidity The maintenance of an attitude or behavioral set when it is no longer appropriate.

Rotation The turning around of letters in a word, for example, *b* for *d.*

Sensorimotor A term applied to the combination of the input of sense organs and the output of motor activity. The motor activity reflects what is happening to the sensory organs, such as the visual, auditory, tactual, and kinesthetic sensations.

Sequential development A step-by-step plan of development wherein one skill is built on another.

Social perception The ability to interpret stimuli in the social environment and appropriately relate such interpretations to the social situation.

Soft neurological signs Behavioral symptoms that suggest possible minimal brain injury in the absence of gross or obvious neurological abnormalities.

Sound blending Ability to synthesize the separate parts of a word and produce an integrated whole.

Spatial orientation Awareness of space around the person in terms of distance, form, direction, and position.

Specific language disability A term traditionally applied to those who have great difficulty learning to read and spell but who are otherwise intelligent and usually learn arithmetic readily. More recently, this term has been applied to any language deficit—oral, visual, or auditory.

Speech clinician A trained specialist who works with students having articulation or language problems, as well as children with more serious speech disorders. Speech therapy services may be provided in individual therapy sessions, in group therapy sessions, or, in many cases, through consultations with the student's teacher.

Splinter skills Highly specific, isolated physical skills that are developed to satisfy academic demands lying beyond a child's regular skill development.

Strauss syndrome The cluster of symptoms characterizing the "brain-injured" child; includes hyperactivity, distractability, and impulsivity.

Strephosymbolia Reversal in perception of left-right order, especially in letter or word order; "twisted symbols."

Surrogate parent A person other than an individual's natural parent who has legal responsibility for the individual's welfare.

Syllabication A word-attack skill consisting of breaking a word down into its appropriate syllables.

Syndrome The cluster or pattern of symptoms that characterizes a specific disorder.

Syntax That part of a grammatical system dealing with the arrangement of word forms to show their mutual relations in the sentence.

Tachistoscope A machine that exposes written material for a short period of time. Practice with such machines is designed to improve rate and span of visual perception of words.

Tactile perception The ability to interpret and give meaning to sensory stimuli experienced through the sense of touch.

Task analysis The technique of carefully examining a particular task to discover the elements it comprises and the processes required to perform it.

Trial lessons A diagnostic technique for discovering how a child learns best. Short lessons are given through the visual, auditory, tactual, and combination approaches. Evaluations of the child's performance on each provides information concerning his or her learning style.

VAKT A multisensory teaching method involving visual, auditory, kinesthetic, and tactile sense modalities; the Fernald "hand-kinesthetic" method.

Verbal expression The ability to express one's concepts verbally.

Vertical Pertaining to the axis from head to foot of the human body.

Vestibular Pertaining to the sensory mechanism for the perception of the organism's relation to gravity.

Vision screening A sampling of visual skills for the purpose of finding visual problems.

Visual association The organizing process by which one is able to relate concepts presented visually.

Visual closure The ability to identify a visual stimulus from an incomplete visual presentation.

Visual discrimination The ability to discern visually similarities and differences.

Visual fusion Coordination of the separate images in the two eyes into one image.

Visual motor The ability to relate visual stimuli to motor responses in an appropriate way.

Visual-motor coordination The ability to coordinate vision with the movements of the body or parts of the body.

Visual perception The identification, organization, and interpretation of sensory data received by the individual through the eyes.

Visual reception The ability to gain meaning from visual symbols.

Visual sequential memory The ability to reproduce sequences of visual items from memory.

Word-attack skills Skills enabling one to analyze unfamiliar words by syllables and phonic elements and to arrive at their pronunciation.

REFERENCES

English, H. B., and A. C. English. *A Comprehensive Dictionary of Psychological Terms.* New York: David McKay Company, 1958.

Frierson, E. C., and W. C. Barbe. *Educating Children with Learning Disabilities.* New York: Appleton-Century Crofts, 1967.

Gearheart, B. R. *Learning Disabilities: Educational Strategies.* St. Louis, Mo.: C. V. Mosby, 1977.

Kaluger, G., and C. J. Kolson. *Reading and Learning Disabilities.* 2nd ed. Columbus, Ohio: Charles E. Merrill, 1978.

Kirk, S. A., and J. J. Gallagher. *Educating Exceptional Children.* 3rd ed. Boston: Houghton Mifflin Company, 1979.

Kirk, S. A., J. M. Kliebhan, and J. W. Lerner. *Teaching Reading to Slow and Disabled Readers.* Boston: Houghton Mifflin Company, 1978.

Kolson, C. J., and G. Kaluger. *Clinical Aspects of Remedial Reading.* Springfield, Ill.: Charles C Thomas, 1963.

Lerner, J. W. *Children with Learning Disabilities: Theories, Diagnoses, and Teaching Strategies.* 2nd ed. Boston: Houghton Mifflin Company, 1976.

Meyen, E. L. *Exceptional Children and Youth: An Introduction.* Denver, Colo.: Love Publishing Company, 1978.

Money, J. *Reading Disability.* Baltimore: The Johns Hopkins Press, 1962.

Myers, P. I., and D. D. Hammill. *Methods for Learning Disorders,* 2nd ed. New York: John Wiley and Sons, Inc., 1976.

Author Index

Subject Index

Academic disabilities, 7
Acalculia, 261
Action Reading: A Participatory Approach, 148
Acuity
  auditory, 6, 8, 100, 117
  visual, 8
Affixes, 195
Aggressive behavior, 4
Agnosia, auditory, 96
Agraphia, 214
Allergies, 9, 68
Alpha I, 148
Alpha Time, 148
Alphabet, teaching order of, 354
Alphabetic phonics approach, 148
American School for the Deaf, 14
Anomia, 157
Anxiety reaction, 33
Aphasia, 96
  auditory expressive, 98–99
  auditory receptive, 98
  formulation, 99
  syntactical, 99
Arithmetic, 261–307
  computation, 298
  conservation of properties, 301
  counting, 295
  diagnosis of learning problems in, 265–291
  fractions, 300
  map and graph reading, 303
  matching, sorting, and classifying, 293
  measurement, 302
  money, 302
  number sense, 292
  numbers and number words, 297

one-to-one correspondence, 294
place value, 299
quantitative language vocabulary of, 296
remediation of learning problems in, 302–307
telling time, 301
types of learning problems in, 262
visualizing groups and sets, 294
Art of Parenting, 325
Articulation disorders, 103, 115, 197
Assertion training, 326
Association
  auditory, 156
  visual, 88
Association for Children with Learning Disabilities (ACLD), 6, 37
Attention
  auditory, 100, 115
  skills, 353
  span, 69
Audiology, 15, 60
Auditory
  acuity, 6, 8, 100, 117
  analysis, 114, 117
  association, 105, 156
  attention, 100, 115
  closure, 107–108
  deficits, 152, 155
  expressive language, 98
  language problems, 95–97
  phonetic methods, 184
  processing dysfunctions, 97
  reception, 103
  sequential memory, 105–106
  strengths, 147

vocal communication system, 95
vocal disorders, 97
Auditory Language Evaluation Summary, 116–118
Automatic level response, 156, 173
Ayres Space Test, 83, 86

Belly button technique, 150–151
Bilingualism, 4, 9
Biochemical imbalance, 74
Blending, 137–139, 148, 155, 189, 205
Blindness, 5, 13
Blood incompatibility, 3
Body image, 78–79
Boehm Test of Basic Concepts, 104
Botel Reading Inventory, 144
Brain dysfunction, 67
Brain injury, minimal, 33
Brainstorming, adjective, 110–111
Bruininks-Oseretsky Test of Motor Proficiency, 83
Buckley amendment, *see* Educational Rights and Privacy Act of 1974
Bureau of Education for the Handicapped, 7

Career development environments, 381–383
Career education, 375–392
  definitions of, 375–376
  goals of, 376–378
  job placement and training, 38‹
  life-centered approach in, 377
  model programs of, 389

To Students

We would like to find out your reactions to *Children with Learning Problems: A Handbook for Teachers.* Your evaluation of the book will help us respond to both the interest and the needs of the readers of future editions. Please fill out the form and return it to: College Marketing, Houghton Mifflin Company, One Beacon Street, Boston, MA 02107.

1. For each chapter that you have read, please mark a check on the corresponding line to indicate your evaluation of the material presented.

	Excellent	Good	Average	Poor
1 Children with Learning Problems	⎯⎯	⎯⎯	⎯⎯	⎯⎯
2 Legal Provisions for Handicapped Children and Youth	⎯⎯	⎯⎯	⎯⎯	⎯⎯
3 Diagnostic and Remedial Considerations	⎯⎯	⎯⎯	⎯⎯	⎯⎯
4 Writing Individualized Education Programs (IEPs)	⎯⎯	⎯⎯	⎯⎯	⎯⎯
5 Selecting the Least Restrictive and Most Productive Type of Program	⎯⎯	⎯⎯	⎯⎯	⎯⎯
6 Diagnosis and Remediation of Social and Behavioral Problems	⎯⎯	⎯⎯	⎯⎯	⎯⎯
7 Diagnosis and Remediation of Perceptual Motor Problems	⎯⎯	⎯⎯	⎯⎯	⎯⎯
8 Diagnosis and Remediation of Visual Perceptual Problems	⎯⎯	⎯⎯	⎯⎯	⎯⎯
9 Diagnosis and Remediation of Auditory Language Problems	⎯⎯	⎯⎯	⎯⎯	⎯⎯
10 Diagnosis of Reading Problems	⎯⎯	⎯⎯	⎯⎯	⎯⎯
11 Instructional Approaches for Various Patterns of Strengths and Deficits	⎯⎯	⎯⎯	⎯⎯	⎯⎯
12 Visual/Sight Word Methods for Teaching Problem Readers	⎯⎯	⎯⎯	⎯⎯	⎯⎯

13 Auditory Phonetic Methods
    of Teaching Reading   _____   _____   _____   _____

14 Diagnosis and Remedia-
    tion of Spelling Problems   _____   _____   _____   _____

15 Diagnosis of Handwriting
    Problems   _____   _____   _____   _____

16 Developing Proficiency in
    Handwriting   _____   _____   _____   _____

17 Diagnosis of Arithmetic
    and Mathematics Problems   _____   _____   _____   _____

18 Remediation of Arithmetic
    and Mathematics Problems   _____   _____   _____   _____

19 Working with Parents of
    Children with Learning
    Problems   _____   _____   _____   _____

20 Record Keeping   _____   _____   _____   _____

21 Teaching Study and Loca-
    tion Skills   _____   _____   _____   _____

22 Programs for Secondary
    School Students with
    Learning Problems   _____   _____   _____   _____

23 Career Education for Students
    with Learning Problems   _____   _____   _____   _____

2. The text includes a variety of forms intended for use in the classroom. Please
    indicate below the extent to which these forms will be useful to you as the
    teacher of children with learning problems.

    _____

    _____

3. Describe the strongest feature(s) of the book.

    _____

    _____

4. Describe the weakest feature(s) of the book.

    _____

    _____

5. Which topics not discussed in the text do you believe should be covered in
    future editions?

    _____

    _____